Excel® 2013
Charts and Graphs

Bill Jelen

800 East 96th Street,
Indianapolis, Indiana 46240 USA

SO-AAC-231

Contents at a Glance

Introduction: Using Excel 2013 to Create Charts 1

1 Introducing Charts in Excel 2013...7
2 Customizing Charts 35
3 Creating Charts That Show Trends 77
4 Creating Charts That Show Differences.....................................113
5 Creating Charts That Show Relationships 147
6 Creating Stock Analysis Charts 171
7 Advanced Chart Techniques..197
8 Creating Pivot Charts and Power View Dashboards 223
9 Using Sparklines, Data Visualizations, and Other
     Nonchart Methods..249
10 Presenting Excel Data on a Map...275
11 Using SmartArt Diagrams and Shapes 287
12 Exporting Charts for Use Outside of Excel................................317
13 Using Excel VBA to Create Charts 333
14 Knowing When Someone Is Lying to You with a Chart................401
A Charting References...411
  Index...417

Excel® 2013 Charts and Graphs

ISBN-13: 978-0-7897-4862-1
ISBN-10: 0-7897-4862-2

Library of Congress Cataloging-in-Publication data is on file.

Printed in the United States of America
Second Printing: April 2013

Trademarks

All terms mentioned in this book that are known to be trademarks or service marks have been appropriately capitalized. Que Publishing cannot attest to the accuracy of this information. Use of a term in this book should not be regarded as affecting the validity of any trademark or service mark.

Warning and Disclaimer

Every effort has been made to make this book as complete and as accurate as possible, but no warranty or fitness is implied. The information provided is on an "as is" basis. The author and the publisher shall have neither liability nor responsibility to any person or entity with respect to any loss or damages arising from the information contained in this book or from the use of the CD or programs accompanying it.

Bulk Sales

Que Publishing offers excellent discounts on this book when ordered in quantity for bulk purchases or special sales. For more information, please contact

U.S. Corporate and Government Sales
1-800-382-3419
corpsales@pearsontechgroup.com

For sales outside of the U.S., please contact

International Sales
international@pearsoned.com

Associate Publisher
Greg Wiegand

Executive Editor
Loretta Yates

Managing Editor
Sandra Schroeder

Development Editor
Charlotte Kughen

Project Editor
Seth Kerney

Copy Editor
Barbara Hacha

Indexer
Ken Johnson

Proofreader
Kathy Ruiz

Technical Editor
Bob Umlas

Publishing Coordinator
Cindy Teeters

Multimedia Developer
Dan Scherf

Interior Designer
Anne Jones

Cover Designer
Anne Jones

Page Layout
Jake McFarland

Contents

Introduction: Using Excel 2013 to Create Charts 1

Choosing the Right Chart Type 1

Using Excel as Your Charting Canvas 2

Topics Covered in This Book 3

This Book's Objectives 4

    Versions of Excel 4

    Conventions Used in This Book 4

    Special Elements in This Book 4

Next Steps 5

1 Introducing Charts in Excel 2013 7

What's New in Excel 2013 Charts 7

Choosing Among the Three Ways to Create a Chart 10

    Creating a Chart from the Quick Analysis Icon 10

    Inserting a Recommended Chart 11

    Creating a Chart Using the Other Icons on the Insert Tab 14

    Creating a Chart Using Alt+F1 15

Changing the Chart Title 16

    Editing a Title in the Formula Bar 16

    Why Can't Excel Pick Up the Title from the Worksheet? 17

    Assigning a Title from a Worksheet Cell 18

Handling Special Situations 19

    Charting Noncontiguous Data 19

    Charting Nonsummarized Data 22

    Charting Differing Orders of Magnitude Using a Custom Combo Chart 23

    Reversing the Series and Categories in a Chart 24

    Changing the Data Sequence by Using Select Data 25

Using the Charting Tools 26

    Introducing the Three Helper Icons 26

    Introducing the Format Task Pane 27

    Using Commands on the Design Tab 30

    Micromanaging Formatting Using the Format Tab 31

    Using Commands on the Home Tab 31

    Changing the Theme on the Page Layout tab 32

Moving Charts 32

    Moving a Chart Within the Current Worksheet 33

    Moving a Chart to a Different Worksheet 34

Next Steps 34

2 Customizing Charts **35**

Accessing Element Formatting Tools 35

Identifying Chart Elements 37

   Recognizing Chart Labels and Axes 37

   Recognizing Analysis Elements...39

   Identifying Special Elements in a 3D Chart 40

Formatting Chart Elements..41

   Moving the Legend 41

   Changing the Arrangement of a Legend 42

   Formatting Individual Legend Entries 43

   Adding Data Labels to a Chart 43

   Adding a Data Table to a Chart...46

   Formatting Axes 47

   Displaying and Formatting Gridlines 55

   Formatting the Plot Area and Chart Area 61

   Controlling 3D Rotation in a 3D Chart 65

   Forecasting with Trendlines 66

   Adding Drop Lines to a Line or Area Chart 69

   Adding Up/Down Bars to a Line Chart 70

   Showing Acceptable Tolerances by Using Error Bars...71

Formatting a Series...72

   Formatting a Single Data Point 73

   Replacing Data Markers with Shapes..73

   Replacing Data Markers with a Picture 73

Changing the Theme Colors on the Page Layout Tab...74

Storing Your Favorite Settings in a Chart Template 75

Next Steps..75

3 Creating Charts That Show Trends..**77**

Choosing a Chart Type 77

   Column Charts for Up to 12 Time Periods 77

   Line Charts for Time Series Beyond 12 Periods 77

   Area Charts to Highlight One Portion of the Line...79

   High-Low-Close Charts for Stock Market Data 79

   Bar Charts for Series with Long Category Labels..79

   Pie Charts Make Horrible Time Comparisons 80

   100 Percent Stacked Bar Chart Instead of Pie Charts 80

Understanding Date-Based Axis Versus Category-Based Axis in Trend Charts 80

   Converting Text Dates to Dates..83

   Plotting Data by Numeric Year 88

   Using Dates Before 1900 89

   Rolling Daily Dates to Months Using a Pivot Chart..91

   Using a Workaround to Display a Time-Scale Axis 93

Communicate Effectively with Charts 96

Using a Long, Meaningful Title to Explain Your Point..96
Highlighting One Column..100
Replacing Columns with Arrows..101
Highlighting a Section of a Chart by Adding a Second Series..................................102
Changing Line Type Midstream...103
Adding an Automatic Trendline to a Chart...105
Showing a Trend of Monthly Sales and Year-to-Date Sales..106
Understanding the Shortcomings of Stacked Column Charts..108
Shortcomings of Showing Many Trends on a Single Chart...110
Next Steps...111

4 Creating Charts That Show Differences...**113**
Comparing Entities..113
Using Bar Charts to Illustrate Item Comparisons...113
Adding a Second Series to Show a Time Comparison...115
Subdividing a Bar to Emphasize One Component...116
Showing Component Comparisons...117
Using Pie Charts..120
Switching to a 100 Percent Stacked Column Chart..126
Using a Doughnut Chart to Compare Two Pies...127
Dealing with Data Representation Problems in a Pie Chart.....................................129
Using a Waterfall Chart to Tell the Story of Component Decomposition.........................136
Creating a Stacked and Clustered Chart...138
Next Steps...145

5 Creating Charts That Show Relationships..**147**
Using Scatter Charts to Plot Pairs of Data Points..148
Creating a Scatter Chart...149
Adding Labels to a Scatter Chart in Excel 2013..149
Showing Scatter Chart Labels in Excel 2010..150
Adding a Second Series to a Scatter Chart...151
Joining the Points in a Scatter Chart with Lines..153
Using a Scatter Chart with Lines to Replace a Line Chart.......................................154
Drawing with a Scatter Chart...155
Testing Correlation Using a Scatter Chart...157
Adding a Third Dimension with a Bubble Chart..159
Using Charts to Show Relationships..161
Using Paired Bars to Show Relationships..161
Using a Frequency Distribution to Categorize Thousands of Points........................163
Using Radar Charts to Create Performance Reviews..166
Using Surface Charts to Show Contrast...167
Using the Depth Axis...168
Controlling a Surface Chart Through 3D Rotation..168
Next Steps...169

6 Creating Stock Analysis Charts **171**

Overview of Stock Charts 171
    Line Charts..171
    OHLC Charts..172
    Candlestick Charts 173

Obtaining Stock Data to Chart 173
    Rearranging Columns in the Downloaded Data...174
    Dealing with Splits Using the Adjusted Close Column 175

Creating a Line Chart to Show Closing Prices 177
    Adding Volume as a Column Chart to the Line Chart...180

Creating OHLC Charts...182
    Producing a High-Low-Close Chart 182
    Customizing a High-Low-Close Chart 183
    Creating an OHLC Chart 184
    Adding Volume to a High-Low-Close Chart 186

Creating Candlestick Charts 191
    Changing Colors in a Candlestick Chart..191
    Understanding High-Low Lines and Up-Down Bars 192

Next Steps..196

7 Advanced Chart Techniques **197**

Mixing Two Chart Types on a Single Chart...197

Moving Charts from One Worksheet to Another 200

Making Columns or Bars Float 200

Using a Rogue XY Series for Arbitrary Gridlines..202

Showing Several Charts on One Chart by Using a Rogue XY Series 207

Creating Bullet Charts in Excel 2013 212

Creating a Thermometer Chart 217

Creating a Benchmark Chart 219

Creating a Delta Chart..220

Next Steps..221

8 Creating Pivot Charts and Power View Dashboards **223**

Creating a PivotChart Using Recommended Charts 223
    Changing the Fields in the Pivot Chart 225
    Sorting the Pivot Chart 226
    Grouping Daily Dates in the Pivot Chart..228
    Filtering Pivot Charts Using the Filter Fly-out Menu 230
    Filtering Pivot Charts Using Slicers 230
    Connecting Multiple Pivot Charts to One Slicer...231

Using PowerPivot and Power View...232
    Enabling PowerPivot and Power View...233
    Loading Your Excel Data to PowerPivot 233
    Adding a Date Lookup Table...234

Format Your Data in PowerPivot 235

VLOOKUPs? Replacing VLOOKUPs with Relationships 236

Creating a Power View Worksheet 237

Every New Dashboard Element Starts as a Table 238

Converting the Table to a Chart 238

Creating a New Element by Dragging..240

Every Chart Point Is a Slicer for Every Other Element 240

Adding a Real Slicer 241

The Filter Pane Can Be Confusing 242

Use Tile Boxes to Filter One or a Group of Charts 243

Replicating Charts Using Multiples 244

Animating a Scatter Chart Over Time 245

Some Closing Tips on Power View 246

Next Steps..247

9 Using Sparklines, Data Visualizations, and Other Nonchart Methods **249**

Fitting a Chart into the Size of a Cell with Sparklines..250

Creating a Group of Sparklines 251

Built-in Choices for Customizing Sparklines...253

Controlling Axis Values for Sparklines...254

Setting Up Win/Loss Sparklines 256

Showing Detail by Enlarging the Sparkline...256

Labeling a Sparkline 257

Using Data Bars to Create In-Cell Bar Charts 259

Creating Data Bars 260

Customizing Data Bars 261

Showing Data Bars for a Subset of Cells...262

Using Color Scales to Highlight Extremes..263

Customizing Color Scales 264

Using Icon Sets to Segregate Data 265

Setting Up an Icon Set 265

Moving Numbers Closer to Icons 266

Showing an Icon for Only the Best Cells...268

Creating a 10-Icon Set Using a Formula...269

Creating a Chart Using Conditional Formatting in Worksheet Cells 271

Creating a Chart Using the REPT Function 273

Next Steps..274

10 Presenting Excel Data on a Map **275**

Plotting Data Geographically...275

Importing Data to MapPoint...275

Creating a Map in Power View 279

Creating a Map in GeoFlow 284

Next Steps..286

11 Using SmartArt Diagrams and Shapes **287**

Using SmartArt 288
    Elements Common Across Most SmartArt 289
    A Tour of the SmartArt Categories 289
    Inserting SmartArt 291
    Micromanaging SmartArt Elements 294
    Changing Text Formatting in One Element 294
    Controlling SmartArt Shapes from the Text Pane 296
    Adding Images to SmartArt 298
    Special Considerations for Organization Charts 299
    Using Limited SmartArt 301

Choosing the Right Layout for Your Message 302

Exploring Business Charts That Use SmartArt Graphics 303
    Illustrating a Pro/Con Decision by Using a Balance Chart 304
    Illustrating Growth by Using an Upward Arrow 304
    Showing an Iterative Process by Using a Basic Cycle Layout 305
    Showing a Company's Relationship to External Entities by Using a Diverging Radial Diagram ...305
    Illustrating Departments Within a Company by Using a Table List Diagram 306
    Adjusting Venn Diagrams to Show Relationships 306
    Understanding Labeled Hierarchy Charts 307
    Using Other SmartArt Layouts 308

Using Shapes to Display Cell Contents 309
    Working with Shapes 311
    Using the Freeform Shape to Create a Custom Shape 311

Using WordArt for Interesting Titles and Headlines 312

Next Steps 315

12 Exporting Charts for Use Outside of Excel **317**

Presenting Excel Charts in PowerPoint or Word 317
    Copying a Document from Excel and Pasting to PowerPoint Sets Up an As-Needed Link 319
    Copying and Pasting While Keeping Original Formatting 323
    Pasting as Link to Capture Future Excel Formatting Changes 324
    Embedding the Chart and Workbook in PowerPoint 325
    Copying a Chart as a Picture 325
    Creating a Chart in PowerPoint with Data Pasted from Excel 327

Presenting Charts on the Web 328

Exporting Charts to Graphics Using VBA 331

Converting to XPS or PDF 332

Next Steps 332

13 Using Excel VBA to Create Charts **333**

Introducing VBA 333
    Enabling VBA in Your Copy of Excel 333
    Enabling the Developer Tab 334
    Visual Basic Tools 335

The Macro Recorder..336
Understanding Object-Oriented Code...336
Learning Tricks of the VBA Trade..337
Writing Code to Handle a Data Range of Any Size...337
Using Super-Variables: Object Variables...339
Using With and End With When Referring to an Object...340
Continuing a Line of Code..340
Adding Comments to Code..341
Understanding Backward Compatibility...341
Referencing Charts and Chart Objects in VBA Code..342
Understanding the Global Settings...342
Specifying a Built-in Chart Type...342
Specifying Location and Size of the Chart...345
Referring to a Specific Chart...345
Creating a Chart in Various Excel Versions..346
Using the .AddChart2 Method in Excel 2013...346
Creating Charts in Excel 2007–2013...348
Creating Charts in Excel 2003–2013...349
Customizing a Chart...350
Specifying a Chart Title...350
Quickly Formatting a Chart Using New Excel 2013 Features..351
Using SetElement to Emulate Changes from the Plus Icon...358
Using the Format Method to Micromanage Formatting Options...................................363
Formatting a Data Series...367
Controlling Gap Width and Series Separation in Column and Bar Charts........................368
Spinning and Exploding Round Charts...369
Controlling the Bar of Pie and Pie of Pie Charts...371
Setting the Bubble Size..375
Controlling Radar and Surface Charts..377
Creating Advanced Charts..381
Creating True Open-High-Low-Close Stock Charts..382
Creating Bins for a Frequency Chart...383
Creating a Stacked Area Chart..386
Exporting a Chart as a Graphic...389
Creating Pivot Charts..390
Creating Data Bars with VBA..392
Creating Sparklines with VBA...395
Next Steps...399

14 Knowing When Someone Is Lying to You with a Chart 401
Lying with Perspective..401
Lying with Shrinking Charts..402
Lying with Scale...403

Lying Because Excel Will Not Cooperate 405

Avoiding Stacked Surface Charts...406

Asserting a Trend from Two Data Points...407

Deliberately Using Charts to Lie...408

Charting Something Else When Numbers Are Too Bad 409

Stretching Pictographs 409

Next Steps...410

A Charting References..411

   Index 417

Dedication

To Zeke Jelen

About the Author

Bill Jelen, Excel MVP and the host of MrExcel.com, has been using spreadsheets since 1985, and he launched the MrExcel.com website in 1998. Bill was a regular guest on *Call for Help* with Leo Laporte and has produced more than 1,500 episodes of his daily video podcast, Learn Excel from MrExcel. He is the author of 39 books about Microsoft Excel and writes the monthly Excel column for *Strategic Finance* magazine. His Excel tips appear regularly in *CFO Excel Pro Newsletter* and *CFO Magazine*. Before founding MrExcel.com, Bill Jelen spent 12 years in the trenches—working as a financial analyst for finance, marketing, accounting, and operations departments of a $500 million public company. He lives near Akron, Ohio, with his wife, Mary Ellen.

Acknowledgments

I wish to thank Gene Zelazny of McKinsey & Company. Gene was generous with his time and feedback. He indirectly taught me a lot about charting more than a decade ago, when I did a six-month stint on a McKinsey project team. Kathy Villella and Tom Bunzel also provided advice on presentations. Mala Singh of XLSoft Consulting vetted the chapter on using VBA to create charts.

Mike Alexander, my coauthor on the *Pivot Table Data Crunching* books, helped outline the table of contents for this book and provided many ideas for Chapter 7.

I enjoy the visual delight of every Edward Tufte book. I apologize in advance to E.T. for documenting all the chartjunk that Microsoft lets us add to Excel charts.

Dick DeBartolo is the Daily GizWiz and has been writing for *Mad* magazine for more than 40 years, since he was 15. The pages of *Mad* were not where I expected to find inspiration for a charting book, but why not? Thanks to Bob D'Amico for illustrating the charts à la *Mad*. The pie chart in Chapter 4 is a Dick DeBartolo original, created especially for this book. Many thanks to Dick for being a contributor.

I was visiting Keith Bradbury's office in Toronto. Keith makes the completely awesome PDF-to-Excel utility at InvestInTech.com. Between parking the car and entering Keith's office, I saw the most amazing store, managed by David Michaelides. SWIPE is a bookstore dedicated to art and design. This is a beautiful store to browse, and if you go in and reveal that you work in Excel all day, they will sympathetically be very nice to you. In a clash of worlds, David has the original 1984 Mac way up above his cash register because it was the start of desktop publishing. I pointed out that the Mac was where Excel 1.0 got its start in 1985, so we had a common thread in our respective backgrounds. Stop by 401 Richmond Street West (two blocks west of Spadina) to take a look the next time you are in Toronto.

Thanks to Jane Liles at Microsoft for guiding the Excel team through Excel 2013. Thanks to Steve Tullis, Dan Battagin, and Melissa MacBeth for making the Excel Web App render charts better every year. Scott Ruble heads up the charting team and was always generous with his time when I ran into a charting quandary. Robin Wakefield provided help with some charting VBA that was eluding me.

At MrExcel.com, thanks to Barb Jelen, Wei Jiang, Tracy Syrstad, Tyler Nash, and Scott Pierson.

The Microsoft MVPs for Excel are always generous with their time and ideas. Over the years, I've learned many cool charting tricks from websites maintained by John Peltier, Andy Pope, and Charley Kyd. Turn to the appendix for links to their respective websites. MVP Bob Umlas (the smartest Excel guy I know) served as a great technical editor. I still smile when I recall Bob pointing out that "9. Repeat step 9 for High, Low, and Close lines." was, in itself, a circular reference.

The great team at Pearson of Loretta Yates, Charlotte Kughen, Barbara Hacha, and Seth Kerney were a pleasure to work with.

Finally, thanks to Zeke Jelen, Dom Grossi, and Mary Ellen Jelen.

We Want to Hear from You!

As the reader of this book, you are our most important critic and commentator. We value your opinion and want to know what we're doing right, what we could do better, what areas you'd like to see us publish in, and any other words of wisdom you're willing to pass our way.

We welcome your comments. You can email or write to let us know what you did or didn't like about this book—as well as what we can do to make our books better.

Please note that we cannot help you with technical problems related to the topic of this book.

When you write, please be sure to include this book's title and author as well as your name and email address. We will carefully review your comments and share them with the author and editors who worked on the book.

Email: feedback@quepublishing.com

Mail: Que Publishing
            ATTN: Reader Feedback
            800 East 96th Street
            Indianapolis, IN 46240 USA

Reader Services

Visit our website and register this book at quepublishing.com/register for convenient access to any updates, downloads, or errata that might be available for this book.

Introduction: Using Excel 2013 to Create Charts

Good charts should both explain data and arouse curiosity. A chart can summarize thousands of data points into a single picture. The arrangement of a chart should explain the underlying data but also enable the reader to isolate trouble spots worthy of further analysis.

Excel makes it easy to create charts. Even though the improvements in Excel 2013 enable you to create a chart with only a few mouse clicks, it still takes thought to find the best way to present your data.

IN THIS INTRODUCTION

Choosing the Right Chart Type.........................1

Using Excel as Your Charting Canvas...............2

Topics Covered in This Book 3

This Book's Objectives 4

Next Steps 5

Choosing the Right Chart Type

Suppose you are an analyst for a chain of restaurants, and you are studying the lunch-hour sales for a restaurant in a location at a distant mall. Corporations surrounding the mall provide a steady lunchtime clientele during the week. The mall does well on weekends during the holiday shopping months but lacks weekend crowds during the rest of the year.

From the data contained in the chart in Figure I.1, you can spot a periodicity in sales throughout the year. An estimated 50 spikes indicate that the periodicity might be based on the day of the week. You can also spot that a general improvement in sales occurs at the end of the year, which you attribute to the holiday shopping season. However, there is an anomaly in the pattern during the summer months that needs further study.

Figure I.1
This chart shows the sales trend for 365 data points.

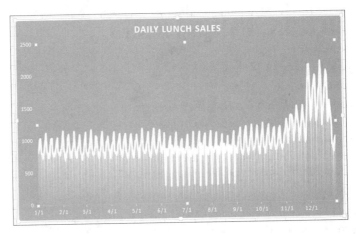

After studying the data in Figure I.1, you might decide to plot the sales by weekday to understand the sales better. Figure I.2 shows the same data presented as seven line charts. Each line represents the sales for a particular day of the week. Friday is the dashed line. At the beginning of the year, Friday was the best sales day for this particular restaurant. For some reason, around week 23, Friday sales plummeted.

The chart in Figure I.2 prompts you to make some calls to see what was happening on Fridays at this location. You might discover that the city was hosting free Friday lunchtime concerts from June through August. The restaurant manager was offered a concession at the concert location but thought it would be too much trouble. Using this pair of charts enabled you to isolate a problem and equipped you to make better decisions in the future.

Figure I.2
When you isolate sales by weekday, you can see a definite problem with Friday sales in the summer.

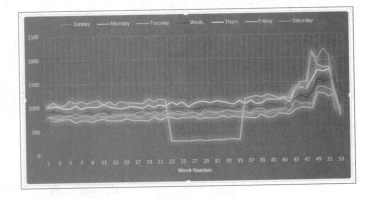

Using Excel as Your Charting Canvas

Excel 2007 offered a complete rewrite of the 15-year-old charting engine from legacy versions of Excel. Unfortunately, Excel 2007 introduced too many new bugs to the charting engine. Much of the effort of the charting team in Excel 2010 went to cleaning up the bugs left over from Excel 2007. Now, in Excel 2013, some amazing leaps have been made with

Recommended Charts and a new set of 153 Chart Styles. Single-series charts no longer get a redundant legend. Chart labels pick up formatting from the source data. Three new helper icons appear to the right of a selected chart, enabling you to add elements, remove totals, and format a chart. A new interface simplifies combo chart creation. Also, data labels can appears as callouts and get their values from cell formulas.

If you have Excel 2013 Pro Plus or Office 365, you also have access to add-ins such as Power View and GeoFlow. Both enable you to use animated charts and maps.

Topics Covered in This Book

This book covers the Excel 2013 charting engine and three types of word-sized charts called *sparklines*. It also covers the Data Visualization and SmartArt Business diagramming tools that were introduced in Excel 2007. If you have Excel 2013 Pro Plus, the new Power View add-in came with your version of Excel and provides animated charts and dashboards.

Besides charts, Excel 2013 offers many other ways to display quantitative data visually. This book explains how to use the new conditional formatting features such as data bars, color scales, and icon sets to add visual elements to regular tables of numbers. In Figure I.3, conditional formatting features make it easy to see that Ontario has the largest population and that Nunavut has the largest land area. You can also add in-cell data bars such as these with a couple of mouse clicks, as described in Chapter 9, "Using Sparklines, Data Visualizations, and Other Nonchart Methods."

The three types of word-sized charts in Excel 2013 called sparklines enable you to create tiny line charts, tiny column charts, and win/loss charts. As shown in Figure I.4, these tiny charts can show win/loss events that paint a better picture than a simple 7–3 record.

Figure I.3
In-cell data bars draw the eye to the largest values in each column.

27	Province	Population	Area
28	Alberta	2974805	639987
29	British Columbia	3907740	926493
30	Manitoba	1119580	551938
31	New Brunswick	729495	71356
32	Newfound and Labrador	512930	370502
33	Northwest Territories	37360	1141108
34	Nova Scotia	908005	52917
35	Nunavut	26745	1925460
36	Ontario	11410045	907656
37	Prince Edward Island	135295	5684
38	Quebec	7237480	1357743
39	Saskatchewan	978930	586561
40	Yukon Territory	28670	474707

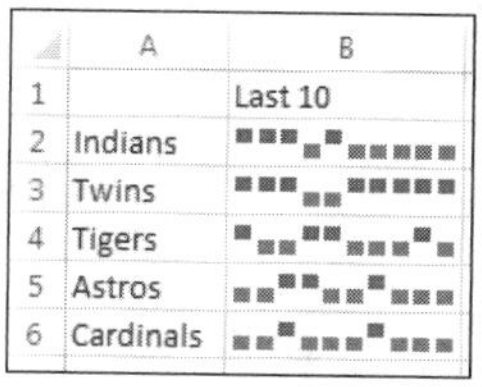

Figure I.4
The Twins baseball team made the post-season in 2009 because they won 8 of their last 10 games while the Tigers struggled.

▲	A	B
1		Last 10
2	Indians	
3	Twins	
4	Tigers	
5	Astros	
6	Cardinals	

This Book's Objectives

The goal of this book is to make you more efficient and effective in creating visual displays of information using Excel 2013.

In the early chapters of this book, you find out how to use the new Excel 2013 charting interface. Chapters 3 through 6 walk you through all the built-in chart types and talk about when to use each one. Chapter 7 discusses creating unusual charts. Chapter 8 covers pivot charts, and Chapter 9 covers creating visual displays of information right in the worksheet. Chapter 10 covers mapping, and Chapter 11 covers the new SmartArt business graphics and Excel 2013's shape tools. Chapter 12 covers exporting charts for use outside of Excel. Chapter 13 presents macro tools you can use to automate the production of charts using Excel VBA. Chapter14 includes several techniques that people can use to stretch the truth with charts. Finally, Appendix A provides a list of resources that will give you additional help with creating charts and graphs.

Versions of Excel

Excel charting was largely unchanged for the dozen years leading up to Excel 2003. This book refers to Excel 2003 and earlier collectively as "legacy" versions of Excel.

This book covers new features in Excel 2013. Many of the concepts were possible in Excel 2010 and earlier, but required more steps.

Conventions Used in This Book

This book follows certain conventions:

- Monospace—Text message you see onscreen or code appears in monospace font.
- **Bold Monospace**—Text you type appears in **bold, monospace** font.
- *Italic*—New and important terms appear in *italics*.
- Initial Caps—Tab names, dialog box names, and dialog box elements are present with initial capital letters so you can identify them easily.

Special Elements in This Book

This book contains the following special elements:

> **NOTE**
> Notes provide additional information outside the main thread of the chapter discussion that might be useful for you to know.

> **TIP**
> Tips provide you with quick workarounds and time-saving techniques to help you do your work more efficiently.

CAUTION

Cautions warn you about potential pitfalls you might encounter. It is important to pay attention to Cautions because they alert you to problems that could cause hours of frustration.

CASE STUDY

Case studies provide a real-world look at topics previously introduced in the chapter.

Next Steps

Chapter 1, "Introducing Charts in Excel 2013," presents the new Excel 2013 interface for creating charts. You discover how to create your first chart and read about the various elements available in a chart.

Introducing Charts in Excel 2013

1

What's New in Excel 2013 Charts

Several charting improvements are introduced in Excel 2013. My favorite new item is the 153 professionally designed chart styles that you can use to format your charts. These styles enable you to apply modern formatting to the chart in a few clicks. They are useful compared to the old gallery of 48 chart styles introduced in Excel 2007.

Other new items in Excel 2013 charting include the following:

- **Recommended charts**—Your starting point for creating a chart should be to select the data and choose Insert, Recommended Chart. Excel applies heuristics and rules to offer charts that will work for your data. There will always be a few different options to choose from. Excel will never offer the bad chart types like pyramid, cone, or 3D charts. If nothing in the Recommended Charts pane works for you, you can use the All Charts tab in the dialog to access another chart style.

- **Charting unsummarized data sets**—Typically, charts should be created from summaries of your detailed data. However, if you select the entire data set and ask for a recommended chart, Excel looks for columns with repeating values and offers to create a pivot chart that summarizes revenue by product or region, for instance.

- **No legend in a single-series chart**—The new default chart always has a chart title. It has a legend only if you have more than one series. This prevents the redundant chart title and data legend that have appeared in Excel charts over the years.

IN THIS CHAPTER

What's New in Excel 2010 Charts.................7

Choosing Among the Three Ways to Create a Chart 10

Changing the Chart Title 16

Handling Special Situations.......................19

Using the Charting Tools..............................26

Moving Charts..32

Next Steps 34

■ **Labels inherit number formatting from the source data**—If you format your source data as currency with 0 decimal places, the data labels and value axis labels have a similar format. This saves you the extra step of figuring out how to change the number format. It is the way it should have worked all along, and hopefully the pivot table team at Microsoft will pick up the cue and make pivot tables work this way in the future.

■ **Quickly add elements using the Plus icon**—When a chart is selected, three new helper icons appear to the right of the chart. The Plus icon (+) holds elements that you can quickly add or remove from the chart. This tiny icon effectively replaces the entire Layout ribbon tab from Excel 2007–2010. (See Figure 1.1.)

■ **Apply formatting using the Paintbrush icon**—The Paintbrush icon holds thumbnails

Figure 1.1
Three new icons hold old and new chart formatting features.

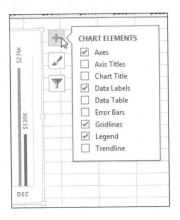

of new chart styles and new color schemes. You can quickly convert a boring chart to a good-looking chart in a few clicks using this icon.

■ **Filter unwanted total rows**—The Funnel icon lets you remove rows or columns from the chart without having to hide them in the worksheet. Suppose that you have 12 monthly data points with four quarterly subtotals interspersed. Typically, you should select the noncontiguous ranges to create the chart. Now you can select the whole data set, create a bad-looking chart, but quickly correct the chart by filtering out the quarterly columns. (See Figure 1.2.)

■ **Data label callouts from cell values**—A new data label callout shape debuts in Excel 2013. Even better, the values for data labels can now come from a range of cells in the worksheet. This enables you to create dynamic chart labels using formulas in the worksheet. (See Figure 1.3.)

■ **Formatting commands move to a task pane**—The Format task pane replaces the Formatting dialog box. You will like that the Format task pane takes up less space on your screen than the old Format dialog box did. However, the commands are now hidden across a three-tier menu system, which takes some getting used to.

Figure 1.2
Rather than select non-contiguous cells, chart all the data and then filter out the subtotal cells.

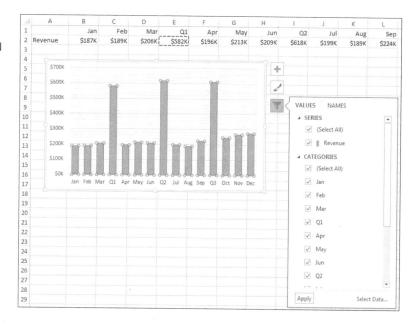

Figure 1.3
Callout text can come from cells on the worksheet.

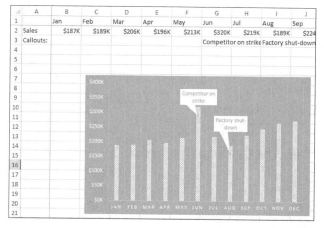

- **New interface for creating combo charts**—The Excel team finally found a logical way to specify combo charts. Excel 2003 offered a few inflexible combo charts. Excel 2007–2010 did away with the canned examples, hoping people would figure out the confusing steps needed to convert a chart into a combo chart. Few people did. Now the Insert Chart dialog offers a custom combo interface. You can choose exactly which series belongs on the secondary axis, and you can choose the chart type for each series. (See Figure 1.4.)

- **Bad charts types are hidden**—Cone, pyramid, and cylinder Charts have been banished to an underground cavern in Kentucky. They were bad chart types. They never should have been in Excel. The chart team finally removed them from the Insert Chart interface. If you are desperate to create misleading charts, you might be able to find similar settings in the Format task pane.

Figure 1.4
A new interface for creating combo charts.

Choosing Among the Three Ways to Create a Chart

There are three entry points for creating a chart. After using Excel 2013 for a while, I believe the Recommended Charts icon is the fastest way to get a good chart. This section reviews all three methods:

- Quick Analysis icon
- Recommended Charts
- Insert tab of the ribbon

Creating a Chart from the Quick Analysis Icon

When you select a range of data in Excel 2013, the Quick Analysis icon appears below the data. (See Figure 1.5.)

Figure 1.5
Select a range of data and the Quick Analysis icon appears.

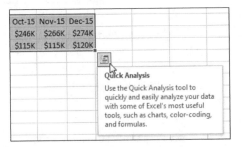

Click the Quick Analysis icon and a menu appears with choices for Formatting, Charts, Totals, Tables, and Sparklines. Click the Charts menu, and the Quick Analysis tool offers a few recommended charts. Hover over any thumbnail to see a live preview of that chart. (See Figure 1.6.)

Figure 1.6
After choosing the Charts category, you can hover, hover, hover to see what each chart would look like.

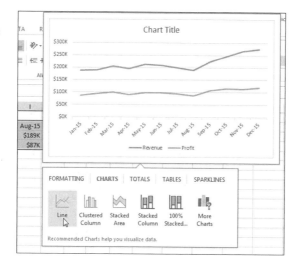

If none of the thumbnails offer what you want, you can click the More Charts icon at the end, which is equivalent to selecting the Recommended Charts icon.

It requires two clicks to get to the Charts section of the Quick Analysis tool, followed by several hovers to review and reject the various suggested charts, and then a third click to get to the recommended charts. It seems easier to skip this entire process and start with Recommended Charts.

Inserting a Recommended Chart

You will likely prefer the Recommended Charts method for creating charts. The icon appears as a large icon on the Charts group on the Insert tab of the ribbon. (See Figure 1.7.) If you end up being a fan of this icon, you can get here by pressing Alt followed by N then R. (Note that you have to press and release Alt before pressing N.) Or you can right-click the Recommended Charts icon and add it to the Quick Access toolbar.

Select the range of data and choose Recommended Charts. Excel displays the Insert Chart dialog and starts on the Recommended Charts tab of the dialog. Here you can see all the thumbnails without having to hover over each one. (See Figure 1.8.) This is better than the Quick Analysis lens.

To blindly accept the first suggestion, use the keystrokes Alt, N, R, Enter. This takes slightly longer than the old Alt+F1 shortcut key for embedding a default chart, but the results are better.

Figure 1.7
The Recommended Charts icon is new in Excel 2013.

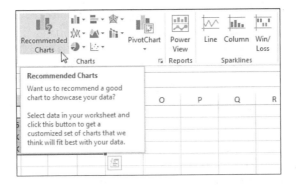

Figure 1.8
You can see thumbnails of each recommended chart.

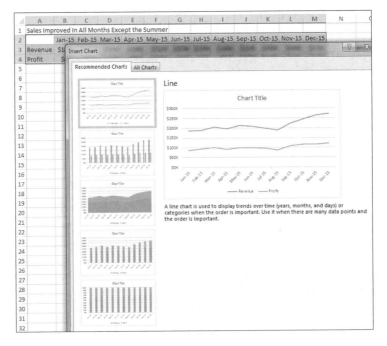

If none of the recommended charts suit you, click the All Charts tab in this dialog to get to all 73 built-in chart types. (See Figure 1.9.) This tab is easier to use than the various icons in the Charts group of the ribbon. The left navigation panel offers all the chart categories, even the Stock and Surface types, which are hidden on the ribbon. The seven thumbnails across the top offer seven types of charts, and the two large thumbnails enable you to choose whether your series should be in rows or columns.

Figure 1.9
You can see thumbnails of each recommended chart.

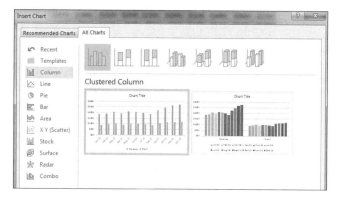

Decoding the Charting Thumbnails

Most of the charting categories offer thumbnail icons across the top of the dialog. These icons usually represent four basic types of charts:

- ■ **Clustered**—This is the top-left chart in Figure 1.10. Each series gets a column, bar, or point that starts from the category axis of the chart. This type of chart makes it easy to compare how each series did over time or across the axis.

- ■ **Stacked**—This is the top-right chart in Figure 1.10. It shows how the three series add up to reach a total value. It is great for communicating the total sales of the three regions, but horrible for seeing how series 2 or series 3 changed over time.

- ■ **100% Stacked**—The actual numbers in the cells are converted to percentages. Each column/bar/line adds up to 100%. This method is horrible for showing total sales and horrible for showing how each series changed over time. This is the bottom-left chart in Figure 1.10.

- ■ **3D Column**—Whereas the preceding three items are available in 3D versions, the column and area charts offer a fourth 3D choice: the 3D column, where the series are shown in a front-to-back arrangement. This works when the series in the front are smaller than the series in the back. Frequently, though, the items in the back series are hidden by items in the front series.

The row of icons in the middle of Figure 1.10 shows how Excel attempts to represent these four chart types for column charts using thumbnails.

As you move to other chart categories, Excel attempts to convey the Clustered, Stacked, and 100% Stacked concepts in a thumbnail representative of that chart category. Figure 1.11 shows the thumbnails used for Column, Line, Bar, and Area charts.

Figure 1.10
These thumbnails represent Clustered, Stacked, 100% Stacked, and 3-D Column.

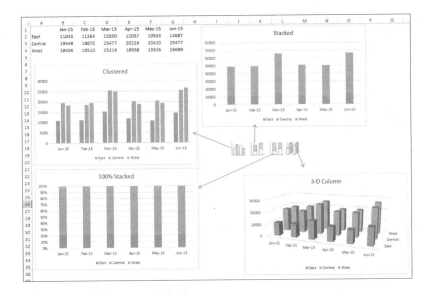

Figure 1.11
The Clustered, Stacked, and 100% Stacked are available in Column, Line, Bar, and Area charts.

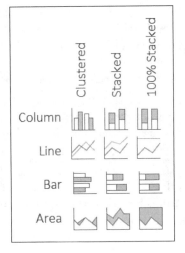

Creating a Chart Using the Other Icons on the Insert Tab

Old habits are hard to break. If you don't embrace the new Recommended Charts icon, you can head directly to one of the eight other charting drop-down menus on the Insert tab of the ribbon. (See Figure 1.12.)

There really should be more icons than the eight that are shown. Bubble charts have been moved to the Scatter Chart icon. Stock and Surface charts are in the Radar chart icon. Cone, Pyramid, and Cylinder charts have been removed from the Column Chart icon and moved to the Formatting task pane. There is no icon for Templates or Recent.

Figure 1.12
The Excel team tried to squeeze 11 charting categories into eight icons.

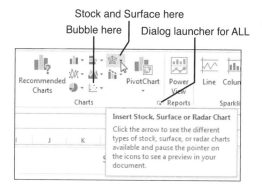

To reach the categories of Templates or Recent, you need to open the All Charts tab of the Insert Chart dialog. Even the tiny dialog launcher shown in Figure 1.12 takes you to the Recommended Charts tab of the Insert Chart dialog. It is easier to click the big Recommended Charts icon and then click All Charts.

Creating a Chart Using Alt+F1

There is a fourth way to create a chart. Select the data and press Alt+F1. Excel creates a default chart in the middle of the current window. Normally, the default chart is a clustered column chart.

If you frequently create a different type of chart, you can set that chart as the default chart that is tied to Alt+F1. In the All Charts dialog, click the small icons across the top and choose Set as Default Chart. (See Figure 1.13.)

Figure 1.13
The command to set the default chart moved in Excel 2013.

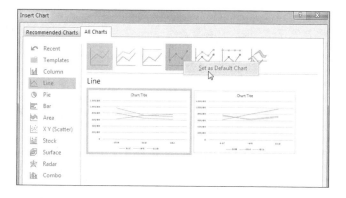

TIP
A custom chart template can be defined as the default chart. This enables you to define custom colors, effects, and settings as the default. See "Creating a Chart Template," near the end of Chapter 2, "Customizing Charts," for more information.

Changing the Chart Title

If you create a chart with a single series, Excel 2013 uses the series label as the chart title. In all other cases, the newly created chart has a generic title of "Chart Title."

In the past, you would typically get no title in a chart.

It was easy to ignore a title that did not exist.

Now that all your charts are going to have a chart title that reads "Chart Title," you are going to have to get very good at changing the title.

Editing a Title in the Formula Bar

If you click the chart title and start typing, the words that you type appear in the Formula Bar. This is disconcerting if you don't know where to look for the words to appear. You might think that nothing is happening or that you accidentally kicked the keyboard cable from the back of the computer.

In Figure 1.14, the Chart Title is selected. Words have been typed, but they are appearing in the Formula Bar instead of in the title. When you finally press Enter to complete the title, the title appears in the chart.

Figure 1.14
Single-click the title, start typing, and the words appear in the Formula Bar until you press Enter.

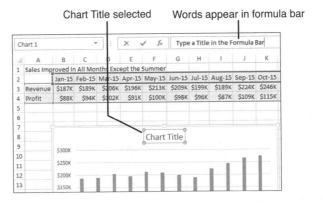

Editing a Title in the Chart

Triple-click the title in the chart and start typing words (see Figure 1.15). The new words that you type replace "Chart Title."

Figure 1.15
Triple-click the title and you can type the words right in the title box.

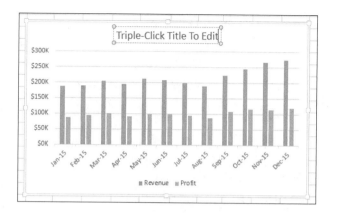

Why Can't Excel Pick Up the Title from the Worksheet?

You might wonder why Excel cannot pick up the title from the worksheet. Before you create a chart, what if you include the title in A1 or A2? Surely, Excel will figure out that you want the long text in that cell to be used as the title. (See Figure 1.16.)

Figure 1.16
You would think titles typed in A1 or A2 would be applied to the title by Excel. They are not.

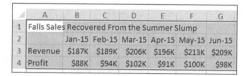

Unfortunately, Excel does not understand that you want that cell to be the title. I've tried it many ways and it never works. Scott Ruble from the Excel team finally confirmed that they will never pick up the title from a data set with two or more series from the worksheet.

Scott did point out that multiple rows of data labels above the chart do get picked up as a hierarchical set of labels, as shown in Figure 1.17. This is a neat trick that has been in Excel for many versions, but it doesn't help with the title.

Figure 1.17
Multiple rows of cell titles get picked up as category axis labels.

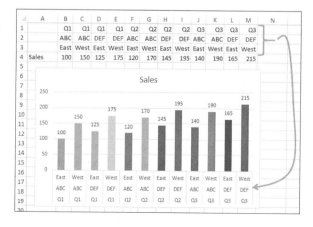

Assigning a Title from a Worksheet Cell

There is a great trick for applying a title from a worksheet cell. Because Excel won't pick up the chart title, you should try this method:

1. Leave space for a chart title somewhere on the worksheet.

2. Create the chart. If there is more than one series, it starts with the default title of Chart Title.

3. Study the chart and find something interesting in the chart. I like to tell my chart audience something about the data. In the current example, type the title **Fall Sales Recovered from the Summer Slump** in cell A1.

4. Click the Chart Title once to select the title.

5. Click in the Formula Bar. Type an equal sign. Click the cell that contains the title. Note that Excel builds the formula as if you are pointing to another worksheet. Because the embedded chart is a foreign object on the worksheet, a formula that points back to the parent worksheet is essentially pointing to another worksheet. (See Figure 1.18.)

Figure 1.18
Select the title. Type an equal sign and then click a cell that contains the title.

Formula in Formula Bar

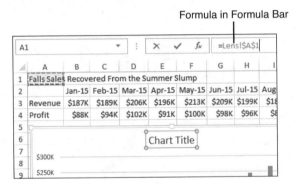

6. Press Enter. The words from the cell appear in the chart title. (See Figure 1.19.) If you later change the text in cell A1, the chart title updates.

Using this trick enables you to create a title that would change over time. For example, you could have a formula in A1 with ="Sales as of "&TEXT(TODAY(),"MMM D, YYYY").

Figure 1.19
It takes four clicks to set
up a dynamic title.

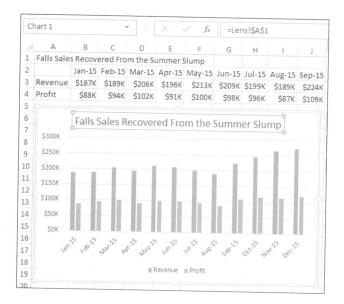

Handling Special Situations

You will frequently run into situations where the source data is not set up perfectly for charting. The techniques in this section assist you in creating the perfect chart from your existing data.

Charting Noncontiguous Data

Sometimes you have some extra rows or columns in your data that do not belong in the chart. The new strategy for Excel 2013 is to first create the chart with the extra cells and then use the Funnel icon to filter those rows or columns out of the chart.

Consider Figure 1.20. The data shows sales for four quarters. Someone added subtotal columns to total Half 1 and Half 2 as well as a grand total column. It is simple enough to not select columns G and H when you create the chart. But the subtotal for Half 1 in column D causes a spike in the middle of your chart.

The easy solution is to select the chart. Three icons appear to the right of the chart. Click the Funnel icon. A list of all your Series and Categories appears. Now uncheck H1 from the list. (See Figure 1.21.)

Figure 1.20
A subtotal for Half 1 is right in the middle of your contiguous data.

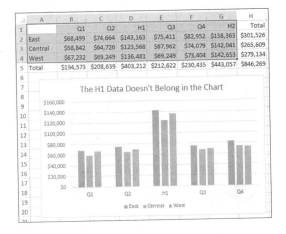

Figure 1.21
Remove H1 from the chart using the Funnel icon.

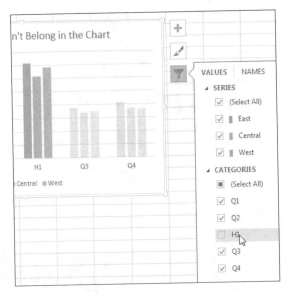

The result is a chart that omits the extra subtotal column. (See Figure 1.22.)

The old strategy is to use the Ctrl key to select noncontiguous data. Suppose you want to create a pie chart showing Profit by Region from the data in Figure 1.23. Follow these steps to select data for creating a chart:

1. Click in cell A1 and drag to cell A10 to select the range of category labels.

2. While holding down the Ctrl key, click in cell F1 and drag down to cell F10 to add F1:F10 to the selection.

3. If you have additional series to plot, repeat step 2 for each additional series.

Figure 1.22
After removing H1, only the quarters remain.

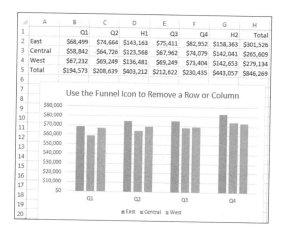

Figure 1.23
Selecting noncontiguous data requires a bit of dexterity because you attempt to drag while holding down the Ctrl key.

	Region	Units	Avg Price	Sales	GP%	Profit
1	Region	Units	Avg Price	Sales	GP%	Profit
2	Pacific Northwest	8564	87.44	748,836	45.7%	342,218
3	Northern California	5291	81.35	430,423	49.8%	214,351
4	Southern California	4977	75.54	375,963	45.0%	169,183
5	Great Plains	7010	81.26	569,633	49.1%	279,690
6	Southwest	5073	91.76	465,498	45.3%	210,871
7	Midwest	6756	76.06	513,861	48.8%	250,764
8	Southeast	7040	90.01	633,670	48.0%	304,162
9	Mid-Atlantic	8177	78.94	645,492	50.0%	322,746
10	Northeast	5644	92.58	522,522	49.7%	259,693

> **CAUTION**
>
> Excel remembers the order in which you selected the data. Although choosing cell A1 and then individually Ctrl+clicking cells F10, F9, B7, B3, F2, and so on could lead to a selection that looks the same as Figure 1.23, it would not create an acceptable chart. You must select the category labels first and then Ctrl+click and drag to select the first series.

The resulting chart is based on column A and column F. (See Figure 1.24.)

Figure 1.24
By selecting noncontiguous ranges, you can avoid using the Funnel icon.

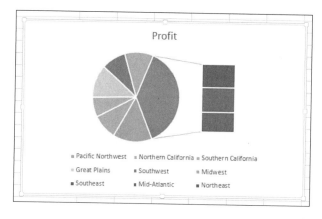

Charting Nonsummarized Data

The new Recommended Charts icon can detect when your data is not summarized and will offer to create a summary chart from the data.

Consider Figure 1.25. This data set contains 500+ rows of detailed data. It looks like a sales database. Creating a chart with 500+ detailed data points would not be a useful chart.

Figure 1.25
This data needs to be summarized before you create the chart.

	A	B	C	D	E	F	G	H	I
1	Region	Product	Date	Year	Customer	Quantity	Revenue	COGS	Profit
551	West	C345	30-Nov-16	2016	Superior Me	700	13314	5929	7385
552	South	A123	1-Dec-16	2016	Best Scoote	600	11628	5082	6546
553	East	A123	9-Dec-16	2016	Safe Aerobi	600	11208	5082	6126
554	South	C345	11-Dec-16	2016	Vivid Yardst	600	12606	5082	7524
555	Central	B234	19-Dec-16	2016	Enhanced E	1000	23990	10220	13770
556	Central	C345	19-Dec-16	2016	Persuasive	700	16408	6888	9520
557	South	F987	22-Dec-16	2016	Vivid Yardst	500	8780	4235	4545
558	East	A123	22-Dec-16	2016	Remarkable	900	18243	7623	10620
559	Central	A123	23-Dec-16	2016	Flexible Ink	200	3802	1694	2108
560	South	C345	26-Dec-16	2016	Alluring Raft	500	10195	4920	5275
561	West	A123	26-Dec-16	2016	Paramount	800	14440	6776	7664
562	West	E654	27-Dec-16	2016	Superior Me	500	11000	5110	5890
563	South	D456	27-Dec-16	2016	Vivid Yardst	400	8592	3936	4656
564	Central	A123	28-Dec-16	2016	Flexible Ink	500	12550	5110	7440

It is surprising that Excel 2013 handles the summarization for you. Select one cell in the data. Go to Insert, Recommended Chart. The Insert Chart dialog is offering Sum of Revenue by Product as the first chart. Excel is analyzing your data, looking for text columns that have a few values that repeat. In this data set, the six products and four regions become the focus of the recommended charts. (See Figure 1.26.)

Figure 1.26
Excel recommends a summary by product.

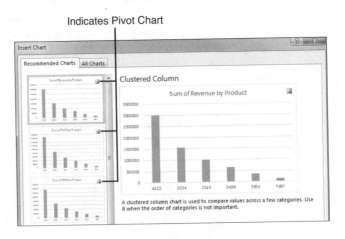

Indicates Pivot Chart

When you insert the chart, a new worksheet is inserted to the left of your worksheet. A summary table appears in A3, and a chart is built from that summary table. (See Figure 1.27.)

Figure 1.27
Excel summarizes the data on a new worksheet and produces a chart.

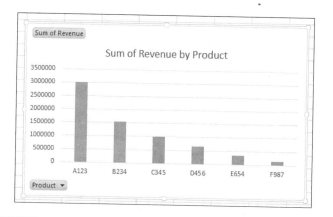

NOTE
The chart in Figure 1.27 is a special type of chart called a PivotChart. You can change the fields in the chart using the PivotChart Fields pane. Read more about pivot charts in Chapter 8, "Creating Pivot Charts and Power View Dashboards."

CAUTION
The algorithm for choosing which fields to summarize is a bit annoying. In this case, Excel chose Region and Product. Excel avoids Customer with 26 unique values, and it avoids Year with 3 unique numeric values. I've tried various tricks to get Year in the chart, to no avail. Rather than going to great lengths to trick Excel into choosing a column, Chapter 8 shows you how to remove Product in the pivot chart and replace it with Year.

Charting Differing Orders of Magnitude Using a Custom Combo Chart

Combo charts let you combine series that have different orders of magnitude. In Figure 1.28, the columns are showing weekly sales. The line is showing accumulated sales. By the end of Week 5, the line is going to be 500% of the size of an average week. As the quarter progresses, the weekly columns will get smaller and smaller compared to the line chart.

The solution is a combo chart with the line plotted on a secondary axis.

Excel 2013 introduces an easy-to-use dialog for creating combo charts. Follow these steps:

1. Select your data.
2. There is a Combo Chart icon on the Insert tab. The icon shows three columns and a line chart above the column chart. Open the Combo Chart drop-down and choose Create a Custom Combo Chart.
3. Excel automatically chooses a Clustered Column chart for Sales and a Line for YTD. Open the Chart Type drop-down for YTD and choose Line with Markers.
4. Check the box for Secondary Axis for the YTD chart.
5. Click OK to create the chart.

Figure 1.28
The new interface for creating combo charts removes the complexity from creating these charts.

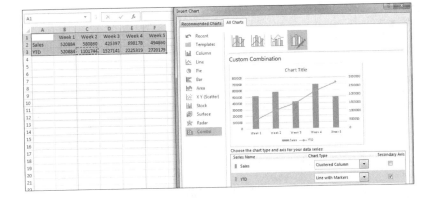

Reversing the Series and Categories in a Chart

Every data set can be plotted with the series coming from the rows or from the columns. When there are more columns than rows, Excel assumes each row is a series. When there are more rows than columns, Excel assumes each column is a series. When the data set is square, each row becomes a series. Although these choices often work, you might need to reverse them.

Figure 1.29 compares two ways to plot data with four seasons and 11 cities. By default, the seasons become the series and the cities become the categories, as in the top chart. You might want to show the data with the seasons as the cities, as in the bottom chart.

Figure 1.29
Both charts are valid ways to plot the data.

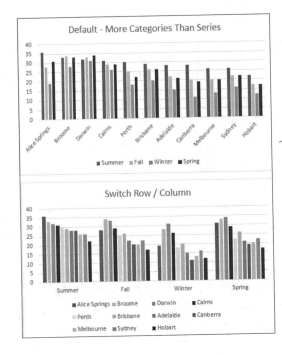

If you are creating the chart using the Insert Chart dialog, Excel 2013 shows you color thumbnails of both choices. The first thumbnail follows the rules for choosing the rows or columns as the series. The second chart has the data reversed. (See Figure 1.30.)

Figure 1.30
The Insert Chart dialog offers two choices, with rows as series or columns as series.

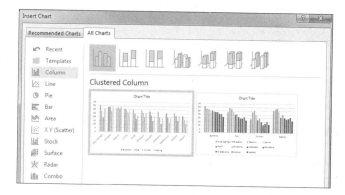

If you used Alt+F1 or any of the small icons in the Charts group to create the chart, you are going to get the default series. A large Switch Rows/Columns icon appears on the Chart Tools Design tab of the ribbon. Click this to switch the series to categories. (See Figure 1.31.)

Figure 1.31
Click this icon to switch the series and categories.

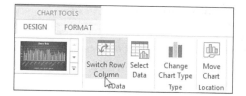

Changing the Data Sequence by Using Select Data

The Select Data icon on the Design tab enables you to change the rows and columns of your data set. The Select Data icon also enables you to resequence the order of the series. When you click this icon, the Select Data Source dialog appears.

As shown in Figure 1.32, buttons in the Legend Entries side of the Select Data Source dialog enable you to add new series, edit a series, remove a series, or change the sequence of a series. A single Edit button on the right side of the dialog enables you to edit the range used for category labels. (See Figure 1.32.)

Figure 1.32
You can use the Select Data Source dialog box for more control over data series.

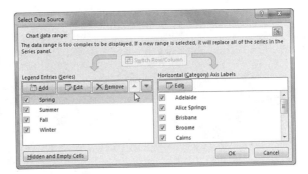

Using the Charting Tools

When you select a chart, a wide variety of charting tools are available to help you format the chart. You've seen a few of these tools already, such as the Funnel icon. All the charting tools are discussed in depth in Chapter 2. This section introduces the tools at your disposal.

Introducing the Three Helper Icons

When you select a chart, three icons appear to the right of a chart:

- **Plus icon** (aka Chart Elements)—This icon lets you quickly toggle various chart elements. Each element has a check box to turn the element on or off. If you hover to the right of an item, an arrowhead appears. Click the arrowhead to open a fly-out menu with more choices. (See Figure 1.33.)

- **Paintbrush icon** (aka Chart Styles)—This icon is possibly the best new icon in all of Excel 2013. Microsoft had 153 new chart styles professionally designed for Excel 2013. Choices in the Paintbrush icon let you apply a style in a few clicks. Your charts will look modern and new. A second menu under the icon lets you change colors. (See Figure 1.34.)

- **Funnel icon** (aka Chart Filters)—This icon lets you hide or show individual rows or columns in the data. You've used this icon previously in Figure 1.21.

Figure 1.33
The Plus icon lets you add elements to your chart.

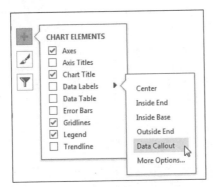

Figure 1.34
The Paintbrush icon quickly applies a style to a chart or changes the colors.

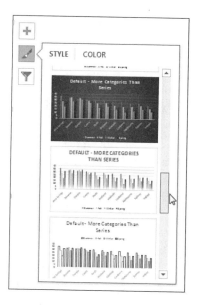

Introducing the Format Task Pane

The old Format dialog box has been replaced by the Format task pane in Excel 2013. If you double-click any element in the chart, you can edit dozens of settings for that element using the choices in the Format task pane.

When the task pane is visible, you can switch to formatting a new element by clicking that element. The choices and menus in the task pane change in response to the current selection.

> **NOTE** In fact, if you click away from the chart, the task pane remains. All the choices are grayed out until you again click a chart, shape, picture, or other object.

The task pane is smaller than the old Format dialog box. This led the Excel team to use a new three-level menu system in the task pane. It becomes quite the guessing game to figure out where you can find a particular setting in the task pane. Refer to Figure 1.35 to locate all three levels of menus:

- The words Format Legend tell you what you are formatting. If you click another element in the chart, these words would change. The drop-down arrow next to the title lets you move the task pane, but it does not let you switch to another element.
- Underneath the large Format Legend are two menus choices, one for Legend Options and one for Text Options. The currently selected choice is green. The drop-down arrow next to the first menu choice lets you change the element that you are

formatting. This arrow really seems like it should be appearing next to the title of the task pane.

- Underneath the two main menu choices, a row of icons appears. Each of these icons is a choice in the second-level menu for the task pane. In Figure 1.35, the icons are a Paint Bucket, Pentagon, and a Chart. The row of icons changes if you choose a different element and when you change to a different level 1 menu item. See Table 1.1 for an attempt to explain the icons you see here.

- Beneath the icons, you see one or more expandable categories in all caps. Click the arrow next to the category to display all the choices for that category. In Figure 1.35, you see Format Legend, Legend Options, Paint Bucket, Border expanded. There is another category for Fill that could be expanded.

Figure 1.35
Formatting choices are hidden among a four-level menu in the task pane.

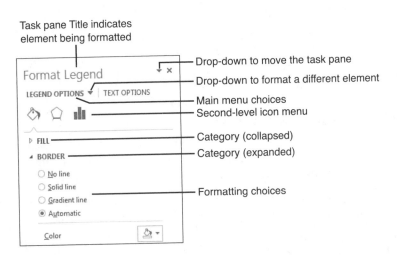

So far, I've managed to get eight different icons to appear in the level-2 menu in the Format task pane. I would not be completely surprised if there are more. Table 1.1 shows each icon and where it is generally used.

Table 1.1   Format Task Pane Icons

Icon	Looks Like	Official Name	Uses
	Paint Bucket	Fill & Line	Fill and border color
	Pentagon	Effects	Shadow, glow, soft edges, 3D format
	Resize	Size & Properties	Location
	Chart	Variously: Table, Axis, Legend, Series, Trendline, Data Label, Error Bar	Good stuff. Always start here.

Icon	Looks Like	Official Name	Uses
A	Text Fill	Text Fill & Outline	Text color
A	Text Effects	Text Effects	Shadow, reflection, glow, soft edges, 3D format, 3D rotation
A	Text Box	Textbox	Alignment
(picture)	Picture	Picture	Corrections, color, crop

1

> **NOTE**
> Even though my friend and tech editor Bob Umlas will protest when this book does not use the correct name for something, I am going to use the names in the Looks Like column of Table 1.1 when referring to the icons in the task pane. The official names simply are not descriptive enough.

> **TIP**
> When you start looking for a setting, see if you have the Chart icon. If you do, start there. The best settings are always under the Chart icon.

Table 1.2 identifies which icons will appear as you are formatting various chart elements.

Table 1.2   Icons Available per Chart Element

Element Being Formatted	Paint Bucket	Pentagon	Resize	Chart	Text Fill	Text Effects	Text Box	Picture
Chart Area	•	•	•		•	•	•	
Plot Area	•	•			•	•	•	
Series	•	•		•				
Data Point	•	•		•				
Data Labels	•	•	•	•				
Chart Title	•	•	•		•	•	•	
Axis (any)	•	•	•		•	•	•	
Axis Title	•	•	•		•	•	•	
Legend	•	•		•	•	•	•	
Gridlines (any)	•	•						
Data Table	•	•		•	•	•	•	
Trendline	•	•		•				

Element Being Formatted	Paint Bucket	Pentagon	Resize	Chart	Text Fill	Text Effects	Text Box	Picture
Series Lines	•	•						
High-Low Lines	•	•						
Error Bar	•	•		•				
Drop Lines	•	•						
Down Bars	•	•						
Up Bars	•	•						
Shape	•	•	•		•	•	•	•
Picture/Clipart	•	•	•					•

Using Commands on the Design Tab

In most cases, the tools available on the Design tab in the ribbon are redundant with commands previously discussed.

The Add Chart Element drop-down is similar to the Plus icon to the right of the chart. The version in the ribbon adds choices for High-Low Lines, Error Bars, and Up/Down Bars.

The Quick Layout drop-down (see Figure 1.36) was a new idea in Excel 2007, and it never caught on. It offers 4 to 12 ways to format the chart. The charts were not professionally designed. These layouts will rarely be exactly what you need. There are 780 quadrillion possible ways to configure a chart, and this layout gallery offers anywhere from 4 to 12 possible layouts. The odds that your desired layout is represented exactly are slim. For the most part, the choices here are not relevant.

Figure 1.36
These old Quick Layout choices never caught on.

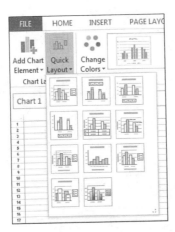

The Change Colors drop-down is identical to the Color menu choice in the Paintbrush icon to the right of the chart.

The Chart Styles gallery is a slightly larger view of the Styles menu in the Paintbrush icon.

The two icons in the Data group let you change the data in the chart.

Change Chart Type is a good place if you decide that you want to change a column chart to an area chart. The same command is in the right-click menu when you click the chart.

Move Chart lets you move a chart to a dedicated chart sheet, in case you want to feel like it is 1985 all over again.

Micromanaging Formatting Using the Format Tab

Everything on the Format tab of the ribbon is redundant with the Formatting task pane. It might be easier to find Shape Fill to change the fill color or Shape Outline to change a border color using the Format tab in the ribbon.

All of the Shape Effects add items like glow, bevel, and so on. Professor Edward Tufte characterizes all this as "chart junk"—effects that add no useful information to the chart.

Using Commands on the Home Tab

If you need to change the font size, color, bold, italic, or typeface, it is easy to select an element in the chart and then use the Font group in the Home tab to format the text.

In Figure 1.37, the title spills to a second line. Click the title once so there is a solid box around the title. You can use the Decrease Font Size icon to make the title size smaller.

Figure 1.37
Use the icons on the Home tab to change the text in the selected chart element.

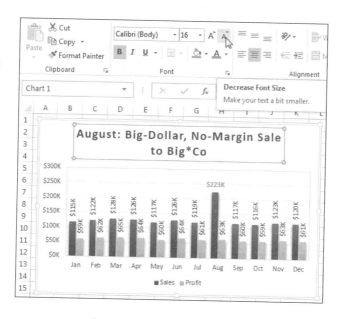

Changing the Theme on the Page Layout tab

The built-in color choices for a chart include variations of six colors. In Excel 2013, the default colors are Blue, Orange, Gray, Gold, Dark Blue, and Green.

You are not stuck with those colors.

Those six colors are part of a theme. Although everyone starts with the same theme, there are 48 themes to choose from on the Page Layout tab of the ribbon.

On the Page Layout tab, click the Themes drop-down to choose from the 48 built-in themes. If you choose a new theme from the Themes drop-down, Excel applies a new color and set of effects to all the charts in the current workbook. If you want to change only the colors or effects, use the Colors or Effects drop-down in the Themes group. Figure 1.38 shows the themes drop-down.

Figure 1.38
Change colors using the Themes drop-down.

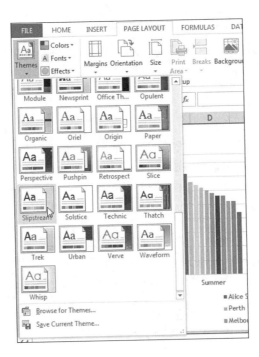

Moving Charts

After creating a chart, you might need to rearrange the data or move the chart to a new location. The topics in this section assist you with these tasks.

Moving a Chart Within the Current Worksheet

In the following case study, you see that Excel had an annoying habit of locating new charts near the bottom of your data set. With a large data set, you might need to move the chart to the proper location thousands of rows away.

There are several ways to move a chart within the current worksheet. Although it is easy to move the chart a few rows in the active window, you should switch to using cut and paste if you have to move the chart hundreds of rows.

Dragging to a New Location in the Visible Window Is Easy

You can drag a chart anywhere in the visible window. Click the border of the chart, avoiding the eight resize handles, and drag. If you try to drag the chart outside of the visible window, the mouse pointer changes to a red "no" symbol. If you release the mouse while it is the no symbol, the chart boomerangs back to its original position.

Dragging Outside of the Visible Window Is Frustrating

If you need to move a chart outside the visible window, drag so that your cell pointer is within one-half row of the edge of the window. Excel slowly starts to scroll in the appropriate direction. As with other Windows programs, you can speed up the scroll by rapidly moving your mouse left and right. However, it is difficult to keep the mouse within the one-half row tolerance while moving left and right.

Adjust the Zoom So New Location Is Within the Visible Window

You are likely to find the scrolling action to be so slow that you will not want to use the previous technique to move the chart to a new location. Another option is to use the Zoom slider to show the worksheet at a 10% zoom. This has the effect of putting about 375 rows in the visible window. If you need to move a chart anywhere from 50 to 375 rows, setting the zoom to 10% and then dragging the chart within the visible window is a fast way to go.

Cut and Paste to Move Thousands of Rows

If your chart is created at the bottom of a 50,000-row data set and you need to move it to the top of the data set, cut and paste might be the fastest way to go. Follow these steps to move a chart within the current worksheet using cut and paste:

1. Select a chart.
2. Press Ctrl+X to cut the chart from the worksheet.
3. Press Ctrl+Home to move to cell A1.
4. Select the cell where you want the top-left corner of the chart to appear.
5. Press Ctrl+V to paste the chart in the new location.

1

CASE STUDY: LOCATING A CHART AT THE TOP OF YOUR DATA SET

The best way to avoid having to move the chart thousands of rows is to have the top of your data set visible before you create the chart.

Suppose that you have 3,000 data points to show on a line chart. If you start in cell A1 and use Ctrl+Shift+down arrow and Ctrl+Shift+right arrow to select the data, you will have row 3000 visible in the window. If you create a chart, the chart appears near row 3000 instead of at the top of the data set.

By changing your workflow slightly, you can make sure the top of the data set is visible before creating the chart.

If you've already selected the data set using Ctrl+Shift+Arrow, use the Ctrl+. (that is, Ctrl+period) shortcut key to move the focus to a new corner of the data. After pressing the shortcut key between one and three times, you will see the top of the data set. Use Alt+F1 or Insert, Recommended Chart to insert the chart near the top of the workbook.

Alternatively, start using Ctrl+* to select the data set. If you start in A2 and press Ctrl+*, Excel selects down to row 3000, but the window stays focused on the top of the worksheet.

Moving a Chart to a Different Worksheet

In Excel 2013, charts always start out as objects embedded in a worksheet. However, you might want to display a chart on its own full-page chart sheet. When this occurs, there are two options for moving a chart:

■ Choose the Move Chart icon at the right edge of the Design tab.

■ Right-click any whitespace near the border of the chart and choose Move Chart.

Either way, the Move Chart dialog appears, offering the options New Sheet and Object In. The Object In drop-down lists all the worksheets in the current workbook. The New Sheet option enables you to specify a name for a new sheet (see Figure 1.39).

Figure 1.39
Move a chart to a different worksheet using the Move Chart dialog.

Next Steps

Chapter 2 describes how to use the Layout tab of the ribbon to toggle on or off individual elements of the chart. It also describes how you can micromanage individual elements using the Format ribbon.

Customizing Charts

Accessing Element Formatting Tools

In Chapter 1, "Introducing Charts in Excel 2013," you learned how to create a chart using the Insert tab. You also learned how to choose built-in chart styles and colors from the Paintbrush icon to the right of the chart.

For many people, using one of the new built-in styles is sufficient. You can live with those defaults and never have to tweak the settings for any chart element.

However, eventually a time may come when a particular manager needs some chart element tweaked on the chart. In those cases, you will have to move beyond the chart styles and learn how to adjust a chart element.

There are also cases where you might need a particular chart element that the built-in chart styles will not offer.

This chapter covers the formatting choices for the individual elements in a chart. Depending on the chart type, there are 36 different types of chart elements that can be customized on a chart.

Unfortunately, all 36 elements are not available in any single list or drop-down in Excel 2013. You can find the tools for adding or editing various elements in the following places:

- The Plus icon to the right of a selected chart lets you add 10 types of chart elements.
- Hover over any item in the Plus icon list to display a fly-out arrow. Click the arrow to show a few choices for that element. This is similar to the choices in the Excel 2007–2010 Layout tab of the ribbon. It is usually a small subset of items available in the Formatting task pane.

2

IN THIS CHAPTER

Accessing Element Formatting Tools 35

Identifying Chart Elements.........................37

Formatting Chart Elements 41

Formatting a Series......................................72

Changing the Theme Colors on the Page Layout Tab...74

Storing Your Favorite Settings in a Chart Template 75

Next Steps 75

- The Add Chart Element drop-down in the Design tab of the ribbon shows all the choices in the Plus icon, with the addition of Drop-Lines and Hi/Lo Lines.

- The Current Selection drop-down in the Format tab of the ribbon offers a comprehensive list of all elements present in the current chart. If you need to edit an existing element, you can choose it from the Current Selection drop-down, and then use the Format Selection icon to display the Formatting task pane for that element. Some changes can be made to the selected element using formatting icons on the Home tab or Format tab of the ribbon.

- If you can see an element in the chart, you can double-click the element to open the Format task pane for that element. You can also right-click and choose Format to get to the same task pane. Or single-click and press Ctrl+1. Sometimes an element appears, but it is too small to be clicked. Then you have to use the Current Selection drop-down in the Format tab of the ribbon.

- When the task pane is already displaying, you can single-click any chart element to change the task pane to format the newly clicked element.

- Some items can be formatted only if you select them first; you will never see a choice to format an individual point in any menu or drop-down list. However, if you single-click a series and then single-click a data point, that point appears in the Current Selection drop-down on the Format tab.

Table 2.1 shows each of the types of chart elements and where you can find the tools to add or format the element.

Table 2.1 Types of Elements in a Chart

Type of Element	Plus Icon	Design Tab	Format Tab
Axes	•	•	•
Axis titles	•	•	‡
Chart title	•	•	‡
Data labels	•	•	‡
Data table	•	•	‡
Error bars	•	•	‡
Gridlines	•	•	‡
Legend	•	•	‡
Lines—drop lines		•	‡
Lines—hi/lo lines		•	‡
Trendline	•	•	‡
Up/down bars	•	•	‡
Chart area			•

Type of Element	Plus Icon	Design Tab	Format Tab
Plot area			•
Series			•
Point			†
Data labels—point			†
Legend entry—point			†
Back wall			3D
Floor			3D
Side wall			3D
Walls			3D

Legend for Table 2.1

• Add or format an element

‡ Format an element that already exists in the chart

† Appears only if you've previously selected the point

> **NOTE**
>
> There are 22 types of elements listed in Table 2.1. An element type can have multiple elements. Seven types of axes may appear in a chart. There are four types of gridlines: major vertical, minor vertical, major horizontal, and minor horizontal. Even Up/Down Bars appear as two elements in the Current Selection drop-down on the Format tab: Up Bars 1 and Down Bars 1. This enables you to format the up bars in one color and the down bars in another color.

3D Appears only when the chart uses a 3D chart type

This chapter walks you through the various chart components that can be customized. It also provides tips and tricks for creating eye-catching but meaningful results.

Identifying Chart Elements

Many elements of a chart can be customized. You rarely want to include all the available elements in a single chart because too many elements detract from the meaning of the data in the chart. Therefore, you should use titles, axes, and gridlines judiciously to help the reader understand the data presented in a chart.

Recognizing Chart Labels and Axes

Figure 2.1 shows a chart that has too many elements. They were included to help identify various elements in the chart.

Figure 2.1 contains the following elements:

Figure 2.1
This chart shows various elements available in a 2D chart.

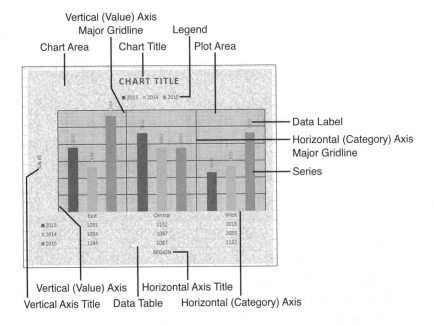

- **Chart area**—The entire range shown in Figure 2.1, including all the area outside the plot area. The chart area is where axis titles, chart titles, and legends often appear.

- **Plot area**—The rectangular area that includes the data series and data points. Gridlines appear inside the plot area. Axes typically appear at one or more edges of the plot area. Data points appear inside the plot area. Data labels usually start inside the plot area but are allowed to spill outside of the plot area.

- **Chart title**—Typically appears in a larger font near the top of the chart. Whereas Excel 2003 always included the chart title outside the plot area, choices in Excel 2013 encourage you to have the title overlaying the plot area.

- **Horizontal axis title**—Identifies the type of data along the horizontal axis. In case it is not clear that "East Central West" represent regions, you can add a horizontal axis title such as the one shown near the bottom of Figure 2.1.

- **Vertical axis title**—Commonly used along the left side of a chart to identify the units along the axis. In Figure 2.1, the word "Sales" along the left side of the chart is the vertical axis title.

- **Legend**—Initially appears below the chart to help identify which color in the chart represents which series. The legend can be dragged anywhere in the chart area or plot area.

- **Data label**—Labels each point with the actual value, percentage, category name, or series name. Data labels are frequently overwritten by gridlines and other charting elements. Far too often, individual data labels need to be nudged so they can be read. New in Excel 2013, a data label can appear in a callout that obscures the underlying gridline.

■ **Data table**—Instead of using data labels, you can have Excel add a spreadsheet, such as a data table beneath the plot area. The data table frequently takes up too much space in the chart area and reduces the size available for the plot area.

■ **Horizontal (category) axis**—Appears along the bottom of the chart for column and line charts and along the left side for bar charts. The horizontal axis is also referred to as the category axis. Your main choice is whether the axis contains a time series. If it does, Excel varies the spacing between the points to represent actual dates.

■ **Vertical (value) axis**—The axis along the left side of the chart in a column or line chart. In some advanced charts, you might have a second vertical axis on the right side of the chart. This axis typically contains values, and your main choice is whether you want the axis scaled in thousands, millions, and so on.

■ **Gridlines**—Typically run horizontally across the plot area and line up with each number along the vertical axis. To show more gridlines, edit the axis scale options. If you do not have data labels on a chart, the horizontal gridlines are particularly useful for telling whether a particular point is just above or below a certain level. It is best to keep gridlines unobtrusive. Some of the best charts include gridlines in a faint color so they do not obscure the main message of the chart. You can have major gridlines and minor gridlines running horizontally and/or vertically in the plot area. If your chart uses a secondary axis, you can have gridlines lined up with either the primary or secondary axis. The chart in Figure 2.1 includes both vertical and horizontal major gridlines.

Recognizing Analysis Elements

The analysis elements include error bars, drop lines, trendlines, up/down bars, and hi/lo lines. Figure 2.2 illustrates some of the analysis elements.

Figure 2.2
This chart shows the various analysis elements.

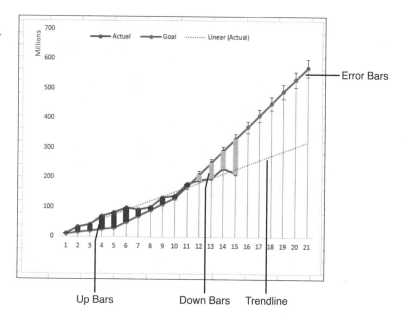

The following are the analysis elements:

- **Trendline**—If you ask for a trendline, Excel uses regression analysis to fit your existing data points to a statistical line. You can have Excel extend this line into future time periods. In Figure 2.2, the dotted trendline shows that unless you alter the system that has been generating those actuals, you will likely miss the goal.

- **Drop lines**—The vertical lines that extend from the data point to the horizontal axis in either line or area charts. Drop lines are helpful because they enable the reader to locate the exact point where the line intersects the axis.

- **Up/down bars**—When you are plotting two series on a line chart, Excel can draw rectangles between the two lines. In Figure 2.2, when the actual exceeds the goal in days 2 through 11, the up/down bars are shown in a dark color. When the goal exceeds the actual in days 11 through 15, the up/down error bars are shown in a contrasting color. If the up/down error bars seem too wide, try using high/low lines.

- **Error bars**—This feature is popular in scientific analysis to show the error of an estimate. You might see these used in business charts to indicate the acceptable tolerance from a quality goal. For example, a quality goal might be to achieve 99.5% quality, with anything between 99% and 100% being acceptable. The error bars could be added to the 99.5% goal series to show whether the actual quality falls within the acceptable tolerance. In Figure 2.2, the error bars are set to 5% above and below the goal value.

Identifying Special Elements in a 3D Chart

Some chart elements are editable only in 3D charting styles. Figure 2.3 shows a 3D column chart.

Figure 2.3
This chart shows the various elements available in a 3D chart.

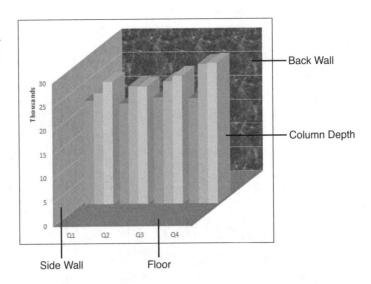

The following are the 3D chart elements:

- **Back wall**—In Figure 2.3, the back wall is formatted with a dark green texture.
- **Side wall**—In Figure 2.3, the side wall is formatted with a gray fill.
- **Floor**—The surface below the 3D columns.
- **Column depth**—One of the many 3D rotation settings you can change. In Figure 2.3, each column appears to be a deep rectangular slab. This effect is created by increasing the column depth. The chart has also been tipped forward a bit, so it appears that the viewer is at a slightly higher viewing angle.

Formatting Chart Elements

When formatting chart elements, you generally start with some of the built-in choices available from the fly-out menus in the Plus icon. You can then move on to full control over the chart element using the Format task pane, the mini toolbar, the Home tab, or the Format tab.

Moving the Legend

When you create a chart with more than one series in Excel 2013, Excel adds a legend. The legend always starts at the bottom of the chart. Charting gurus suggest that the legend should appear above or to the left of the chart. The built-in choices for the legend include having the legend outside the left, right, bottom, or top of the plot area. If you move the legend to the left or right, Excel rearranges the legend in a vertical format, as shown in Figure 2.4.

Some charts don't need a legend. Having category name labels on a pie chart or including a data table can make the legend redundant. To remove the legend, choose Design, Add Chart Element, Legend, None. Or click the legend in the chart and press Delete.

By default, the legend is always outside of the plot area. You can drag the legend and drop it inside the plot area. New in Excel 2013, the Format Legend task pane offers a check box for Show the Legend Without Overlapping the Chart. Uncheck this setting to have the legend overlay the plot area.

Figure 2.4
The reader should encounter the legend before the chart. Position the legend above or to the left of the chart.

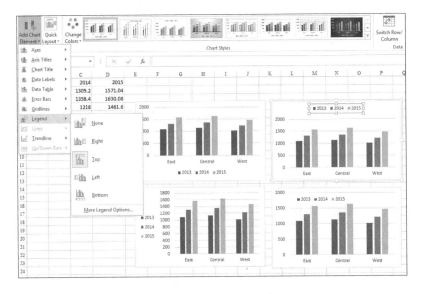

Changing the Arrangement of a Legend

Excel decides if a legend will be horizontal or vertical. You can override the default behavior. Click the Legend to activate the resizing handles. Drag the corner resize handle. Figure 2.5 shows the original horizontal legend. Drag the legend into a square shape to have a 2×2 arrangement. Drag the legend into a vertical shape to have a vertical legend.

Starting in Excel 2010, the legend has no fill or outline. This can cause the gridlines to show through the legend, as in the top example in Figure 2.5. The second example has a white fill but no outline. With the legend selected, choose Format Shape Fill, White.

The third legend has a white fill and a black outline. After changing the fill, go to Format, Shape Outline, Black to add an outline.

Figure 2.5
You have some control over the arrangement of the labels in the legend when you resize the legend border.

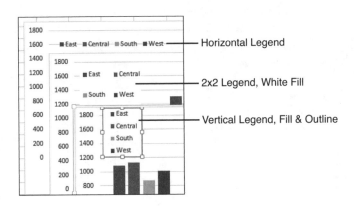

Formatting Individual Legend Entries

A feature in Excel 2013 is the capability to format or resize the individual legend entries. This proves particularly useful when one entry is longer than the other entries. To format an individual legend, follow these steps:

1. Click the legend so the entire legend is selected.
2. Click the legend entry you want to change.
3. To change the font size, right-click the text and use the options in the mini toolbar. To change anything else, use the Home tab or the Format tab. To delete that particular legend entry, press Delete.

Deleting a legend is useful when you are using extra series to add elements to a chart. Several examples in Chapter 7, "Advanced Chart Techniques," utilize this method.

Adding Data Labels to a Chart

By default, your chart does not have labels on each point. To add labels, click the Plus icon, hover over data labels, click the fly-out arrow, and choose one of the chart label locations: Center, Inside End, Inside Base, Outside End, or Data Callout. (See Figure 2.6.) Note that Outside End is not available for stacked column or bar charts.

Figure 2.6
Use the Plus icon to add data labels to the chart.

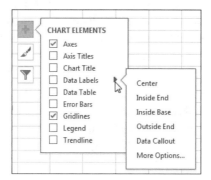

The five label locations are shown in Figure 2.7. Assuming that you are showing the numeric value in the label, it is better to have the label near the top of the column, either using Inside End, Outside End, or Data Callout.

Figure 2.7
You have five choices for the label location.

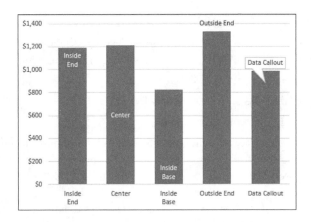

Correcting Data Labels Crossed Out by Gridlines

If your chart has dark gridlines, it might appear that one or more data labels is crossed out by the gridline. There are several solutions to this problem.

- It is tedious, but you can nudge an individual data label. Click any data label to select all labels for that series and then click the label being crossed out. You've now selected a single data label. Drag the label up or down slightly so it does not hit the gridline. After you have a single data label selected, you can single-click any other label to select that label. Note that when your data changes, you might have to repeat this process. Consider using one of the other methods.

- The problem happens in the first place because the box holding a data label is transparent. A quick solution is to add a white fill to the box. Select the labels. On the Format tab, choose Shape Fill and choose white.

- Convert the labels to use a Data Callout. You can do this with the Plus icon, hover over Data Labels, open the fly-out menu, and choose Data Callout.

Figure 2.8 compares the three methods.

Figure 2.8
When gridlines and data labels intersect, you have three alternatives to alleviate the problem.

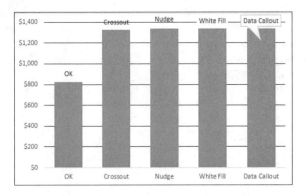

Changing the Content in the Label

Most often, data labels contain the value from that point. However, at times you may want to show a combination of the category name as well as the value. The Format Data Labels task pane offers any combination of Series Name, Category Name, and Value. Certain charts, such as pie charts, allow you to choose a percentage. You can specify that each part of the data label is separated by a comma, space, new line, and so on. New in Excel 2013, the text for the label can come from other cells in your workbook. This enables you to use formulas to calculate the data labels.

To access the Format Data Labels task pane, double-click any data label. Click the Chart icon in the task pane and then expand the Label Options category. In Figure 2.9, the data label contains the category name and value, separated by a space.

Figure 2.9
You can choose which content to include in the data labels.

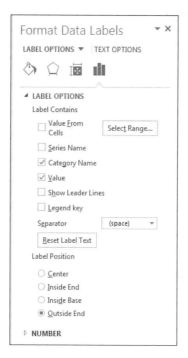

Making Wide Labels Fit in a Chart

In Excel 2013, the numeric format for the data label in a chart comes from the format in the underlying cells. If you are trying to label a chart with 12 columns of monthly data, the labels will likely be too large to fit.

In the top-left chart in Figure 2.10, the labels use a format of $143,390 and many labels are running into adjacent labels. There are three easy solutions.

- Double-click the values along the vertical axis to display the Format Axis task pane. Click the Chart icon. Expand the Axis Options. Change the Display Units drop-down to Thousands. A Display Units label displays next to the axis. The labels automatically shorten to show $143 to represent about $143,000 instead of $143,390. (See the top-right chart in Figure 2.10.)

- Double-click any column in the chart to display the Format Data Series task pane. Drag the Gap Width slider from 150% to about 40%. This makes the columns wider. Click any label to display the Format Data Labels task pane. Choose the Chart icon and then expand the Number category. Type a custom number format code into the Format Code box and click Add. For example, to display numbers in thousands, use #,##0,K. (See the bottom-left chart in Figure 2.10.)

- Rotate the labels. Click any label and then use the Orientation icon in the Alignment group of the Home tab. Choose Rotate Text Up to rotate the data labels as shown in the bottom-right chart of Figure 2.10.

Figure 2.10
Shorten or rotate the data labels to make them fit.

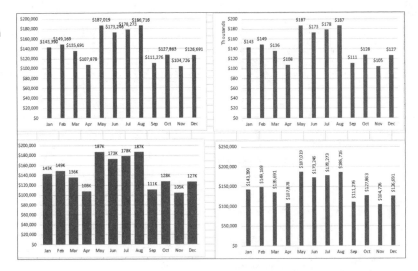

Adding a Data Table to a Chart

A data table is a miniworksheet that appears below a chart. In it, Excel shows the values for each data point in the table. One advantage of a data table is that you can show the numbers that would normally be shown with data labels without adding any elements to the plot area.

There are two built-in options in the Data Table fly-out menu: You can show the data table with legend keys or without legend keys.

The data table takes up a fair amount of space at the bottom of the chart. Putting the legend keys in the table allows you to regain some of that space by eliminating the legend element from the chart.

When you choose More Options to get to the Format Data Table task pane, you can toggle on or off the horizontal or vertical lines between cells in the table. You can use the text formatting tools on the Home tab to apply a new font, font color, or size. The numeric format shown in the table is the same as the number format applied to the source cells in the worksheet.

In the chart in the top in Figure 2.11, the legend keys appear in the chart. In the chart on the bottom, the legend keys are not shown. The font has been changed. The vertical gridlines are removed.

Figure 2.11
A data table provides a concise grid for the actual values without adding extra data to the plot area itself.

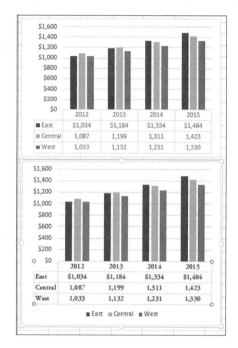

	2012	2013	2014	2015
■ East	$1,034	$1,184	$1,334	$1,484
■ Central	1,087	1,199	1,311	1,423
■ West	1,033	1,132	1,231	1,330

	2012	2013	2014	2015
East	$1,034	$1,184	$1,334	$1,484
Central	1,087	1,199	1,311	1,423
West	1,033	1,132	1,231	1,330

■ East ■ Central ■ West

Formatting Axes

Unlike the previously described elements that are fairly cosmetic, the axis options have major ramifications on how the chart will appear. Changing the minimum and maximum bounds for the value axis controls how the chart zooms in on the data. Setting the Units in the Axis Options affects the appearance of major and minor gridlines in a chart.

Most charts (column, line, bar, area, XY scatter) have two axes. A pie chart actually has no axes. A radar chart has one axis. A surface chart has three axes. When you create a combo chart and check Secondary Axis, you add a third axis to column, line, bar, and area charts. The same setting in an XY Scatter chart adds a third and fourth axis (see Figure 2.12).

Figure 2.12
Depending on the chart settings, you will have zero to four axes.

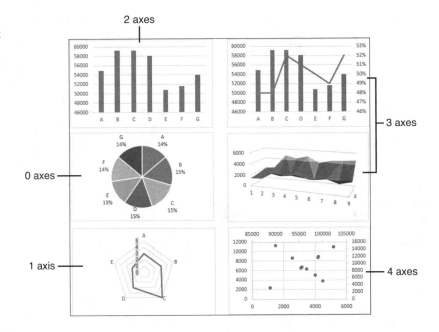

Axes can either represent Value or Categories. In a typical line or column chart, the values axis is the vertical axis. The category axis appears along the bottom of the chart. These are reversed in a bar chart; the category axis appears along the side and the values appear across the top. In XY Scatter charts, all the axes represent values.

Changing the Scale of a Values Axis

Typically, a chart has a vertical axis that runs from zero to a value larger than the largest value in the data set. There are exceptions.

- Excel breaks this rule when the range between the minimum and maximum value in the chart is less than 20% of the minimum and 1/6th of the maximum. For example, suppose that your values are between 100 and 200. The range is 100. This is 100% of the minimum and 50% of the maximum, so Excel shows a zero-based scale. However, if your data runs from 500 to 600, the range is 100. This is 20% of the minimum and 16.6667% of the maximum, so Excel automatically adjusts the chart to show 440 to 620. Sometimes this is good. Sometimes it is bad. In the top-left chart of Figure 2.13, Excel automatically chose an axis starting at 150,000. This makes it look like sales from 2012 to 2015 grew sixfold. This is not true. Sales are up, but only by 16.7%.

- You can choose to change the bounds when you want to zoom in on a part of the chart. In the top-right chart in Figure 2.13, the values are expected to fall in the 156,000 to 156,200 range. If you use a zero-based axis, none of the variability shows through. By changing the axis bounds to 156,000 to 156,120, you can see the variability from hour to hour as shown in the bottom-right chart.

■ When you are using a secondary axis, you might want both the primary and secondary axes to have identical scales. In this case, you will want to override the automatic settings. Even if Excel calculates automatic values of 180,000, you should type 180,000 in the bounds box to change the setting from Auto to Manual. This prevents Excel from later changing the bounds.

Figure 2.13
Change the bounds for the axis to convey the proper message in the chart.

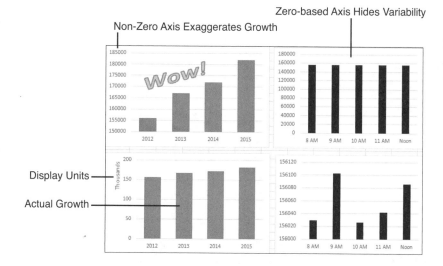

To change the axis bounds, follow these steps:

1. Double-click the numbers along the axis. Excel displays the Format Axis task pane.

2. In the task pane, click the Chart icon. Open the Axis Options category. You see settings for Minimum, Maximum, Major, and Minor. The word Auto to the right of the value means that this is an automatic setting that Excel might later change if the values change. Reset means that someone has explicitly typed a manual value. In Figure 2.14, the chart has been forced to have a minimum of zero. The maximum is recalculated by Excel. The Major setting of 50,000 forces Excel to show an axis label every 50,000 units.

3. Near the bottom of the Axis Options category, a drop-down appears for Display Units. Change this value to hundreds, thousands, millions, billions, or trillions to prevent an unruly number of zeroes appearing in the axis labels. In Figure 2.15, the United States National Debt chart can be shown with an axis of trillions.

Figure 2.14
Change the bounds for the axis to convey the proper message in the chart.

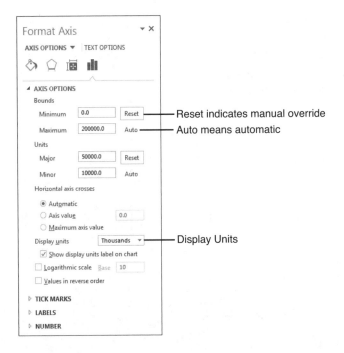

Reset indicates manual override
Auto means automatic

Display Units

Figure 2.15
Change the Display Units to get rid of the extra zeroes in the axis labels.

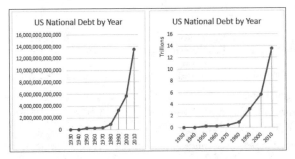

Showing Different Orders of Magnitude Using a Logarithmic Axis

Logarithmic axis is a useful choice when you need to compare numbers of different scales along the same series. Although the concept of logarithmic axes sounds scary, there is a simple use for it.

Suppose that you have a series of data with both large and small data values, such as sales by model line. Your company probably has high-flying models that account for 80% of your revenue, and then has some older-model lines that are still hanging around. When you try to plot these items on a chart, Excel must make the axis scale large enough to show the sales of the best-selling products. This causes the detail for the smaller product lines to become lost because the values are a relatively small percentage of the entire scale.

In Figure 2.16, there is important data regarding the first three product lines. However, when looking at the chart, no one will be able to see if the sales of these products were near the forecast.

When this occurs, the solution is to convert the axis to a logarithmic axis. In a logarithmic axis, the distance from 1 to 10 is the same as the distance from 10 to 100, and so on. This enables you to see detail of the product selling a few hundred units as well as the products selling 100,000 units.

To convert to a logarithmic scale, double-click the value axis labels. In the Format task pane, choose the Chart icon, Axis Options, and Logarithmic Scale. New in Excel 2013, you can change the base of the logarithm from 10.

In Figure 2.16, the Minimum has been changed from 1 to 100 to avoid extra whitespace in the bottom of the plot area.

Figure 2.16
The bottom chart uses a logarithmic scale.

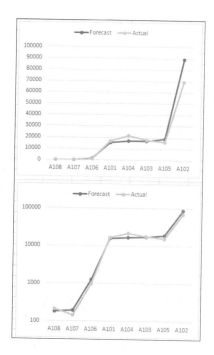

> **NOTE**
> Scientists might say that I would be remiss for not defining a logarithm. A logarithm is the power to which a base, such as 10, must be reduced to produce a given number. Luckily, you do not have to understand that sentence in order to use this setting to improve your charts that show a range of magnitudes.

┌─ C A U T I O N ───
│ The log scale cannot be used if your data contains negative numbers. There is no way to raise 10 to a
│ power and get a negative number. It would be helpful if Excel could actually use the log concept to
│ show negative numbers—sort of a pseudo-log scale.
└──

Controlling Labels Along the Category Axis

The category axis, which contains the category labels, appears along the bottom of the
chart in column, line, area, and stock charts. It appears along the left side of the chart in
bar charts. When your chart has many data points, Excel tries to fit as many labels along
the axis as possible. In Figure 2.17, the top chart spans from 1965 to 2012. Excel decided to
skip every other label, creating labels of 1965, 1967, 1969, and so on. You can override this
choice.

1. Double-click the numbers along the category axis. Excel opens the Format Axis task
    pane.

2. In the task pane, choose the Chart icon and then expand the Labels category.

3. Change the Interval Between Labels from Automatic to 5. This forces Excel to show
    labels at 1965, 1970, 1975, and so on.

Note that the category labels always start by displaying the first value. Had the data run
from 1961 to 2012, there would not be a good way to have the years ending in 5 and 0
appear as the labels.

Figure 2.17
Control the axis labels.

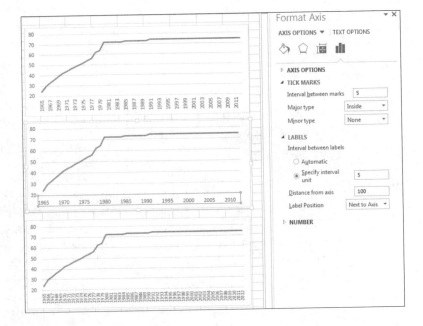

Showing Years in Reverse for Annual Reports

Typically, the financial charts in the Annual Report show the most recent year at the left side of the chart. Excel offers a choice to reverse the order of the years, but this choice also moves the vertical axis labels to the right side of the chart.

Follow these steps to create the chart in Figure 2.18:

1. Double-click the years along the category axis. Excel displays the Format Axis task pane.

2. In the task pane, click the Chart icon.

3. Expand the Axis Options category.

4. At the bottom of the category, choose Categories in Reverse Order. Excel moves the most recent year to the left side of the chart, as shown in Figure 2.18.

5. Display the Format tab of the ribbon. In the Current Selection drop-down, the Horizontal (Category) Axis is shown.

6. Single-click the labels along the vertical axis in the chart. These numbers are along the right side of the chart. When you select this axis, the task pane still shows Format Axis, but the settings change. Look in the ribbon to see that the current selection is the Vertical (Value) Axis.

7. In the task pane, choose the Chart icon and then expand the Labels category. Change the Label Position drop-down to High. It might make no sense semantically, but this moves the vertical axis labels next to the highest year, which is on the left side of the chart.

Figure 2.18
Reverse the order of the years in the category axis.

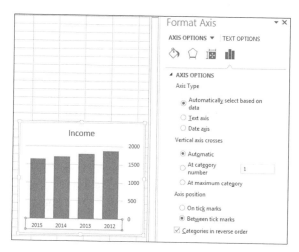

Choosing Date Versus Text-Based Axes

In most Excel charts, the points along the horizontal axis are equidistant. This makes sense when you are comparing departments or regions, or even when comparing months of the year.

At times, the horizontal axis might be based on dates that have points that might not be equally spaced. In Figure 2.19, the top chart positions each point at an equidistant location along the horizontal axis. By using a date axis, Excel spaces the points based on the number of days between the points. Perhaps this data shows random quality testing. The two data points in April are only a week apart. The bottom chart shows those points as closer together.

Figure 2.19
Using a date axis spaces the points out according to the number of days between the points.

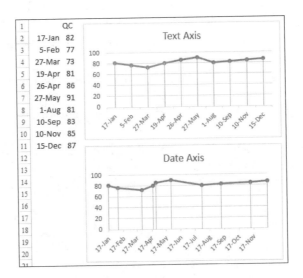

Excel automatically detects a date axis or a text axis. To override the automatic setting, double-click the labels along the axis. Click the Chart icon, then Axis Options, and choose either Text Axis or Date Axis from the Axis Type.

Several examples in Chapter 3, "Creating Charts That Show Trends," show how to format the category axis when you have dates or time in the axis. See the section "Understanding Date-Based Axis Versus Category-Based Axis in Trend Charts."

Labeling Monthly Charts with JFMAMJJASOND

A popular financial chart in the *Wall Street Journal* and other financial presses abbreviates the month names with the initial letter of each month. Thus, you have J for January, F for February, M for March, and so on.

The left chart in Figure 2.20 requires a lot of space for the angled labels of 1/1/2015, 2/1/2015, 3/1/2015, and so on. The chart on the right takes less space by using the month abbreviations.

To create the chart with the initial letter of each month, follow these steps:

1. Make sure that your original data contains dates. The dates can be from the first of the month or the last of the month, but they have to contain dates.

2. Create a chart with dates along the category axis.

3. Double-click the dates along the category axis. Excel displays the Format Axis task pane.

4. In the task pane, choose the Chart icon and then expand the Number category.

5. The Category drop-down should already read Date.

6. Open the Type drop-down and choose the fourteenth item, which is "M." All the entries in this drop-down show the number format applied to March 14, 2001. "M" is the initial letter in March and is the desired number format.

7. Use the resize handles to make the chart narrower.

8. Optionally, click any chart column to select the series. In the Format Series task pane, drag the gap width slider to the left to make the columns wider.

Figure 2.20
Abbreviate the dates with the first initial of the month name to save space in the chart axis.

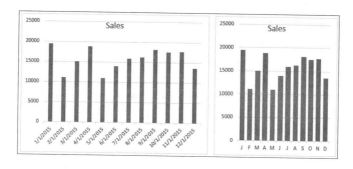

Displaying and Formatting Gridlines

Gridlines help the reader locate data on a chart. Without gridlines, it is difficult to follow the plotted points over to the vertical axis to figure out the value of a point.

Gridlines work in conjunction with the Major Unit and Minor Unit settings in the Format Axis task pane (refer to Figure 2.14). If you display major gridlines, they appear at the interval specified for Major Unit. If you display minor gridlines, they appear at the interval specified for the Minor Unit.

Figure 2.21 shows four versions of the same chart. In this chart, the major unit is 50, and the minor unit is 10.

Open the Plus icon and choose Gridlines. Excel adds major gridlines as shown in the lower-left chart of Figure 2.21. If you hover over Gridlines in the Plus icon menu and open the fly-out menu, you can choose minor gridlines. Displaying minor gridlines instead, as in the top-right chart, causes Excel to draw 25 horizontal lines on the chart. This might seem like overkill because it is difficult to follow the gridlines across the chart. The bottom-right chart shows major and minor gridlines.

Figure 2.21

Four variations of the same chart include major and/or minor gridlines.

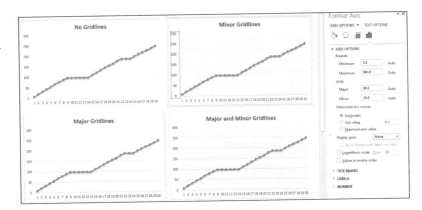

Creating Unobtrusive Gridlines

Gridlines should not overpower the series line. Go with thin gridlines in a gray color that almost disappear into the background. Someone who needs to figure out the value for a point can follow the gridline across.

You can override the default formatting for either the major or minor gridlines. When you click a gridline to select it, do not click the top gridline. Click a gridline in the middle. Clicking the top gridline selects the plot area instead of the gridline. If you've effectively selected the gridlines, you should see a column of selection circles down the right side of your chart. If you see a solid box instead, you've selected the plot area.

After selecting a gridline, you can quickly apply many changes using the Shape Outline drop-down in the Format tab of the ribbon. Using the Shape Outline, you can choose an unobtrusive gray, use the Weight fly-out menu to make the gridlines thinner, and use the Dashes fly-out menu to make the gridlines dotted or dashed. (See Figure 2.22.)

If you opt to use the Format Gridlines task pane, click the Paint Bucket icon and then expand the Line category (see Figure 2.23). You can apply arrowheads to the gridlines, apply a gradient, and more.

Figure 2.22
Change the gridline color or weight using this drop-down on the Format tab.

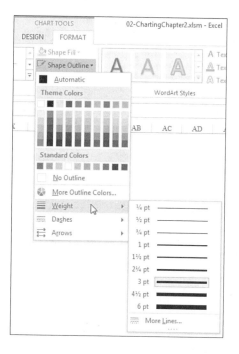

Figure 2.23
Choices in the Format task pane enable you to create pointless effects, such as gradients or arrows.

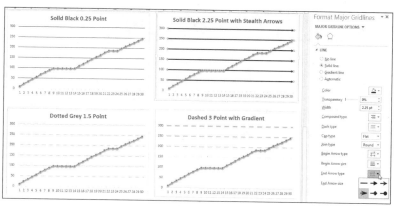

Controlling Placement of Major and Minor Gridlines

Settings in the Format Axis task pane can be used to control the placement of major and minor gridlines. For the vertical axis, you can change the Major Unit and Minor Unit settings to control the spacing of the horizontal gridlines. Even though you are allowed to choose something else, for best results, the major unit should be a multiple of the minor unit.

The top and left charts in Figure 2.24 show various settings for the major and minor units and their effect on the gridlines.

To control the placement of vertical gridlines, you have to format the horizontal axis. There is a setting called Interval Between Tick Marks. In the lower-right chart shown in Figure 2.24, the interval has been increased to 5. This causes Excel to display a vertical gridline after every five points.

Figure 2.24
By changing the units on the Format Axis dialog, you can control the spacing between horizontal gridlines.

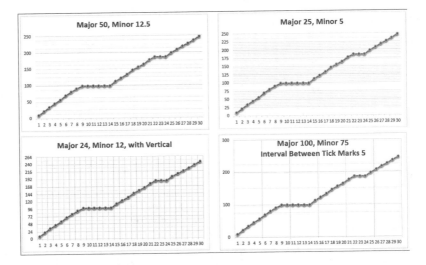

CASE STUDY: CHANGING THE TITLE TO ALL CAPS

As discussed in Chapter 1, the new Paintbrush icon offers professionally designed chart styles that you can quickly apply to a chart. I think these styles look great. They contain clever combinations of effects that have been available in the past few versions of Excel. Although you might never have thought of combining the various effects, everything that is offered would have been possible in Excel 2007 or Excel 2010, all by using the formatting steps in this chapter.

To prove this, it is interesting to try to go from a plain vanilla chart to one of the professionally designed chart styles by using regular formatting tools instead of the Paintbrush icon.

Consider the chart style shown in Figure 2.25. As you set out to replicate this style, the biggest mystery is how they converted "YTD Ski Vacation Bookings" in cell A2 to the all-caps "YTD SKI VACATION BOOKINGS" in the chart title. Initially, you might think the Excel charting team switched to a font that offers all caps in place of lowercase letters. But that font in the chart is Calibri—the body font for the Office theme.

If you use Word or InDesign, there are settings to display text stored as lowercase as uppercase. Have you ever seen such a setting in Excel? It certainly is not in the Home tab of the ribbon.

Right-click the chart title and choose the Font menu item. (See Figure 2.26.)

You now arrive at a Font dialog box that offers choices that you won't ever see in the Format Cells dialog box. Many of the choices are the same. Change the Font Style from Normal to Bold. Some of the settings in Effects are different from the Format Cells choices. Choose All Caps to convert the text stored in A2 to the chart title in all caps. Figure 2.27 shows the results of choosing All Caps and Bold. This is slightly different from the chart title offered by the professionally designed style.

Figure 2.25
How does this chart make
the title be all caps?

Cell contains upper & lower case

Title is all caps

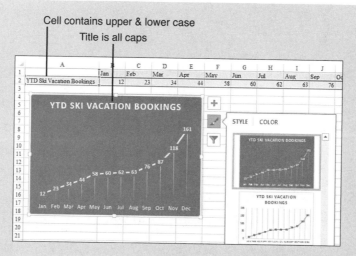

Figure 2.26
Choose Font from the
context menu.

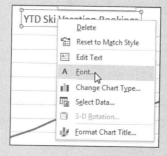

Figure 2.27
Choose Bold and All Caps
to convert the title.

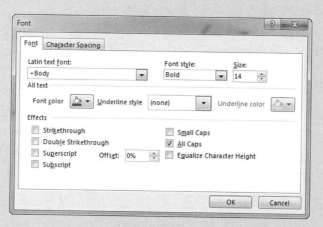

Go to the Character Spacing tab in the Font dialog. Change the spacing to Expanded by 1 Point. This creates the same effect as in the professionally designed style. (See Figure 2.28.)

Figure 2.28
Stretch the title by using Expanded Character Spacing.

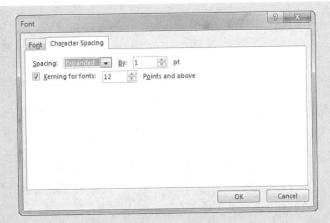

The point of the professionally designed chart styles is to show off the effects that have been in Excel but few people were using. You've probably never noticed this unusual version of the Font dialog. I went back to Excel 2010 and the same choices are there, but I had never discovered them on my own. Now, thanks to this professionally designed chart style, you've learned a new trick for formatting text inside of text frames. Unfortunately, there is no way to apply the formatting to regular text in cells in Excel.

Although this case study is primarily about the All Caps setting, here are the steps to convert a regular chart into the formatted chart. Step 1 has already been completed.

1. Get the title in all caps: right-click Title, Font, All Caps, Bold, Character Spacing, Expanded, 1 point.

2. Change the chart fill to blue: Chart area, Format, Shape Fill, Blue.

3. Change all chart fonts to white: Chart area, Home tab, Font Color drop-down, White.

4. Delete numbers along the left axis: Vertical (Value) axis, press Delete key.

5. Select Gridlines, Delete.

6. Select Design, Add Chart Element, Lines, Droplines.

7. Display data labels directly where the data point should be: Plus icon, check Data Labels. Hover for the fly-out arrow, click the fly-out arrow, More Data Label Options, Chart icon, Label Options, Center.

8. Make the data label cause a break in the line: in Format Data Labels, select Label Options, Paint Bucket icon, Fill, Solid Fill, Blue.

9. With the data labels selected, click the Bold icon in the Home tab.

10. Draw the series line in white: Format, Current Selection "Series YTD Ski Vacation Bookings," Format Selection, Paint Bucket, Line, Solid Line, Color White.

11. Select Format Drop Lines, Paint Bucket icon, Line, Gradient Line, Type Linear, Angle 270, First Gradient Stop, Blue, Second Gradient Stop, White, 77%, Third Gradient Stop, White.

12. Select Horizontal Axis, Axis Options, Paint Bucket Icon, Line, No Line.

All these steps could have been done in Excel 2010—there is nothing new in the steps. However, although it is possible to replicate all the steps to create the chart, the brilliant part is that the professional chart designers thought up the unique combination of steps to create this chart style.

Formatting the Plot Area and Chart Area

Two separate areas of a chart can be formatted: the chart area and the plot area. These areas can be filled with a solid color, a pattern, a texture, a gradient, or even a picture. But more importantly, either area can be set to No Fill, which allows the underlying element to show through.

In Figure 2.29, the underlying cells have a blue fill; the chart area has a gradient fill; and the plot area has a pattern fill. Think of the cells being on the bottom, then the chart area, then the plot area. Changes to the plot area cover changes to the chart area.

Figure 2.29
You can separately format the plot area and the chart area.

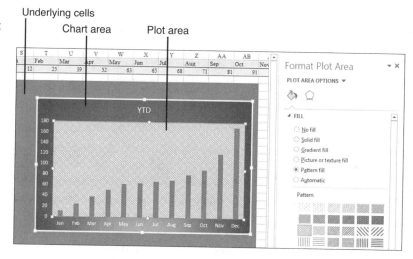

Default charts in Excel 2013 have the plot area set to No Fill. Thus, any formatting changes to the chart area also show through on the plot area.

If you also set the chart area to No Fill, you could see through the chart to the underlying cells. You can even stack two charts. If the top chart has no fill, you can see through to the underlying chart. This allows some very unusual combo charts.

Using a Gradient for the Plot Area

Setting up a simple two-color gradient has become far more difficult in Excel 2013 than it used to be. Microsoft offers many more choices for controlling the gradient, but this causes the process of setting up the gradient to be more difficult.

The first set of choices involves selecting whether the gradient should be linear, radial, or rectangular, or whether it should follow the path of the shape. Within the linear gradients, you can specify a direction, such as 90 degrees for top to bottom or 180% for right to left. With the radial and rectangular gradients, you can specify whether the gradient radiates from the center or from a particular corner. The path type creates a gradient that is relative to the shape of the bounding object. Figure 2.30 shows a variety of gradient types.

Figure 2.30
The gradient types can be linear, radial, or rectangular.

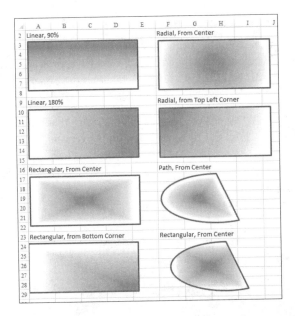

The next choice involves the number of colors. You can choose a predefined color scheme from the Preset drop-down, or you can specify your own color scheme by defining a number of gradient stops. Each stop is assigned a color, transparency, and position ranging from 0% to 100%. Excel 2013 offers an improved Gradient Stop bar (see Figure 2.31) that enables you to visualize the position of each stop in the gradient. Click a stop to move it or adjust the settings for that stop. Use the + or X icons to the right of the Gradient Stops bar to add or remove stops. You can edit only one gradient stop at a time.

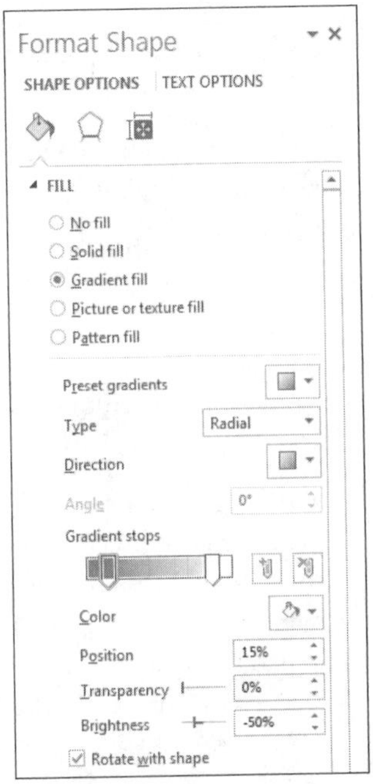

Figure 2.31
The Gradient Stops bar enables you to control the gradient.

Creating a Custom Gradient

Suppose you want the plot area to contain a two-color gradient, flowing from green on the top to white on the bottom. This was simple in Excel 2003, but it is difficult to set up in Excel 2013 for the first chart. However, if you have many charts to format in the same Excel session, the settings from the first gradient remain in the Format Plot Area task pane, which makes it easier to format subsequent charts. You might decide that the top 5% of the chart should be solid green, the bottom 5% of the chart should be solid white, and everything in between should be a gradient from green to white.

A gradient stop consists of a position, a color, and a transparency value. The first gradient stop indicates a color green and 5% as the position. The second gradient stop indicates a color of white and 95% as the position. Everything from 5% to 95% would be a blend from green to white. To use a lighter color green, you can increase the transparency of the green stop.

If you have previously created a chart with a predefined gradient, you might find that the default gradient has three through six stops already defined. If this is the case, select the later stops and click Remove to remove them.

Complete the following steps to set up a two-color gradient:

1. Select a chart. From the Format tab, choose the plot area. Click Format Selection. Excel displays the Format Plot Area task pane.

2. Choose the Paint Bucket icon. In the Fill category, choose Gradient Fill.

3. Change the Type to Linear.

4. Change the Angle to 90 degrees.

5. Each chevron shape on the Gradient Stops bar indicates a gradient stop. If there are more than two stops, select the last stop and click the X button to remove that stop. Continue removing any stops higher than Stop 2.

6. Click the first stop chevron to work with Stop 1. Choose a green color. Set the stop position at 5% by either using the spin button or by dragging the chevron. Set the transparency to 25% to make a lighter green.

7. Click the Stop 2 chevron. Choose white as the color. Set the stop position at 95%.

The result is a two-color gradient ranging from dark green at the top to white at the bottom. Figure 2.32 shows the gradient and the setting for Stop 1.

Figure 2.32
Creating a two-color gradient requires many more steps in Excel 2013 than in legacy versions.

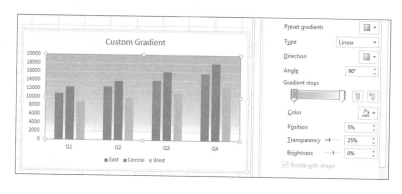

Using a Picture or Texture for the Plot Area

You have many options available when you want to use a texture or a picture for the plot area. When choosing Picture or Texture Fill, a Texture drop-down appears, with the same two dozen textures that have been in Office for years. To use a picture instead of a texture, click the File button and browse your drives to locate a picture to insert.

When you choose a picture, it is stretched or shrunk to fill the plot area completely. This might cause your logo to be a little squashed, as shown in the top-left chart in Figure 2.33. To make your picture keep its correct aspect ratio, select the Tile Picture as Texture check box in the Format Plot Area dialog.

When you choose to tile the picture, a number of choices are available in the Tiling Options section. In the top-right chart in Figure 2.33, the Scale X and Scale Y options are set to 30% to create a repeating pattern of logos. The first logo is aligned with the top left of the plot area.

You can choose alternating tiles of the image to be mirror images of the first. However, this is not appropriate when using logos. In the bottom-right chart in Figure 2.33, the logo is set to show both a horizontal and vertical mirror image of the picture.

To lighten the picture, adjust the Transparency slider to the right. The bottom-left chart in Figure 2.33 has an 80% transparency.

Figure 2.33
You can stretch or tile a picture fill.

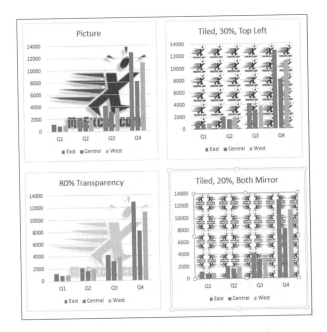

Controlling 3D Rotation in a 3D Chart

A number of options are available for rotating a 3D chart. To access the 3D Rotation settings, select the plot area and choose Format Selection. In the Format Plot Area task pane, choose the Pentagon icon. Expand the 3D Rotation category.

Of the available options, you are most likely to change the X rotation and leave the other angles alone:

- **X rotation**—Choose a value from 0 to 359.9 degrees to rotate the floor of the chart counterclockwise. The chart at the top-right of Figure 2.34 has been rotated 50 degrees from the default rotation. This rotation forces the series names to move clockwise to the left. In some cases, it might be easier to see a short series by rotating the x-axis.

- **Y rotation**—Choose a value from –90 degrees to 90 degrees to change the height of the viewer with respect to the chart. In the default 15% Y rotation, it appears that the reader is slightly above the chart. For a 0-degree rotation, the view appears that the reader is at about eye level with the chart, as shown in the chart at the top left of Figure 2.35. At a 90-degree rotation, the reader appears to be looking straight down on the chart, which makes it impossible to judge the height of any columns. Negative rotations create a view where the reader is actually looking up at the chart from underneath a transparent floor. The bottom-left chart in Figure 2.34 shows a Y-rotation of 40 degrees.

- **Perspective**—The Perspective setting is grayed out until you uncheck Right Angle Axes. Choose a value from 0 to 120 to distort a chart further. If you have used a wide-angle lens on a camera, you might have noticed that items in the foreground appear unusually large, whereas items in the background appear unusually small. Increasing the perspective is similar to using a wide-angle camera. The chart at the bottom right of Figure 2.34 has an increased perspective. Note how the Q4 bars seem to shrink in this view.

- **Depth**—Choose a value from 0% to 2000% of the base. Decreasing the ratio of depth to the base creates a chart where the columns become wide rectangles.

- **Height**—Clear the Autoscale check box to enable the Height setting. You can choose a value from 0% to 500% of the base. The bottom-right chart in Figure 2.34 shows a chart with an increased height:width ratio.

Figure 2.34
Rotating the X-axis turns
the floor of the chart
clockwise.

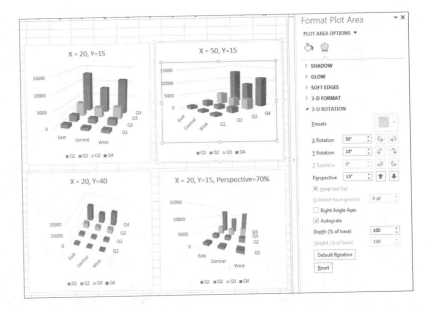

Forecasting with Trendlines

A trendline attempts to fit existing data points to a formula and extend that formula into the
future. When a trendline is added to a chart, Excel uses least-squares regression to find the
best line to represent the data points. Excel can either draw the trendline for existing points
to indicate if the points are trending up or down, or it can extend the trendline into the
future to project whether you will meet a goal.

In Figure 2.35, actual progress toward a goal is tracked in column B. Note that because the
project is in process, several points in the data set are not yet filled in. New in Excel 2013,
those cells need to be filled with =NA() instead of being left empty.

Figure 2.35
This chart shows the
actual points and a goal
line that indicates how
much progress should be
made each day to reach
the project completion.

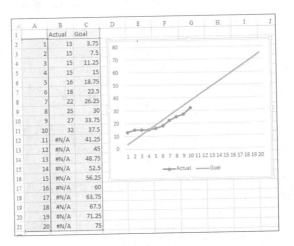

Adding a trendline enables you to project when the project will finish if you continue working at the current pace. To add a trendline, click the Plus icon and choose Trendline. The Add Trendline dialog asks if you want the trendline applied to the Actual or Goal series. Choose Actual and click OK.

Excel adds a new virtual series to the chart. This series is plotted out to the end of the data series. In Figure 2.36, you can see that the linear trendline is projecting that you will have just under 50 units complete by the 20th day.

Figure 2.36
The trendline indicates that based on your current run rate, you will severely miss the deadline.

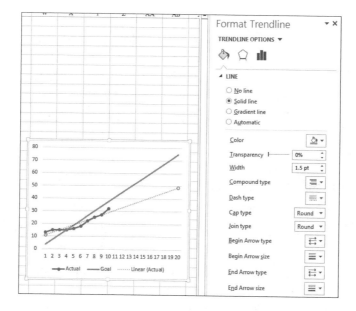

Although creating a trendline requires only a few clicks, several trendline options are worth learning. These are described in the following subsections.

Formatting a Trendline

To format a trendline, double-click the trendline to display the Format Trendline task pane. Options under the Paint Bucket icon enable you to format the color and size of the line. I usually leave the trendline as a dashed line to indicate that it is not actual data, but a computer projection. I also change the color, often to red. When a project is falling behind schedule, the red dashed trendline becomes a call to action. The trendline says, "You need to pick up the pace of production—not just for one day, but for several sustained days."

Suppose you suddenly do 10 units of production on the 11th day. This brings the project back on track with 42 units complete, when 41.25 are needed to stay headed toward the goal. However, when the trendline looks at your average daily production, it sees that you spend 10 days only averaging 3 units a day. The trendline is not convinced that just because you had one good day, you will make the final goal. In this case, the trendline adjusts the projection from 50 to about 57. This makes the trendline seem like a bit of a cynic. However, in reality, the trendline is using simple math to analyze your behavior as you have worked on this project up to this day.

Figure 2.37 shows the trendline after day 11. It also displays the Trendline Equation, which is described next.

Figure 2.37
An equation can be added to a chart to see how Excel is fitting the chart to the line.

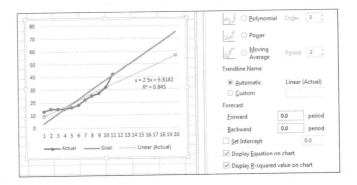

Adding the Trendline Equation to a Chart

To help understand how a trendline is calculated, you can display the equation on the chart.

In the Trendline Options category of the Format Trendline dialog, select Display Equation on the Chart. For a linear trendline, Excel displays a trendline in the form of y = mx + b.

Alternatively, you can choose to force the y-intercept to be zero or display the R-squared value on the chart. R-squared is a measure of how closely the trendline fits the existing points. Although R-squared can range from 0 to 1, values closer to 1 indicate that the trendline is doing a good job of representing the data points.

In Figure 2.37, the equation predicts that you magically started with 6.8 units done on day 0 and then have averaged 2.5 units a day thereafter. This is pretty good because in this case, several units were finished in the previous month but did not make up a full case pack, so their totals were added to day 1 of the current month. The R-squared of 0.845 says that the trendline is a pretty good fit. The bottom line is that you need to focus on production for the next nine days if you want to make the goal.

Choosing a Forecast Method

In business, a linear trendline is used most often, which assumes a constant rate of progress throughout the life of the chart. Several other forecast methods are available for trendlines:

- **Exponential trendline**—Used most often in science. Describes a population that is rapidly increasing over successive generations, such as the number of fungi in a Petri dish over time.

- **Logarithm trendline**—Results when there is an initial period of rapid growth that levels off over time.

- **Polynomial trendline**—Can describe a line that undulates due to two to six external factors. When you specify a polynomial trendline, you have to specify which order of polynomial. For example, in a third-order polynomial, the line is fit to the equation $y = b + c1x + c2x^2 + c3x^3$.

- **Power trendline**—Fits the points to a line, where $y = cx^b$. This describes a line that increases at a specific exponential rate over time.

- **Moving average trendline**—Used to smooth out data that fluctuates over time. A typical trendline would use a three-month moving average.

Adding Drop Lines to a Line or Area Chart

Area and line charts are great at showing trends, but it is often difficult for the reader to figure out the exact values for data points. Because the line is floating in space, you are counting on the viewer's eye being able to travel from the horizontal axis straight up to the data series line.

A drop line is a vertical line that extends from a line or area chart down to the horizontal axis. As shown in the lower chart in Figure 2.38, the drop lines help you see that the March point is exactly at 300. This would be difficult to discern in the chart shown at the top of Figure 2.38.

Drop lines are one of the few features that were left out of the Plus icon. To add a drop line, select the chart. In the Design tab of the ribbon, choose Add Chart Element, Lines, Drop Lines.

Figure 2.38
Drop lines help you visualize the exact value of each point along the horizontal axis.

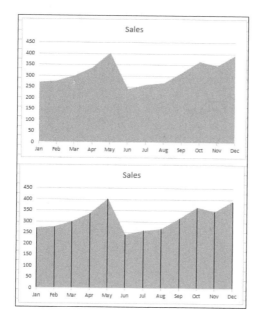

Adding Up/Down Bars to a Line Chart

If you have a line chart with two different data series, you might want to compare the series at each point along the horizontal axis. Yu can use two different options for this comparison.

In the top chart in Figure 2.39, high-low lines extend from one line to the other line. These are created using Design, Add Chart Element, Lines, High-Low Lines.

In the bottom chart in Figure 2.39, up/down bars extend from one line to the other line. These bars appear in contrasting colors, depending on which line is higher at that particular point. To add up/down bars, use the Plus icon and select Up/Down Bars.

Figure 2.39
High-low lines and up/down bars help show the relationship between two series at specific points along the X-axis.

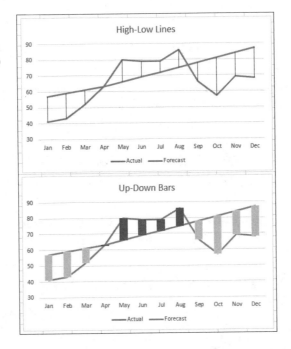

When you add Up/Down bars, two new elements appear in the Current Selection drop-down. You can separately format Down-Bars1 and Up-Bars1. In Figure 2.39, the Down bars started as black and the Up bars as white. Without a shape outline, the white bars faded into the background. The bars in the figure have a light gray fill applied.

Showing Acceptable Tolerances by Using Error Bars

I used to run monthly sales and operations planning meetings. In these meetings, the leaders of the sales, marketing, engineering, and manufacturing departments would decide on the production plan for each sales model. During the next month's meeting, a chart would compare the previous month's forecast to actual demand. If the demand was more than 20% above or below the plan, someone had to present the root causes for that variance. The discussion was often lively: Did the east region really have no clue that Customer XYZ was about to order 1,000 units, or was it sandbagging so it could have a lower quota?

To figure out which products required this scrutiny, both the forecast and actual performance were plotted for each product line. Error bars showing the acceptable 20% tolerance were added to the forecast line. If the actual line was within the 20% tolerance, no discussion was needed.

Error bars are tricky to format because they start out so small.

Follow these steps to add and format the error bars:

1. Start out with a chart that has forecast and actual. Perhaps you've formatted the values axis to show the appropriate bounds and changed to a logarithmic scale if appropriate. Decide which series the error bars should apply to.

2. On the Format tab, select that series from the Current Selection drop-down.

3. Click the Plus icon and choose Error Bars. It is likely that the default error bars might not even show up. You might get a warning about logarithmic scales not working for negative numbers. This warning is a bug; you have not introduced anything that is negative. Click OK to dismiss the warning.

4. On the Design tab, open the Current Selection drop-down. You should see Series Forecast Y Error Bars. If your chart contains an XY series, you might also see Series Forecast X Error Bars. If there is an extra set of error bars, choose those from the Current Selection drop-down and press Delete to delete them.

5. On the Design tab, open the Current Selection drop-down and choose Error Bars. Click Format Selection. Excel displays the Format Error Bars task pane.

6. In the task pane, click the Chart icon. The Error Amount can be set to a fixed value, a percentage, a standard deviation, standard error, or a custom value. In Figure 2.40, the error bars are set to a percentage of 20%.

7. While the error bars are selected, use the Shape Outline drop-down on the Format tab to adjust the color and weight of the lines.

Figure 2.40
The error bars show an acceptable tolerance or a margin of error around each point.

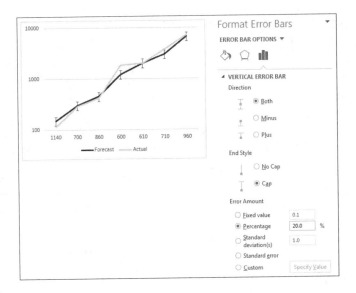

Formatting a Series

There is not a button on the Plus icon for the Series element. Depending on your chart type, various settings will be available for the series element.

In Figure 2.41, the top charts have a normal Gap Width between the columns. The bottom charts have a narrow gap width, which makes the columns wider. The bottom-right chart also uses a negative value for Series Overlap. To format the series, double-click one of the markers for the series. If the points are too small to click, you can select the series from the Current Selection drop-down. All the chart-type-specific settings are under the Chart icon in the task pane.

Figure 2.41
Change the Gap Width and Series Overlap settings to make the columns wider.

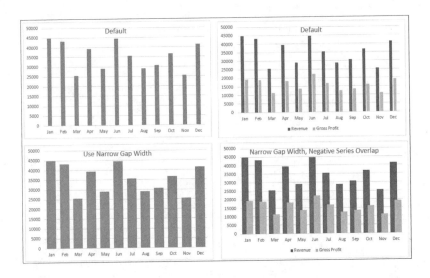

Formatting a Single Data Point

The first click on a data series selects the entire series. If you pause for a moment and then perform a second click on a data point, the Current Selection drop-down indicates that you have selected an individual data point. The drop-down might say Series "Sales" Point "Dec."

It is interesting that the only way to perform this selection is by performing two single-clicks on the chart. The Current Selection drop-down does not offer a list of all the data points.

After selecting a data point, any changes that you make in the ribbon or the Format task pane apply only to that point. This is a good way to change the color for a single column in a chart.

Replacing Data Markers with Shapes

Instead of using columns for your data markers, you can replace the column with either some clip art or a shape from the Shapes gallery.

Figure 2.42 shows a chart with Arrows instead of columns. To create this chart, follow these steps:

1. Create a column chart.
2. Select any cell in the worksheet. Use Insert, Shapes. Select one of the block arrows. Click and drag in the worksheet to draw the arrow.
3. With the arrow selected, press Ctrl+C to copy the arrow to the Clipboard.
4. Select the chart. Click any column to select the series.
5. Press Ctrl+V to paste the arrow shape instead of the columns.

Figure 2.42
Copy a shape and paste on the series to change the column to the shape.

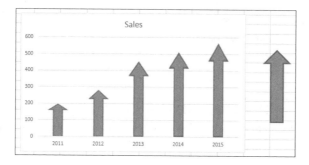

Replacing Data Markers with a Picture

Office Online offers thousands of free clip art images. You can insert any of these images in a chart to replace the data markers. Follow these steps to create a pictograph:

1. In a 2D column chart, select a data series. Right-click the data series and select Format Data Series.

2. In the Format Data Series task pane that appears, choose the Paint Bucket icon. In the Fill category, choose Picture or Texture Fill.

3. Click the Online button.

4. In the Search Office.com text box, type a keyword to describe the clip art and then click the magnifying glass.

5. Browse through the returned images. You are looking for something that is cartoonish and narrow. Rather than clip art with a detailed background, look for clip art where only the character appears. When you find an acceptable image, click OK.

The result is a chart similar to the chart in Figure 2.43. The clip art is stretched to indicate the height of the bar.

Figure 2.43
Create visual interest by replacing the columns with clip art.

> **TIP**
>
> Fans of Edward Tufte may point out that he rails against pictographs in his books. However, what Tufte complained about was both the width and height of the clip art changing in response to increased numbers. Microsoft does not increase the width of the bars, only the height, ensuring that the area of the image stays roughly proportional to the data that it is representing.

Changing the Theme Colors on the Page Layout Tab

The six accent colors and the built-in effects are different in each of the 60+ themes that ship with Office 2013. You can change to any of the themes or create your own theme to access new colors and effects.

On the Page Layout tab, click the Themes drop-down to choose from the 60 built-in themes. If you choose a new theme from the Themes drop-down, Excel applies a new color and set of effects to all the charts in the current workbook. If you want to change only the colors or effects, use the Colors or Effects drop-down in the Themes group.

Storing Your Favorite Settings in a Chart Template

Suppose you need to create a series of charts. You spend some time to perfectly format the first chart. You would like all the other charts to have a similar look and feel.

The solution is to build one chart and then save that chart as a template. If you indicate that the template is the default chart type, you can quickly create new charts by using the Alt+F1 keyboard shortcut.

Follow these steps to create the template:

1. Create a chart and apply any formatting.
2. Right-click the chart and choose Save as Template.
3. On the Design tab, select Save as Template. Give the template a name, such as BudgetChart.
4. On the Design tab, select Change Chart Type. Click the Templates category. Right-click the BudgetChart thumbnail and choose Set as Default Chart.

After completing these steps, you can create a chart with your favorite settings by selecting the data to be charted and pressing Alt+F1. Excel creates a chart with all your favorite settings.

Next Steps

In Chapter 3, you see examples of charts that show trends, such as column and line charts. You also learn how to use a trendline to project a trend into the future.

Creating Charts That Show Trends

3

Choosing a Chart Type

You have two excellent choices when creating charts that show the progress of some value over time. Because Western cultures are used to seeing time progress from left to right, you are likely to choose a chart where the axis moves from left to right—whether it is a column chart, line chart, or area chart.

> **NOTE**
> The new Sparklines feature is another way to show trends with tiny charts. See Chapter 9, "Using Sparklines, Data Visualizations, and Other Nonchart Methods."

Column Charts for Up to 12 Time Periods

If you have only a few data points, you can use a column chart because they work well for 4 quarters or 12 months. If your data set contains 12 or fewer data points that represent a time period, choose a column chart to illustrate the trend over time.

Line Charts for Time Series Beyond 12 Periods

When you get beyond 12 data points, you should switch to a line chart, which can easily show trends for hundreds of periods. Line charts can be designed to show only the data points as markers, or data points can be connected with a straight or smoothed line.

Figure 3.1 shows a chart with only nine data points, where a column chart is appropriate. Figure 3.2 shows a chart of 100+ data points. With this detail, you should switch to a line chart to show the trend.

IN THIS CHAPTER

Choosing a Chart Type 77

Understanding Date-Based Axis Versus Category-Based Axis in Trend Charts 80

Communicate Effectively with Charts 96

Adding an Automatic Trendline to a Chart... 105

Showing a Trend of Monthly Sales and Year-to-Date Sales 106

Understanding the Shortcomings of Stacked Column Charts.............................. 108

Shortcomings of Showing Many Trends on a Single Chart.. 110

Next Steps 111

Figure 3.1
With 12 or fewer data points, column charts are viable and informative.

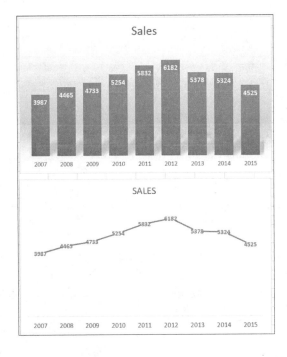

Figure 3.2
When you go beyond 12 data points, it is best to switch to a line chart without individual data points. The middle chart in this figure shows the same data set as a line chart.

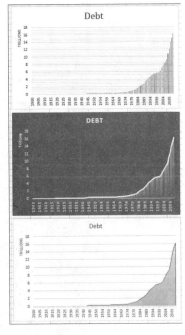

Area Charts to Highlight One Portion of the Line

An *area chart* is a line chart where the area under the line is filled with a shading or color. This can be appropriate if you want to highlight a particular portion of the time series. If you have fewer data points, adding drop lines can help the reader determine the actual value for each time period.

High-Low-Close Charts for Stock Market Data

If you are plotting stock market data, use stock charts to show the trend of stock data over time. You can also use high-low-close charts to show the trend of data that might occur in a range, such as when you need to track a range of quality rankings for each day.

Bar Charts for Series with Long Category Labels

Even though bar charts can be used to show time trends, they can be confusing because readers expect time to be represented from left to right. In rare cases, you might use a bar chart to show a time trend. For example, if you have 40 or 50 points that have long category labels that you need to print legibly to show detail for each point, consider using a bar chart. Another example is shown in Figure 3.3, which includes sales for 45 daily dates. This bar chart would not work as a PowerPoint slide. However, if it is printed as a full page on letter-size paper, the reader could analyze sales by weekday. In the chart in Figure 3.3, weekend days are plotted in a different color than weekdays to help delineate the weekly periods.

Figure 3.3
Although time series typically should run across the horizontal axis, this chart allows 45 points to be compared easily.

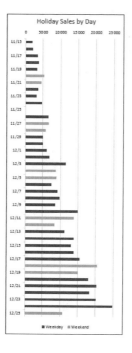

Pie Charts Make Horrible Time Comparisons

A pie chart is ideal for showing how components that add up to 100% are broken out. It is difficult to compare a series of pie charts to detect changes from one pie to the next. As you can see in the charts in Figure 3.4, it is difficult for the reader's eye to compare the pie wedges from year to year. Did market share increase in 2013? Rather than using a series of pie charts to show changes over time, use a 100 percent stacked column chart.

Figure 3.4
It is difficult to compare one pie chart to the next.

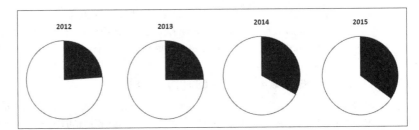

100 Percent Stacked Bar Chart Instead of Pie Charts

In Figure 3.5, the same data from Figure 3.4 is plotted as a 100 percent stacked bar chart. Series lines guide the reader's eye from the market share from each year to the next year. The stacked bar chart is a much easier chart to read than the series of pie charts.

Figure 3.5
The same data presented in Figure 3.4 is easier to read in a 100 percent stacked bar chart.

Understanding Date-Based Axis Versus Category-Based Axis in Trend Charts

Excel offers two types of horizontal axes in a trend chart. Having the proper setting can ensure that your message is accurate.

If the spacing of events along the time axis is uniform, it does not matter whether you choose a date-based axis or a text-based axis because the results will be the same. When this occurs, it is fine to allow Excel to choose the type of axis automatically.

However, if the spacing of events along the time axis is haphazard, you definitely want to make sure that Excel uses a date-based axis.

Accurately Representing Data Using a Time-Based Axis

Figure 3.6 shows the spot price for a certain component used in your manufacturing plant. To find this data, you downloaded past purchase orders for that product. Your company doesn't purchase the component on the same day every month; therefore, you have an incomplete data set. In the middle of the data set, a strike closed one of the vendors, spiking the prices from the other vendors. Your purchasing department had stocked up before the strike, which allowed your company to slow its purchasing dramatically during the strike.

In the top chart in Figure 3.6, the horizontal axis is set to a text-based axis, and every data point is plotted an equal distance apart. Because your purchasing department made only two purchases during the strike, it appears the time affected by the strike is very narrow. The bottom chart uses a date-based axis. In this axis, you can see that the strike actually lasted for half of 2013.

3

Figure 3.6
The top chart uses a text-based horizontal axis: Every event is plotted an equal distance from the next event. This leads to the shaded period being underreported.

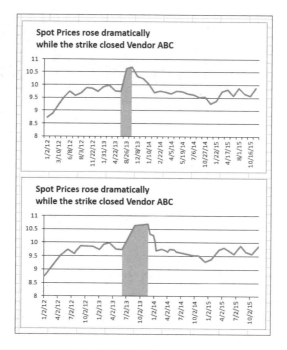

NOTE To learn how to highlight a portion of a chart as shown in Figure 3.6, see "Highlighting a Section of Chart by Adding a Second Series," later in this chapter.

Usually, if your data contains dates, Excel defaults to a date-based axis. However, you should always check to make sure Excel is using the correct type of axis. A number of potential problems force Excel to choose a text-based axis instead of a date-based axis. For example, Excel chooses a text-based axis when dates are stored as text in a spreadsheet and when dates are represented by numeric years. The list following Figure 3.7 summarizes other potential problems.

To explicitly choose an axis type, follow these steps:

1. Right-click the horizontal axis and select Format Axis.

2. In the Format Axis task pane that appears, select the Axis Options at the top, then the chart icon, and then expand the Axis Options category.

3. As appropriate, choose either Text Axis or Date Axis from the Axis Type section (see Figure 3.7).

Figure 3.7
You can explicitly choose an axis type rather than letting Excel choose the default.

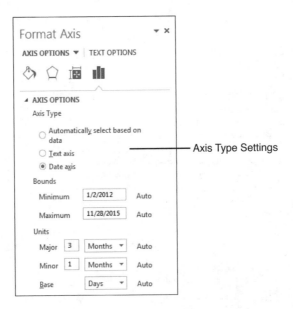

Axis Type Settings

A number of complications that require special handling can occur with date fields. The following are some of the problems you might encounter:

- **Dates stored as text**—If dates are stored as text dates instead of real dates, a date-based axis will never work. You have to use date functions to convert the text dates to real dates.

- **Dates represented by numeric years**—Trend charts can have category values of 2008, 2009, 2010, and so on. Excel does not naturally recognize these as dates, but you can trick it into doing so. Read "Plotting Data by Numeric Year" near Figure 3.15 in this chapter.

- **Dates before 1900**—If your company is old enough to chart historical trends before January 1, 1900, you will have a problem. In Excel's world, there are no dates before 1900. For a workaround, read "Using Dates Before 1900" near Figure 3.16.

- **Dates that are really time**—It is not difficult to imagine charts in which the horizontal axis contains periodic times throughout a day. For example, you might use a chart like this to show the number of people entering a bank. For such a chart, you need a time-based axis, but Excel will group all the times from a single day into a single point. See "Using a Workaround to Display a Time-Scale Axis" near Figure 3.19 for the rather complex steps needed to plot data by periods smaller than a day.

Each of these problem situations is discussed in the following sections.

Converting Text Dates to Dates

If your cells contain text that looks like dates, the date-based axis does not work. The data in Figure 3.8 came from a legacy computer system. Each date was imported as text instead of as dates.

This is a frustrating problem because text dates look exactly like real dates. You may not notice that they are text dates until you see that changing the axis to a date-based axis has no effect on the axis spacing.

If you select a cell that looks like a date cell, look in the formula bar to see whether there is an apostrophe before the date. If so, you know you have text dates (see Figure 3.8). This is Excel's arcane code to indicate that a date or number should be stored as text instead of a number. Or, if the number format drop-down on the Home tab indicates that the cell is formatted as text, then you might have text dates.

Figure 3.8
These dates are really text, as indicated by the apostrophe before the date in the formula bar.

D	E
	Cost
1/1/2015	20
2/15/2015	20
4/1/2015	20
5/15/2015	455
6/1/2015	45
6/8/2015	45
6/15/2015	145
6/22/2015	45

┌───┐
CAUTION

Selecting a new format from the Format Cells dialog does not fix this problem, but it might prevent you from fixing the problem! If you import data from a .txt file and choose to format that column as text, Excel changes the numeric format for the range to be text. After a range is formatted as text, you can never enter a formula, number, or date in the range. People try to select the range, to change the format from text to numeric or date, hoping this will fix the problem, but it doesn't. After you change the format, you still have to use a method described in the "Converting Text Dates to Real Dates" section, later in this chapter, to convert the text dates to numeric dates.

However, it is still worth changing the format from a text format to General, Date, or anything else. If you do not change the format, and then insert a new column to the right of the bad dates, the new column inherits the text setting from the date column. This causes your new formula (the formula to convert text to dates) to fail. Therefore, even though it doesn't solve your current problem, you should select the range, click the Dialog Launcher icon in the lower-right corner of the Number group on the Home tab, and change the format from Text to General. Figure 3.9 shows the Dialog Launcher icon.
└───┘

Figure 3.9
Many groups on the ribbon have this tiny Dialog Launcher icon in the lower-right corner. Clicking this icon leads to the legacy dialog box.

Dialog launcher

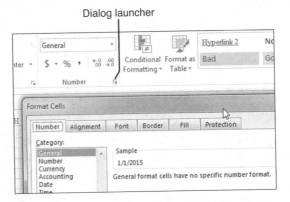

CASE STUDY: COMPARING DATE SYSTEMS

Complete the following case study to see firsthand how important date systems information really is.

1. Enter the number 1 in cell A1.

2. Select cell A1 and then press Ctrl+1 to access the Format Cells dialog.

3. Change the numeric formatting to display the number as a date, using the *Wednesday, March 14, 2001 type. On a PC, you see that the number 1 is January 1, 1900.

4. Type 2 in cell A1. The date changes to January 2, 1900.

Now try this:

1. Select cell B5. Press Ctrl+; to enter today's date in the cell.

2. Again, select cell B5. Press Ctrl+1 to display the Format Cells dialog.

3. Change the number format from a date to a number. Your date changes to a number in the 40,000 to 42,000 range, assuming you are reading this in the 2013–2015 time period.

This might sound like a hassle, but it is worth it. If you store dates as real dates (that is, numbers formatted to display as a date), Excel can do all kinds of date math. For example, you can figure out how many days exist between a due date and today by subtracting one date from another. You can also use the WORKDAY function to figure out how many workdays have elapsed between a hire date and today.

If you type **60** in cell A1, you see Wednesday, February 29, 1900—a date that did not exist! When Mitch Kapor was having Lotus 1-2-3 programmed in 1982, the programmers missed the fact that there was not to be a leap year in 1900. Lotus was released with the mistake, and every competing spreadsheet had to reproduce the same mistake to make sure that the billions of spreadsheets using dates produced the same results. Although the 1900 date system works fine and reports the right day of the week for the 40,300 days since March 1, 1900, it reports the wrong day of the week for the 59 days from January 1, 1900, through February 28, 1900.

3

Excel provides a complete complement of functions to deal with dates, including functions that convert data from text to dates and back. Excel stores times as decimal fractions of days. For example, you can enter noon today as =TODAY()+0.5 and 9:00 a.m. as =TODAY()+0.375. Again, the number format handles converting the decimals to the appropriate display.

Converting Text Dates to Real Dates

The DATEVALUE function converts text that looks like a date into the equivalent serial number. You can then use the Format Cells dialog to display the number as a date.

The text version of a date can take a number of different formats. For example, your international date settings might call for a month/day/year arrangement of the dates. Figure 3.10 shows a number of valid text formats that can be converted with the DATEVALUE function.

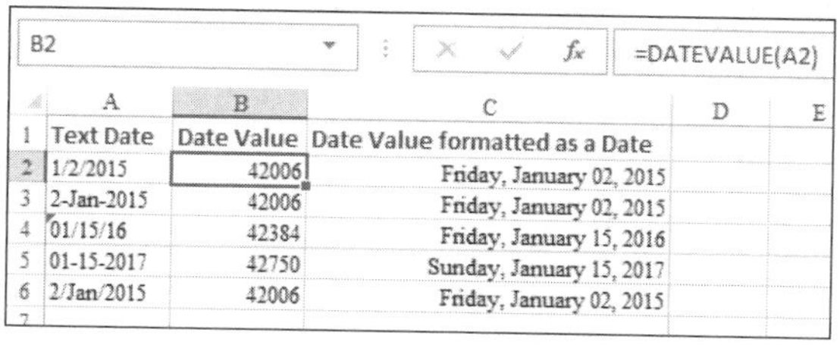

Figure 3.10
The DATEVALUE function can handle any of the date formats in column A.

	A	B	C	D	E
	Text Date	Date Value	Date Value formatted as a Date		
2	1/2/2015	42006	Friday, January 02, 2015		
3	2-Jan-2015	42006	Friday, January 02, 2015		
4	01/15/16	42384	Friday, January 15, 2016		
5	01-15-2017	42750	Sunday, January 15, 2017		
6	2/Jan/2015	42006	Friday, January 02, 2015		

B2 — fx =DATEVALUE(A2)

Figure 3.11 shows a column of text dates. Follow these steps to convert the text dates to real dates:

1. Insert a blank column B by selecting cell B1. Select Home, Insert, Insert Sheet Columns. Alternatively, you can use the legacy shortcut Alt+I+C.

2. In cell B2, enter the formula =DATEVALUE(A2). Excel displays a number in the 40,000 range in cell B2. You are halfway to the result. You still have to format the result as a date.

3. Double-click the fill handle in the lower-right corner of cell B2. The fill handle is the square dot in the lower-right corner of the active cell indicator. Excel copies the formula from cell B2 down to your range of dates.

4. Select Column B2. On the Home tab, select the drop-down at the top of the Number group and choose either Short Date or Long Date. Excel displays the numbers in Column B as a date (see Figure 3.12). Alternatively, you can press Ctrl+1 and select any date format from the Number tab. If some of the dates appear as #######, you need to make the column wider. To do so, double-click the border between the column B and column C headings.

5. To convert the live formulas in column B to static values, while the range of dates in Column B is selected, press Ctrl+C to copy. Press Ctrl+V to paste. Press Ctrl to open the Paste Options dialog. Press V to paste as values.

6. Delete the original column A.

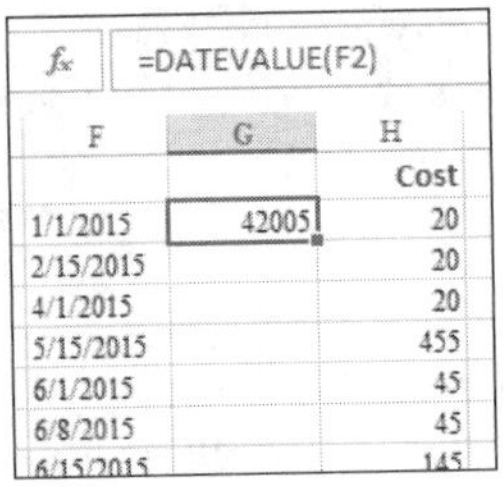

Figure 3.11
The result of the DATEVALUE function is a serial number.

There are other methods for converting the data shown in Figure 3.11 to dates. Here are two methods:

■ **Method 1**—Select any empty cell. Press Ctrl+C to copy. Select your dates. On the Home tab, select Paste, Paste Special. In the Paste Special dialog, choose Values in the Paste section and Add in the Operation section. Click OK. The text dates convert to dates.

■ **Method 2**—Select the text dates, select Text to Columns on the Data tab, and then click Finish.

After converting the text dates to real dates, insert a line chart with markers. Excel automatically formats the chart with a date-based axis. In Figure 3.13, the top chart reflects cells that contain text dates. The bottom chart uses cells in which the text dates have been converted to numeric dates.

Figure 3.12
Choose a date format from the Number drop-down on the Home tab.

Figure 3.13
When your original data contains real dates, Excel automatically chooses a more accurate date-based axis. The bottom chart reflects a date-based axis.

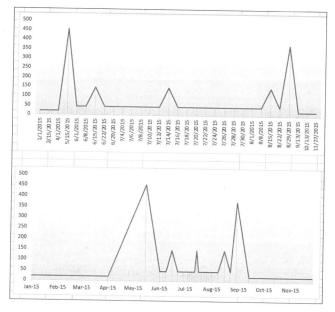

Converting Bizarre Text Dates to Real Dates

When you rely on others for source data, you are likely to encounter dates in all sorts of bizarre formats. For example, while gathering data for this book, I found a data set where each date was listed as a range of dates. Each date was in the format 2/4-6/15. I had to check with the author of the data to find out if that meant February 4th through 6th of 2015 or February 4th through June 15th. It was the former.

Used in combination, the functions in the following list can be useful when you are converting strange text dates to real dates:

- =DATE(2015,12,31)—Returns the serial number for December 31, 2015.
- =LEFT(A1,2)—Returns the two leftmost characters from cell A1.

■ =RIGHT(A1,2)—Returns the two rightmost characters from cell A1.

■ =MID(A1,3,2)—Returns the third and fourth characters from cell A2. You read the function as "return the middle characters from A1, starting at character position 3, for a length of 2."

■ =FIND("/",A1)—Finds the position number of the first slash within A1.

Follow these steps to convert the text date ranges shown in Figure 3.14 to real dates:

Figure 3.14
A mix of LEFT, RIGHT, MID, and FIND functions parse this text to be used in the DATE function.

	A	B	C	D	E
1	**Date**	**Year**	**Month**	**Day**	**Date**
2	2/1-4/15	2015	2	1	2/1/2015
3	2/9-11/15	2015	2	9	2/9/2015
4	2/15-12/15	2015	2	15	2/15/2015
5	12/19-21/15	2015	12	19	12/19/2015
6	*B2: =RIGHT(A2,2)+2000*				
7	*C2: =LEFT(A2,FIND("/",A2)-1)*				
8	*D2: =MID(A2,FIND("/",A2)+1,FIND("-",A2)-FIND("/",A2)-1)*				
9	*E2: =DATE(B2,C2,D2)*				

1. Because the year is always the two rightmost characters in column A, enter the formula =RIGHT(A2,2)+2000 in cell B2.

2. Because the month is the leftmost one or two characters in column A, ask Excel to find the first slash and then return the characters to the left of the slash. Enter =FIND("/",A2) to indicate that the slash is in second character position. Use =LEFT(A2,FIND("/",A2)-1) to get the proper month number.

3. For the day, either choose to extract the first or last date of the range. To extract the first date, ask for the middle characters, starting one position after the slash. The logic to figure out whether you need one or two characters is a bit more complicated. Find the position of the dash, subtract the position of the slash, and then subtract 1. To see the formula in action, select the cell and choose Formulas, Evaluate Formula, and click Evaluate 10 times. Use this formula in cell D2:
   =MID(A2,FIND("/",A2)+1,FIND("-",A2)-FIND("/",A2)-1)

4. Use the DATE function as follows in cell E2 to produce an actual date:
   =DATE(B2,C2,D2)

Plotting Data by Numeric Year

If you are plotting data where the only identifier is a numeric year, Excel does not automatically recognize this field as a date field.

For example, in Figure 3.15 data are plotted once a decade for the past 50 years and then yearly for the past decade. Column A contains four-digit years, such as 1960, 1970, and so on. The default chart shown in the top of the figure does not create a date-based axis. You know this to be true because the distance from 1960 to 1970 is the same as the distance from 2000 to 2001.

Figure 3.15
Excel does not recognize years as dates.

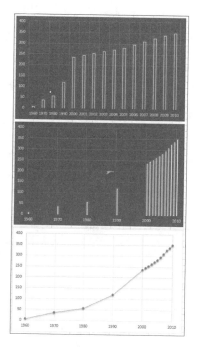

Listed here are two solutions to this problem:

- Convert the years in column A to dates by using **=DATE (A2,12,31)**. Format the resulting value with a yyyy custom number format. Excel displays 2015 but actually stores the serial number for December 31, 2015.

- Convert the horizontal axis to a date-based axis. Excel thinks your chart is plotting daily dates from May 13, 1905, through July 2, 1905. Because no date format has been applied to the cells, they show up as the serial numbers 1955 through 2005. Excel displays the chart properly, even though the settings show that the base units are days.

Using Dates Before 1900

In Excel 2013, dates from January 1, 1900 through December 31, 9999 are recognized as valid dates. However, if your company was founded more than a demisesquicentennial before Microsoft was founded, you will potentially have company history going back before 1900.

Figure 3.16 shows a data set stretching from 1787 through 1959. The accompanying chart would lead the reader to believe that the number of states in the United States grew at a constant rate. This inaccurate statement would cause Mr. Kessel, my eighth-grade geography teacher, to give me an F for this book.

Figure 3.16
Dates from before 1900 are not valid Excel dates. A date-based axis is not possible in this case.

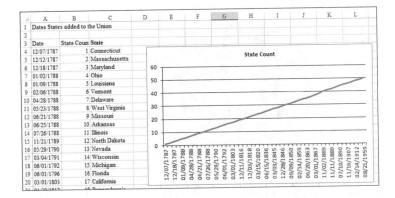

As mentioned previously, formatting the chart to have a date-based axis will not work because Excel does not recognize dates before 1900 as valid dates. Possible workarounds are discussed in the next two subsections.

Using Date-Based Axis with Dates Before 1900

In Figure 3.17, the dates in Column A are text dates from the 1800s. Excel cannot automatically deal with dates from the 1800s, but it can deal with dates from the 1900s.

Figure 3.17
Transforming the 1800s dates to 1900s dates and clever formatting allows Excel to plot this data with a date axis.

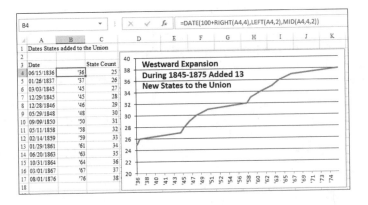

One solution is to transform the dates to dates in the valid range of dates that Excel can recognize. You can use a date format with two years and a good title on the chart to explain that the dates are from the 1800s. However, keep in mind that this solution fails when you are trying to display more than 100 years of data points.

To create the chart in Figure 3.17, follow these steps:

1. Insert a blank column B to hold the transformed dates.

2. Enter the formula =DATE(100+RIGHT(A4,4),LEFT(A4,2),MID(A4,4,2)) in cell B4. This formula converts the 1836 date to a 1936 date.

3. Select cell B4. Press Ctrl+1 to open the Format Cells dialog. Select the date format 3/14/01 from the Date category on the Number tab. This formats the 1936 date as 6/15/36. Later, you will add a title to indicate that the dates in this column are from the 1800s.

4. Double-click the fill handle in cell B4 to copy the formula down to all cells.

5. Select the range B3:C17.

6. From the Insert tab, open the Line Chart drop-down and choose the first line chart icon.

7. Double-click the vertical axis along the left side of the chart to display the Format Axis task pane.

8. In the task pane, click the Chart icon.

9. For the Minimum value, type a value of 20.

10. Click the dates in the horizontal axis in the chart. Excel automatically switches to formatting the horizontal axis, and the settings in the Format task pane redraw to show the settings for the horizontal axis. In the Axis Type section, select Date Axis.

11. From the Plus icon to the right of the chart, hover over Chart Title and then click the arrowhead that appears. Select Centered Overlay Title.

12. Click the State Count title. Type the new title `Westward Expansion<enter>During 1845-1875 Added 13<enter>New States to the Union`. Click outside the title to exit Text Edit mode.

13. Click the title once. You should have a solid selection rectangle around the title. On the Home tab, click the Decrease Font Size button. Click the Left Align button.

14. Carefully click the border of the title. Drag it so the title appears in the top-left corner of the chart.

15. Select the dates in B4:B17. Press Ctrl+1 to access the Format Cells dialog. On the Number tab, click the Custom category. Type the custom number format `'yy`. This changes the values shown along the horizontal axis from m/d/yy format to show a two-digit year preceded by an apostrophe.

The result is the chart shown in Figure 3.17. The reader might believe that the chart is showing dates in the 1800s, but Excel is actually showing dates in the 1900s.

Rolling Daily Dates to Months Using a Pivot Chart

Suppose that you have daily data that you would like to summarize by month. You might think that you can use the Units drop-downs in the Format Axis task pane, under the Chart icon, Axis Options to solve the problem. Here you'll see three settings:

- Major Units: *N* Days/Months/Years
- Minor Units: *N* Days/Months/Years
- Base: Days/Months/Years

In the first two bullet points, *N* is the number entered in the text box.

The Major Units setting is useful for controlling the labels along the date axis. The top-left chart in Figure 3.18 is plotting one point per day, but the labels are readable because the Major unit is set to 1 month instead of 1 day.

The lower-left chart is also using a Base of Days, but the Major Unit is 2 Months. Using the Number category at the bottom of the task pane, adjust the date format to mmm and you get month abbreviations instead of individual dates.

If you attempt to change the Base field from Days to Months, the result is not a summary by month, as you might have expected. The top-right chart is a Line with Markers chart where the Line is set to No Line so you can see the points. By rolling the Base field to Months, Excel plots all the points that occurred in January in a single column. This might be interesting for showing the range of daily sales, even perhaps the distribution of daily sales. But it is not a method for summarizing the daily dates.

Figure 3.18
The settings in the Format Axis task pane control the axis labels, but cannot summarize by months.

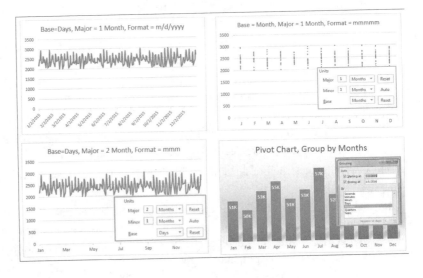

Excel can roll the daily dates up and summarize by month, but you need to start with a pivot chart instead of a regular chart. Pivot charts are covered in detail in Chapter 8, "Creating PivotCharts and Power View Dashboards." Here are the steps to create the bottom-right chart in Figure 3.18.

1. Select the range of sales by date.

2. Choose Insert, PivotChart.

3. The Create PivotChart dialog will offer to create the chart on a New Worksheet. Because a pivot chart includes an associated summary pivot table, it is best to build the chart on a new worksheet and then move the chart when it is done. Accept the default settings in the Create PivotChart dialog and click OK.

4. A new worksheet is inserted to the left of the old worksheet. A PivotTable Fields task pane appears with a list of field. Check both the Date and Sales field. You end with a table of daily dates, identical to what you started with.

5. In the Excel worksheet, choose a cell in the new table that contains a date. The ribbon changes to show a tab called PivotTable Tools Analyze. The third group in this ribbon tab is called Group. Choices there include Group Selection and Group Field. Be sure that you have a date cell selected and choose Group Field. Excel displays the Grouping dialog box. You can see this dialog in the inset of the bottom-right chart of Figure 3.18.

6. Select Months (or Quarters) from the Grouping dialog. If your data spans more than one year, be sure to include years. To group by Week, choose only Days and then use the Number of Days spin button to go to seven-day periods. Click OK.

The pivot table and pivot chart changes to show one column per month instead of daily dates. You can use normal chart formatting to customize the chart. After the chart is formatted, right-click the chart and choose Move Chart to move to the desired worksheet.

Using a Workaround to Display a Time-Scale Axis

The developers who create Microsoft Excel are careful in the Format Axis dialog box to call the option a date axis. However, the technical writers who write Excel Help refer to a time-scale axis. The developers get a point here for accuracy, because Excel absolutely cannot natively handle an axis that is based on time.

A worksheet in the download files is used to analyze queuing times. In the first column, it logs the time that customers entered a busy bank. Times range from when the bank opened at 10:00 a.m. until the bank closed at 4:00 p.m.

Based on the staffing level and the number of customers in the bank, further calculations determine when the customer will move from the queue to an open teller window and when the customer will leave the window, based on an average of three minutes per transaction.

A summary range records the number of people in the bank every time someone enters or leaves. This data is definitely not spaced equally. Only a few customers arrive in the 10:00 hour, whereas many customers enter the bank during the lunch hour.

The top chart in Figure 3.19 plots the number of customers on a text-based axis. Because each customer arrival or departure merits a new point, the one hour from noon until 1:00 p.m. takes up 41 percent of the horizontal width of the chart. In reality, this one-hour period merits only 16% of the chart. This sounds like a perfect use for a time-series axis, right? Read on for the answer.

3

The bottom chart is an identical chart where the axis is converted to show the data on a date-based axis. This is a complete disaster. In a date-based axis, all time information is discarded. The entire set of 300 points is plotted in a single vertical line.

Figure 3.19
Excel cannot show a
time-series axis that
contains times.

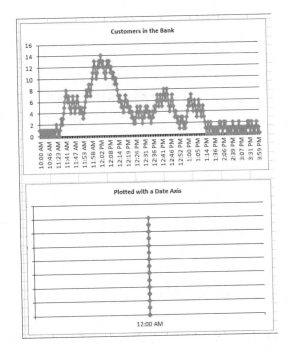

The solution to this problem involves converting the hours to a different time scale (similar to the 1800s date example in the preceding section). For example, perhaps each hour could be represented by a single year. Using numbers from a 24-hour clock, the 10:00 hour could be represented by 2010 and the 3:00 hour could be represented by 2015.

In this example, you manipulate the labels along the vertical axis using a clever custom number format. A few new settings on the Format Axis dialog ensure that an axis label appears every hour.

Follow these steps to create a chart that appears to have a time-based axis:

1. In cell L2, enter the following formula to translate the time to a date:

   `=ROUND(DATE(HOUR(I2)+2000,1,1)+MINUTE(I2)/60*365,0)`

   Because each hour represents a single year, the years argument of the DATE function is =HOUR(I2)+2000. This returns values from 2010 through 2015. The month and day arguments in the date function are 1 and 1 to return January 1 of the year. Outside the date function, the minute of the time cell is scaled up to show a value from 1 to 365, using MINUTE(I2)/60*365. The entire formula is rounded to the nearest integer because Excel would normally ignore any time values.

2. With cell L2 selected, press Ctrl+1 to display the Format Cells dialog. On the Number tab, choose the Custom category. In the Type box, enter yy":00". This format displays the year of the date with two digits. Hence, all dates in 2010 display as "10". Excel appends whatever is in quotes after the year. Because you've put :00 after the year, a date in 2010 displays as 10:00. A date in 2015 displays as 15:00. It is up to you to convince your manager that you have to use the 24-hour clock.

3. Select cell L2. Double-click the fill handle to copy this formula down to all the data points. The result of this formula ranges from January 1, 2010, which represents the customer who walked in at 10:00 a.m., to 12/25/2015, which represents the customer who walked in at 3:57 p.m. However, thanks to the formatting in step 2, you have a series of cells that all display 10:00, then more cells that display 11:00, and so on.

4. Select cells L1:M303.

5. From the Insert tab, select Recommended Charts, OK. The resulting chart is almost perfect. The only glitch: Each "hour" along the bottom axis appears three times.

6. Double-click the labels along the horizontal axis to display the Format Axis task pane. Choose the Chart icon and then expand the Axis Options category. You see the Major Unit is set to 4 Months. Change the Months to Years. Change the 4 to 1. The chart now displays one label per year, which on the chart looks like one label per hour.

As you see in Figure 3.20, the chart now allocates one-sixth of the horizontal axis to each hour. This is an improvement in accuracy over either of the charts in Figure 3.19. The additional chart in Figure 3.20 uses a similar methodology to show the wait time for each customer who enters the bank. If my bank offered 12-minute wait times, I would be finding a new bank.

Figure 3.20
These charts show the number of customers in the bank and their expected wait times.

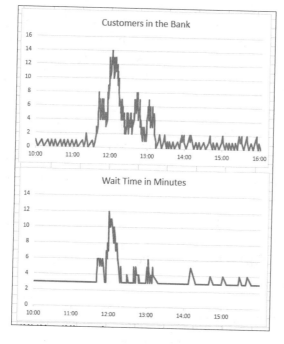

Communicate Effectively with Charts

A long time ago, a McKinsey & Company team investigated opportunities for growth at the company where I was employed. I was chosen to be part of the team because I knew how to get the data out of the mainframe.

The consultants at McKinsey & Company knew how to make great charts. Every sheet of grid paper was turned sideways, and a pencil was used to create a landscape chart that was an awesome communication tool. After drawing the charts by hand, they sent off the charts to someone in the home office who generated the charts on a computer. This was a great technique. Long before touching Excel, someone figured out what the message should be.

You should do the same thing today. Even if you have data in Excel, before you start to create a chart, it's a good idea to analyze the data to see what message you are trying to present.

The McKinsey & Company group used a couple of simple techniques to always get the point across:

- To help the reader interpret a chart, include the message in the title. Instead of using an Excel-generated title such as "Sales," you can use a two- or three-line title, such as "Sales have grown every quarter except for Q3, when a strike impacted production."

- If the chart is talking about one particular data point, draw that column in a contrasting color. For example, all the columns might be white, but the Q3 bar could be black. This draws the reader's eye to the bar that you are trying to emphasize. If you are presenting data onscreen, use red for negative periods and blue or green for positive periods.

The following sections present some Excel trickery that enables you to highlight a certain section of a line chart or a portion of a column chart. In these examples, you spend some time up front in Excel adding formulas to get your data series looking correct before creating the chart.

 TIP If you would like a great book about the theory of creating charts that communicate well, check out Gene Zelazny's *Say It with Charts Complete Toolkit* (McGraw-Hill, 2006, ISBN: 978-0-07-147470-2). Gene is the chart guru at McKinsey & Company who trained the consultants and taught me the simple charting rules. Although *Say It with Charts* doesn't discuss computer techniques for producing charts, it does challenge you to think about the best way to present data with charts and includes numerous examples of excellent charts at work. Visit www.zelazny.com for more information.

Using a Long, Meaningful Title to Explain Your Point

If you are a data analyst, you are probably more adept at making sense of numbers and trends than the readers of your chart. Rather than hoping the reader discovers your message, why not add the message to the title of the chart?

Figure 3.21 shows a default chart in Excel. Because this chart contains a single series, the label "Share" from the original data becomes the title.

Figure 3.21
By default, Excel uses an unimaginative title taken from the heading of the data series.

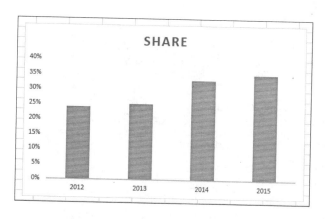

Follow these steps to create the chart in Figure 3.22:

1. Select the data for the chart. Use Insert, Recommended Chart, Column Chart, OK.
2. Use the Paintbrush icon. Choose a Chart Style.
3. Click the Plus icon. Put a check next to Data Labels.
4. Click the title in the chart. Click again to put the title in Edit mode.
5. Backspace to remove the current title. Type `Market share has improved`, press Enter, and type `13 points since 2012`.
6. To format text while in Edit mode, you would have to select all the characters with the mouse. Instead, click the dotted border around the title. When the border becomes solid, you can use the formatting icons on the Home tab to format the title. Alternatively, right-click the title box and use the Mini toolbar to format the title.
7. On the Home tab, select the icon for Align Text Left and then click the Decrease Font Size button until the title looks right.
8. Click the border of the chart title and drag it so the title is in the upper-left corner of the chart.

The result, shown in Figure 3.22, provides a message to assist the reader of the chart.

Figure 3.22
Use the title to tell the reader the point of the chart.

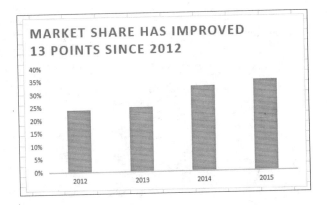

Resizing a Chart Title

The first click on a title selects the title object. A solid bounding box appears around the title. At this point, you can use most of the formatting commands on the Home tab to format the title. Click the Increase/Decrease Font Size buttons to change the font of all the characters. Excel automatically resizes the bounding box around the title. If you do not explicitly have carriage returns in the title where you want the lines to be broken, you are likely to experience frustration at this point.

When you have the solid bounding box around the title, carefully right-click the bounding box and select Edit Text. Alternatively, you can left-click a second time inside the bounding box to also put the title in Text Edit mode. Note that the dashed line in the bounding box indicates the title is in Text Edit mode. Using Text Edit mode, you can select specific characters in the title and then move the mouse pointer up and to the right to access the mini toolbar and the available formatting commands. You can edit specific characters within the title to create a larger title and a smaller subtitle, as shown in Figure 3.23.

Figure 3.23
By selecting characters in Text Edit mode, you can create a title/subtitle effect.

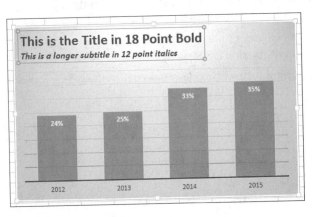

You cannot move the title when you are in Text Edit mode. To exit Text Edit mode, right-click the title and select Exit Edit Text, or left-click the bounding box around the title.

When the bounding box is solid, you can click anywhere on the border except the resizing handles and drag to reposition the title.

When you click a chart title to select it, a bounding box with four resizing handles appears. Actually, they are not resizing handles even though they look like it, which means that you do not have explicit control to resize the title. It feels like you should be able to stretch the title horizontally or vertically, as if it were a text box, but you cannot. The only real control you have to make a text box taller is by inserting carriage returns in the title. Keep in mind that you can insert carriage returns only when you are in Text Edit mode.

Deleting the Title and Using a Text Box

If you are frustrated that the title cannot be resized, you can delete the title and use a text box for the title instead. The title in Figure 3.24 is actually a text box. Note the eight resizing handles on the text box instead of the four resizing handles that appear around a title. Thanks to all these resizing handles, you can actually stretch the bounding box horizontally or vertically.

Figure 3.24
Instead of a title, this chart uses a text box for additional flexibility.

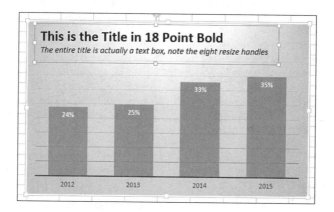

To create the text box shown in Figure 3.24, follow these steps:

1. Click the Plus (+) icon. Uncheck the box next to Chart Title to remove the title. Excel resizes the plot area to fill the space that the title formerly occupied.

2. Select the plot area by clicking some white space inside the plot area. Eight resizing handles now surround the plot area. Drag the top resizing handle down to make room for the title.

3. Make sure the chart is still selected. On the Insert tab, click the Text Box icon.

4. Click and drag inside the chart area to create a text box.

5. Click inside the text box and type a title. Press the Enter key to begin a new line. If you do not press the Enter key, Excel wordwraps and begins a new line when the text reaches the right side of the text box.

6. Select the characters in the text box that make up the main title and use either the mini

toolbar or the tools on the Home tab to make the title 18 point, bold, and Times New Roman.

7. Select the remaining text that makes up the subtitle in the text box, and use the tools on the Home tab to make the subtitle 12 point, italic, Times New Roman.

Microsoft advertises that all text can easily be made into WordArt. However, when you use the WordArt drop-downs in a title, you are not allowed to use the Transform commands found under Text Effects on the Drawing Tools Format tab. When you use the WordArt menus on a text box, however, all the Transform commands are available (see Figure 3.25).

A text box works perfectly because it is resizable, and you can use WordArt Transform commands. If you move or resize the chart, the text box moves with the chart and resizes appropriately.

Figure 3.25
Using a text box instead of a title allows more formatting options.

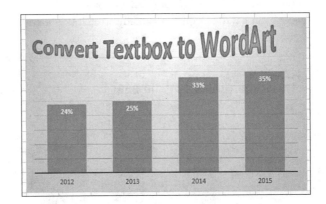

Highlighting One Column

If your chart title is calling out information about a specific data point, you can highlight that point to help focus the reader's attention on it, as shown in Figure 3.26. Although the tools on the Design tab do not allow this, you can achieve the effect quickly by using the Format tab.

Figure 3.26
The column for Friday is highlighted in a contrasting color, and it is also identified in the title.

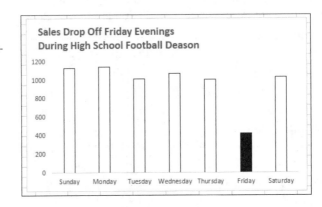

To create the chart in Figure 3.26, follow these steps:

1. Create a column chart by selecting Column, Clustered Column from the Insert tab.

2. Click any of the columns to select the entire series.

3. On the Format tab, select Shape Fill, White. At this point, the columns are invisible. Invisible bars are great for creating waterfall charts, which is discussed in Chapter 4, "Creating Charts That Show Differences." However, in this case, you want to outline the bars.

4. From the Format tab, select Shape Outline, Black. Select Shape Outline, Weight, 1 point. All your columns are now white with black outline.

5. Click the Friday column in the chart. The first click on the series selects the whole series. A second click selects just one data point. If all the columns have handles, click Friday again.

6. From the Format tab, select Shape Fill, Black.

7. Using the Plus icon, turn off Gridlines.

8. Type a title, as shown in Figure 3.26, pressing Enter after the first line of the title. On the Home tab, change the title font size to 14 point, left aligned.

The result is a chart that calls attention to Friday sales.

Replacing Columns with Arrows

Columns shaped like arrows can be used to make a special point. For example, if you have good news to report about consistent growth, you might want to replace the columns in the chart with arrow shapes to further indicate the positive growth.

Follow these steps to convert columns to arrows:

1. Create a column chart showing a single series.

2. In an empty section of the worksheet, insert a new block arrow shape. From the Insert tab, select Shapes, Block Arrows, Up Arrow. Click and drag in the worksheet to draw the arrow.

3. Select the arrow. Press Ctrl+C to copy the arrow to the Clipboard.

4. Select the chart. Click a column to select all the columns in the data series.

5. Press Ctrl+V to paste the arrow. Excel fills the columns with a picture of the block arrow.

6. If desired, select Format Selection from the Format tab. Reduce the gap setting from 150 percent to 75 percent to make the arrows wider.

The new chart is shown in the bottom half of Figure 3.27. After creating the chart, you can delete the arrow created in step 2 by clicking the arrow and pressing the Delete key.

Figure 3.27
Arrows can be used to emphasize the upward growth of sales.

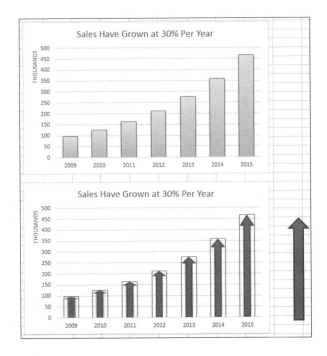

Highlighting a Section of a Chart by Adding a Second Series

The chart in Figure 3.28 shows a sales trend over one year. The business was affected by road construction that diverted traffic flow from the main road in front of the business.

Figure 3.28
Highlight the road construction months in the chart to emphasize the title further.

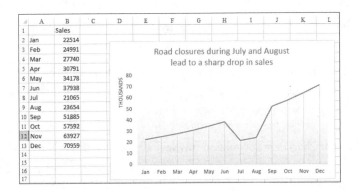

The title calls out the July and August time period, but it would be helpful to highlight that section of the chart. Follow these steps to add an area chart series to the chart:

1. Begin a new series in column C, next to the original data. To highlight July and August, add numbers to column C for the July and August points, plus the previous point, June. In cell C7, enter the formula of =B7. Copy this formula to July and August.

2. Click a blank area inside the chart. A blue bounding box appears around B2:B13 in the worksheet. Drag the lower-right corner of the blue bounding box to the right to extend the series to include the three values in Column C. Initially, this line shows up as a red line on top of a portion of the existing blue line.

3. On the Layout tab, use the Current Selection drop-down to select Series 2, which is the series you just added.

4. While Series 2 is selected, select Design, Change Chart Type. Select the first area chart thumbnail. Click OK. Excel draws a red area chart beneath the line segment of June through August.

5. On the Format tab, use the Current Selection drop-down to reselect Series 2. Open the Shape Fill drop-down. Choose a fill color. The fourth row, first column offers a ToolTip of White, Background 1, Darker 25% and is suitable.

The top chart in Figure 3.29 shows the highlight extending from the horizontal axis up to the data line for the two line segments. Alternatively, you can replace the numbers in column C with 70,000 to draw a shaded rectangle behind the months, as shown in the bottom chart in Figure 3.29.

Figure 3.29
A second series with only three points is used to highlight a section of the chart.

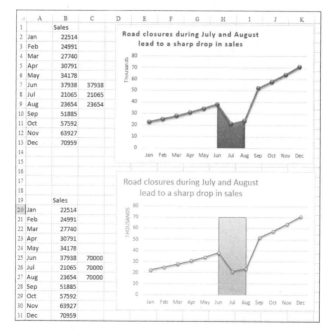

Changing Line Type Midstream

Consider the top chart in Figure 3.30. The title indicates that cash balances improved after a new management team arrived. This chart initially seems to indicate an impressive turn-around. However, if you study the chart axis carefully, you see that the final Q3 and Q4 numbers are labeled Q3F and Q4F to indicate that they are forecast numbers.

Figure 3.30
It is not clear in the top chart that the last two points are forecasts.

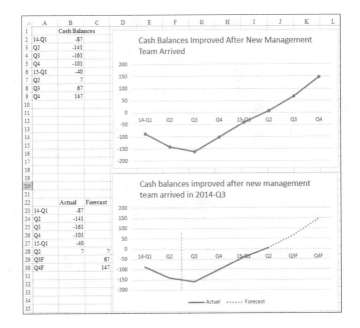

It is misleading to represent forecast numbers as part of the actual results line. It would be ideal if you change the line type at that point to indicate that the last two data points are forecasts. To do so, follow these steps:

1. Change the heading above column B from Cash Balances to Actual.

2. Add the new heading **Forecast** in column C.

3. Because the last actual data point is for Q2 of 2014, move the numbers for Q3 and Q4 of 2014 from column B to column C.

4. To force Excel to connect the actual and the forecast line, copy the last actual data point (the 7 for Q2) over to the Forecast column. This one data point—the connecting point for the two lines—will be in both the Forecast and Actual columns.

5. Change the last two labels in column A from Q3F to just Q3 and from Q4F to just Q4.

6. Click the existing chart. A bounding box appears around the data in column B. Grab the lower-right blue handle and drag outward to encompass B & C. A second series is added to the chart as a red line.

7. Click the red line. In the Format tab, you should see that the Current Selection drop-down indicates Series "Forecast."

8. Select Format, Shape Outline, Dashes and then select the second dash option. The red line changes to a dotted line.

9. While the forecast series is selected, select Design, Change Chart Type. Select a chart type that does not have markers.

10. The chart title indicates that a new management team arrived, but it does not indicate when the team arrived. To fix this, change the title to indicate that the team arrived in Q3 of 2014.

11. On the Insert tab, select Shapes, Line. Draw a vertical line between Q2 and Q3 of 2014, holding down the Shift key while drawing to keep the line vertical.

12. While the line is selected, on the Format tab, select Shape Outline, Dashes and then select the fourth dash option to make the vertical line a dashed line. Note that this line is less prominent than the series line because the weight of the line is only 1.25 points.

The final chart is shown at the bottom of Figure 3.30.

Adding an Automatic Trendline to a Chart

In the previous example, an analyst had created a forecast for the next two quarters. However, sometimes you might want to allow Excel to make a prediction based on past results. In these situations, Excel offers a trendline feature in which Excel draws a straight line that fits the existing data points. You can ask Excel to extrapolate the trendline into the future. If your data series contains blank points that represent the future, Excel can automatically add the trendline. I regularly use these charts to track my progress toward a goal.

The easiest way to add a trendline is to build a data series that includes all the days that the project is scheduled to run. In Figure 3.31, column A contains the days of the month and column B contains 125 for each data point. Therefore, Excel draws a straight line across the chart, showing the goal at the end of the project. Column C shows the writing progress I should make each day. In this particular month, I am assuming that I will write an equal number of pages six days per week. Column D, which is labeled Actual, is where I record the daily progress toward the goal.

The chart is created as a line chart with the gridlines and legend removed. The trendline is formatted as a lighter gray. The actual line is formatted as a thick line. The top chart in Figure 3.31 shows the chart before the trendline is complete. Notice that the thick line is not quite above the progress line.

To add a trendline, follow these steps:

1. Right-click the series line for the Actual column. Select Add Trendline. A default linear trendline is added to the chart. The Format Trendline task pane appears. Your choices in the task pane are for trendlines that use Exponential, Linear, Logarithmic, Polynomial, Power, or Moving Average. Leave the choice at Linear for this example.

2. In the Trendline Name section, either leave the name as Linear (Actual) or enter a custom name such as Forecast.

Figure 3.31
In the top chart, the actual line is running behind the target line, but it seems close.

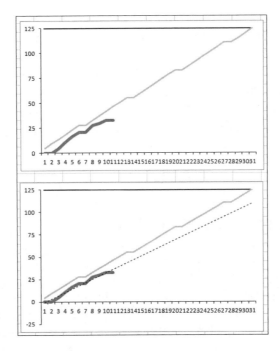

3. When forecasting forward or backward for a certain number of periods, leave both of those settings at 0 because this chart already has data points for the entire month. There are also settings where Excel shows the regression equation on the chart. Add this if you desire.

4. Right-click the trendline to select it. On the Format tab, select Shape Outline, Dashes and then select the fourth dash option. Also, select Shape Outline, Weight, 3/4 point.

The trendline is shown at the bottom of Figure 3.31. In this particular case, the trendline extrapolates that if I continue writing at the normal pace, I will miss the deadline by 15 pages or so.

Excel's trendline is not an intelligent forecasting system. It merely fits past points to a straight line and extrapolates that data. It works great as a motivational tool. For example, the current example shows that it would take a few days of above-average production before the trendline would project that the goal would be met.

Showing a Trend of Monthly Sales and Year-to-Date Sales

In accounting, sales are generally tracked every month. However, in the big picture you are interested in how 12 months add up to produce annual sales.

The top chart in Figure 3.32 is a poor attempt to show both monthly sales and accumulated year-to-date (YTD) sales. The darker bars are the monthly results, whereas the lighter bars are the accumulated YTD numbers through the current month. To show the large YTD number for November, the scale of the axis needs to extend to $400,000. However, this makes the individual monthly bars far too small for the reader to be able to discern any differences.

The solution is to plot the YTD numbers against a secondary vertical axis. My preference is that after you change the axis for one series, you should also change the chart type for that series. Follow these steps to create the bottom chart in Figure 3.32:

1. Select the chart. In the Design tab, choose Change Chart Type.

2. In the left panel of the Change Chart Type dialog, choose Combo. Change the YTD series to a Line chart. Choose the Secondary Axis box for YTD. Click OK. The YTD line is now plotted on the second axis, allowing the columns for months to fill most of the plot area.

3. From the plus icon, uncheck gridlines.

4. From the plus icon, choose Axis Titles. Excel adds the words "Axis Title" to the left, bottom, and right side of the chart.

5. Double-click the numbers along the left axis to display the Format Axis task pane. At the top of the task pane, leave Axis Options selected. From the row of icons, choose the Chart icon. Expand the Axis Options category. Open the Display Units drop-down and choose Thousands. Uncheck the box for Show Display Units Label on Chart, because you will note the units when you edit the axis title.

6. Without closing the task pane, single-click the numbers along the right axis. Open the Display Units drop-down and choose Thousands. Uncheck the box for Show Display Units Label on Chart.

7. Click the bottom Axis Title and press the Delete key to delete that axis title.

8. Double-click the left axis title. Type `Monthly Sales ($000)`.

9. Double-click the right axis title. Type `YTD Sales ($000)`.

10. Click the legend and drag it to appear in the upper-left corner of the plot area.

11. Click the plot area to select it. Drag one of the resizing handles on the right side of the plot area to drag it right to fill the space that used to be occupied by the title.

12. To present your charts in color, change the color of text in the primary vertical axis to match the color of the monthly bars. To change the color, click the numbers to select them. Use the Font Color drop-down on the Home tab to select a color, such as blue. This color cue helps the reader realize that the blue left axis corresponds to the blue bars.

The resulting chart is shown at the bottom of Figure 3.32. The chart illustrates both the monthly trend of each month's sales and the progress toward a final YTD revenue number.

Figure 3.32
The size of the YTD bars obscures the detail of the monthly bars.

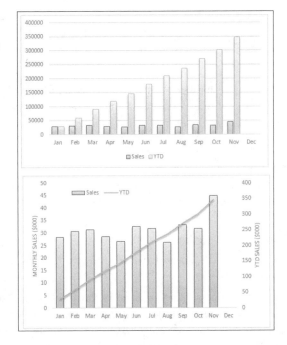

Understanding the Shortcomings of Stacked Column Charts

In a stacked column chart, Series 2 is plotted directly on top of Series 1. Series 3 is plotted on top of Series 2, and so on. The problem with this type of chart is that the reader can't tell whether the values in the individual series is increasing or decreasing. The reader also might not be able to tell if Series 1 is increasing or decreasing. However, because all the other series have differing start periods, it is nearly impossible to tell whether sales in Series 2, 3, or 4 are increasing or decreasing. For example, in the top chart in Figure 3.33, it is nearly impossible for the reader to tell which regions are responsible for the increase from 2010 to 2015.

Stacked column charts are appropriate when the message of the chart is about the first series. In the lower chart in Figure 3.33, the message is that the acquisition of a new product line saved the company. If this new product line had not grown quickly, the company would have had to rely on aging product lines that were losing money. Because this message is about the sales of the new product line, you can plot this as the first series so the reader of the chart can see the effect from that series.

Figure 3.33
In the top chart, readers are not able to draw conclusions about the growth of the three regions located at the top of the chart.

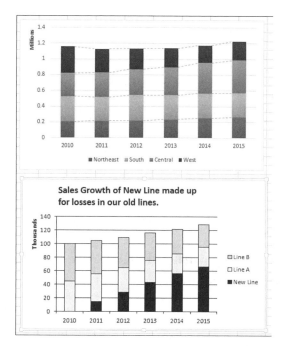

The chart in Figure 3.34 uses a combination of a stacked column chart and a line chart. The stacked column chart shows this year's sales, broken out into same-store sales and new-store sales. In this case, the same-store sales are plotted as the first series in white. The new-store sales are the focus and are plotted in black.

The third series, which is plotted as a dotted line chart, shows the prior-year sales. Although the total height of the column is greater than last year's sales, some underlying problem exists in the old stores. In many cases, the height of the white column does not exceed the height of the dotted line, indicating that sales at same store are down. To create this chart, follow these steps:

1. Set up your data with months in column A, old-store sales for this year in column B, new-store sales for this year in column C, and last year's sales in column D.

2. Select cells A1:D13. Choose Insert, Recommended Charts. Click the All Charts tab in the Insert Chart dialog. Choose Combo chart from the left panel.

3. In the bottom of the Insert Chart dialog, change the Chart Type for Old Stores to Stacked Column. The Chart Type for New Stores will automatically change as well. Leave Last Year as a Line chart. Do not check Secondary Axis for any of the charts. Click OK.

4. Use the Format tab to format the third series as a dotted line. Format the colors of the first two series as shown in Figure 3.34.

Figure 3.34
Current-year sales are shown as a stacked column chart, with last year's sales as a dotted line.

Shortcomings of Showing Many Trends on a Single Chart

Instead of using a stacked column chart, you might try to show many trendlines on a single line chart, which can be confusing. For example, in the top chart in Figure 3.35, the sales trends of five companies create a very confusing chart.

If the goal is to compare the sales results of your company against those of each major competitor, consider using four individual charts instead, as shown at the bottom of Figure 3.35. In these charts, the reader can easily see that your company is about to overtake the long-time industry leader MegaCo, but that quick growth from NewCo might still cause you to stay in the second position next year.

Figure 3.35
Instead of using a single chart with five confusing lines, compare your company to each other competitor in smaller charts.

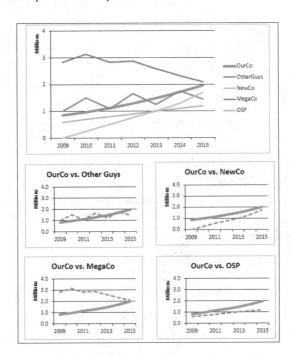

Next Steps

In Chapter 4, you discover charts used to make comparisons, including pie, radar, bar, donut, and waterfall charts.

3

Creating Charts That Show Differences

Comparing Entities

Whereas Chapter 3, "Creating Charts That Show Trends," was concerned with the progression of a trend over time, this chapter focuses on demonstrating the differences between entities. For example, you can use Excel charts to compare each sales region versus the others or your company versus the competitors. In addition, when you want to compare the differences among a handful of entities, a bar chart is the perfect choice because the reader can clearly see the differences between the entities.

The only time you should use a pie chart is when you want to show how components add up to a whole entity. Pie charts are vastly overused, and many guidelines contraindicate their use. You should often instead consider 100% stacked column charts, bar of pie charts, or pie of pie charts. These last charts are a bit tricky to master but have some amazing flexibility.

Finally, in this chapter you find out how to use some more Excel trickery to build a waterfall chart. This type of chart is perfect for telling the story of how a whole entity breaks down into components.

Using Bar Charts to Illustrate Item Comparisons

Bar charts are perfect for comparing items. Bar charts offer a few advantages over column charts for comparing sales of various items:

- People tend to associate column charts—or any other chart in which the data progresses from left to right—as having a time-based component. When you turn the columns on their sides and make them horizontal bars, people tend not to read time into the equation.

4

IN THIS CHAPTER

Comparing Entities..113

Using Bar Charts to Illustrate Item Comparisons 113

Showing Component Comparisons..............117

Using a Waterfall Chart to Tell the Story of Component Decomposition 136

Next Steps 145

■ With a bar chart, the category names can appear in a horizontal orientation, giving plenty of room for longer names. For example, in the chart shown in Figure 4.1, the category names take almost half the chart. However, there is room to get the point across that the "Excel for" series is not selling as well as the general-purpose Excel books.

Figure 4.1
A bar chart allows for lengthy category names and a comparison of different product lines.

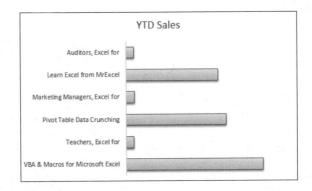

Bar charts are oriented with the first item in the list closest to the bottom of the chart. If you expect people to read a chart from top to bottom, you should sort the categories into descending alphabetical sequence by clicking the ZA button in the Data tab. The bar chart in Figure 4.2 compares sales of six product lines. It is easy to spot the winners in the chart because the original data set is sorted to have the VBA title at the top of the spreadsheet.

Figure 4.1 uses a clustered bar chart type, although it has only one series to report.

For a more powerful arrangement of data, you can sort these categories by sales in ascending sequence. Excel then plots the largest category at the top of the chart. Even more than the chart in Figure 4.1, you can see that the chart in Figure 4.2 depicts a clearer delineation between the winners and losers than the chart in Figure 4.1.

Figure 4.2
Sort the data by ascending sales to show the largest bars at the top of the chart.

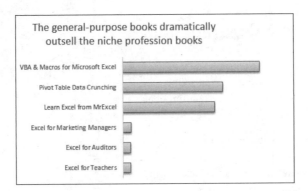

If you think it is silly to sort your data into the reverse order from which you want to present it in the chart, there is a setting in the Format Axis task pane that you can use to correct this logic. Double-click the labels along the category axis. In the task pane, click the Chart icon and then expand the Axis Options category. Choose Categories in Reverse Order to show the first row in your data set at the top of the chart. (See Figure 4.3.)

Figure 4.3
Instead of sorting your data in reverse order, you can sort the data in normal order and then specify reverse order for the categories.

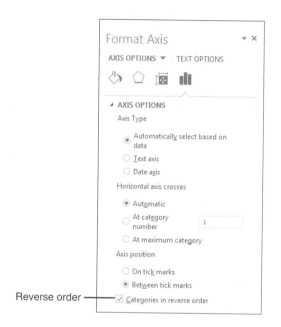

Reverse order

Adding a Second Series to Show a Time Comparison

In Figure 4.4, two series are plotted on the bar chart. The original series presents sales data from this year. This data was moved to Series 2 to continue to be plotted as the top bar. The new Series 1 contains sales data from last year, for reference.

Because the main message is current-year sales, those bars are formatted with a black fill to draw attention to them. The bars for last year are shown as white with black outlines.

The addition of data from the previous year adds a bit of context to the chart. The reader can tell that Products 2, 3, and 5 are new this year and have no sales history from the previous year. Product 4 was the previous market leader, but its sales have fallen off sharply. Product 1 has experienced good year-to-year growth; it will be interesting to see if the newly emerging products show similar growth in Year 2.

To create the chart in Figure 4.4, follow these steps:

1. Enter product names in column A.

2. Enter last-year sales in column B and this-year sales in column C.

Figure 4.4
In this chart, the sales for this year are moved to Series 2. A new Series 1 shows sales from last year—a bit of additional data to show whether sales are increasing or decreasing.

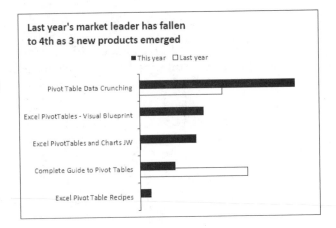

3. Sort the data so that the largest sales from this year are at the bottom of the chart.

4. From the Insert tab, select Bar, 2D Bar, Clustered Bar.

5. Click a gridline and press the Delete key to delete the gridlines. Note that there are gridlines at 0, 1000, 2000, ..., 7000. To delete the gridlines, select one of the gridlines between 1000 and 6000. Selecting the gridline at 0 or 7000 selects the plot area.

6. Click the numeric axis labels at the bottom of the chart and press the Delete key to delete those labels.

7. Select the Plus icon, Legend, Top.

8. Click in the title area. Type the first line of the title, press Enter, and type the second line of the title.

9. Click the outline of the title to exit Text Edit mode. On the Home tab, click the Left Align button and the Decrease Font Size button. Drag the title to the left.

10. Click a bar from this year. On the Format tab, select Shape Fill and then select black.

11. Right-click the black bar and select Format Data Series. Change the Series Overlap setting to 25%.

12. Click one of the bars for last year. On the Format tab, select Shape Fill, White. On the Format tab, select Shape Outline and then select black.

13. Grab one of the resizing handles in the corner of the chart and drag outward to resize the chart.

Subdividing a Bar to Emphasize One Component

Excel offers a stacked bar chart type that allows you to break a bar, such as total sales, to show components. In the top chart in Figure 4.5, only one component is isolated as the black portion of the bar. The subject of the chart is this one component of product cost, showing how Company A has a significant cost advantage.

You should use this chart type sparingly. The reader of the chart is able to make a judgment about the size of the black bar for the major subcomponent. The reader is also able to make a judgment about the total size of the bar. However, it is difficult to make a judgment about the size of the white component of the bars. Can you tell which company has the lowest other cost? (The answer is Company B.)

The problem becomes worse if you try to show more than two components in the stacked bar chart. For example, the bottom chart in Figure 4.5 is trying to compare the costs of four major components. However, the reader will not be able to learn anything about the additional components.

Figure 4.5
A stacked bar chart allows the reader to judge the size of the total bar and the first component bar. Beyond that, it is difficult to make a comparison from one bar to the next.

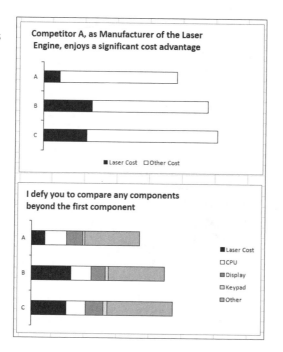

Showing Component Comparisons

A component comparison chart is useful when you want to show several parts that add up to a whole. You can use this type of chart to show these concepts:

- The market share of several competitors in a market
- The cost breakdown of a product by subcomponent
- The breakdown of time spent in a day
- The relative size of five major customers and all other customers as a group

These are also all great concepts to show using a pie chart or a 100% stacked bar/column chart. Unfortunately, pie charts are overused in business today. People try to use pie charts to compare items that do not add up to a whole. For example, in Figure 4.6, someone tried to use a pie chart to compare product prices. Without reading the individual prices labeling each pie slice, it is difficult to figure out whether the Hummer H3 or the Ford Escape hybrid costs more. As discussed in the previous section, using a bar chart is best when you are trying to compare items. The bottom chart in Figure 4.6 shows the same data as the pie chart. However, in this case, it is plotted on a bar chart, which makes it easier to understand.

Figure 4.6
An attempt to use a pie chart to compare prices is misguided. The bar chart in the lower half of the figure is more effective.

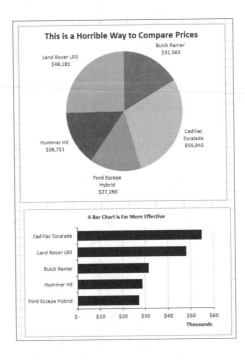

Some of the frustrations with pie charts are humorously summarized by Dick DeBartolo, *Mad*'s Maddest Writer, in the chart in Figure 4.7 that he prepared for this book.

> **NOTE**
> Dick Debartolo has been writing for *Mad* magazine for more than 40 years. If you are a fan of *Mad*, check out his book, *Good Days and MAD: A Hysterical Tour Behind the Scenes at MAD Magazine*. Dick also hosts the Daily Giz Wiz podcast, which is a review of the latest gadgets and those gadgets that once seemed like a good idea but are now collecting dust in Dick's Gadget Warehouse.

When you are performing component comparisons, the following chart types are effective:

- A pie chart is appropriate when you are comparing 2 to 5 components.
- A pie of pie chart is appropriate for comparing 6 to 10 components.
- A bar of pie chart can handle 6 to 15 components.

Figure 4.7
Pay close attention to this
chart. Most people's eyes
will glaze over by the
second slice.

- You should use a 100% stacked column chart when you want to have two or more pies, such as to compare market share from this year to last year. The 100% stacked bar, 100% stacked line, and 100% stacked area are all variations of the 100% stacked column chart.

- A doughnut chart is a strange chart that can occasionally be used to compare two pie charts. However, a 100% stacked column chart is usually better for this type of comparison.

Figure 4.8 illustrates when to use which type of chart.

Figure 4.8
Choose the proper type
of pie chart based on the
number of categories in
your data.

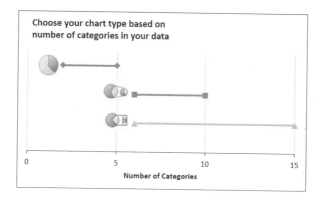

The following sections describe the ins and outs of using pie, 100% stacked column, and the other previously mentioned charts.

Using Pie Charts

Pie charts are great for comparing two to five different components. You typically select a range that contains category labels in column A and values in column B. Often, the categories are sorted so that the largest value is at the top and the remaining categories are sorted in descending order.

To create a pie chart, from the Insert tab, select the Pie drop-down, as shown in Figure 4.9. The following six icons are located in this drop-down:

Figure 4.9
You commonly use the first icon to create a 2D pie chart.

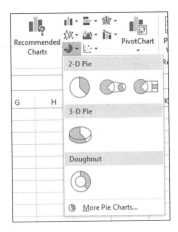

■ **2D Pie**—The pie chart type used most frequently.

■ **Pie of Pie or Bar of Pie**—Both of these chart types are effective for dealing with data sets that have too many slices and when you care about the small pie slices.

■ **3D Pie**—This is a regular pie chart tipped on its side so you can see the "edge" of the pie. This is a cool effect when you are trying to decorate a PowerPoint chart. However, it is not as effective if you want someone to read and understand the data.

■ **Doughnut**—A doughnut chart shows two or more pie charts in concentric circles.

The default pie chart has no labels and includes a legend on the bottom to help identify the pie slices. Initially, the first data item appears starting at the 12 o'clock position, and additional wedges appear in a clockwise direction, as shown in Figure 4.10.

In black and white, it is particularly difficult to match the tiny color swatches used in the legend with the pie slices. For this reason, you nearly always want to delete the legend and add data labels, as discussed in the next section.

Figure 4.10
The default pie chart uses a legend that is too small and too far from the chart to be effective.

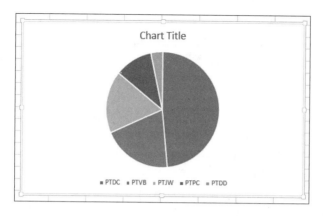

Labeling a Pie Chart

Because a pie chart does not have a lengthy axis running along one edge of the chart, choosing the data labels is an important consideration. To get full control over your data labels, use the Format Data Labels task pane. First, add data labels by choosing them in the Plus icon to the right of the chart. Then, double-click a label to open the task pane.

Excel displays the Label Options page of the Format Data Labels task pane, as shown in Figure 4.11.

Figure 4.11
Double-click a data label to arrive at this task pane.

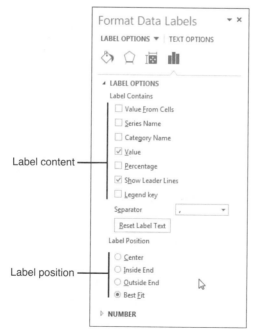

You have options for what the label should contain, including the following:

- **Value from Cells**—This is new in Excel 2013. You can point to a range of values or formulas that generate the labels.

- **Series Name**—This option does not make sense in a pie chart because every slice has a series name, such as Sales.

- **Category Name**—Choose this option to show the names of items represented by the individual pie slices. When you turn this item on, you can set Legend to None.

- **Value**—Choose this option to show the actual numeric value for this slice from the cells in the spreadsheet. Either the Value or Percentage numeric values are used most often.

- **Percentage**—Choose this option to have Excel calculate the percentage of the pie allocated to each pie slice. This is a number that is not typically in your spreadsheet.

- **Show Leader Lines**—It is recommended that you leave this setting on. If you later reposition a label, Excel draws a line from the label to the pie slice associated with that label.

- **Legend Key**—Use this option to add a tiny bit of color next to the label. This color matches the color of the associated wedge.

- **Label Position**—The usual choices for the label position on a pie chart are to either show the label outside the pie slice, indicated by Outside End, or inside the pie slice, indicated by Center.

The final choice in the Label Options page of the Format Data Labels dialog is the Separator drop-down. This option becomes important when you have chosen two items in the Label Contains section. For example, if you have selected Category Name and Percentage, Excel's default choice for a comma as the separator shows the label East, 33 percent. To remove the comma from the pie chart labels, choose either (space) or (New Line) from the Separator drop-down.

Figure 4.12 shows a pie chart with category names and percentages at the outside end of each slice. The data label is separated by a newline character.

Figure 4.12
Displaying the labels at the outside end ensures that the labels can be read.

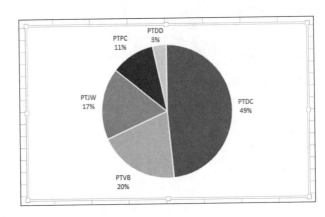

Rotating a Pie Chart

There is an ongoing argument about the rotation of a pie chart. Many people say that the first pie slice should start at the 12 o'clock position, and subsequent pie slices should appear in a clockwise direction. I disagree with this philosophy, from a purely practical point of view. I think that the smallest pie slices should be rotated around so that they appear in the lower-right corner of the pie. This location provides the most room for the labels of the small pie slices to appear without overlapping.

You have control over the rotation of a pie chart. You can right-click a pie chart and select Format Data Series. On the Format Series task pane that appears, you can change the setting for Angle of First Slice. For example, in Figure 4.13, the bottom pie chart has been rotated 195 degrees, which prevents labels from appearing on top of each other.

Figure 4.13
You can change the angle of the first slice to rotate the pie until the data labels have the most room to appear without overlapping each other.

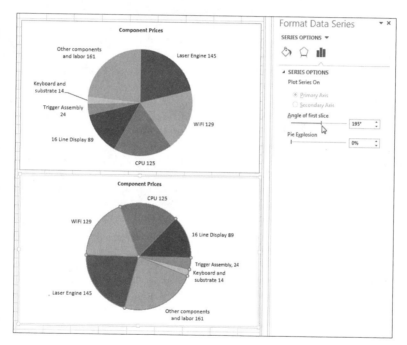

Moving an Individual Pie Slice Label

In a pie chart that has long category names and many slices, you might not be able to find an angle of rotation that enables all the labels to have sufficient room. In this case, you need to move an individual pie slice label.

The first time you click a data label, all the data labels are selected. At this point, you can use icons on the Home tab to change the font or font size.

Clicking a second time on a data label selects only that particular label. You can click the border of the label and drag it to a new position. If the Leader Lines option remains selected (refer to Figure 4.11), Excel automatically connects the label and the pie slice with a leader line. In Figure 4.14, the label for the keyboard has been moved so that it does not crash into the label for the trigger assembly.

Figure 4.14
After a second single-click, only one label is selected. You can drag an individual data label into a new position.

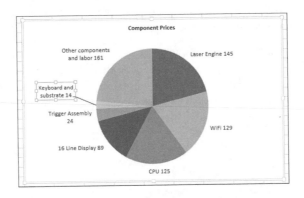

Highlighting One Slice of a Pie by Exploding

The first time you click a pie selects the data series, which means it selects all the pie slices. If you then drag outward from the center of the pie as you click, you explode all the slices of the pie.

If you want to explode the whole pie, you have to be fairly deliberate about it. If you click once to select all the slices and then click again to drag the slices outward, the second click selects only a single slice and explodes only a single slice. Click outside the pie to select the entire chart and then click the pie and drag outward. This action selects the pie and explodes it in a single step.

The charts in Figure 4.15 show various levels of explosion. The top-left chart uses a 15% explosion factor. Excel allows you to specify up to a 400% explosion factor, which really looks pretty silly.

A better technique is to explode just the one slice that is the subject of the pie. For example, in Figure 4.16, a large order cannot ship because of shortages of a tiny assembly. The plant managers had previously decided to cut safety stock on this component. To illustrate that this might have been a poor decision, you can explode just that slice of the pie.

To explode one slice of the pie, click once on the pie to select the entire series. Then click the slice in question one more time to select only that slice. Drag the individual slice outward to explode only that slice, as shown in Figure 4.16.

Figure 4.15
Drag outward while a data series is selected to select the entire pie.

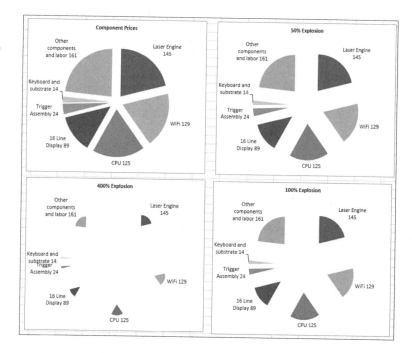

Figure 4.16
You can explode one piece of the pie to call attention to that piece.

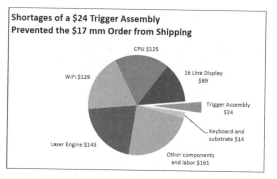

Highlighting One Slice of a Pie with Color

Instead of exploding a slice of a pie, you can highlight that slice using a contrasting color. A single black pie slice in an otherwise white pie instantly draws the reader's eye, as shown in Figure 4.17.

To format the chart as shown in Figure 4.17, follow these steps:

1. Click anywhere on the pie to select the entire pie.
2. On the Format tab, select Shape Fill, White. The entire pie disappears.
3. On the Format tab, select Shape Outline and then select black. The pie is now a white pie outlined in black.

Figure 4.17
You can plot one slice of the pie in a contrasting color to draw attention to that slice.

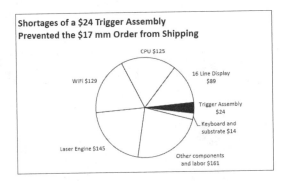

4. Click the one pie slice that you want to highlight.

5. On the Format tab, select Shape Fill and then select black. The single pie slice now stands out from the other slices.

Switching to a 100 Percent Stacked Column Chart

It is difficult for a reader to track the trends from one pie to the next when you are trying to show a trend by using multiple pie charts, as shown in Figure 4.18.

Figure 4.18
It is hard to track trends by looking at multiple pies.

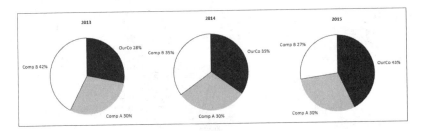

Instead of using pie charts, you can switch to one of Excel's 100% charts. For example, in the 100% stacked column chart, Excel stacks the values from Series 1, Series 2, Series 3, and so on but scales the column so that each column is the same height. This gives the effect of dividing a column into components, just as in a pie chart.

Excel offers 100% versions of column charts, bar charts, area charts, and line charts. To find them, in the Insert Chart dialog, look for charts where both the left and right elements are the same height (see Figure 4.19).

Figure 4.20 shows examples of 100% stacked column, area, bar, and line charts. The 100% stacked column chart is probably the easiest to interpret. In a 100% stacked chart, the reader is able to judge the growth or decline of both the first series and the last series.

Figure 4.19
These icons all create 100% stacked charts.

Figure 4.20
For year-over-year comparisons, a 100% stacked column chart is easier to read than multiple pie charts.

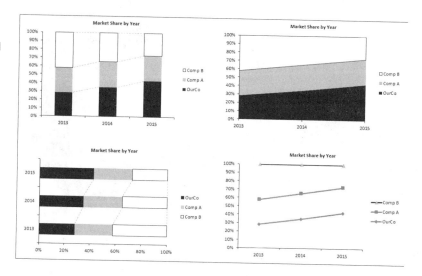

Using a Doughnut Chart to Compare Two Pies

Excel offers another chart type—the doughnut chart—that attempts to compare multiple pies. In a doughnut chart, one pie chart encircles another pie chart.

A reader of the chart in Figure 4.21 can see that the market share for OurCo increased between 2014 and 2015 and that the market share for Comp B decreased between 2014 and 2015. However, it is unlikely that the reader can draw any conclusions about Comp A based on this chart.

In creating the chart in Figure 4.21, you need to go through a number of maddening steps, including the steps listed here:

1. Select the Plus icon, Data Labels, More Options to display the Format Data Labels task pane. Choose the Chart icon and then expand the Label Options category. Choose only Series Name in the Label Contains. You probably need to leave the legend turned on with this chart because there is not space to legibly fit OurCo 2014 in the thin ring of the doughnut.

2. Changing the colors using the Format tab is a tedious process. You cannot format both OurCo sections simultaneously. Instead, click the 2014 ring, and then click 2015 OurCo. Select Format, Shape Fill, and then select black. Repeat these steps for the other five pieces of the doughnut chart.

3. To make some data labels white, select the labels for Series 1, then select just one label, and then use the Font Color drop-down on the Home tab. Repeat this step for OurCo for Series 2.

Figure 4.21
Doughnut charts are generally difficult to read, although this one does effectively communicate some information.

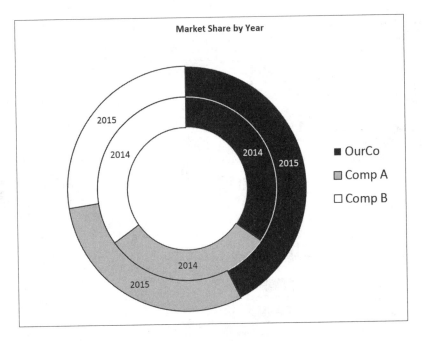

One interesting setting for the doughnut chart is the doughnut hole size. When you right-click the inner series of the doughnut chart and select Format Data Series, the Format dialog box appears. You can use this dialog to change the doughnut hole size; valid values range from 10% to 90%. The doughnut chart in Figure 4.22 uses a hole size of 10%. Reducing the hole size makes the chart more readable in this case.

Figure 4.22
Reduce the doughnut hole size to allow more room for labels on the chart.

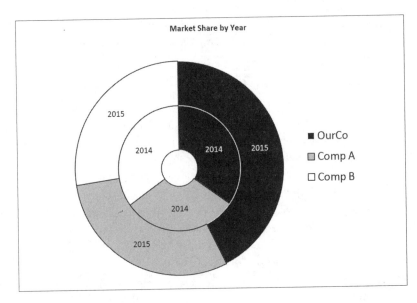

Dealing with Data Representation Problems in a Pie Chart

The 80/20 rule comes into play with pie charts. In many component comparisons, 20% of the categories make up 80% of the pie. In this case, the tiny pie slices at the end of the pie contain too much detail and are not useful. If you attempt to leave these slices in the pie, the labels needlessly complicate the chart, as shown in Figure 4.23.

As noted in the "Using Pie Charts" section earlier in this chapter, there are several methods that enable you to create the chart shown in Figure 4.23. For example, you can rotate a pie chart and move individual pie labels. However, the process is tedious with this amount of data.

Figure 4.23
The 20 pie slices make this chart difficult to read.

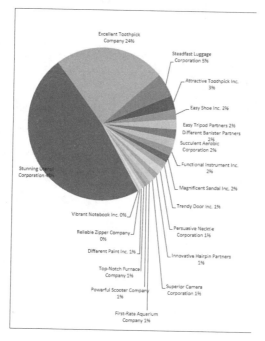

In addition, the data used in Figure 4.23 might not be entirely realistic. Usually, a company has a few major accounts and dozens of minor accounts. If you need a list of all your accounts, you should really show it in a table that lists the customers, sorted in descending sequence.

Usually a pie chart is focused on the top four to five accounts. The message for the reader of the chart in Figure 4.23 is that two major accounts make up 75% of the revenue stream. If anything happens to either of those accounts, this company will be in for tough times. To communicate this message, you can replace the last 16 pie slices with a single slice labeled 16 Other Accounts.

4

Other times you may need to show the detail of the small accounts, such as to grow some new megacustomers. In this case, you can switch to a bar of pie or pie of pie chart. These options are discussed in the next sections.

Replacing Smaller Slices with an Other Customer Summary

Replacing smaller slices with an Other Customer summary does not require magic. Instead, you look through your customer list and identify a logical breakpoint between major customers and customers that should be listed as "other."

The example shown in Figure 4.24 includes two customers that are not exactly major to help communicate how quickly sales fall off.

Figure 4.24
The low-tech solution is to add a formula to the worksheet to total all the smaller accounts.

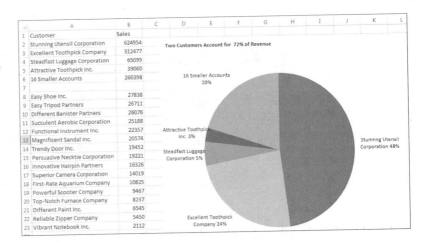

To create this chart, insert a few blank rows to separate the major accounts from the other accounts. In the worksheet, add the label 16 Smaller Accounts. Then enter a SUM function to total all the smaller customers. Finally, change the chart range to include only the major customers and the Other line.

You do not have to re-create the chart to specify a new data range. If you click once on the chart, Excel draws a blue rectangle around the data included in the chart. Grab the blue resizing handle at the bottom of the data range and drag upward to include only the major customers and the Other Total row.

In Figure 4.24, the chart is less busy than in Figure 4.23. The title has been improved, and each data label now includes both the category name and percentage.

Using a Pie of Pie Chart

A pie of pie chart shows the smallest pie slices in a new, secondary pie chart. The true volume of the small slices is shown in a slice marked Other in the original pie. Series lines extend from the Other slice to the secondary pie.

This chart type can be used when the focus of your chart is the small slices, such as when the focus is on the emerging markets (see Figure 4.25). Together, the five markets in this chart account for a 19% share. However, the markets are not doing equally well. The pie of pie chart shows which of the new markets are growing the fastest.

Figure 4.25
A secondary pie shows the detail of the emerging markets.

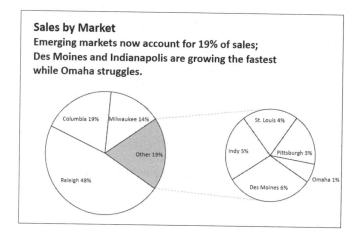

> → Creating the chart in Figure 4.25 requires some tricky steps that are described later in this chapter, in the "Customizing the Split in the 'Of Pie' Charts" section.

Several interesting settings are available in the "of pie" charts. In both the pie of pie and bar of pie charts, you can control the size of the secondary plot compared to the primary pie. You can control the gap between the plots and choose whether the series lines extend from one chart to the next. To access these settings, click inside the chart but outside the pie to deselect the pie. Right-click the pie and select Format Data Series; then the Format Data Series dialog appears, as shown in Figure 4.26.

Figure 4.26
The pie of pie and bar of pie charts offer new settings in the Series Options tab of the Format Data Series dialog.

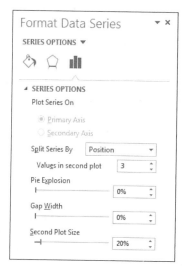

In the Format Data Series dialog, you can set the gap between the pies from 0% to 500%. The gap size is expressed as a percentage of the radius of the main pie. In other words, when you select 100%, the gap between the pies is equal to the radius of the main pie, which is 50% of the width of the main pie.

You can also set the secondary plot size to be anywhere from 5% to 200% of the main pie chart. The default setting is 75%.

Adjusting either the gap setting or the secondary plot size changes the size of both pies. If you make either the gap or the secondary plot size larger, Excel has to make the main pie smaller to fit all three elements into the same plot area. This requires a little bit of high school algebra. For example, if the plot area is 500 pixels wide and the width of the main pie is a variable n, you might encounter these settings:

■ With a gap of 100% and a secondary plot size of 75%, the original pie is n pixels wide, the gap is $0.5n$ pixels wide, and the secondary pie is $0.75n$ pixels wide. This means the total width is $2.25n=500$, so n is 222. This results in a main pie width of 222 pixels, a gap of 111 pixels, and a secondary plot size of 166.50.

■ If you increase the secondary plot size to 100% and increase the gap to 150%, the original pie is n pixels wide, the gap is $0.75n$ pixels wide, and the secondary pie is n pixels wide. This means the total width is $2.75n=500$. The main pie is 181 wide, the gap is 136 wide, and the secondary pie is 181 pixels wide.

As you increase the size of either setting, the main pie gets smaller. Table 4.1 shows the horizontal size of the main pie, the gap, and the secondary pie for various combinations of gap width and secondary plot size. For example, the main pie can occupy as much as 83% of the plot area width if you select a 0% gap and a secondary plot size of 20%. As you increase the gap and secondary plot size, you might end up with a main pie that occupies as little as 18% of the width of the plot area.

Here is an example of how to read the table. The first cell in the table indicates 83%/0%/17%. This means that if you choose a secondary plot size of 20% and a gap size of 0%, the main pie occupies 83% of the width, the gap is 0%, and the secondary plot occupies 17%. This happens because 17% is 20% of 83%.

For another example, read across row 2. In all these examples, the secondary plot is to be 50% of the primary pie. In the first column, with a gap size of 0%, the main pie takes 67%, the gap is 0%, and the secondary pie is 33%. Move right to the 100% Gap Size column. Now the gap is set to be 100% of the second pie. The table shows 50%/25%/25%, meaning that the main pie takes up 50% of the width, the gap takes up 25% of the width, and the second pie takes up 25% of the width.

Table 4.1   Width of Main Pie/Gap/Second Pie

Secondary Plot Size	Gap Size				
	0%	**50%**	**100%**	**250%**	**500%**
20%	83%/0%/17%	69%/17%/14%	59%/29%/12%	41%/51%/8%	27%/68%/5%
50%	67%/0%/33%	57%/14%/29%	50%/25%/25%	36%/45%/18%	25%/63%/13%
75%	57%/0%/43%	50%/13%/38%	44%/22%/33%	33%/42%/25%	24%/59%/18%
100%	50%/0%/50%	44%/11%/44%	40%/20%/40%	31%/38%/31%	22%/56%/22%
150%	40%/0%/60%	36%/9%/55%	33%/17%/50%	27%/33%/40%	20%/50%/30%
200%	33%/0%/67%	31%/8%/62%	29%/14%/57%	24%/29%/47%	18%/45%/36%

Figure 4.27 shows the extremes for the gap size and secondary plot size settings.

Figure 4.27
Changing the gap width and secondary plot size can create vastly different looks for the chart.

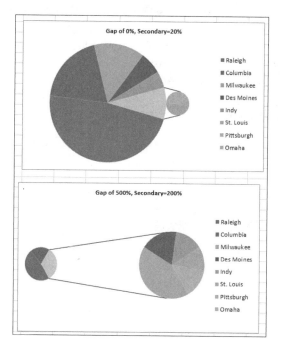

Excel also offers a robust system for choosing which slices should be in the secondary plot. The following section applies to both pie of pie and bar of pie charts.

Customizing the Split in the "Of Pie" Charts

With an "of pie" chart, you have absolute control over which slices appear in the main pie and which slices are sent to the secondary plot. Excel offers a surprising array of ways to control this setting.

When you right-click the pie and select Format Data Series, the Format Data Series dialog appears. The top setting in the dialog is the drop-down Split Series By, which offers the following options:

- **Split Series by Position**—You can change the spin button to indicate that the last n values should be shown in the secondary pie. Excel then uses the last n values from the original data set in the secondary pie.

- **Split Series by Value**—When you enter a value in the text box, Excel moves any slices with a value less than the entered value to the secondary pie.

- **Split Series by Percentage Value**—You can use the spin button to enter a value from 1% to 99%. Any slices smaller than the entered percentage move to the secondary plot. Note that if there are no slices smaller than that value, the secondary plot appears as an empty black circle.

- **Split Series by Custom**—This is a flexible setting where you can choose which slices to send to the secondary pie. After choosing Custom from the drop-down, you click an individual slice in the chart. Then, in the Format Data Point dialog, you indicate that the point belongs to the second plot or the first plot. You continue selecting additional slices in the chart and indicating the location for those points.

4

CASE STUDY: CREATING A PIE OF PIE CHART

At this point, you have enough information to create the chart shown previously in Figure 4.25. Follow these steps to create that chart:

1. Enter `markets` in column A and `sales` in column B.

2. Sort by sales in descending order.

3. Select the markets and sales cells.

4. From the Insert tab, select Pie, 2D Pie, Pie of Pie. Excel creates a pie with three items in the secondary plot, a legend, and no labels.

5. Click the Legend and press the Delete key.

6. Right-click the pie and select Format Data Series. Select Split Series by Position. Set the Values in Second Plot to 5.

7. With the entire pie still selected, select Shape Outline from the Format tab, and then select black. Select Shape Fill, White to outline all the pie slices but fill them with white.

8. From the Plus icon, select Data Labels, More Options. Select Category Name and Percentage. Clear the Value check box. Change the separator from a comma to a space.

9. Click the Other slice in the left pie. If the current selection drop-down in the Layout or Format tab does not indicate that you selected Series x, Point n, click the Other slice again.

10. From the Format tab, select Shape Fill, and then select light gray.

11. In the Current Selection drop-down of the Format tab, select Series Lines 1. In the Format tab, select Shape Outline and then select gray. Select Shape Outline, Dashes, and then select the fourth dash choice.

12. Enlarge the chart by clicking one of the resizing handles in the border around the chart. Drag out from the center to enlarge the chart.

13. If a chart title is not visible, on the Layout tab, select Chart Title, Above Chart.

14. Click in the chart title twice. Select the characters and type a new title, such as `Sales by Market`, and then press the Enter key. Type the remaining three lines of the title.

15. Select the characters in the top line of the title. On the Home tab, select 20 Point. Select the remaining lines of the title. On the Home tab, select 18 Point.

16. Click the border of the title. On the Home tab, click Left Align. Drag the title so that it is left-justified above the chart.

Using a Bar of Pie Chart

The bar of pie chart is similar in concept to the pie of pie chart. In the case of bar of pie, the large slices are plotted on a main pie. The smaller slices are moved over to a column chart on the right side of the chart area. All the settings for gap width, series lines, secondary plot size, and which slices move to the second plot area are valid for the bar of pie chart.

Figure 4.28 shows a bar of pie chart. Technically, this should be called a column of pie chart.

Figure 4.28
In a bar of pie chart, the smaller slices are grouped into Other, and the detail is shown in a column chart.

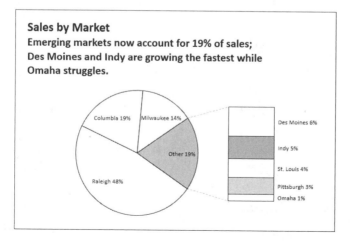

Sales by Market
Emerging markets now account for 19% of sales;
Des Moines and Indy are growing the fastest while
Omaha struggles.

Columbia 19%   Milwaukee 14%

Other 19%

Raleigh 48%

Des Moines 6%

Indy 5%

St. Louis 4%

Pittsburgh 3%

Omaha 1%

Using a Waterfall Chart to Tell the Story of Component Decomposition

As mentioned in Chapter 3, I spent a few months as a team member of a McKinsey & Company consulting gig when they were brought in to turn around the company where I used to work. McKinsey consultants were experts at creating cool charts, including the waterfall chart that is closely associated with that firm.

The waterfall chart is a useful chart because it tells a story. For example, if you are an NPR fan, you might have listened to Ira Glass's "This American Life" weekly radio show. Glass describes the show as a series of stories in which, "this happens, and then this happens, and then this happens, and then this happens...." Similarly, a waterfall chart makes a simple table into a story.

For example, waterfall charts in Figure 4.29 are used to analyze the profitability of a proposal. The chart starts with a tall column on the left side to show the total list price of the products you are selling. The next column appears to float in midair, dropping down from the total list price column to show the total discount that the sales team is proposing. The next column shows net revenue. The rest of the chart is a series of floating columns that show where all the revenue went. A tiny column on the right side shows the profit from the deal.

Figure 4.29
A waterfall chart breaks a single component chart out over several columns.

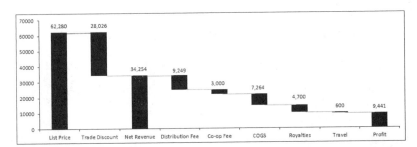

The trick to making the middle columns float is to use a stacked column chart. The second series is the actual columns that appear on the chart. The first series is changed into an invisible color without any lines in order to make the bars in the second series appear to float.

You might start with values such as those shown in columns A and B of Figure 4.30. The trick to creating a waterfall chart is to move those values into two series. The second series is the height of each column that is actually seen. The first series is an invisible column that makes the other bars appear to float.

Follow these steps to create the chart shown in Figure 4.30:

1. For the three columns in the chart that touch the horizontal axis, set the invisible column to zero and the visible column to the number from column B.

Figure 4.30
Break the series in column B into two series in E and F.

▲	A	B	C	D	E	F
1					Invisible	Visible
2	List Price	62,280		List Price	0	62,280
3	Trade Discount	28,026		Trade Discount	34,254	28,026
4	Net Revenue	34,254		Net Revenue	0	34,254
5	Distribution Fee	9,249		Distribution Fee	25,005	9,249
6	Co-op Fee	3,000		Co-op Fee	22,005	3,000
7	COGS	7,264		COGS	14,741	7,264
8	Royalties	4,700		Royalties	10,041	4,700
9	Travel	600		Travel	9,441	600
10	Profit	9,441		Profit	0	9,441

2. The goal for trade discount is to have a floating bar that extends from 62,280 down to 34,254. To have the bar float at this level, you need an invisible bar that is 34,254 tall. Therefore, in cell E3, enter the formula =F4.

3. The height of the floating bar needs to extend from 34,254 to 62,280, so enter the formula =F2-E3 in cell F3.

4. After the Net Revenue bar are all the SG&A expenses. The height of each floating bar should be the amount of the expense. Therefore, in cell F5, enter the formula =B5. Copy this down to cells F6:F9.

5. The formula for the invisible portion of the bars is often difficult to figure out. In this case, starting at the final bar might make this easier. The Travel bar representing $600 needs to float just above the Profit bar of 9,441. Therefore, enter the formula =F10 in cell E9.

6. The Royalties bar of 4,700 needs to float just above the level of the Travel bar. The height of the Travel bar is the height of the invisible bar (9441 in E9) and the height of the visible bar (600 in F9). Therefore, in cell E8 enter =E9+F9. You now have a formula that can be copied.

7. Copy cell E8 to the blank cells in E7:E5.

8. Select the Range D1:F10. From the Insert tab, select Column, Stacked Column.

9. Turn off the legend by selecting the Plus icon and unchecking the Legend.

10. Click the lower Trade Discount bar. On the Format tab, select Shape Fill, White. The lower columns disappear.

11. Select the top column. On the Format tab, select Shape Fill, and then select black.

12. Turn off the gridlines by selecting the Plus icon and unchecking Gridlines.

13. Right-click a top column and select Add Data Labels.

14. Grab each label individually and move it to the top of the column.

> **NOTE** Normally, you will choose to put the data labels at the outside end. However, because this is a stacked column chart, the outside end is not an option in the Format Data Labels dialog.

15. To finish the waterfall chart, you need to draw connecting lines from the bottom of one column to the next column. Therefore, on the Insert tab, select Shapes, Line. While holding down the Shift key, draw a line from the top of the first column to the top of the next column. Select Format, Shape Outline, and then select black to darken the line. Repeat this step to connect all the columns.

You can use a waterfall chart in many situations to turn a single component column chart into a whole-page chart. These charts present a dramatic picture of all the components in a process.

4

Creating a Stacked and Clustered Chart

In my seminars, people ask about creating both a stacked and clustered column for each time period, as shown in Figure 4.31. This type of chart can be used to show components of a cost figure compared to a total revenue figure.

Figure 4.31
Cost components stack up against revenue for each quarter.

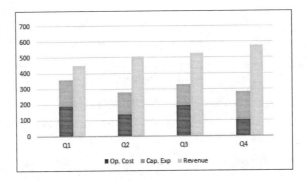

Creating this chart is fairly difficult in Excel because it combines both a stacked column chart and a clustered column chart. Even if you can figure out how to create this chart, Excel has roadblocks to prevent the chart from looking good.

Secret 1: Combining Stacked Columns and Clustered Columns

Suppose you started out with three series of data and create a stacked revenue chart, as shown in Figure 4.32. You need to move the Revenue portion of the column next to stacked cost components.

Figure 4.32
Start with all series stacked.

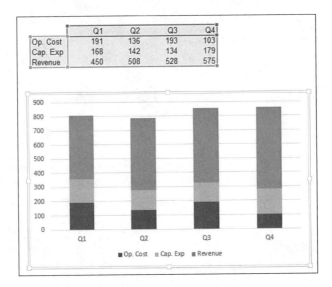

	Q1	Q2	Q3	Q4
Op. Cost	191	136	193	103
Cap. Exp	168	142	134	179
Revenue	450	508	528	575

1. Double-click the Revenue portion of one of the columns. Excel displays the Format Data Series task pane. Click the chart icon.

2. In the task pane, select Plot Series On: Secondary Axis.

By moving this series to the secondary axis, Excel removes Revenue from the stack of Operating Cost and Capital Expense. That is a good thing, but then Excel plots the Revenue column directly in front of the stacked columns. You cannot see the stacked columns, except in Q1 and Q3. (See Figure 4.33.)

Figure 4.33
Change Revenue to be a clustered column.

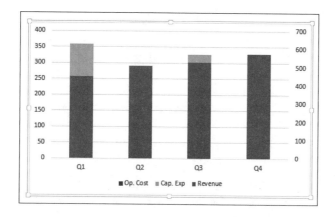

Secret 2: Moving a Series Over by Using Blank Series

To solve the problem in Figure 4.33, you can use another bit of chart magic—inserting some zero series to shift the revenue series to the right. In Figure 4.34, two dotted columns represent the series I call Blank 1 and Blank 2. By plotting these series and Revenue as a clustered column chart on the secondary axis, you force the Revenue column to the right, so you can see the stacked column underneath. Eventually, both of the blank series will have no fill and no line and will be invisible. In Figure 4.34, I've outlined them in dashes so you can see the role they play in forcing revenue over to the right.

Figure 4.34
The two extra series force the Revenue column to move to the right.

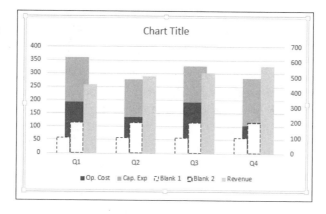

You want to have Operating Cost and Capital Expenses as a stacked column chart. You are then going to have three series: Blank1, Blank2, and Revenue as a clustered column chart on the secondary axis. Insert two extra rows in your data set, as shown in Figure 4.35. When you select the data to create the chart, do not select the revenue row yet.

Figure 4.35
Add Blank 1 and Blank 2 to your data set with zeroes.

	A	B	C	D	E	F
90						
91						
92			Q1	Q2	Q3	Q4
93		Op. Cost	191	136	193	103
94		Cap. Exp	168	142	134	179
95		Blank 1	0	0	0	0
96		Blank 2	0	0	0	0
97		Revenue	450	508	528	575

CAUTION

Excel 2013 introduced the new interface for creating combo charts. Although I like this interface, a problem becomes evident in this example. For this chart, you are about to create a data set with four quarters of columns and five rows of data.

In the Insert Chart dialog, if you choose most chart types, such as column, line, or area, you would have two thumbnails from which to choose: one plotting the quarters as series and one plotting the quarters as categories.

However, when you choose a combo chart in the Insert Chart dialog, Excel chooses the default and does not provide a way for you to move the quarters from Series to Categories. This is bad in the current situation. Setting up a combo chart with quarters as series does not get you any closer to the desired chart.

There are two workarounds, neither of which are fun.

- Workaround 1 is to create a stacked column chart from the five series, making sure to choose the second thumbnail with the quarters going across the horizontal axis instead of the quarters as series. After you've created this chart, you go back to the dialog via the Change Chart Type icon and begin setting up the combo chart in earnest.

- The second method is easier and involves a trick. Because the fourth row and the fifth row have the same combo settings, you can create the combo chart from the first four rows and then quickly add the fifth row to the finished chart.

Although the second workaround is easier, it is less intuitive, because you cannot see the Revenue series in the preview as you are building the combo chart.

The following steps, which solve this problem, assume that you deleted the chart from Figure 4.33 and are starting over.

1. As shown previously in Figure 4.34, add two new rows called Blank 1 and Blank 2 before the Revenue row. Select the data, leaving out the Revenue series for now.

2. Select Insert, Recommend Charts, All Charts, Combo. The dialog starts off with two Clustered Column series and two Line series, as shown in Figure 4.36.

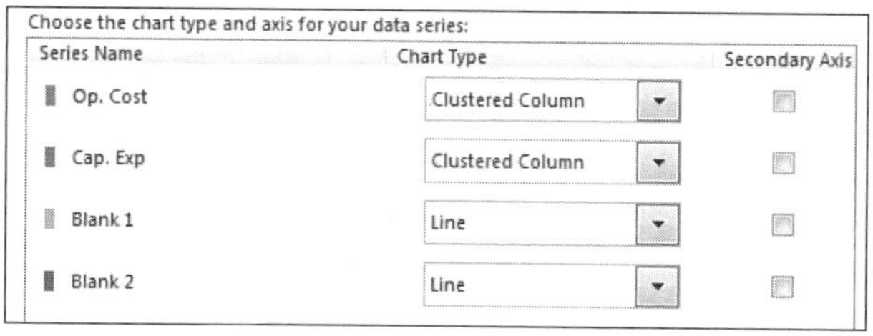

Figure 4.36
Initially, the dialog offers clustered column and line charts.

3. Add a check for Secondary Axis for Blank 1 and Blank 2. Do this first, to make sure that Excel won't automatically change the chart type for these series when you change the chart type for the first two series.

4. Change the Chart Type for Operating Cost to a Stacked Column. Note that because Operating Cost and Capital Expense are on the same axis with a clustered chart type, changing one of the drop-downs to Stacked automatically changes both drop-downs to stacked. You do not have to touch the Capital Expense drop-down; it is already fixed for you after you fix the first drop-down. I tend to blindly change both drop-downs, choosing the "other" type of column chart. Changing the second series also changes the first series, and I end up with everything back as a clustered column chart. This is wrong. Change Operating Cost to Stacked and then do not touch Capital Expense.

5. Change the Chart Type for Blank 1 to Clustered Column.

6. Change the Chart Type for Blank 2 to Clustered Column. This doesn't happen automatically. You are allowed to mix clustered columns and lines on the same axis. At this point, your dialog should look like Figure 4.37.

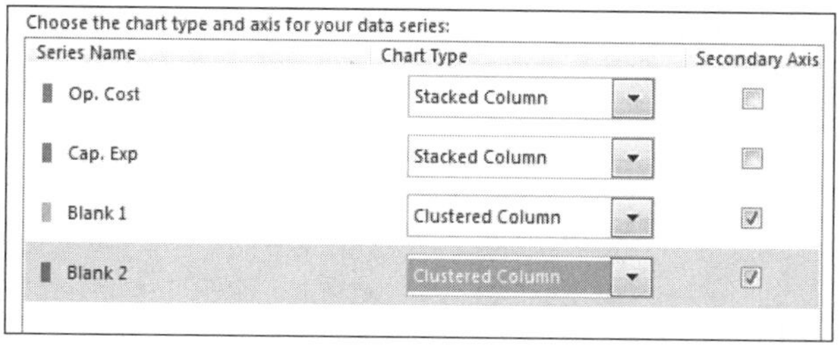

Figure 4.37
Change to two Stacked Column series and two Clustered Column series.

7. Click OK to create the chart. Don't worry that you can't see Revenue yet. You will solve that in step 8. Note that although the chart is selected, three parts of your chart data are outlined. The series labels in B93:B96 have a red outline. The category labels in C92:F92 have a purple outline. The actual numbers in C93:F96 have a blue outline. There is a square handle in each of the four corners of the outline. (See Figure 4.38.)

Figure 4.38
Drag this handle down to add Revenue to the chart.

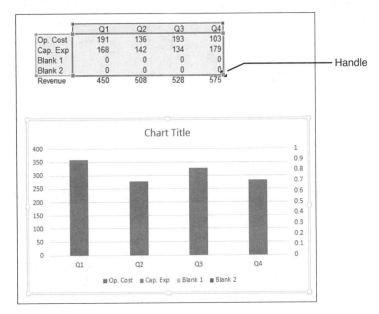

8. Drag the handle from the bottom-right corner of cell F96 down one row to add Revenue to the chart. You now effectively have a cluster-stack chart, but there are still several tweaks to make the chart correct. (See Figure 4.39.)

Figure 4.39
Add Revenue to the chart, and you have a cluster-stack chart.

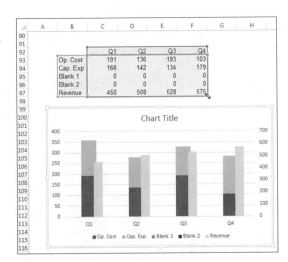

Although you have overcome the major hurdle in completing the chart, you still have some problems with this chart. The revenue column is narrower than the cost columns. The blank series are showing up in the legend. In addition, the biggest problem is that the revenue column at 450 is showing up shorter than the cost columns that only total 359.

Secret 3: Increasing Gap Width Makes Columns Narrower

Double-click one of the Cost series in the chart. There is a setting in the Format Data Series task pane called Gap Width. As you increase the gap between the series, the net effect is that the column becomes narrower.

There is not a perfect rule to figure out the correct gap width. Try 350% and see if the size of the cost columns appears to be about the same width as the size of the revenue column.

Secret 4: Removing Items from the Legend Box

You can remove items from the legend, although it requires a bit of tenacity.

Click the legend once to select the entire legend. Next, click the Blank 1 legend entry to select only that entry. Press the Delete key to delete that entry.

Deleting a legend entry also deselects the legend. Single-click the legend to select the entire legend. Single-click the Blank 2 entry to select that one entry. Press Delete.

Secret 5: Adjusting Y-Axis Scale When There Are Two Axes

Sometimes you move a series to a secondary axis to show two series that have different orders of magnitude. In this case, you want the revenue and cost series to have the same scale.

You can solve this problem, but there is a cost. Normally, Excel chooses the scale automatically based on the data. If you later plug in new data for this chart and the revenue increased above 700, the upper limit for the chart grows automatically.

You have to turn off the automatic behavior for both the left and right axis. This means that if the data later grows larger than the chart, you have to revisit the Format Axis task pane to adjust.

1. Double-click the numbers along the left axis. Excel displays the Format Axis task pane. Click the chart icon. Expand the Axis Options category. Initially, settings for Minimum, Maximum, Major Unit, and Minor Unit are all set to Auto.

2. The minimum setting is currently 0, which might seem correct. You must click into that box and type a new setting of zero. When you tab out of the box, Excel changes the word "Auto" to a button that reads Reset. This means that you have turned off Excel's capability to automatically change the minimum. By typing zero in the box, you are changing from "0 Auto" to "0 Manual". Back in Excel 2010, you actually had an option button to switch from Auto to Manual. Now in Excel 2013, you have to type a zero in place of the existing zero. It makes sense, after you get used to it.

3. Change the Maximum setting to 750.

4. Change the Major Unit setting to 250. This setting controls where the gridlines are drawn.

> **NOTE**
> I prefer fewer gridlines, so a setting of 250 feels right to me. However, you might prefer a setting of 125 or 100.

At this state, the chart is not yet fixed. You have formatted the left axis to run from 0 to 750. However, the right axis is still running from 0 to 700.

With the Format Axis task pane still open, click the right axis in the chart. Make changes to the settings as described in steps 2 through 4. You briefly see that the right axis is now at the same scale as the left axis, as shown in Figure 4.40.

When you are sure the axes are set to the same scale, it seems redundant to have the numbers on the right side. In the Format Axis task pane, expand the Labels category. Change the Label Position drop-down to None.

Figure 4.40
Adjust the right axis to be the same as the left.

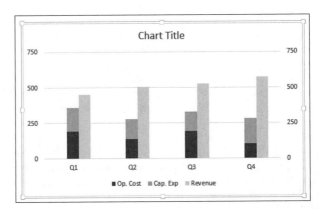

The final chart is shown in Figure 4.41.

Figure 4.41
The final chart makes it look easy.

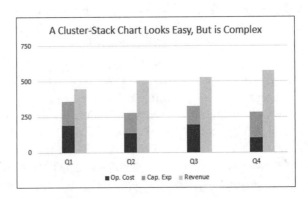

N O T E   Excel MVP Jon Peltier sells a Cluster-Stack add-in utility which dramatically simplifies the process of creating these charts. Search Bing for Peltier Cluster Stack for current pricing information.

Next Steps

In Chapter 5, "Creating Charts That Show Relationships," you find out how to create charts that highlight relationships. Scientists often use scatter charts. However, you see how to use scatter charts in a variety of ways in business to demonstrate a correlation, or the lack of a correlation. In addition, you discover that radar charts can be used to conduct annual performance reviews. Chapter 5 also takes a look at surface charts and frequency distributions.

4

Creating Charts That Show Relationships

5

The chart types discussed in this chapter are unusual. Scatter, radar, bubble, and surface charts are probably the least understood Excel charts.

Both scatter and bubble charts show the interplay between two or three different variables. They require a bit of care in setting up the data. A scatter chart can help you to figure out whether a correlation exists between two variables. A bubble chart has the unique ability to provide data about a third dimension. The first section in this chapter covers the mechanics of creating scatter charts.

When you are thinking about creating scatter charts to show a relationship, you might need to consider alternative charts, such as a paired bar chart, paired chart, or frequency distribution. The second section in this chapter compares the message that you convey with the various chart types.

Radar charts are rarely used, but they are great for providing performance reviews. For example, a radar chart can show how a person scored on 5 to 10 key indicators as spokes emanating from a central point.

Surface charts attempt to show a 3D surface floating above an x,y grid. It is difficult to find a data set that looks cool with a surface chart, and after you have found an appropriate data set, it is often difficult to make out the valleys that might occur within the data set.

The first part of this chapter discusses scatter charts in detail. Although it is easy enough to create a simple scatter chart, many annoying complications can occur when you want to add new data series to the chart or when you want to try to label the chart.

IN THIS CHAPTER

Using Scatter Charts to Plot Pairs of Data Points 000

Using Charts to Show Relationships 000

Using Surface Charts to Show Contrast 000

Next Steps 000

Using Scatter Charts to Plot Pairs of Data Points

Figure 5.1 shows a table of average January temperatures for selected U.S. cities. There is no trend or pattern to this data.

Figure 5.1
When this data is plotted on a column chart, there is no pattern to the data.

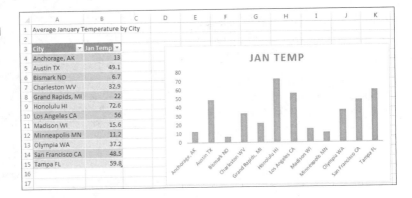

What are the likely causes of variability in January temperature? You might theorize that the most likely cause would be distance from the equator. In Figure 5.2, a new column B shows the latitude of each city. This data set is perfect for a scatter chart. (Note: The terms scatter chart and XY chart are interchangeable). The latitudes in column B represent an independent variable. The temperatures in column C represent a dependent variable. A scatter chart plots one data marker for every pair of latitude and temperature data. In this case, the latitude is plotted along the x-axis, and the temperature is plotted along the y-axis.

Figure 5.2
You can plot latitude and temperature on a scatter chart to understand the relationship between the values.

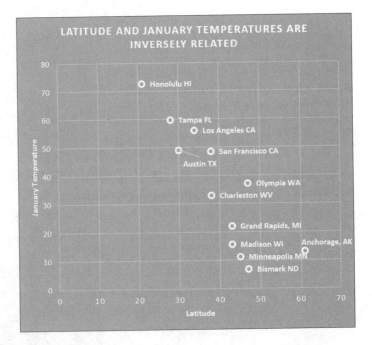

The chart in Figure 5.2 shows a relationship between latitude and temperature: As latitude increases, temperature decreases. Therefore, you can say that latitude and temperature are inversely related.

Creating a Scatter Chart

Scatter charts have always been a bit different from regular charts. Although Excel has always tracked the X and Y numeric value for each point, it historically never had a built-in way to track the text label for each point.

In the past, you would create a scatter chart by selecting B1:C13 in Figure 5.2. Now you are allowed to include the labels by selecting A1:C13. However, the label information is initially discarded, so it does not matter which method you choose.

Follow these steps to create a scatter chart:

1. Select A1:C13.

2. Select Insert, Recommended Chart. The second recommended chart is a scatter chart. Select this chart and choose OK.

   Every scatter chart that you create should have both axis titles and no legend. The Quick Layout drop-down on the Design tab offers 11 different layouts, none of which adds the axis titles without adding a legend. None of the 12 chart styles adds axis titles. You are going to have to tweak this chart manually.

3. From the Plus icon, choose Axis Titles. This adds the words "Axis Title" to both the horizontal and vertical axes.

4. Click the horizontal axis title. In the formula bar, type an equal sign. Click the X axis heading in cell B1. Press Enter.

5. Click the vertical axis title. In the formula bar, type an equal sign. Click the Y axis heading in cell C1. Press Enter.

6. The Chart Title is redundant with the vertical axis title. Edit it to offer some analysis, such as "January Temperature and Latitude Are Inversely Related."

Adding Labels to a Scatter Chart in Excel 2013

Excel 2013 finally offers a built-in way to label scatter charts. In all prior versions of Excel, you had to either resort to a VBA macro or use Rob Bovey's Chart Labeler utility to get the labels to appear. (Read more about this utility in the next section.)

You might still have to resort to one of those methods if you plan to share your charts with someone who has Excel 2010 or earlier.

In Excel 2013, follow these steps to add the labels from A2:A13 to the chart.

1. Verify that your sheet name does not contain anything that looks like a decimal. A sheet name of "Example 5.2" is legal in Excel, but the charting engine cannot create labels that point to a sheet. "Sheet 5" is fine. "My.Example" is fine. "5.2" is not.

5

2. Select the chart so that the three icons appear to the right of the chart.

3. Click the Plus icon. Choose Data Labels. Excel labels each point with the Y value.

4. Double-click one of the data labels. Excel displays the Format Data Labels text pane. The Chart icon should already be selected, and the Label Options category will be expanded.

5. Uncheck Y Value.

6. Choose Value from Cells. Excel displays the Data Label Range dialog. Specify A2:A13 as your data label range. Click OK.

7. Change the Label Position option button from Above to Right. Make sure that Show Leader Lines is selected.

8. Study the labels. Do any of the labels run into other labels? In Figure 5.3, the label for Austin, TX, is running into the point for San Francisco. To move an individual label, click the label once to select all labels. Click the label a second time to select that one label. You can now drag the label to a new location. Drag the label far enough, and a leader line appears.

Figure 5.3
The label for Austin needs to be moved.

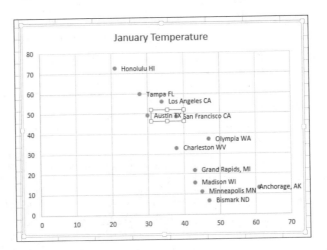

Showing Scatter Chart Labels in Excel 2010

If you create labels using the new functionality in Excel 2013, those labels will not work in Excel 2010. Anyone opening the workbook in Excel 2010 sees all the labels read [CELLRANGE] as shown in Figure 5.4.

To create scatter chart labels that work in all versions of Excel, you can download a free add-in, the XY Chart Labeler, from Rob Bovey, at http://www.appspro.com/Utilities/ChartLabeler.htm.

Figure 5.4
The new labels don't work in Excel 2010.

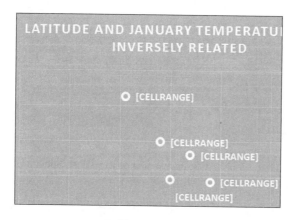

LATITUDE AND JANUARY TEMPERATU
INVERSELY RELATED

[CELLRANGE]

[CELLRANGE]
[CELLRANGE]

[CELLRANGE]
[CELLRANGE]

Adding a Second Series to a Scatter Chart

You can compare two or more populations on the same scatter chart. This is useful for seeing how the populations differ. For example, Figure 5.5 shows education level and monthly
salary for a number of employees. You've split the list into those with college and those
without.

Figure 5.5
Plot two populations on a single scatter chart.

	A	B	C	D	E	F	G
1	Monthly Salary as a Function of Years of Education						
2							
3	Name	Education	No College		Name	Education	College
4	KATHRYN SIMON	12	1012.8		STEPHEN RIDDLE	21	3195.083
5	BILLY SCOTT	12	1268.8		VERONICA BUSH	20	3323.667
6	DENISE HENSLEY	12	1003.2		KEVIN BASS	16	4409.167
7	DONALD SIMPSON	12	1201.6		LUZ CHAPMAN	17	4963.417
8	RAMONA MEYERS	12	1276.8		JOSHUA RHODES	16	5554.083
9	WILMA HEBERT	12	1264		SEAN ANTHONY	17	5778
10	KIMBERLY GONZALES	11	1206.4		CAROLINE MAYS	18	6032
11	JUAN ROY	11	1272		MARGUERITE WARE	19	3629.083
12	MYRTLE MCDOWELL	11	996.8		SEAN CALDWELL	19	3902
13	WILLIAM WARREN	11	1124.8		NINA WADE	18	5078.5
14	DENNIS LE	11	1086.4		CARLOS MENDEZ	17	4114.833
15	JIMMY STEVENSON	11	1243.2		MARVIN DEAN	18	5111.167
16	LINDSAY FRAZIER	12	1121.6		LAWRENCE WORKMAN	16	5832.75
17	ANTONIO TYLER	12	1116.8		CHRISTY HIGGINS	22	5404.75
18	AMANDA NICHOLSON	12	982.4				

The easiest way to create this chart is to create a scatter chart for the first population. You
can then use Copy and Paste Special to add the second series to the chart.

1. Select B3:C26 in Figure 5.5.
2. On the Insert tab, open the Scatter Chart icon and choose the first scatter chart.
3. Select F3:G17. Press Ctrl+C to copy.
4. Select the chart you created in step 2.
5. On the Home tab, go to the bottom of the Paste icon and open the drop-down. Ignore
the Paste icons and choose the words Paste Special, as shown in Figure 5.6.

5

Figure 5.6
Select Paste Special from
the Home tab.

6. Excel displays a useful chart-specific version of the Paste Special dialog as shown in
   Figure 5.7. Most of the settings will be correct. You need to choose the box Categories
   (X Values) in First Column.

Figure 5.7
This chart-specific Paste
Special dialog lets you
avoid the complicated
Select Data dialog.

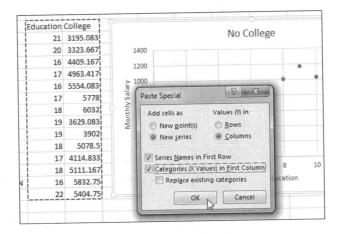

7. Click OK.

8. Click the Plus icon to the right of the chart. Hover over the Legend, click the arrowhead, and choose Top to display the legend at the top of the chart.

The resulting chart in Figure 5.8 shows the differences between the two populations.

Figure 5.8
Two populations appear
on the same scatter chart.

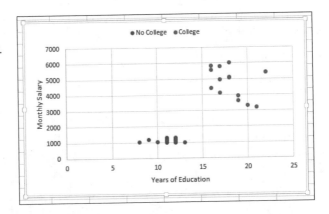

Joining the Points in a Scatter Chart with Lines

So far in this chapter, you've seen scatter charts without lines. The Scatter category of the Insert Chart dialog offers several scatter charts with lines.

Whereas the dot version of a scatter chart can be sequenced in any order, chaos results if you try to join the dots with lines. In Figure 5.9, a familiar curve turns to spaghetti when the dots are joined with lines.

Figure 5.9
Chaos results when you add a line to an unsorted scatter chart.

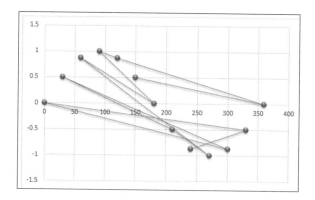

Before adding lines, make sure that your data is sorted by the x-axis value. In Figure 5.10, using a line to join exactly the same data set as in Figure 5.9 appears orderly.

In the Design tab, choose Change Chart Type. Several thumbnails are available: Markers only, Markers with Straight Line, Markers with Smooth Line, No Markers Straight Line, No Markers Smooth Line.

The bottom chart in Figure 5.10 uses Scatter with Smooth Lines and Markers. The middle chart in Figure 5.10 uses Scatter with Straight Lines and Markers. When you choose straight lines, Excel draws lines from one point to the next. If you have sparse data, choose the smooth line. Excel attempts to interpolate the missing points with a smooth curve.

5

Figure 5.10
It is important to use a smoothed line with sparse data.

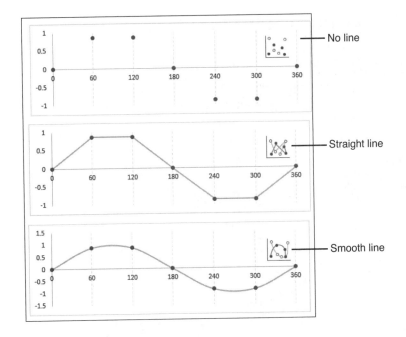

Using a Scatter Chart with Lines to Replace a Line Chart

Way back in Figure 3.19, a chart with times along the X axis did not plot correctly. Rather than converting times to years to force the chart to draw correctly, you could plot the same data as a scatter chart with straight lines.

The data in this chart uses time, but the points are not spaced evenly. A new record is generated every time a customer enters or leaves the bank. The Date-axis doesn't work with times. The Category axis assumes every event is spaced equally. While updating Chapter 3, I was surprised when the Recommended Charts feature suggested a scatter chart to solve this problem. A scatter chart solves all these problems. The scatter chart has no problem plotting the times along the horizontal axis.

In Figure 5.11, the top chart shows a regular line chart with a category axis. The customers entering the bank during lunch should be tightly centered in the Noon and 1:00 p.m. hours, but the top chart stretches those customers out until they fill 60% of the chart.

The bottom chart uses a scatter chart with straight lines and represents the actual times very well.

The difficult part in creating the bottom chart in Figure 5.11 was to get the axis labeled correctly; 10:00 a.m. is 10/24 of a day, but I haven't memorized the decimal equivalents of 5/12, 33/48, or 1/24. In a blank section of the worksheet, enter 10:00 a.m., 4:30 p.m., and 1:00 a.m. Format those cells as numbers with 5 decimal places. 10 a.m. is equivalent to 0.41667. 4:30 p.m. is equivalent to 0.6875. The one-hour figure is equivalent to 0.4167.

Figure 5.11
The Recommended
Charts feature suggested
the solution in the bot-
tom.

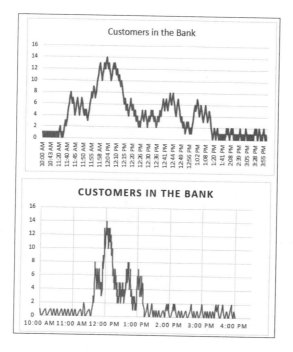

Double-click the horizontal axis. In the Format Axis dialog, choose the Chart icon and then expand the Axis Options category. As shown in Figure 5.12, use 0.41667 as the minimum. Use 0.6875 as the maximum. Use 0.04167 as the major unit. These three settings cause the horizontal axis labels to snap into 10:00 a.m., 11:00 a.m., and so on.

Figure 5.12
A major unit of 0.04167
corresponds to an hour.

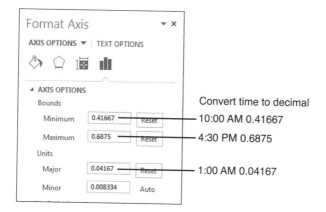

Drawing with a Scatter Chart

An unusual use for XY scatter charts with straight lines is to make crude drawings on a chart.

To create a drawing, it helps to trace your drawing onto quadrille graph paper first. You need to choose a point where the left edge and bottom edge cross, which, in this case, will be the (0,0) point. For every point in the drawing, you enter the x and y location. The x location is the number of gridlines from the left edge of the chart to that point. The y location is the distance from the bottom of the chart to the point.

If you need to draw a curve, you can choose as many points as possible around the perimeter of the curve. The more points you can plot, the smoother the curve.

Figure 5.13 shows an x and y data set where the coordinates from the drawing have been entered as Cartesian coordinates.

Figure 5.13
Transfer points from a drawing into columns for x and y.

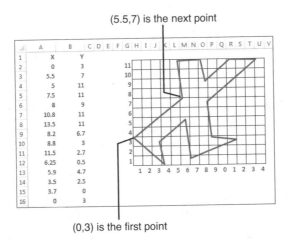

(5.5,7) is the next point

(0,3) is the first point

Next, select the data from A2:B16. From the Insert tab, select Scatter, Scatter with Straight Lines, which is the thumbnail with straight lines and no markers. Excel creates the chart shown in Figure 5.14.

Figure 5.14
Excel connects the x and y points to create a simple drawing.

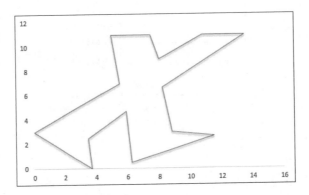

Testing Correlation Using a Scatter Chart

A scatter chart is showing the relationship of two variables for every row in the data set. If there is a relationship between those two variables, the chart shows the points arranged in a diagonal line. Although you can get a feel based on looking at the chart, a trendline with formula enables you to test the correlation.

In Figure 5.15, the data in B2:C15 represents a price survey of regional car dealerships for a particular model of vehicle. Each pair of numbers in a row represents the data for a single car. Mileage is in the first column, and price is in the second column. In theory, you would expect that as the miles go up on a car, the price would come down.

If you select the data from B2:C15 and insert a scatter chart, Excel plots the points shown in Figure 5.15. The axis titles have been edited to label each axis.

Figure 5.15
Create a scatter chart from the two potentially correlated variables.

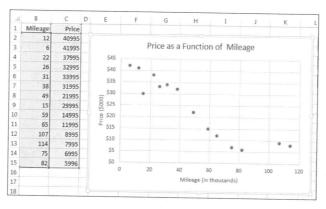

In Figure 5.15, it appears that there is a fairly strong relationship between mileage and price. Because the dots slant from top left to bottom right, the variables have an inverse relationship. You can ask Excel to do a least-squares regression and fit a trendline to the points plotted on the chart. One of the trendline options is to display the regression equation and the R-squared value on the chart.

To create a trend line and measure the R-squared, follow these steps:

1. Click the Plus icon to the right of the chart. Hover over Trendline. Click the arrowhead that appears. Choose More Options. Excel defaults to adding a linear trendline and opens the Format Trendline task pane. The Chart icon should be selected and the Trendline Options category should be expanded.

2. Near the bottom of the task pane, choose both Display Equation on Chart and Display R-Squared Value on Chart.

3. The equation and R-squared are added to a text box on the chart. You can move the text box so it is not near the points. Add a solid white fill using Format, Fill, White.

As shown in Figure 5.16, the straight-line regression formula shows that Price is about $41K minus $360 per thousand miles. The R-squared value is 0.849, which means there is a pretty good correlation between mileage and price based on this population of 14 vehicles.

Figure 5.16
Based on the R-squared value of 0.849, mileage is a fairly good predictor of used car price.

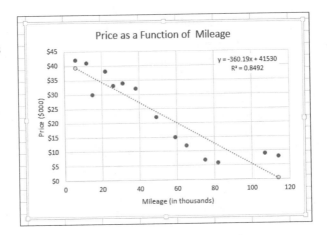

> **NOTE**
> Remember that R-squared is a measure of how well a trendline matches the points. R-squared ranges from 0 to 1, with 1 meaning a nearly perfect correlation.

Figure 5.17 shows three different scatter charts. The top chart has a perfect correlation and an R-squared value of 1. The next chart has just a small bit of variation. Individual points appear close to the trendline but are sometimes a bit above or below it. This provides an R-squared value of 0.995. The bottom chart looks like a shotgun blast. There does not appear to be any correlation between those variables, and Excel reports an R-squared value of 0.003. If the data set is truly random, the trendline is often a straight horizontal line, drawn through the value that marks the average of all the points.

Figure 5.17
R-squared is a measure of how well a trendline fits the points in a chart.

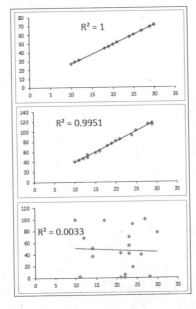

Adding a Third Dimension with a Bubble Chart

A bubble chart attempts to add a third piece of information to each point in a scatter chart. In a bubble chart, the size of the marker varies, based on the third data point for each marker.

The best time to use a bubble chart is when you have a sparse data set. The size of the bubbles makes it difficult to read the chart when you have too many data points on the chart.

Figure 5.18 shows a bubble chart. The size of each bubble is based on the selling price for a particular model of car. The location of the bubble along the horizontal axis indicates the age of the car. The location of the bubble along the vertical axis shows the mileage of the car.

In theory, cars that are older or have higher mileage should have lower prices. However, you can find some bubbles where the seller of an older car is asking for more money.

Here are some tips for creating bubble charts:

- You should always leave the heading off the top-left cell in the data range. This rule applies anytime you have numbers as the first column of your data set. It is particularly important with bubble charts.

- The initial size of the bubbles is always too large because it is initially scaled to 100%. If you see too much overlap in the bubbles, you can right-click a bubble and select Format Data Series. In Figure 5.18, the bubbles are scaled down to 30 percent to prevent excessive overlapping.

- There is a Size Represents option in the Format Series task pane. The default value is Area. Never choose Width. Like cone and pyramid charts, using Width misrepresents your data.

Figure 5.18

This bubble chart shows the relationship between age, mileage, and price.

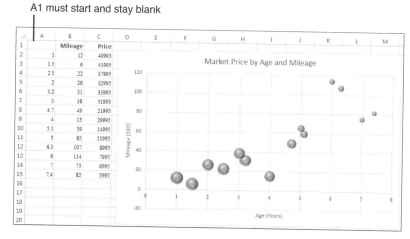

In both charts shown in Figure 5.19, each bubble is two times larger than the previous bubble. The top chart includes the option that the size of data in the third column affects the area of the bubble. This is the default setting, and it is the correct setting. If you instead decide to tie the data in the table to the width of the bubble, you violate the pictograph rule. When you are using pictures for markers, you should increase the marker in only one dimension, not in both dimensions.

Figure 5.19
The width setting in the bottom chart creates the false impression that the bubble is four times larger than the previous bubble.

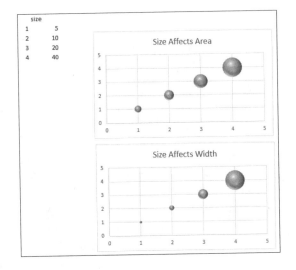

To create the chart in Figure 5.18, follow these steps:

1. Set up your data with age in column A, mileage in column B, and price in column C. It is okay to have headings above the data in columns B and C. The heading above the first column must be blank.

2. Select cells A1:C15.

3. Choose Insert, Recommended Charts, All Charts, Scatter, Bubble with a 3D Effect.

4. Right-click one bubble and select Format Series. Change the Scale Bubble Size value from 100 to 30.

5. Right-click the numbers along the vertical axis and select Format Axis. Change Minimum to Fixed, 0.

6. Edit the chart title.

7. Click the Plus icon and choose Axis Titles. Edit the default axis titles to show Mileage and Age.

When you need to show the relationship between three variables and you have only a few points to compare, a bubble chart creates an effective presentation of the data.

→ Power View lets you add a fourth dimension to your scatter charts. See Chapter 8, "Creating Pivot Charts and Power View Dashboards," for an example.

Using Charts to Show Relationships

Beyond scatter charts, you can use several types of charts to illustrate the relationship between two variables, including the following:

■ In some cases, a pair of matching charts allows the reader to compare two variables to see whether a relationship exists.

■ Radar charts are rarely used charts that enable you to see the relationship between four to six variables.

■ In some cases, you might have a population of results and be trying to figure out whether any patterns exist in one variable. In these cases, use of the FREQUENCY function enables you to make sense of the data by grouping members into similar categories and then comparing the categories.

Using Paired Bars to Show Relationships

Suppose that you want to compare survey responses from two populations. For each question, you want to compare male and female responses. Scatter charts do not compare these populations.

If you need to compare two variables and have around a dozen points, a paired bar chart can be more effective than a scatter chart. For example, Figure 5.20 shows a preference for ice cream, based on a survey of two groups: kids and adults.

The chart is sorted by the kids' preference. Any bars toward the bottom of the chart that have a sizable presence on the right are flavors that grow in popularity as the respondents mature.

Figure 5.20
A paired bar chart allows you to compare values for two populations.

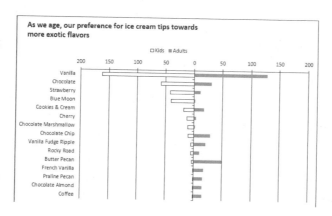

To create this chart in Excel, you need to use a little trickery in several steps. Because this is a stacked bar chart, the values for the left bar have to be in the Excel table as negative to force them to stretch leftward from the axis.

Follow these steps to create the chart in Figure 5.20:

1. Sort your original data by the first series so that it is in descending order.

2. Copy the data set to the right of the original data set. In the copy of the data set, enter the formula -B39 in cell F39 to create a negative value for the first series (see Figure 5.21).

Figure 5.21
Use a formula to make the first series negative.

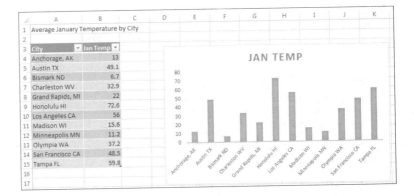

3. Select the data for your chart. Press Ctrl+1 to display the Format Cells dialog box. On the Number tab, select the Custom category and type the custom number code 0;0. Click OK. The negative numbers in Column F are displayed without the minus sign.

> **NOTE**
> Although you are likely to type only a single format as your custom number format, the field is allowed to have up to four "zones," separated by semicolons. If you have two zones, the first format is for positive numbers, and the second format is for negative numbers. For example, the code 0;-0 displays numbers as positive and negative. The code 0;(0) displays the negative numbers in parentheses. The code 0; hides the negative numbers. The code 0;0 forces the negative numbers to display without the minus sign and without parentheses. It is difficult to imagine why anyone would want to show negative numbers without the minus sign, until you consider our current example where it certainly comes in handy.

4. From the Insert tab, select Recommended Charts. The third recommendation is a stacked bar chart. Choose this and click OK to create the chart.

5. Click the Plus icon to the right of the chart. Hover over Legend. Click the arrowhead that appears. Select Top to move the legend to the top.

6. Resize the chart vertically to allow enough room for each category name to appear along the axis.

7. Double-click one of the ice cream flavor labels near the center axis. In the Format Axis task pane, choose the Chart icon and then expand the Axis Options category. Select the Categories in Reverse Order check box, which is the fourth selection in the Axis Options panel.

8. (Optional) Initially, the category labels overwrite the left bars. You have to decide how annoyed you are by this. It might be best to keep the labels there. If you want to move them to the left, select Low from the Axis Labels drop-down.

9. (Optional) The initial chart is not quite symmetrical, running to 200 on the kids' side and to only 150 on the adults' side. To correct this, click the horizontal axis. Specify a fixed minimum of –200 and a fixed maximum of 200 for the horizontal axis.

Using a Frequency Distribution to Categorize Thousands of Points

Suppose your data set had results of 3,000 trials. Figuring out how to present this data can be difficult. The chart in Figure 5.22 is a first attempt. The data is sorted by the trial number in column A. A line chart is based on columns A and B. You cannot tell much of anything from this chart. You can tell that the range is from 20 to 100, but that is about it.

Figure 5.22
This cannot be the best way to plot this data.

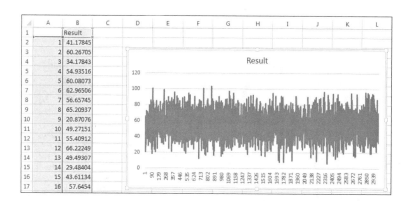

If you sort the data by the result field in column B, the chart changes into a smooth line, as shown in Figure 5.23. Again, you can tell that the range is from 20 to 100 and that for 60 percent of the chart, the data ranges from 40 to 60.

Figure 5.23
Some might be able to draw conclusions from this chart, but it is not obvious.

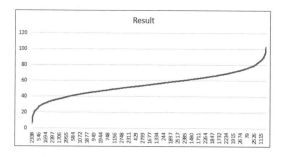

To create a more useful chart with this data, you need to use a somewhat obscure function. You use the FREQUENCY function to group the data into bins. This function is one of the few functions that returns several answers all at once. These functions, called array functions, require special care and handling.

Creating Bins

To make sense of the data in column B in Figure 5.23, you need to group the results into equal-sized bins. You need to type limits for each bin in a range, going down a column of the worksheet.

If your first bin is the number 0, the FREQUENCY function shows all the trial results less than 0 next to that bin. If the next bin is the number 15, the FREQUENCY function shows all the trial results from the last bin (0) to the current value (15).

To create bins that contain ranges of 15 units each, follow these steps:

1. Type **0, 15, 30, 45, 60, 75, 90, 105,** in cells E2:E9. Remember that this range contains eight cells.

2. Because the FREQUENCY function returns one more value than the number of bins that you have, select the empty cells F2:F10, as shown in Figure 5.24. The additional bin is for any results larger than your last bin value.

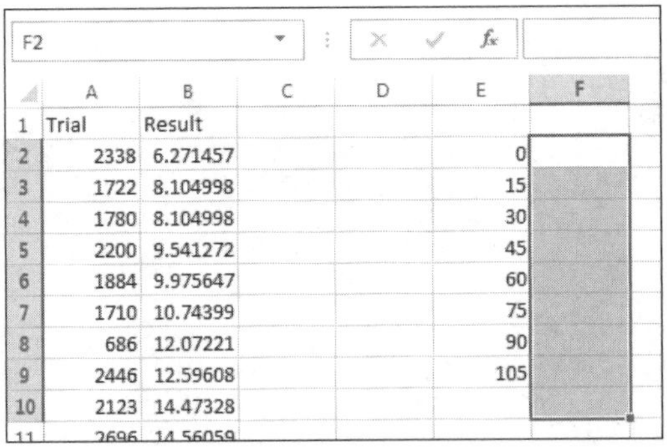

Figure 5.24
Select one more cell than you have bins.

▲	A	B	C	D	E	F
1	Trial	Result				
2	2338	6.271457			0	
3	1722	8.104998			15	
4	1780	8.104998			30	
5	2200	9.541272			45	
6	1884	9.975647			60	
7	1710	10.74399			75	
8	686	12.07221			90	
9	2446	12.59608			105	
10	2123	14.47328				
11	2696	14.56059				

3. Type **=FREQUENCY(**.

4. When Excel asks for the data array, enter the trial results from B2:B3001. Type a comma.

5. When Excel asks for the Bins array, enter the values from E2:E9. If you were actually entering nine copies of this formula, you would have to put dollar signs in all those references. However, this is one single formula that returns nine results, which means that you do not need dollar signs.

6. Type the closing parenthesis, but do not press Enter (see Figure 5.25).

7. Hold down Ctrl+Shift while pressing Enter. Excel returns all nine answers at once. You now have one formula entered in nine cells. The results are shown in column F of

Figure 5.26. Because those results are difficult to understand, you can build a second table to the right of the results table with labels to define the limits of each bin.

=frequency(B2:B3000,E2:E9)

E	F	G	H
0	=frequency(B2:B3000,E2:E9)		
15			
30			
45			
60			
75			
90			
105			

Figure 5.25
It might feel strange, but you are entering one formula in this range.

=E2&"-"&E3

E	F	G	H	I
				Frequency
0	0		<0	0
15	10		0-15	10
30	130		15-30	130
45	607		30-45	607
60	1149		45-60	1149
75	826		60-75	826
90	243		75-90	243
105	34		90-105	34
	0		105-	0

Figure 5.26
After getting the results in F2:F10, add a new table in H and I to make sense of the results.

You have to "know the code" to figure out what is going on here. There is a 0 next to the 0, and a 10 next to the 15. This means that none of the results was less than 0 and 10 of the results were between 0 and 15. At the other end of the range, there is a 34 next to the 105, and a 0 below that. This means that there are 34 results between 90 and 105. The final 0 means that there were no results above 105. When you set up the bin range, you should always bracket the expected results with one bin above and below your expected results. Having a 0 end up as the first and last result means that you have accurately captured all your results.

Creating the Frequency Distribution Chart

The results in column F in Figure 5.26 are somewhat difficult to decode, but you can improve the appearance of the labels along the axis of the chart.

In Figure 5.26, the formulas in H3:H9 concatenate the bins so that they make more sense. The formula `=E2&"-"&E3` concatenates the bin in the previous row, a dash, and the bin in the current row. The formulas in Column I copy the results from the current row of the array formula in F.

To create the frequency distribution chart shown in Figure 5.27, follow these steps:

1. Select cells H3:I9.

2. From the Insert tab, select Recommended Charts, All Charts, Column, Clustered Column.

3. Normally, there is a fair-sized gap between the columns. If you prefer that the columns touch each other, or even that there be less of a gap, you can change the gap width by right-clicking a column, choosing Format Data Series, and then dragging the Gap Width slider to zero percent.

Figure 5.27
After adjusting the axis labels, you have this chart.

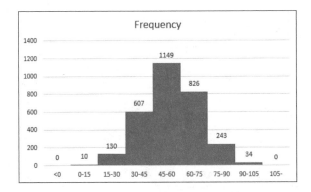

Using Radar Charts to Create Performance Reviews

Radar charts are designed for showing a person's or a company's rating along several performance areas. Here are some typical usages:

■ **Employee performance review**—A manager might rate an employee using a one-to five-point rating scale in areas such as efficiency, accuracy, timeliness, and so on. Although this data can be presented in a table, a radar chart provides an interesting alternative presentation.

■ **Customer satisfaction results**—A marketing manager could use a radar chart to summarize the results of a customer satisfaction survey. In this case, one line can be used to show customer satisfaction along rating areas such as speed, accuracy, and value.

If you want to summarize customer satisfaction results for two companies, you can present the results as two series on a single chart, as shown in Figure 5.28.

You can choose to fill in the chart area or to show the series as a line. You should leave the chart unfilled when you put two series on one chart.

To create the radar chart shown in Figure 5.28, follow these steps:

1. Set up your data as shown in A1:C6 of Figure 5.28. The category in A2 appears at 12:00 on the chart. The remaining categories are arranged in clockwise order.

Figure 5.28
Radar charts can compare several values from two entities.

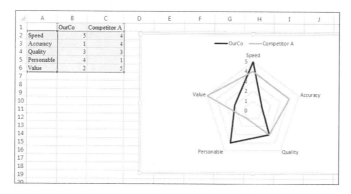

2. Select Cells A1:C6. From the Insert tab, open the radar chart drop-down. Choose Radar with Markers.

3. Click the line from your company. Use Format, Shape Outline, Black.

Using Surface Charts to Show Contrast

Not many data sets can be plotted as a surface chart, which look like topographic maps. Because you use a surface chart to represent a 3D surface on a 2D piece of paper, it is particularly important that your surface be generally sloping toward the front of the chart. Otherwise, you will never see the details hidden by the hill at the front of the chart.

Before you start to build a data set, you should look at Figure 5.29. The data for the chart is in C3:L12. Each data point requires two headings. Headings for the front axis are in C2:L2. Headings for the side axis are in B3:B12.

Figure 5.29
Study this table and chart to understand how surface charts work.

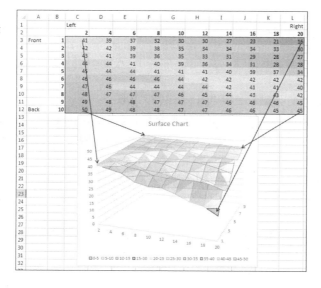

Data at the top of the table appear at the front edge of the chart. Data in the last row of the table appear at the back of the chart. The Front and Back labels in column A are there to help you keep track of this.

Data in the left column of the table appear in the left side of the chart. The four arrows point out where each corner of the data table ends up in the chart.

To create this chart, you select Cells B2:L12. From the Insert tab, open the radar chart drop-down. Select 3D Surface.

> **NOTE** In Excel 2010, surface, radar, and stock charts were grouped under a drop-down called Other Charts. In Excel 2013, they are grouped in the radar chart drop-down.

When the front wall of the surface chart is higher than the other points, you can use the techniques that follow to create the other three charts.

Using the Depth Axis

One element unique to surface charts is the depth axis. This is the axis that falls along the right side of the chart in the default orientation.

In the top-right chart in Figure 5.30, the chart has been turned around by having the orientation of the depth axis changed. Follow these steps to create this effect:

1. From the Layout tab, select Current Selection, Depth (Series) Axis.
2. Click Format Selection.
3. Select Series in Reverse Order.

Because the depth axis is treated as a category axis, you do not have control over the minimum or maximum values along the axis. The Format dialog box is limited to settings for the interval between tick marks and labels and where the tick marks and labels appear.

Controlling a Surface Chart Through 3D Rotation

You can spin a surface chart by rotating it. To access the rotation settings, select 3D Rotation from the Layout tab. This takes you to the 3D Rotation category of the Format Chart Area dialog, which has the following settings:

- **X Rotation**—This setting ranges from 0 degrees to 359.9 degrees. It rotates the floor of the chart in a clockwise direction, when you are looking down at the chart from above.
- **Y Rotation**—This setting starts at +15 degrees. It is your viewing angle in relation to the baseline of the chart. With an angle of 15 degrees, you are looking slightly down at the chart. With an angle of 0 degrees, many of the 3D effects disappear. As you increase

from 10 to 80 degrees, you have slightly different views of the chart. At 90 degrees, the chart becomes flat, because you are looking directly down from above. You can also enter negative values from 0 to –90. As you move from –10 to –80, you look at the chart from underneath. This might allow you to see better detail. When you reach –90, the chart turns flat again, because you are looking directly up at the chart from below.

Perspective ranges from 0 to 120. A value of 0 creates the least distortion. As you increase to 120, the foreshortening increases, creating distortion similar to what you get with an ultra-wide-angle lens on a camera.

Figure 5.30
All four charts represent the same data. Each chart provides a different view angle.

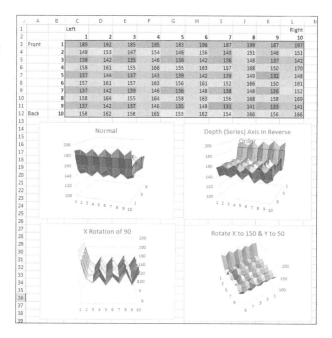

Next Steps

In Chapter 6, "Creating Stock Analysis Charts," you find out about the process of creating charts to show the performance of stocks and securities. Although Excel offers four types of built-in stock charts, they appear dated in light of modern stock charts available on numerous websites. Chapter 6 shows you how to go beyond the four built-in charts to create modern-looking stock charts.

Creating Stock Analysis Charts

Overview of Stock Charts

Excel provides four basic types of stock analysis charts: high-low-close, open-high-low-close, volume-high-low-close, and volume-open-high-low-close. These built-in charts are helpful when you need to display a stock trend for use in an executive dashboard.

Unfortunately, like the old charting in legacy versions of Excel, the stock charts are showing signs of age. If you are familiar with the charts in the *Wall Street Journal* or on http://finance.yahoo.com, you can see that charting technology has definitely left Excel behind.

This chapter guides you on how to coax acceptable results out of the Excel charting engine. However, sometimes it is easier to ditch the Excel stock charts and design your own chart using a line chart.

If you are planning to do dashboard reporting, this chapter provides a few tips to help make your charts smaller than usual, while maintaining readability.

Typically, stock charts in the newspaper or online are represented by one of three chart types: line charts, open-high-low-close (OHLC) charts, or candlestick charts. The following sections discuss each of these chart types.

Line Charts

A line chart shows the closing price of a security every day for a month, quarter, half year, year, or longer. A line chart may show a second series of volume represented as a column chart at the bottom of the chart. For example, in Figure 6.1 a line chart shows the closing price for a security for one year. A volume chart at the bottom shows unusually high activity for the security in May.

IN THIS CHAPTER

Overview of Stock Charts 171

Obtaining Stock Data to Chart 173

Creating a Line Chart to Show Closing Prices 177

Creating OHLC Charts 182

Creating Candlestick Charts 191

Next Steps 196

Figure 6.1
A line indicates the closing price of the security
each day for a year. The
column chart at the bot-
tom shows the volume of
shares traded each day.

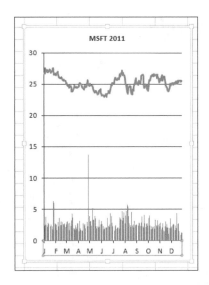

When creating a line chart in Excel, you do not have to use stock chart types. Instead, you can simply choose a line chart.

One advantage of line charts is that it is easy to add a second security to a line chart to show how the original security is doing compared to an index or a competitor.

OHLC Charts

An OHLC chart shows a vertical line extending from the low price to the high price for a given period. A dash on the left side of the line indicates the opening price. A dash on the right side of the line indicates the closing price. For example, the chart in Figure 6.2 shows that January opened at 325, the price ranged from 324 to 349, and January closed at 339.

Figure 6.2
This is a true OHLC chart.
Excel's built-in types omit
the marker for the open-
ing price.

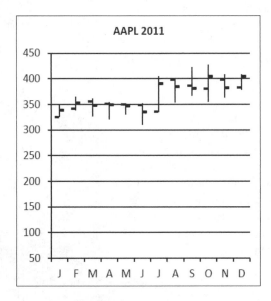

6

Excel does not have a built-in style for OHLC charts, but it can create a variant of this chart. Excel's high-low-close chart shows the vertical line and the closing line on the right side of the line. However, it is missing the marker for the opening price. Excel's volume-high-low-close chart is a variant of the OHLC chart that is coupled with a volume chart showing trading volume.

■ If you absolutely need to show the opening price, see the "Creating OHLC Charts" section later in this chapter.

Candlestick Charts

A candlestick chart has a vertical line that indicates the range of low to high prices for a security. A thicker column indicates the opening and closing prices. If the price of the security closed up, the thicker column appears in white or green. If the price of the security closed down, the thicker column appears in black or red.

This stock chart was named a candlestick chart because each shape appears as a candle with a wick sticking out of the top and the bottom. For example, in Figure 6.3, the security declined in the four months from March through June, before gaining in July.

Excel creates candlestick charts using the open-high-low-close chart type. In another variant, volumes for each period are plotted on a second axis. You can quickly scan this type of chart to see whether the stock has had more winning periods than losing periods.

Figure 6.3
The thicker column indicates the open and closing prices. The thinner line indicates the high-to-low range.

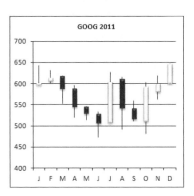

Obtaining Stock Data to Chart

There are plenty of free sources of historical data to chart. To obtain stock data to chart, you can go to http://finance.yahoo.com or another such site and follow these steps:

1. If you do not know the stock ticker symbols for the company of interest, use the Symbol Lookup link that appears next to the Go button in the top navigation bar of the page.

2. Enter a stock ticker symbol in the Get Quotes text box and press the Go button. Yahoo! returns a table and a chart showing information about the current day.

3. Click Historical Prices in the left navigation bar. Enter a starting date and an ending date and choose whether you want the data summarized daily, weekly, or monthly. Click Get Prices to generate new results. Yahoo! shows columns for date, open, high, low, close, volume, and adjusted close. A minor annoyance is that it shows about 50 dates on a page and then offers a Next link.

4. Instead of copying a page at a time, scroll down and select the Download to Spreadsheet link that appears below the results.

5. In the File Download dialog that appears, click Save. An unimaginative name of table.csv is proposed. Save using this name or something more specific, such as MSFTDaily2011.csv.

6. In Excel 2013, select File, Open. In the Open dialog that appears, in the Files of Type drop-down, select Text Files (*.prn, *.txt, *.csv).

7. Browse to the downloaded .csv file and click Open. Excel opens the file. Column A, which contains dates, is typically too narrow, as shown in Figure 6.4. Double-click the border between the column A and B headings to make column A wider.

Figure 6.4
After the CSV file opens in Excel, you need to adjust the column widths.

	A	B	C	D	E	F	G
1	Date	Open	High	Low	Close	Volume	Adj Close
2	########	26	26.12	25.91	25.96	27395700	25.45
3	########	25.95	26.05	25.86	26.02	22616900	25.51
4	########	26.11	26.15	25.76	25.82	29822500	25.32
5	########	25.96	26.14	25.93	26.04	21287200	25.53
6	########	25.91	26.04	25.73	26.03	23205800	25.52
7	########	25.82	25.86	25.48	25.81	35794100	25.31
8	########	26.01	26.19	25.44	25.76	64132500	25.26
9	########	25.86	26.1	25.81	26.03	60767600	25.52
10	########	26.02	26.12	25.46	25.53	52258300	25.03

8. The data is always sorted with the most recent data first. Therefore, click a cell in column A and select Data, AZ to sort the date into ascending sequence by column.

9. If you have more than one screen of data, from the View tab, select Freeze Panes, Freeze Top Row to ensure that you can always see the headings at the top of the screen.

10. CSV files are not good places to store Excel charts. Before creating any charts, select File, Save As. Select to save as an Excel macro-enabled workbook.

Rearranging Columns in the Downloaded Data

If you are using one of the Excel built-in stock charts, you should know that Excel is very particular about the sequence of the columns. For example, in a high-low-close chart, the date should be in the first column, followed by a High column, a Low column, and a Close column. This does not match the sequence of the data downloaded from Yahoo.com. You need to be prepared to insert new columns, and then cut and paste data from one column to another to sequence your data as necessary. The following list shows the required sequence of columns for each chart type:

- **Line chart**—Date in column A and Close in column B
- **Line chart with volume**—Date in column A, Close in column B, and Volume in column C
- **High-low-close**—Date in column A, High in column B, Low in column C, and Close in column D
- **Volume-high-low-close**—Date in column A, Volume in column B, High in column C, Low in column D, and Close in column E
- **Open-high-low-close as candlestick**—Date in column A, Open in column B, High in column C, Low in column D, and Close in column E
- **Open-high-low-close as OHLC**—Date in column A, High in column B, Low in column C, Close in column D, and Open in column E
- **Volume-open-high-low-close as candlestick**—Date in column A, Volume in column B, Open in column C, High in column D, Low in column E, and Close in column F
- **Volume-open-high-low-close as OHLC**—Date in column A, Volume in column B, High in column C, Low in column D, Close in column E, and Open in column F

> **TIP**
> Although you might be tempted to delete the unused columns, it is better to leave them to the right of the data to be charted. This way, if you decide to add a series to the chart later, it is easy to do so.

Dealing with Splits Using the Adjusted Close Column

Before charting data, you should look at the earliest data point and compare the Close column to the Adjusted Close column. If they differ, you know that one of two events happened during the period in question:

- The company declared a dividend. For example, if the company pays out three cents per share, the adjusted price is reduced by three cents for all months that occurred earlier than the dividend.
- If the company declares a stock split, the adjusted close shows the closing price, which pretends the split had occurred previously.

Figure 6.5 shows an example of a stock split. Six Flags stock began June 2011 at a price of $79.61 and closed the month at $37.45. The stock did not really incur a huge drop during the month.

Six Flags had declared a two-for-one stock split on June 28, 2011. Every person who had 100 shares on that day watched those shares change into 200 shares. The value of each share was cut in half at the time of the split. In this case, if you start the month with 100 shares of Six Flags, valued at $7,961, you will end the month with 200 shares of Six Flags, valued at $7,490. This is a drop, but not a massive 50% drop.

6

Figure 6.5
At first glance, it appears that Six Flags stock took a nosedive in June.

	A	B	C	D	E	F	G
1	Date	Open	High	Low	Close	Volume	Adj Close
2	1/3/2011	54.71	60.6	53.96	59.34	171800	28.43
3	2/1/2011	59.74	66.5	58.24	62.36	232700	29.9
4	3/1/2011	62.52	72.42	60.16	72	276500	34.52
5	4/1/2011	72.48	73.99	66.5	68.53	208900	32.86
6	5/2/2011	68.59	80.5	68.35	79.7	441400	38.25
7	6/1/2011	79.61	80.19	36.2	37.45	704100	35.94
8	7/1/2011	37.4	39.99	33.68	35.21	463500	33.79
9	8/1/2011	35.5	35.69	28.56	33.55	556800	32.2
10	9/1/2011	33.44	34.15	27.7	27.72	425100	26.65
11	10/3/2011	27.47	36.92	24.72	35.9	597700	34.52
12	11/1/2011	34.69	38.24	34.24	38	329100	36.54
13	12/1/2011	38.2	41.64	36.86	41.24	325800	39.72

To learn when the split or dividend occurred, you have to look through the table on http://finance.yahoo.com, which shows splits and dividends. This information is not downloaded in the CSV file.

If you are plotting a line chart showing the closing price, you can deal with the split by using the Adjusted Close column. Notice in Figure 6.5 that the Adjusted Close column for January 2011 is $28.43, half the real closing price of $59.34. Yahoo goes to the trouble of adjusting the closing price to provide a comparable view of the closing price.

If you are plotting a chart showing high, low, and close, you have to add some additional calculations. To do so, follow these steps:

1. Add the new column headings Date, High, Low, Close to H1:K1.
2. Copy the formula =A2 from cell H2 down to all rows. This formula is for the date.
3. Copy the formula =G2 from cell K2 down to all rows. This formula is for the adjusted close.
4. Copy the formula =C2*($G2/$E2) from cell I2 down to all rows in columns I and J.

> **NOTE**
> This formula in step 4 adjusts the high price from column C by the same ratio as Adjusted Close to Close. You might change it in some rows. The dollar signs before columns G and E enable you to copy the formula to column J for the adjusted low as well.

5. Manually fix any dates where a split occurred.
6. Create your stock charts from the data in columns H:K, as shown in Figure 6.6.

Figure 6.6
Most of the adjusted columns are a formula, but you need to use special care in the months in which a stock split occurred.

▲	A	B	C	D	E	F	G	H	I	J	K
1	Date	Open	High	Low	Close	Volume	Adj Close	Date	High	Low	Close
2	1/3/2011	54.71	60.6	53.96	59.34	171800	28.43	1/3/2011	29.03367	25.85242	28.43
3	2/1/2011	59.74	66.5	58.24	62.36	232700	29.9	2/1/2011	31.88502	27.92457	29.9
4	3/1/2011	62.52	72.42	60.16	72	276500	34.52	3/1/2011	34.72137	28.84338	34.52
5	4/1/2011	72.48	73.99	66.5	68.53	208900	32.86	4/1/2011	35.47806	31.88662	32.86
6	5/2/2011	68.59	80.5	68.35	79.7	441400	38.25	5/2/2011	38.63394	32.80285	38.25
7	6/1/2011	79.61	80.19	36.2	37.45	704100	35.94	6/1/2011	40.095	34.7404	35.94
8	7/1/2011	37.4	39.99	33.68	35.21	463500	33.79	7/1/2011	38.37723	32.3217	33.79
9	8/1/2011	35.5	35.69	28.56	33.55	556800	32.2	8/1/2011	34.25389	27.41079	32.2
10	9/1/2011	33.44	34.15	27.7	27.72	425100	26.65	9/1/2011	32.8318	26.63077	26.65
11	10/3/2011	27.47	36.92	24.72	35.9	597700	34.52	10/3/2011	35.50079	23.76976	34.52
12	11/1/2011	34.69	38.24	34.24	38	329100	36.54	11/1/2011	36.77078	32.92446	36.54
13	12/1/2011	38.2	41.64	36.86	41.24	325800	39.72	12/1/2011	40.10526	35.50144	39.72

> **NOTE**
> The original data showed a high price of $80.19 for June 2011. You can assume that this high happened before the split. In cell I7, divide C7 by 2 to adjust the high to $40.095. If you need the chart to be completely accurate, go back to http://finance.yahoo.com and run a daily report for the month in question. Find the high price after the split and compare it to the calculated high of $40.095. If higher, replace the calculation with the actual high from after the split. The original data showed a low price of $36.20 for June 2011. Mentally double this value to see if any of the pre-split lows were below 72.40. If they were, enter a new low of 50% of the pre-split low.

Creating a Line Chart to Show Closing Prices

A line chart is the easiest type of stock chart to create. Instead of using Excel's built-in stock charting types, you use a line chart. Follow these steps to create a line chart:

1. Download data for the security from http://finance.yahoo.com.

2. Sort the data into ascending sequence by date.

3. Insert a blank column B after the Date column.

4. Copy the Adjusted Close column from column H to the new column B.

5. Delete the extra column H.

6. Clear the date in cell A1.

> **TIP**
> Whenever your row labels contain dates, the top-left cell of the chart range should be blank.

7. Replace the Adjusted Close heading in B1 with the security symbol and time period, such as MSFT 2011.

8. Select your data in columns A and B.

9. On the Insert tab, select Recommended Charts. Excel recommends a line chart. Click OK. Excel creates the chart shown in Figure 6.7.

Figure 6.7
Excel creates a line chart showing closing prices.

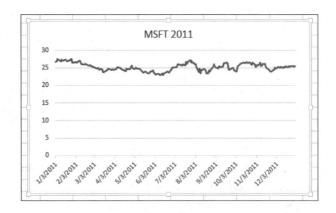

10. The value axis currently runs from a low of 0 to a high of 30. During 2011, the security closing prices ran in a range from $23 to $30. If you want to show more detail in the chart, double-click the value axis to open the Format Axis task pane. Click the chart icon near the top. Expand the Axis options category. Change the Minimum setting from 0 to 20. Keep the Maximum setting at 30. Keep the task pane open for step 11.

11. The dates in the horizontal axis are already showing one date per month, but the date appears in m/d/yyyy format. To display the initial letter of the month (JFMAMJJASOND), do the following:

   ■ Assuming the Format task pane is still open, click the horizontal axis labels. The task pane changes to show settings for the horizontal axis.

   ■ On the Axis Options category, change the Axis Type to Date axis.

   ■ The Units should show Major of 1 Months, and a Base of Days. The base makes sure that you have one data point per day. The Major makes sure the labels appear once per month. There is a bug in Excel 2013. After you choose a number format to display the initial letter of the month name, the major setting changes to 7 Days. To prevent this, change the Major from Months to Days. Then change it from Days back to Months. This turns off the Auto setting for Major units and prevents Excel from changing this setting.

   ■ Click the Number category at the bottom of the Format Axis task pane to expand the Number category.

   ■ The Category drop-down should already show Date.

   ■ Open the Type drop-down. There are 17 options. The 14th option is simply "M". Choose this. The Format Code shows a locale code and then mmmmm;@. The mmmmm custom type displays a single letter for each month. In the English version of Excel, it displays JFMAMJJASOND, a format regularly seen in the *Wall Street Journal*. If the axis labels change instead to JJJJFFFFMMMMAAAAMMMM... you are going to run into a second bug. If you go back to the axis options, the Major Units are still showing 1 Month. This is not correct. Excel failed to update the setting. To see the correct setting, click the vertical axis and then back on the horizontal axis to force Excel to display the erroneous setting of 7 days. You should now return the setting to 1 Month.

12. Resize the chart so that it is narrower than the default chart. Click the chart border to select the chart. Drag the right resizing handle to the left.

The resulting chart is shown in Figure 6.8.

Figure 6.8
When you zoom in on the $20–$30 price range, more details are visible.

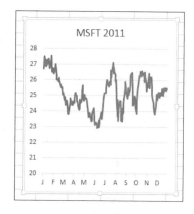

┌ C A U T I O N ──

The behavior of the date axis in Excel 2013 is different from Excel 2010. If you had a chart displaying "J F M A M J J A S O N D" successfully in Excel 2010 and open that chart in Excel 2013, the labels along the axis repeat each month label two to five times. When this happens, double-click the axis labels to open the Format Axis task pane. In the task pane, choose the Chart icon and then Axis Options. Change the Major Unit back to 1 Month. (See Figure 6.9.) This problem happens only with the "M" number format. If you use M-YY, the axis behaves normally. Unfortunately, the universal format is the "M" format for stock charts.

Figure 6.9
Reset the major units to 1 Month to prevent the axis label problem.

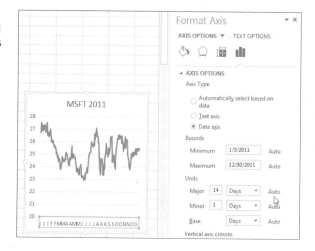

Adding Volume as a Column Chart to the Line Chart

A popular option in stock charts is to add a column chart that shows volume of shares traded. This chart usually appears at the bottom of the trend chart.

Continuing with the example from the preceding section, to plot prices in the $15–$35 range with volumes in the 15–300 million range, the volumes have to be plotted on a secondary axis. One trick is to inflate the maximum artificially for the secondary axis by a factor of three or four to keep the volume chart in the lower portion, which is the lower quarter to third of the chart.

Follow these steps to create a chart that shows closing prices and volume:

1. Download data from `http://finance.yahoo.com`.
2. Sort the data into ascending sequence by date.
3. Insert blank columns B and C after the Date column.
4. Cut the Adjusted Close column from column I to the new column B.
5. Cut the Volume column from column H to the new column C.
6. Clear the heading from cell A1.
7. Select your data in columns A:C.
8. Excel 2013 offers a new dialog for creating combo charts in one step. Getting to the dialog is tricky. Select Insert, Recommended Charts. In the Insert Chart dialog, click the All Charts tab across the top. In the left navigation panel, choose Combo.
9. In the bottom of the dialog, change the Chart Type for MSFT 2011 to Line. Change the Chart Type for Volume to Clustered Column. Choose the Secondary Axis check box for the Volume Series. (See Figure 6.10.) Click OK.

Figure 6.10
Create a combo chart using this new dialog in Excel 2013.

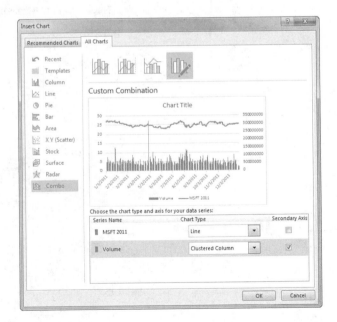

10. Click the Legend and press the Delete key. Excel removes the legend from the chart.

11. Edit the Chart Title to read MSFT 2011. Using the Plus sign icon, change Chart Title to Centered Overlay.

12. The value axis currently runs from a low of $0 to a high of $30. Although prices of Microsoft (MSFT) stock never dipped below $23 in 2011, you can leave that space to hold the volume portion of the chart. The highest volume was about 300 million shares traded. If you scale the secondary axis to have a maximum value of 600 million shares traded, the volume portion of the chart occupies the lower half of the chart. Double-click the secondary value axis to open the Format Axis task pane. Click the chart icon at the top of the task pane and then expand the Axis Options category. The Maximum currently shows 3.5E8. Change this to 6E8 (which is 600,000,000). The tallest column in the volume area of the chart stays below the gridline for $20. Keep the task pane open for steps 13 and 14.

13. Usually, the analyst does not care how many shares are traded; he or she is interested in the relative scale of the shares being traded. From the chart, you can tell that something remarkable happened in May when Microsoft traded three times more shares than usual. Thus, you do not need to have any volume numbers along the right side of the chart. In the task pane, expand the Tick Marks category. Change the Label Position drop-down to None.

14. The dates in the horizontal axis are trying to show month, day, and year, as in the original data set. To display one label for each month, do the following:

    ■ Click the dates along the horizontal axis.

    ■ Back in the task pane, go back to the Axis Options category. The Units section currently shows 1 Months Auto. You need to set this setting so it won't change. Change the Major Units setting from Months to Days temporarily. Change the setting back to Months. Now the setting shows 1 Months Reset. The Reset button is the indicator that you have overridden the Automatic setting. In the Axis Options dialog, select Major Unit, Fixed, 1, Month. The fact that you have to do this seems to be a bug.

    ■ Expand the Number category in the task pane.

    ■ Open the Type drop-down and choose the M setting. This type displays only the first letter of each month name. Therefore, it appears as JFMAMJJASOND.

15. Resize the chart so that it is narrower than the default chart. Click the chart border to select the chart. Drag the right resizing handle to the left.

16. If the Draft mode indicator appears on the chart, open the Draft mode indicator and select Turn Off Draft Mode.

Figure 6.11 shows the resulting chart.

The process of creating line charts is quite straightforward. Although a certain amount of tweaking needs to happen, it is about normal for a chart. In contrast, when creating OHLC charts, you must jump through more hoops, as described in the next section.

6

Figure 6.11
The final chart shows closing price as a line chart and volumes as columns at the bottom of the chart.

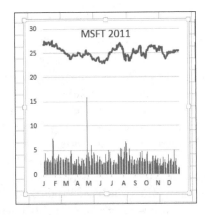

Creating OHLC Charts

Excel offers two built-in chart types that come close to the OHLC chart shown earlier in Figure 6.2. The built-in types both ignore the left-facing dash used to indicate the opening price each day.

The Excel team is not being dense here. Instead, a fundamental flaw exists in the underlying chart engine that makes it difficult to show the left-facing marker. This is why Microsoft does not support the open marker in the built-in charts. As you see in the sections that follow, you can work around this flaw.

Producing a High-Low-Close Chart

Before progressing to a true OHLC chart, it is best to start with Excel's built-in high-low-close chart. Follow these steps to produce a high-low-close chart in Excel 2013:

1. Download data from `http://finance.yahoo.com`. Because you cannot save a chart in a CSV file, use the Save As command to save the file as a regular Excel file type.

2. Move the Open data from column B to the blank column H. Delete the now-empty column B. This leaves you with dates in column A, High in column B, Low in column C, and Close in column D.

3. Select your data in columns A:D.

4. On the Insert tab, select Recommended Charts. Click the All Charts tab across the top. Along the left, choose Stock. The default stock chart is high-low-close. Click OK. Excel creates the default chart shown in Figure 6.12.

The default chart leaves a lot to be desired. For example, when looking at the vertical line extending from low to high, notice that it is nearly impossible to see the marker for the close. In addition, the legend at the bottom does not add useful information to the chart.

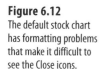

Figure 6.12
The default stock chart has formatting problems that make it difficult to see the Close icons.

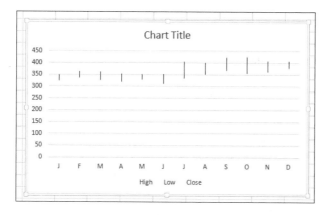

As I previously have mentioned, the Paintbrush icon often provides solutions to your charting problems. Not so in this case. There are 11 styles offered in the gallery and none of them add a suitable marker for the Close series. If you choose any of these, the close markers change from being imperceptibly small to being far too large.

Customizing a High-Low-Close Chart

It is possible to make an acceptable high-low-close chart in Excel 2013. After you delete extraneous chart elements and zoom in, you need to format and change the marker style for the Close series. Here's how you do it:

1. Click the Legend and press the Delete key to remove the legend from the chart.
2. Double-click the Vertical Axis to display the Format Axis task pane.
3. Click the Chart icon at the top of the task pane. Expand the Axis Options category. Change the Minimum to a number that is a bit lower than the low value in the chart. In the current example, a low value of 300 is appropriate. Keep the Format task pane open for steps 4 through 12.
4. On the Format tab in the ribbon, open the Current Selection drop-down and select Series "Close".
5. Back in the task pane, click the Paint Bucket icon. Underneath the row of icons, choose Marker. Expand the Series Options category.
6. Increase the Size setting to 9 to ensure that the markers are visible.
7. Expand the Fill category in the task pane. Select Solid Fill and then select the black color.
8. Expand the Border category in the task pane. Select Solid Line and then select the black color.
9. Click the horizontal gridlines in the chart.
10. Back in the task pane, for Line Color, select Solid Line. From the Color drop-down, select gray.
11. Change the width to 0.5 points.

12. Edit the Chart Title to say AAPL 2011.

13. Using the Plus icon to the right of the chart, select Chart Title, Centered Overlay.

14. Click the chart border. Drag the right resizing handle to the left to shrink the chart.

Figure 6.13 shows the resulting chart.

Figure 6.13
After formatting the high-low-close chart, you can actually see the close markers.

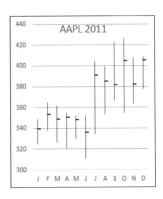

Creating an OHLC Chart

The fundamental barrier to creating a true OHLC chart is that Excel does not offer a left-facing dash as a built-in marker for a chart. However, you can import your own image to use as a marker.

Alternatively, you can use Photoshop to create a new graphic. For example, I created a graphic that was 11 pixels wide and 3 pixels tall. The leftmost five columns of pixels in this graphic are black, and the remaining pixels are transparent. I saved this file as a GIF image named LeftDash.gif. However, if you do not want to take the time to create an image like this, you can download this graphics from the web page of examples for this book at http://www.MrExcel.com/chart2013data.html.

The trick to creating an OHLC chart is to start with a high-low-close chart and add the Open series with a custom marker style. Follow these steps to create an OHLC chart in Excel 2013:

1. Start with data that has Date in column A, High in column B, Low in column C, Close in column D, and Open in column E. Do not include the Open data in the initial selection. Select the data in A:D.

2. From the Insert tab, select Insert, Recommended Charts, All Charts, Stock, High-Low-Close. Excel draws a chart. A blue box surrounds the charted data in B2:D13.

3. Click the blue handle in cell D13. Drag to the right to include the Open data on the chart. Excel adds the Open data in a format similar to the Close data.

4. On the Format tab in the ribbon, select Series Close from the Current Selection drop-down. Click Format Selection to display the Format Data Series task pane. Choose

the Paint Bucket icon. Choose the Marker item below the icons. Expand the Series Options category.

5. Leave the marker as the built-in right-facing dash and change the size to 7.

6. Expand the Fill category. Select Solid Fill. Select black from the color drop-down.

7. Expand the Border category. Select Solid Line. Select black from the color drop-down.

8. Without closing the Format task pane, select Series Open from the Current Selection drop-down in the ribbon. In the task pane, go to Paint Bucket, Marker, Series Options.

9. Change the Marker Type setting from None to Built-in. Temporarily, choose the Right-Facing Dash as the Type and set the Size to 9.

10. In the Type drop-down, select the tenth marker, which is a tiny version of the Picture icon that is prevalent throughout Excel. The Insert Picture dialog displays. Navigate to and select the LeftDash.gif that you downloaded from the sample files page for this book. Click Insert. The marker looks "wrong" because there is still an outline around the transparent portion of the marker. Change the Marker Border to No Line.

11. In the chart, delete the Legend.

12. Edit the title to show AAPL 2011.

13. Resize the chart so that it is horizontally smaller.

14. Double-click the numbers along the vertical axis to display the Format Axis task pane. Select the Chart icon, Axis Options. For this data set, you could use a Minimum of 300, Maximum of 450, and a Major Unit of 25.

Figure 6.14 shows the final chart.

Figure 6.14
The markers for the Open series are image files created in Photoshop.

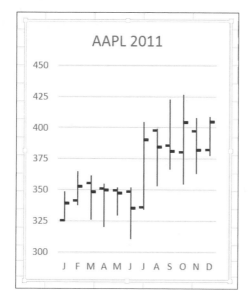

If you are going to add volume to the chart later, you can allow the vertical scale to run from 0 to 450.
If you are showing only OHLC on the chart, you can scale the vertical axis from 300 to 450.

The process of adding the open markers adds complexity to creating this chart. However, if you frequently need to create OHLC charts, you can save this chart type as a template to streamline the process in the future. To save a chart as a template, select the chart and then select Save as Template from the Type group on the Design tab.

Adding Volume to a High-Low-Close Chart

There are two ways to add a volume column chart to a high-low-close chart:

- Microsoft offers a built-in volume-high-low-close chart. However, this built-in chart automatically moves the prices from the left axis to the right axis.
- You can add volume while keeping the prices along the left axis.

Creating a Built-in Volume-High-Low-Close Chart

Follow these steps to create a built-in volume-high-low-close chart:

1. Arrange your data with Date in column A, Volume in column B, High in column C, Low in column D, and Close in column E.

2. If you have actual dates in column A, remove the Date heading from the top-left corner cell.

3. Select the range of data in A:E.

4. Select Insert, Recommended Charts, All Charts, Stock, Volume-High-Low-Close. Excel creates the chart shown in Figure 6.15.

Figure 6.15
The volume columns hide the high-low-close markers for most of this chart.

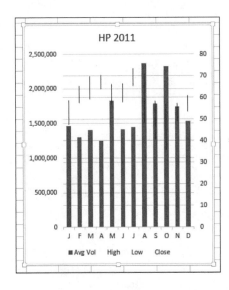

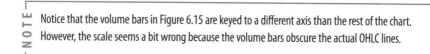

> **NOTE** Notice that the volume bars in Figure 6.15 are keyed to a different axis than the rest of the chart. However, the scale seems a bit wrong because the volume bars obscure the actual OHLC lines.

5. Click the Legend and then press the Delete key.

6. Double-click the numbers along the left side of the chart to display the Format Axis task pane. Choose the Chart icon and then expand the Axis Options category.

7. Set the Maximum to triple the current value. This shrinks the size of the volume columns. In this example, you triple the original value of 2.5E6 to 7.0E6.

8. To remove the axis labels for the Volume columns, expand the Labels category. Change the Label Position drop-down in the center of the Format Axis dialog to None.

9. On the Format tab of the ribbon, open the Current Selection drop-down. Select Series Close.

10. In the Format Data Series task pane, choose the Paint Bucket icon, Marker, Series Options. Increase the size drop-down from 5 to 9.

11. The gridlines are showing for both the Volume Axis and the Price Axis. To remove the Volume gridlines, click the chart and then click the Plus icon to the right of the chart. Hover to the right of the Gridlines entry and a right-arrow head appears. Click the arrow to open a list of Gridlines. Uncheck Primary Horizontal Gridlines.

12. Click one of the remaining gridlines in the chart. The task pane now shows Format Major Gridlines.

13. In the task pane, the Line category should display. Select Solid Line. In the Color drop-down, choose a light gray color to make the gridlines less obtrusive.

14. Click the Chart Title. Type **HP 2011** and press Enter.

15. Reduce the horizontal size of the chart by clicking the right resizing handle and dragging toward the center of the chart.

Figure 6.16 shows the resulting chart. However, it can be a bit disconcerting to have the axis scale appear on the right side of the chart when 99 percent of the charts in the Western world have the axis appear on the left side of the chart. A solution for this problem is provided in the next section.

6

Figure 6.16
After a number of adjustments, the built-in volume-high-low-close chart does the job, although the axis appears on the wrong side.

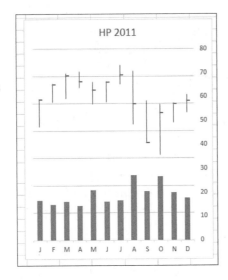

Adding Volume to the Right Axis of an Open-High-Low-Close Chart

In this section, you abandon stock charts completely. In reality, there is nothing magical about a stock chart. The vertical line between the High and Low series is a special element called a High-Low line. The High and Low series "appear" on the chart with neither a marker nor a line. Their only purpose is to make the high-low lines work. The Open and Close series are a line chart with markers where the line is set to no line. The volume chart at the bottom is a clustered column chart.

The following steps add volume to the open-high-low-close chart shown earlier in Figure 6.14.

Follow these steps to create a volume-open-high-low-close chart:

1. Download two years of daily historical data from http://finance.yahoo.com. The data is fine in the original order of Date, Open, High, Low, Close, Volume.

2. Remove the Date heading from the top-left cell in the range.

3. Select the data in columns A:F.

4. Select, Insert, Recommended Charts, All Charts, Combo. You have to use some care in choosing the chart type for each series. For Open and Close, choose Line with Markers. For High and Low, choose Line, which removes the markers. Change the Volume series to a Clustered Column and choose the Secondary Axis box for this series. The dialog box displays as shown in Figure 6.17. As you might be able to see in the preview, the chart doesn't look anything like the desired chart. Click OK to create the chart. This chart has 500 data points, so make the chart as large as possible.

5. Edit the Chart Title to show NFLX 2011-12.

Figure 6.17
This line chart appears to
be a long way from the
OHLC format you desire.

6. Edit the right axis. You goal is initially to triple the maximum for the axis. In the Format Axis dialog, choose the Chart icon, Axis Options and change the Maximum. This particular chart has a pretty severe tumble for the right 60% of the chart, and the usual trick of tripling the volume axis does not effectively separate the volume columns from the stock price. Try a Maximum that is four times the original value, or 2.0E8. While you are in the Format Axis task pane, expand the Labels category and choose None as the Label Position.

7. You don't always have to use the task pane. Click one gridline to select it. On the Chart Tools Format tab in the ribbon, open the Shape Outline drop-down and choose a gray color for the gridlines.

   At this point, you have four line charts in place of the OHLC markers. You have to edit the series one at a time. It is going to be tough to select a series by clicking the chart, so you select the series from the first drop-down on the Chart Tools Format tab in the ribbon. The High and Low series will be edited to have no line. They already have no markers. The Close series will use a small right-facing dash as a marker but no line. The Open series will have a marker and no line.

8. Select Series High from the Current Selection drop-down in the Format tab. In the Format Data Series task pane, choose the Paint Bucket, Line, No Line. Repeat for Series Low.

9. Select Series Close from the Current Selection drop-down in the Format tab. In the Format Data Series task pane, choose the Paint Bucket, Marker, Series Options,

Built-In. For the Type, choose the right-facing dash. Size 3. In the Fill, choose Solid Fill and black. In the Border category, choose No Line.

10. Select Series Open from the Current Selection drop-down in the Format tab. In the Format Data Series task pane, choose the Paint Bucket, Marker, Series Options, Built-In. For the Type, choose the full dash. Size 3. In the Fill, choose Solid Fill and black. In the Border category, choose No Line. Go back to the Built-In drop-down and choose Image. Choose LeftDash.gif from the download files in this book. The image appears too large. Go back to Built-In and re-choose the full-dash icon. For some bizarre reason, the dash appears only on the left side of the vertical bar now.

11. Click the Legend and press the Delete key.

The final chart is shown in Figure 6.18. It is a bit ironic that the best stock chart is created by not using stock charts at all. For all the love and attention that the Excel team put into the Paintbrush icon to the right of the chart, with 153 new chart styles, the entire stock chart category was certainly neglected.

Figure 6.18
Here is a true OHLC chart with volume.

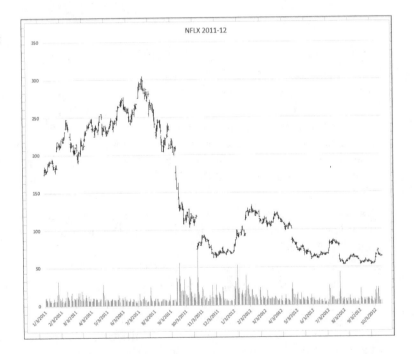

The next section describes candlestick charts, which require the least customization because Excel includes good built-in charts to create candlestick charts.

Creating Candlestick Charts

A basic candlestick chart requires a data range that includes a date in the first column, and open, high, low, and close values in the remaining columns. To create a candlestick chart, follow these steps:

1. Download data from `http://finance.yahoo.com`. Your data is in the correct sequence, with Date in column A, Open in column B, High in column C, Low in column D, and Close in column E.

2. Select your data in columns A:E.

3. On the Insert tab, select Recommended Charts, All Charts, Stock, Open-High-Low-Close. Excel creates the chart in Figure 6.19.

Figure 6.19
A default candlestick chart.

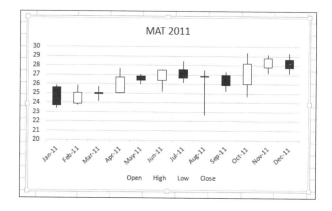

4. Click the legend and press Delete.

5. Double-click the numbers along the vertical axis. Specify a fixed minimum value that is greater than zero but lower than the low value for the range in question.

6. Click the dates along the bottom. In the Format Axis task pane, choose the Chart icon and then choose Number. Change the Category drop-down to Date. Change the Type drop-down to M. This changes the bottom axis to use the JFMAMJJASOND labels.

7. Edit the title.

8. Reduce the horizontal size of the chart.

Changing Colors in a Candlestick Chart

By default, Excel makes the candlestick charts monochrome. Stock price increases are shown with white columns. Stock price declines are shown with black columns. If you will be presenting the chart in color, you might prefer another system, such as red for declines and green for increases. If this is the case, it is easy to customize the colors in a chart.

6

The white up bars and the black down bars are actually two separate objects in the chart. Therefore, first you need to format the up bars and then format the down bars. To change the color of the bars, follow these steps:

1. On the Format tab, select Current Selection, Up Bars 1.
2. Select Format, Shape Fill and then select green. (In color stock charts, up periods are typically shown in green.)
3. On the Format tab, select Current Selection, Down Bars 1.
4. Select Format, Shape Fill and then select red. (In color stock charts, up periods are typically shown in red.)

Figure 6.20 shows the final candlestick chart.

Figure 6.20
With minimal formatting, you can create a candlestick stock chart.

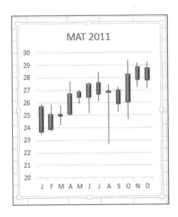

Excel offers a built-in chart you can use to create a candlestick chart that includes volume bars. However, as with the volume-high-low-close chart, the height of the volume bars is often too large. Plan to adjust the volume axis so the maximum is three times the original value.

Understanding High-Low Lines and Up-Down Bars

To make your own stock charts, you need to have a good understanding of how Excel draws in high-low lines and up/down bars. This section explains the rules for high-low lines and up/down bars.

Figure 6.21 shows four line series on a single chart. The first series is the thick solid line from lower left to upper right. The second series is the dotted line at the top of the chart. The third series starts out as the lowest dashed line but crosses to become the second-lowest line late in the chart.

Lines, Trendlines, and Drop-Bars are three chart elements that are not listed in the Plus Sign icon to the right of the chart. Instead, you have to go to the Design tab in the ribbon and open the Add Chart Element drop-down on the left side of the ribbon. Here, you discover a menu almost identical to the Plus icon, with the addition of Lines, Trendlines, and Up/Down Bars.

Figure 6.21
These four series are used to illustrate the different behavior of high-low lines and up/down bars.

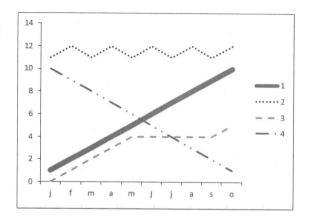

To add high-low lines to a chart, select Design, Add Chart Element, Lines, High-Low Lines. Figure 6.22 shows that the vertical lines extend from the lowest value at each data point to the highest value at each data point. In February, the line extends from the 1 in Series 3 up to the 12 in Series 2. In October, the high-low line extends from the 1 in Series 1 to the 12 in Series 2.

Figure 6.22
High-low lines look at all the line series in the chart and extend from the lowest to the highest at each data point.

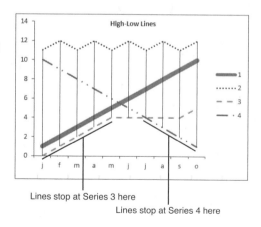

In contrast to high-low lines, up/down bars always extend from the first series line to the last series line. In Figure 6.23, the up/down bars always start at the solid line for Series 1 and extend to the dash-dot line for Series 4. It seems like there should be a setting that you could use to specify that the up/down bars should extend from any specific series to another specific series, but there is not. Instead, Excel always draws the up/down bars from the first series to the last series (see Figure 6.23).

Figure 6.23
Up/down bars always start at the first series and extend to the last series.

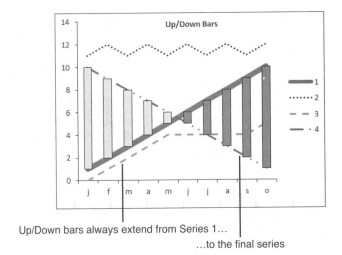

Up/Down bars always extend from Series 1...

...to the final series

Both the high-low lines and up/down bars are valid only for series that are plotted as line charts. You are allowed to use the No Line setting to make the line invisible.

To see how up/down bars and high-low lines work in conjunction, try to build a candle that is 10 units tall. A wick sticks out 3 units above the candle. The wick should not stick out below the candle. You set up four series like this:

- The first series is the bottom of the candle. Call this series A and have it start at 1.

- The last series is the top of the candle. Call this series D and have a value of 11, which is 10 higher than the series A value.

- In between these series, have a B series for the bottom of the wick and a C series for the top of the wick. Note that B and C apply only to the wick if they are the MIN and MAX of the four series. The value for C should be 3 above the value for D, or 14.

In Figure 6.24, the data has three additional data points. Column 2 will show a candle that is 3 units shorter than column 1. Column 3 gets shorter still. The wick protrudes a small bit below the candle for columns 2 and 3. Column 4 is reversed, where the value in A is less than the value in D.

Figure 6.24
Series A and D control the up/down bars.

	Col 1	Col 2	Col 3	Col 4	Explanation
A	1	1	1	11	*First Series is Bottom of Drop Bar*
B	1	0.75	0.25	1	*Min value is bottom of wick*
C	13.5	12	10	13	*Max value is top of wick*
D	11	8	5	1	*Last Series is Top of Drop Bar*

Create a line chart without markers from the four series. (See Figure 6.25.)

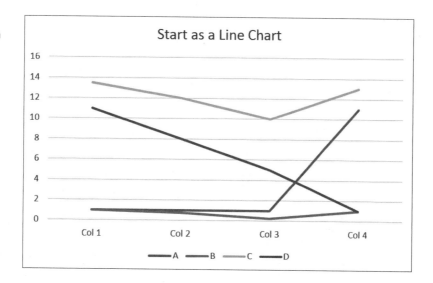

Next, mark each series as No Line. Double-click one line to open the Format Data Series task pane. Choose the Paint Bucket icon, Line, No Line. The line disappears. Click the next line to select that line. The task pane stays on the same panel, so you can quickly choose No Line. Repeat for the two remaining lines. In Figure 6.26, the four series are still plotted, but no lines and no markers are showing. You can see the selection handles around the four data points from the last series.

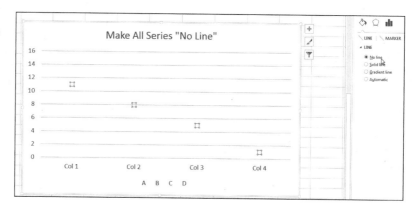

Finally, go to the Design tab in the ribbon. Open the Add Chart Element drop-down. Choose Lines, High-Low Lines. Open the same drop-down and choose Up/Down Bars. The chart in Figure 6.27 has a few additional tweaks, such as a title, no legend, and a bevel from the Shape Effects drop-down on the Format tab in the ribbon.

6

Figure 6.27
The lines and markers don't appear, but are placeholders that allow the high-low lines and up/down bars to work.

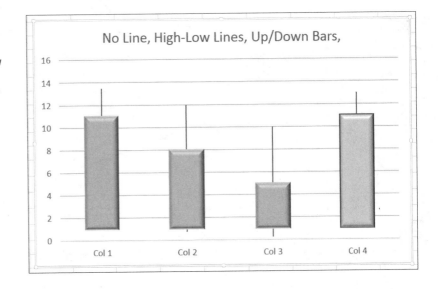

Next Steps

In this chapter, you discovered that at times you need to think creatively to coax an "impossible" chart out of Excel. In Chapter 7, "Advanced Chart Techniques," you find out how to use Excel's built-in charting tools to create charts that you do not normally see in Excel.

Advanced Chart Techniques

7

As the host of MrExcel.com, I get to see a lot of wild spreadsheets that people create. I have seen some amazing things come across my desk. This chapter covers some of the usual advanced charting tricks, and some unusual charts that you do not typically see in Excel. At the end of the chapter are a few examples of some charts that impressed me, so that you can see some of the cool things people can coax out of Excel.

The ideas in this section can be useful on most chart types that you work with. They include many techniques that you will come to realize are the basic, why-didn't-I-think-of-doing-that kind of ideas.

Mixing Two Chart Types on a Single Chart

You can represent a chart's series with different chart types. Instead of two lines on a chart, you can show one series as a line and one series as columns. Or you can mix columns and area charts, as shown in Figure 7.1.

Combo charts in Excel 2013 are controlled using the Custom Combination settings shown in Figure 7.2. The settings are the same whether they are in the Insert Chart dialog or the Change Chart Type dialog.

If you are initially creating a chart, choose Insert, Recommended Charts, All Charts, Combo to reach the dialog. If you are adjusting an existing chart, use the Change Chart Type icon.

IN THIS CHAPTER

Mixing Two Chart Types on a Single Chart ... 197

Moving Charts from One Worksheet to Another 200

Making Columns or Bars Float 200

Using a Rogue XY Series for Arbitrary Gridlines 202

Showing Several Charts on One Chart by Using a Rogue XY Series 207

Creating Bullet Charts in Excel 2013 212

Creating a Thermometer Chart 217

Creating a Benchmark Chart 219

Creating a Delta Chart 220

Next Steps 221

Figure 7.1
To emphasize one series, you can mix chart types on a single chart.

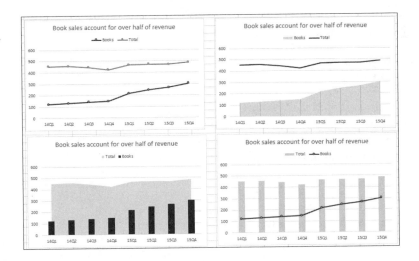

When you change the chart type of a series in a chart, you set up a new chart group. Suppose you have a stacked column chart with five series. When you change Series D and E to be a stacked line chart, chart group 1 contains the three series in the stacked columns. Chart group 2 contains the line series.

If you then change Series C to be an area chart, that creates a third chart group. The original chart group now contains only the two series that remain in the stacked columns. In Figure 7.2, five series occupy three chart groups.

In general, every different chart type in the same chart is in a new group. Moving one or more series to the secondary axis also creates a new chart group. Certain settings, such as the width of the column markers, apply to all the series in the same group. Some of the examples in this chapter purposely move a series to the second axis or change the chart type of a series to create a different group where different settings can apply. If you need to mix clustered and stacked columns, you have to use this technique.

→ To see how combo charts are used to combine stacked and clustered column charts, see "Creating a Stacked and Clustered Chart" in Chapter 4, "Creating Charts That Show Differences."

For best results when mixing chart types, follow these guidelines:

- You should stick with 2D chart types. Excel does not let you mix 3D charts.
- You cannot stack markers from chart group 2 on top of markers from chart group 1. Every chart group starts stacking from the category axis.
- Although Excel lets you do it, you should not mix vertical types with horizontal types. Figure 7.3 shows a chart where one series is moved to a bar chart. Most people are not able to glean anything from this chart (other than perhaps that you have no sense of design).

■ You can mix circular charts. For example, you can change one series of a doughnut chart to a pie chart.

■ Remember that in many cases, a line chart can be changed to an XY scatter with line series. The advantage is that up/down bars and high-low lines ignore an XY scatter chart line.

Figure 7.2
Stacked columns, stacked lines, and an area chart create three chart groups.

Figure 7.3
Although Excel lets you mix column and bar charts, I am not sure why you would.

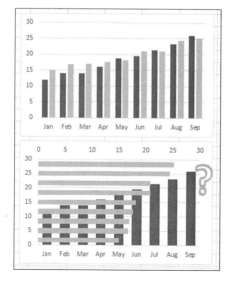

Moving Charts from One Worksheet to Another

You can combine charts from many worksheets into a single dashboard by moving the charts from their original locations.

For example, if your sales data is on a sales worksheet, you can build the chart on the sales worksheet. When the chart is selected, you select Move Chart from the Design tab. You can then choose to move the chart to a different worksheet (see Figure 7.4).

The chart continues to point to data on the original worksheet, but you end up with an uncluttered screen of just charts. Even though the charts are on a new worksheet, they still respond to data changes on the source worksheets.

Figure 7.4
You use the Move Chart dialog to build a dashboard of charts on a single sheet.

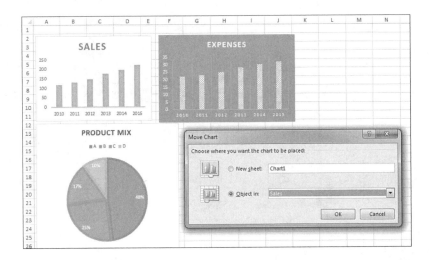

Making Columns or Bars Float

In Figure 7.5, the black bars appear to float in midair. This type of chart is good for showing the components of a whole.

The secret is that you plot the floating bars as Series 2. Series 1 is a dummy series that you fill using No Fill and No Outline in Excel.

There are some interesting settings involved in creating the charts shown in Figure 7.5. Follow these steps to create the chart in the figure:

1. Set up a data table to split the single series into two series. In Figure 7.6, column B shows the sales for each category. The formulas in column C:E are the data used to create the chart. The formulas in column C copy the values from column A. The formulas in column E copy column B.

2. Enter 0 in cell D2. This is the "height" of the invisible column. For the first series, the height is zero.

Figure 7.5
The floating columns or bars demonstrate how components make up a whole.

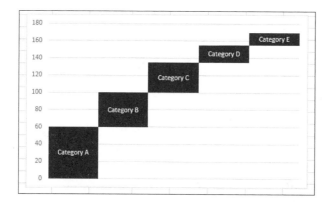

3. In cell D3, enter =D2+E2. This formula adds the starting height of the last column (D2) and the height of the previous column (E2).

4. Double-click the fill handle in cell D3 to copy the formula down to the rest of the series. Your data should now look like the data shown in Figure 7.6.

Figure 7.6
Formulas in column D show the starting point for each column. That series will later become invisible.

	A	B	C	D	E	F
		Sales		Invisible	Sales	
1		Sales		Invisible	Sales	
2	Category A	60	Category A	0	60	
3	Category B	40	Category B	60	40	
4	Category C	35	Category C	100	35	
5	Category D	20	Category D	135	20	
6	Category E	15	Category E	155	15	

D4 · · × ✓ *fx* =D3+E3

5. Select cells C1:E6. From the Insert tab, select Recommended Charts. Choose the third choice, a stacked column chart. Excel creates the chart shown in Figure 7.7.

Figure 7.7
You can see the Invisible series before it disappears.

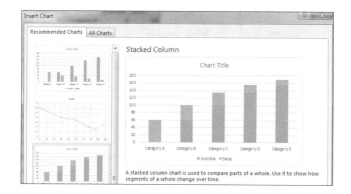

6. Click the Legend and press the Delete key to delete the legend.

7. Click the Title and press the Delete key to delete the title.

8. Click the labels along the bottom axis and press the Delete key to delete the axis labels.

9. Click any of the lower columns to select the first series. From the Format tab, select Shape Fill, No Fill. You might think that Excel is still outlining the first series, but those lines are the selection border. Click away from the series to make the selection disappear completely.

10. Double-click the visible series to display the Format Data Series task pane. Click the Chart icon in the task pane and select Format Data Series. In the Series Options category, set Gap Width to 0%.

11. The second series is whichever color happens to be the second accent color in the current theme. While the series is selected, select Shape Fill and select a desired color.

12. While the second series is selected, use the Plus icon to the right of the chart. Check Data Labels. Excel adds the value to the center of each column. Click a data label to change the task pane to Format Data Labels. In the task pane, click the Chart icon. In the Label Options category, uncheck Value. Check Category Name.

13. With the data labels selected, select Font Color on the Home tab and then select a font color that contrasts with the column.

The preceding steps create the column chart shown in Figure 7.5.

Using a Rogue XY Series for Arbitrary Gridlines

The chart in Figure 7.8 shows annual scores against a government performance index. The top chart uses gridlines that are a fixed space apart. In reality, the index is converted into named scores using the table shown in Figure 7.9. The bottom chart in Figure 7.8 replaces the built-in gridlines with lines showing where the category changes.

The goal is to draw gridlines at unevenly spaced locations of 7.5, 12.5, 18.5, 23.5, and 28. There is not a good way to adjust the gridlines to show horizontal lines for each category. The main problem is that Excel treats the collection of horizontal gridlines as a single object. When you format one major gridline, all major gridlines change. If each gridline could be formatted individually, you could draw a gridline every one unit and make most of the gridlines invisible. The solution is to add the gridlines' locations to the chart using an XY-Scatter series. You can hide the marker for this series and add a horizontal error bar to simulate the line.

This is a fairly complex set of steps, but the results are worth the work. If you try it a few times, you will realize how perfectly it works and appreciate the flexibility to both replace the gridlines with new gridlines and to replace the vertical axis labels with new labels. This example includes more figures than usual so you can easily see how it works.

Figure 7.8
The top chart has automatic gridlines. The bottom chart's gridlines have actual meaning.

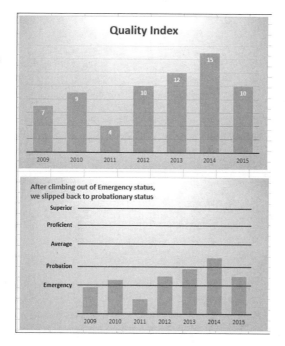

Figure 7.9
The numeric rating is translated to words based on these ranges.

	Rating	
10	Rating	
11	0-7	Emergency
12	8-12	Probation
13	13-18	Average
14	19-23	Proficient
15	24-28	Superior
16		

Follow these steps to convert the top chart to use arbitrary gridlines and labels:

1. Somewhere on the worksheet, build a table of the locations for each arbitrary gridline. The table should have 0 in the first column and the location for the gridline in the secondary column. In this case, you want the gridlines to be drawn between 7 and 8, so use numbers such as 7.5, 12.5, and so on.

2. Select the range of values from step 1. Press Ctrl+C to copy. Select the chart. On the Home tab, open the Paste drop-down and choose Paste Special.

3. In the Paste Special dialog, New Series should already be selected. Choose Categories (X Labels) in First Column. (See Figure 7.10.) Excel adds the new series as a clustered column chart as shown in Figure 7.11.

Figure 7.10
Copy the location for the gridlines and paste special as a new XY series.

Figure 7.11
Excel initially adds the new series as a clustered column series.

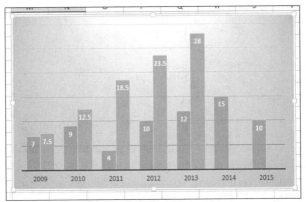

4. Choose Design, Change Chart Type. Choose a Combo chart. In the custom Combo settings, change the second series to a scatter chart. When you choose Scatter, Excel assumes you want the series on the secondary axis. Uncheck secondary axis. You now have a marker and a data label where each gridline should appear (see Figure 7.12).

5. Remove the old gridlines. One fast way to do it is to click the second gridline to select all gridlines and then press the Delete key. This doesn't work if you choose the top gridline, because you will select the plot area instead.

6. Remove the data labels on the columns. Click any column label and press Delete.

Figure 7.12
Change the new series to a scatter chart on the original axis.

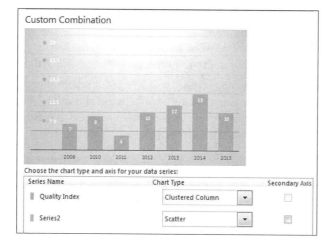

7. The markers that will soon become gridlines have a label showing the Y-value. Click one label. The task pane changes to show Format Data Labels. In the Format Data Labels task pane, click the Chart icon and expand the Label Options category. Before unchecking the Y Value check box, choose Value from Cells. Select a range that contains the words that you want to appear on each gridline. You now have labels such as "Superior, 28" to the right of a marker. You can now uncheck the Y Value box. In the task pane, change the Label Position to Left. On the Home tab, choose a dark font color for the labels.

8. If the labels are long, they may not have room to appear to the left of the marker. Click any blank space in the middle of the chart to select the plot area. Eight resize handles appear. Drag the left resize handle toward the center of the chart until there is room for the labels to appear. Your chart looks pretty good—you still have to convert the dot markers into solid gridlines. (See Figure 7.13.)

Figure 7.13
Add labels to the XY Markers.

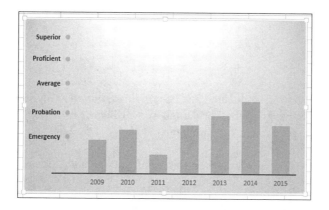

9. Click one of the dot markers to select the second series. In the Format Data Series dialog, choose the Paint Bucket icon. Underneath the row of task bar icons, choices appear for Line or Marker. Click Marker. Expand the Marker Options category. Choose None. The markers now disappear, even though they are still selected.

10. While the now-invisible markers are still selected, click the Plus icon to the right of the chart and choose Error Bars. You automatically get the wrong error bars. There is not a way to control what error bars appear. Although it seems frustrating, it is best to let Excel draw the wrong error bars in and then make the corrections. Steps 11 through 15 fix the error bars.

11. Go to the Format tab in the ribbon. Open the top-left drop-down in the ribbon. Excel has automatically added Series 2 Y Error Bars and Series 2 X Error Bars. From the drop-down, choose Series 2 Y Error Bars. Press the Delete key to delete the vertical error bars.

12. In the same drop-down, choose Series 2 X Error Bars. Just below the drop-down, choose Format Selection. The Format Error Bars task pane appears.

13. In the task pane, click the Chart icon. In the Horizontal Error Bar category, choose a direction of Plus. Choose an End Style of No Cap. For the Error Amount, choose Fixed Value. Count the number of columns in your chart. Add one to the column count and use that for the fixed value. Because the current chart has seven columns, use eight for the Fixed Value. The task pane settings are shown in Figure 7.14.

Figure 7.14
From the invisible marker, draw an error bar extending eight columns to the right.

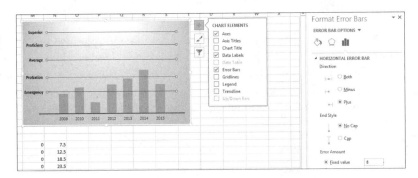

14. The error bars appear, looking just like gridlines, but unevenly spaced. While the error bars are selected, go to the Format tab in the ribbon. Open the Shape Outline drop-down. Open the Weight fly-out menu and choose 1/5 point.

The chart is shown in Figure 7.15. At this point, you can add a title or make other formatting changes.

If you try the steps a few times, this workaround starts to seem natural and almost poetic. The rogue XY series comes into play in the next example, which involves stacking many charts on a single chart.

Figure 7.15
Those gridlines are really plus error bars attached to an invisible XY marker.

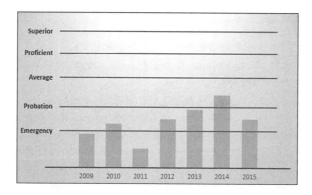

Showing Several Charts on One Chart by Using a Rogue XY Series

Figure 7.16 shows a single chart that appears to stack up four different charts. This chart is especially useful because one of the middle series, which is the subject of the chart, has a particularly low Q3 value. If you used a series of overlaid area charts, you would never be able to see the Q3 value in question. Note that it is important that all four charts in the stack have the same scale. Even with the current arrangement, it is difficult to compare one year to another. Which Q1 is largest? Without looking at the data, you cannot really tell.

The chart is actually a stack of seven area charts. The second, fourth, and sixth charts are invisible charts that are the complements to the first, third, and fifth charts. For example, if you have decided that the range for each chart should be 0 to 250, the formula for each point in the second series will be 250 minus the corresponding point in the first series.

Figure 7.16
The four stacked area charts are easy; getting the correct labels takes most of the work.

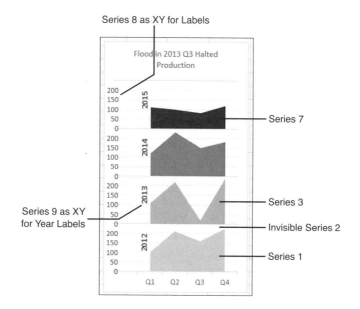

7

Follow these steps to set up the data for this chart stack:

1. Insert blank columns before years 2, 3, and 4.

2. The formula in the blank column should be 250 minus the column to the left. Copy this formula to all three blank columns.

3. Choose Insert, Recommended Charts. Across the top, choose the All Charts tab. Along the left, choose Area. From the Area chart icons, choose the second icon for Stacked Area. There are two chart previews available. Choose the second preview. (See Figure 7.17.) Caution: Using the Recommended Charts icon is better than choosing from the Stacked Area chart icon. If you choose from the Stacked Area icon, Excel 2013 plots the data with columns as the series, and the chart will be incorrect.

Figure 7.17
Insert three extra series to represent the whitespace between each chart.

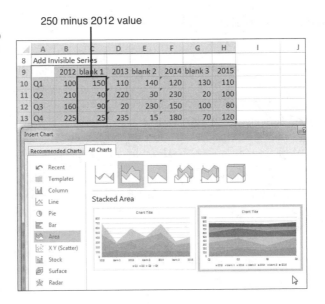

4. In the chart, click the Blank 1 series. From the Format tab, select Shape Fill, No Fill. Click the Blank 2 series. Press F4 to repeat the No Fill command. Repeat for Blank 3. You now have four stacked charts. The main problem is that the axis labels go from 0 to 1000 instead of repeating 0 to 250.

5. You are going to replace the vertical axis labels with scatter labels. Build a column of 0, 50, 100, ... 950. These values will be the height of the label. To the right of those numbers, repeat 0, 50, 100, 150, 200, 0, 50, ... as shown in Figure 7.18. This column will be the actual label that appears in the chart. To the left of the numbers, fill the column with zero. This is the location along the horizontal axis where the label will appear.

6. Copy the first two columns of the range from step 5. Press Ctrl+C to copy. Select the chart. Use Alt+E+S+F+Enter to Paste Special the data as a new series on the chart. The chart appears to be ruined. You will fix it in steps 7 and 8.

Figure 7.18
Paste a new XY series to hold the fake axis labels.

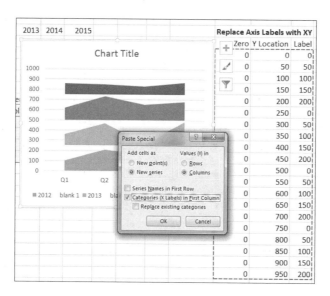

7. A large area chart extends to the right of the four smaller charts. Click this part of the chart to select Series8. If you are not sure that you have selected Series8, look in the first drop-down in the Format tab of the ribbon to see that Series8 is selected. Step 8 requires that only Series8 is selected.

Figure 7.19
Although it appears that your chart is ruined, select Series8.

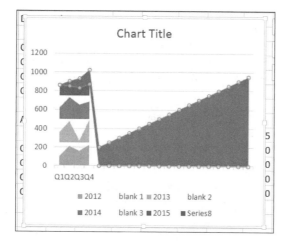

8. Make sure that only Series8 is selected. On the Design tab, choose Change Chart Type. In the Change Chart Type dialog, you should see All Charts, Combo, Custom Combination. At this point, all eight series should be listed as Stacked Area. If they are not, you did not have only Series8 selected. Click Cancel and go back to step 7. If all eight series are listed as Stacked Area, open the drop-down for Series8. Change the

7

chart type to Scatter. Excel defaults to using the Secondary Axis for Series8. Uncheck Secondary Axis. (See Figure 7.20.)

Figure 7.20
The dots along the left represent future axis labels.

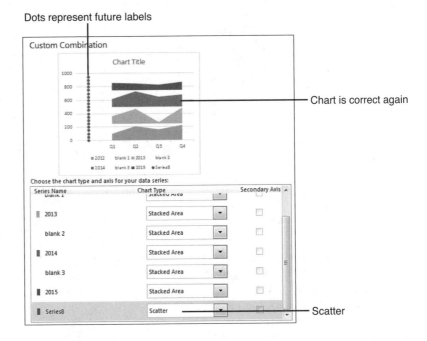

Dots represent future labels

Chart is correct again

Scatter

9. Repeats steps 5 and 6 to build a series to hold the year labels. This time, the X value is 0.3, the Y value is 150, 400, 650, 900, and the Labels are 2012, 2013, 2014, 2015. When you use Paste Special, Series9 appears as a scatter chart, so there is no need to repeat steps 7 and 8. Figure 7.21 shows the copied range and the new series markers on the chart.

Figure 7.21
Four dots will later hold the year labels.

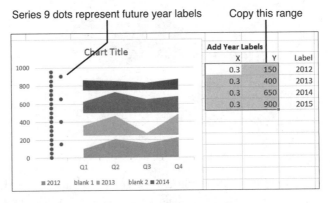

Series 9 dots represent future year labels   Copy this range

10. Double-click the numbers along the vertical axis to open the Format Axis task pane. In the task pane, choose the Chart icon. In the Axis Options category, set the minimum

to 0, Maximum to 1000, Major to 250, Minor to 50. In the same task pane, open the Labels category. Set the Label Position to None.

Believe it or not, you are almost done! You need to add and format labels for Series8, Series9, then hide the markers for those series. Steps 11 through 16 get the year markers on the chart. It is very important that you follow the sequence of these steps exactly.

11. Click one of the four Series9 markers to select Series 9. These are the four dots that appear to the left of Q1.

12. With Series9 selected, choose the Plus icon to the right of the chart and then choose Data Labels. Excel incorrectly adds data labels of 150, 400, 650, and 900. You should not delete those labels until you add new labels to replace them.

13. Open the Plus icon again. Hover over Data Labels until the fly-out arrow appears. Click the fly-out arrow and choose More Options to open the Format Data Labels task pane.

14. In the task pane, choose the Chart icon and then expand the Label Options category. Choose Value from Cells. Excel asks for the range that contains labels. Choose the range with 2012:2015. You now have labels that show both the year and the Y Value. Uncheck the Y Value in the task pane to leave only the Year label.

15. While the year labels are selected, go to the Home tab of the ribbon. In the Alignment group is a drop-down with a diagonal "ab" symbol. This is the Orientation drop-down. Open the drop-down and choose Rotate Text Up. If desired, make the year labels bold, change the font, font color, or size. At this point, you have the year label appearing, plus the Series9 marker. (See Figure 7.22.) You will get rid of the marker in step 16.

16. Getting rid of the Series9 markers requires five mouse clicks. Click one of the four dots to select Series9. The Format Data Series task pane appears. Click the Paint Bucket icon in the task pane. Two menu items appear below the Paint Bucket icon: Line and Marker. Click Marker. Click the Marker Options category to expand it. Change the Marker Options to None. You now have made Series9 invisible, except for the year labels.

Figure 7.22
The whole point of Series9 is to provide an X,Y location for the year labels.

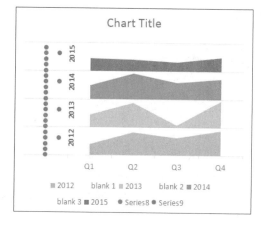

17. Repeat steps 11 through 14 and 16 to replace the Series8 markers with labels. In Step 11, click one of the Series8 markers. In step 14, use the range of 0, 50, 100, 150, 200 repeated four times. Also in step 14, choose a label location of Left of the marker.

18. Add minor gridlines. Click the Chart. Click the Plus icon. Expand the Gridlines fly-out menu. Primary Major Horizontal is already selected. Add Primary Minor Horizontal.

19. Extra series are appearing in the legend. It requires three clicks to remove each extra item from the legend. Click the legend to select it. Click blank 1 to select it. Press Delete. After deleting a legend entry, the legend becomes unselected. To delete the blank 2 from the legend, you have to click the legend, click blank 2, and press Delete. Continue deleting blank 3, Series8, Series9 from the legend. You now have a chart similar to Figure 7.23.

Figure 7.23
From here, you have simple formatting to finish the chart.

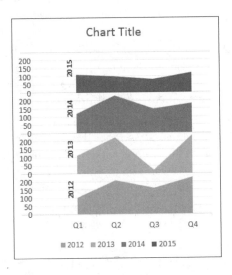

All that is left is to adjust the title, fill color, and location of the legend. To move the year labels closer to the area charts, increase the 0.3 X value next to each year to 0.5.

Creating Bullet Charts in Excel 2013

Charting guru Stephen Few has been promoting bullet charts as a space-saving alternative over dial charts. A bullet chart shows all the information typically in a dial chart:

■ The chart shows three (or more) ranges. These could be red/yellow/green or varying shades of gray.

■ A dark indicator shows the current value. You can see at a glance if the current value is in the red, yellow, or green zones.

■ An extra marker can either indicate the target or quota for the value, or show the same value from a prior period.

I am not a fan of bullet charts. Just like the thermometer chart shown later in this chapter, you are using massive amounts of ink to convey two or three pieces of information. Why not just display the current value and use conditional formatting to show the value in red, yellow, or green?

However, to Few's credit, the bullet chart does use less ink than the dial chart, so it is worthy of discussion here.

Figure 7.24 shows a horizontal bullet chart.

Figure 7.24
The current value for East sales is in the good zone and beyond the quota.

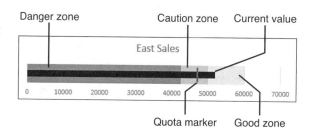

Bullet charts can also be created in a vertical orientation, as shown in Figure 7.25. The process for creating the quota marker is slightly different for vertical charts than for horizontal charts. (The process for creating the quota marker for both horizontal and vertical charts is described later in this section.)

Figure 7.25
A bullet chart can appear in a vertical orientation.

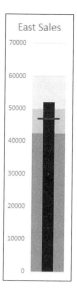

A bullet chart is composed of three series. The first and third series provides shading to highlight the danger, caution, and good zones of the chart. In Figure 7.26, these series are called One Side and Other Side. The formula for One Side uses the ranges in row 2 and calculates the incremental size of that zone. The formula for Other Side is a formula that copies One Side.

7

Figure 7.26
The first and third series provide the shading for the bullet chart.

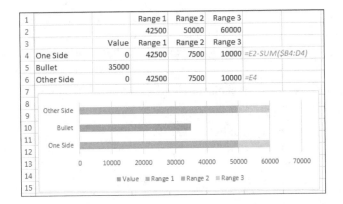

Double-click any part of the bullet chart to display the Format Series task pane. Set the Gap Width to zero to make the three series appear as a continuous field of color (see Figure 7.27).

Figure 7.27
Set the Gap Width to 0.

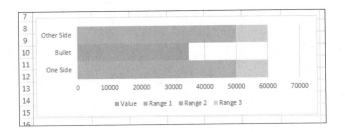

In Figure 7.27, the area beyond the bullet value is white. You need formulas to fill in the remaining bits of color after the bullet series. The formula in E5 starts out as =SUM($B4:E4)-SUM($B5:D5). This formula says to add up all the color ranges to this point and subtract all the bullet value and partial color ranges to the left of the current cell. In Figure 7.28, this works out great. The danger zone goes through 42,500. The bullet value is $35,000. Thus, you need another $7500 of the danger color to appear after the bullet.

In Figure 7.28, the chart uses a Line color of black around each series so you can visualize how the $7500, $7500, and $10,000 fill the whitespace to the right of the bullet.

However, that formula would fail in Figure 7.29. Here, the bullet value is $48,000. The formula would calculate that you need –$5500 of the danger zone color. You never want any numbers in the bullet chart to be negative. A great way to make sure that a number is positive is to take the MAX of zero and the formula. Thus, the formula in E5 is =MAX(SUM($B4:E4)-SUM($B5:D5),0). Copy this formula to C5 and D5.

The formulas in row 5 always fill in enough color after the bullet to appropriately fill the whitespace from Figure 7.27.

Figure 7.28
The formula in row 5 fills in the area to the right of the bullet.

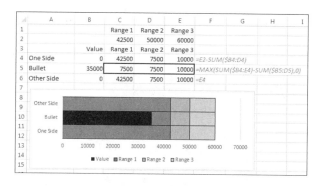

Figure 7.29
When the bullet value is in the caution zone, cell D5 calculates just enough of the caution color.

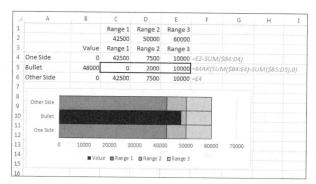

When the bullet value is in the good zone, C5 and D5 are zero. E5 calculates enough of the good color to fill the whitespace to the right of the bullet. (See Figure 7.30.)

Figure 7.30
When the bullet value is in the good zone, cell E5 calculates just enough of the good color to fill to the right of the bullet.

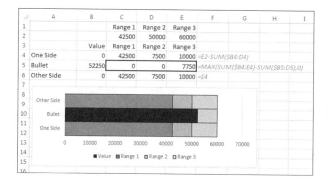

To finish the main portion of the chart, make the chart shorter. Remove the Shape Outlines from all series. The chart now looks almost like a Bullet chart. The only thing missing is the quota marker.

The quota marker is really a Y-Error bar drawn from a single-point scatter series. To draw the quota at 47,000, use an X value of 47000 and a Y value of 1. Copy those two cells. Select the chart and Paste Special. Choose New Series and Categories (X Labels) in First Column. Click OK. (See Figure 7.31.)

Figure 7.31
Create a single scatter point and paste to the chart as a new series.

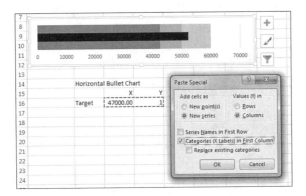

Follow these steps to format the quota marker:

1. In the ribbon, go to the Format tab. Choose Series 4 from the first drop-down in the Format tab.

2. Choose Design, Change Chart Type, Combo. Change Series 4 to a Scatter Chart. You are forced to have the series on the secondary axis because bar charts and scatter charts cannot use the same axis.

3. A new set of axis labels appears at the right side of the chart. Double-click those labels to display the Format Axis task pane. In the task pane, choose the Chart icon and then Axis Options. Set the Minimum to 0, the Maximum to 2, and the Major to 1.

4. Select Series 4 again.

5. Click the Plus icon and then choose Error Bars. This adds X-Error Bars and Y-Error Bars.

6. Open the first drop-down on the Format tab of the ribbon. Choose X-Error Bars to select them. Press the Delete key to delete the X-Error bar.

7. Open the first drop-down of the Format tab of the ribbon. Choose Y-Error Bars. Click the Format Selection icon in the ribbon to display the Format Error Bars task pane.

8. In the task pane, choose the Chart icon. The Direction should be Both. The End Style should be No Cap. Choose Fixed Amount and 0.75.

9. While the error bar is selected, choose Format, Shape Outline, Weight, 2.25 point to make the quota marker thicker.

10. Select Series 4 again. The task pane changes to Format Data Series. Click the Paint Bucket icon, then Marker, Marker Options, None. The bullet chart is nearly done, as shown in Figure 7.32.

11. You can click the 2, 1, 0 axis labels at the right side of the chart to select them; then press Delete to delete them.

Figure 7.32
After adding the quota marker, the chart is nearly complete.

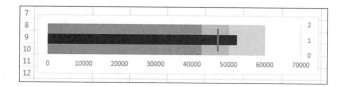

The process for creating a vertical bullet chart is similar to the previous steps. Choose a Stacked Column Chart instead of a bar chart. The data point for the quota marker shows 2 as the X-value and the quota as the Y-value. Paste the new data as a new series. When you select the combo chart, make Series 4 a scatter chart, but leave it on the primary axis. This time, you keep the X-Error bar and delete the Y-Error bar. The size of the X-Error bar is 1.0 in each direction.

Figure 7.33
For a vertical chart, the X value is 2 and the Y value is the quota.

	A	B	C
8			
9	Vertical Bullet Chart		
10		X	Y
11	Target	2	47000.00
12			
13	Horizontal Bullet Chart		
14		X	Y
15	Target	47000.00	1
16			

Creating a Thermometer Chart

A thermometer (see Figure 7.34) chart is a big way to display a single number. It is great for use on a dashboard display where you want everyone to see progress toward a goal.

Figure 7.34
This chart is a single column based on the number in cell A1.

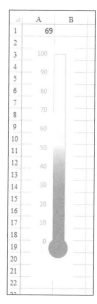

To create a thermometer chart like the one shown in Figure 7.34, follow these steps:

1. Enter a number between 0 and 100 in cell A1.

2. Select cell A1. From the Insert tab, select Recommended Chart, Clustered Column.

3. Click the number 1 below the chart. Press the Delete key to delete the Primary Horizontal Axis Label.

4. Click any gridline to select the gridlines. Press the Delete key to delete the gridlines.

5. Double-click the single column to display the Format Data Series task pane. Choose the Chart icon. Change Gap Width to 0%.

6. Click the Paint Bucket icon in the task pane. For the Fill, choose Gradient Fill. The Type is Linear. The direction is Linear Down (the second icon in the Direction drop-down). The Angle is 90%.

7. You want four gradient stops. You initially start with 2 or 3 symbols under Gradient Stops. Click the + symbol in the Gradient Stops area until you have four gradient stops. (See Figure 7.35.) You have to click each Gradient Stop symbol and set the settings as follows.

8. For the first gradient stop, leave the color as white and the position at 0%.

9. For the second gradient stop, the color is yellow. The position is 25%.

10. For the third gradient stop, the color is orange. The position is 60%.

11. For the fourth gradient stop, the color is red. The position is 100%.

Figure 7.35

Set up the gradient.

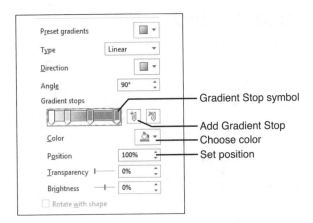

12. Select Plot Area from the drop-down on the Format tab. Choose Shape Outline and choose an orange color.

13. Select the chart area and format the Shape Outline as No Outline.

14. Delete the Chart Title.

15. Resize the chart area so that it is narrow and long.

16. Double-click the numbers along the vertical axis. In the Format Axis task pane, choose the Chart icon, Axis Options. Change Minimum to 0, Maximum to 100, and Major to 10.

17. With the axis labels still selected, select Font Color and then select orange on the Home tab.

18. Select the plot area. Drag the bottom resizing handles up so that there is space between the bottom of the plot area and the bottom of the chart area.

19. From the Insert tab, select Shapes, Basic Shapes and then select an oval. Hold down the Shift key while you draw a circle at the bottom of the chart. Note that the Shift key forces the oval shape to be drawn as a circle.

20. From the Format tab, select Shape Fill, and then select red for the ball at the bottom of the thermometer.

Creating a Benchmark Chart

A benchmark chart shows sales for each period as a column chart. The quota, goal, or benchmark for the period is shown as a cap. If the sales exactly meet the quota, the sales column fits perfectly into the cap. If sales fell short of the quota, you see some whitespace between the cap and the column.

Follow these steps to create a benchmark chart like the one in Figure 7.36:

1. Enter Months in column A, Sales in column B, and Quota in column C.

2. Create a clustered 2D column chart from the data. Delete the legend. Delete the Chart Title.

3. Click the Quota series in the chart. From the Design tab, select Change Chart Type. Select the Combo category. Change the Chart Type for Quota to Scatter. Uncheck Secondary Axis. Click OK. You now have a marker dot where each quota should be.

4. Click one of the quota data markers to select that series. Use the Plus icon to the right of the chart. First, choose Error Bars. Then expand the Error Bars menu and choose More Options to display the Format Error Bar task pane. In the task pane, choose the Chart icon. Choose Cap. Choose Fixed Value of 0.2. In the ribbon, choose Format, Shape Outline, Weight, 2.25 width.

5. Select Series Quota Y Error Bars from the current selection drop-down. Press the Delete key to delete the Y error bars.

6. Select Series Quota from the Current Selection drop-down. In the task pane, choose the Paint Bucket icon, then Marker, Marker Options, None.

7

Figure 7.36
The horizontal markers on each column indicate where the quota had been for that month.

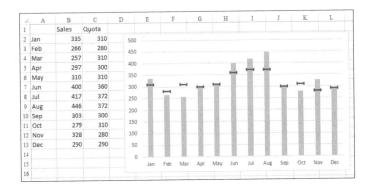

Creating a Delta Chart

You can use a delta chart to plot revenue and a quota as line charts. A special data marker appears halfway between the two lines to show the percentage of quota (see Figure 7.37). The hard part of creating a delta chart is getting the labels to float halfway between the two lines.

Figure 7.37
The labels automatically float halfway between the two lines.

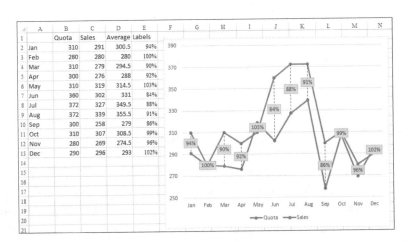

Follow these steps to create a delta chart:

1. Set up a data set with months in column A, quota in column B, and sales in column C.

2. In column D, enter the following formula to average revenue and quota:

   `=AVERAGE(B2:C2)`

   This is the location point for the data label. Copy the formula down the column.

3. In column E, enter the formula `=C2/B2` to hold the label. This formula shows the percentage to quota. Format the results as a percentage with zero decimal places and copy the formula down the column.

4. Create a chart from cells A1:D13. From the Insert tab, select Recommended Chart, All Charts, Line, Line with Markers.

5. Double-click the labels along the vertical axis. In the Format Axis task pane, choose the Chart icon, Axis Options. Specify appropriate Minimum and Maximum values. For the chart in Figure 7.37, you could use 250 and 390.

6. Select Series Average from the Current Selection drop-down on the Layout tab. In the Format Data Series task pane, choose the Paint Bucket icon. Choose Line, No Line. Choose Marker, No Marker.

7. Click the Plus icon to the right of the chart. Choose Data Labels. Expand the Data Labels menu and choose More Options. In the Format Data Labels task pane, choose Value from Cells. Specify E2:E13 as the range with label values. Uncheck Value. For the Label Position, choose Center.

8. While the labels are selected, choose Format, Shape Fill, light orange. Choose Format, Shape Outline, dark orange.

9. You need to add High-Low lines, but these are not available from the Plus icon to the right of the chart. Instead, go to the Design tab in the ribbon. Use the Add Chart Element drop-down. Choose Lines, High-Low Lines. Excel draws lines from the Quota to the Sales.

10. Select High-Low Lines 1 from the Current Selection drop-down on the Format tab. After the lines are selected, use Format, Shape Outline, Dashes, and choose a dashed line.

11. Click the Average entry in the legend. The first click selects the whole legend. The second click selects just the Average entry. Press Delete to remove that entry.

Next Steps

In Chapter 8, "Creating Pivot Charts and Power View Dashboards," you learn how to summarize thousands of rows of detailed data into a summary chart and then show those charts in a dashboard.

7

Creating Pivot Charts and Power View Dashboards

8

Pivot tables are the most powerful feature in Excel. A pivot table enables you to summarize a million records of transactional data in Excel with a few mouse clicks. A pivot chart is an extension of the pivot table concept. You start with detailed data, Excel summarizes that data in a pivot table, and then the summary data is charted.

Pivot charts are easier than ever to create thanks to the Recommended Charts feature in Excel 2013. You can go from a detailed data set to a summary chart in a few clicks. From there, even if the recommended chart is not exactly what you envisioned, you can quickly add or remove fields.

IN THIS CHAPTER

Creating a PivotChart Using
Recommended Charts 223

Using PowerPivot and Power View 232

Next Steps 247

Creating a PivotChart Using Recommended Charts

The data set in Figure 8.1 has more than 500 rows of transactional data with Sector, Region, Product, Date, Customer, Quantity, Revenue, COGS, and Profit. In the past, creating a chart from this data would lead to absolute chaos.

However, starting in Excel 2013, you can select one cell in the data. Use Insert, Recommended Charts. The Insert Chart dialog offers eight choices. The first six are pivot charts. The last two charts are chaos, just in case you were trying to create a chart with 500+ points.

The first chart is Sum of Profit by Sector. Not a bad guess.

The next five charts are

- Sum of Revenue by Region
- Sum of Revenue by Product
- Sum of Profit by Product

■ Sum of Quantity by Region

■ Sum of Profit by Region

A little reverse engineering of the algorithm suggests that Excel is looking for text columns with very few unique values. This is why Sector, Region, and Product are the "by" fields. Then Excel offers to show the sum of various numeric fields by those text fields. Excel definitely prefers fields called Revenue and Profit. If you try the same steps on an identical data set with random headings instead of Revenue and Profit, you will get different suggestions.

I always want the Recommend Chart algorithm to offer Revenue by Customer, but because I have 26 unique customers, it is never offered. But that is okay. It is easy enough to accept Profit by Sector and to swap out Revenue for Profit and Customer for Sector.

As shown in Figure 8.1, anytime you see the Pivot icon on the chart thumbnail, you will be getting a pivot chart.

Figure 8.1
Go ahead, create a chart from this detailed data.

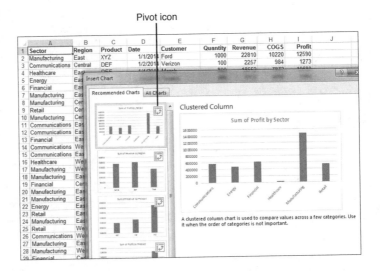

After you click OK to accept the recommended chart, you land on a new worksheet to the left of the original data. Excel inserted this worksheet for you. There is a lot to notice in Figure 8.2:

■ Your pivot chart showing Sum of Profit by Sector is in C3:J19.

■ The range in A3:B9 is the pivot table that Excel created to summarize the original records. Don't delete this, because your chart is based on it.

■ Three new ribbon tabs with the heading PivotChart Tools appear when you have the chart selected. The Analyze tab contains tools for pivoting. The Design and Format tabs are like the Chart Tools tabs.

■ A PivotChart Fields pane appears. Notice that Sector and Profit are checked. If you uncheck Sector and Profit and choose Customer and Revenue, your chart and pivot table change to summarize Revenue by Customer. (However, you have to manually edit the chart title.)

Figure 8.2
Use the check boxes to change what data is summarized in the chart.

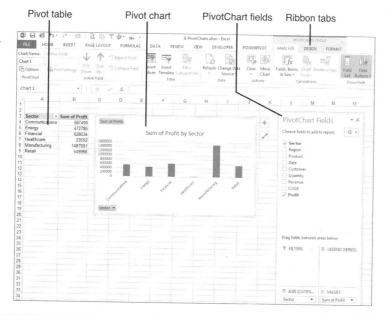

Pivot table   Pivot chart   PivotChart fields   Ribbon tabs

T I P   By default, the pivot chart and the associated pivot table are created on the same worksheet. This is a welcome improvement: You can now easily see the relationship between the pivot table and the pivot chart. If you want to print only the pivot chart, you can either set the print range to include just the chart, select the chart before printing, or you can select the Charting Tools Analyze tab and then select the Move Chart icon to move the pivot chart to a new worksheet.

Changing the Fields in the Pivot Chart

When the pivot chart is selected, you can adjust the fields in the PivotChart Fields pane to change the report.

Suppose you wanted to replace Profit with Revenue. It takes two clicks. You check Revenue and clear the check mark from Profit.

Figure 8.3 shows the pivot chart after checking Revenue. Wait—this chart looks pretty good! Maybe your manager would like to see this instead.

To remove Profit from the chart, uncheck the Profit field from the top of the PivotChart Fields pane.

8

Figure 8.3
Halfway to replacing
profit with revenue, this
intermediate chart looks
useful, too.

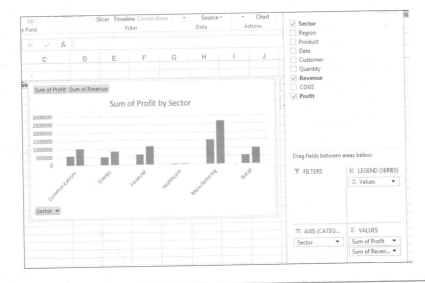

> **NOTE**
>
> As an aside, if you were really planning to use the chart in Figure 8.3, you should add a legend, change
> the title, and reverse the order of Profit and Revenue. The first two items have been covered through-
> out this book. Reversing the order of Profit and Revenue is simple. In the bottom-right corner of the
> PivotChart Fields, two tiles appear in the Values drop zone. Simply drag the Sum of Profit tile down and
> drop it beneath Sum of Reven...

You now have a chart summarizing the detail data set, showing sales by sector. The sectors
appear alphabetically, with Communications, Energy, and Financial appearing first. The
chart might have more impact if it was sorted so the largest sectors appeared first.

Sorting the Pivot Chart

The pivot chart has Field Buttons on the chart. The Field Buttons have come and gone
over the various versions of Excel. They were gone in Excel 2007, back in 2010, and continue to appear in Excel 2013.

My first step with any new pivot chart is to remove the field buttons by toggling the Field
Buttons icon in the Analyze tab of the ribbon. However, it happens that the Sector field
button assists in changing the sort order of the pivot chart. If you have not hidden the field
buttons, you can change the sort order by following these steps:

1. Open the Sector drop-down on the Pivot Chart.
2. Choose More Sort Options. Excel displays the Sort (Sector) dialog.
3. Choose Descending.
4. Open the drop-down below Descending. Change from Sector to Sum of Revenue. (See
   Figure 8.4.)
5. Click OK.

Figure 8.4
Change the sort order of a pivot chart.

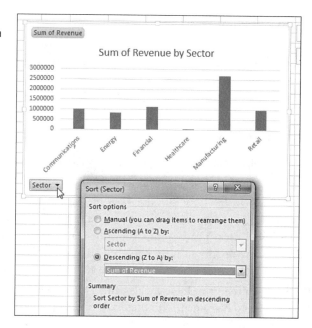

Figure 8.5
The sectors appear with the largest sector first.

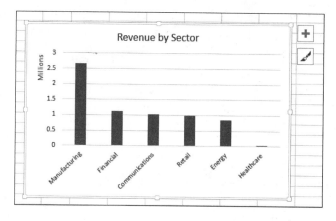

The sectors are now sorted with Manufacturing first, Financial second, and so on. (See Figure 8.5.)

It is easy to format your chart using the methods described in Chapters 1 and 2 of this book. In Figure 8.5, the vertical scale is shown in Millions. Just as with a regular chart, you double-click the axis and in the Format Axis task pane, choose the Chart icon and change the Display Units drop-down to Millions.

Grouping Daily Dates in the Pivot Chart

Because the pivot chart is created from detailed data, your dates will often be daily instead of being summarized by month, quarter, or year. Pivot tables make it very easy to group daily dates up to months, quarters, or years.

The icon that is used to group dates is missing from the PivotChart Tools Analyze tab. Expect this to happen a lot. It is not a problem, because you can quickly switch to the pivot table tools to make the change.

Follow these steps to roll daily dates up to years and add years as an axis field to the pivot chart:

1. Up to this point, the chart has been selected. Instead, choose a cell inside the pivot table, such as A3 or B4. Two important things happen. First, the PivotChart Fields pane changes to PivotTable Fields. The Legend drop zone is now Columns. The Axis drop zone is now Rows. More importantly, the three PivotChart Tools tabs in the ribbon change to two PivotTable Tools tabs. You now have access to more commands.

2. Check the Date field in the PivotTable Fields pane. Don't even look at the chart, because it now appears to be ruined, with hundreds of data points across the horizontal axis.

3. Choose any date cell in the pivot table. In Figure 8.6, cell B4 is selected.

4. Choose the Group Field icon in the Analyze tab of the ribbon.

Figure 8.6
The pivot table tools offer Group Field for grouping dates.

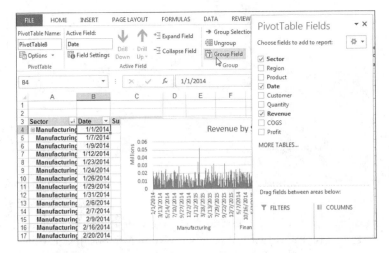

5. The Grouping dialog lets you group by Months, Quarters, and Years. Months is the default. Choose Years instead, as shown in Figure 8.7. Click OK.

   The result shown in Figure 8.8 is a little strange. Both Sector and Date are stacked as Rows fields. This is not what you want, but it is almost what you want.

Figure 8.7
Group the dates by Years.

Figure 8.8
The Date field now contains years.

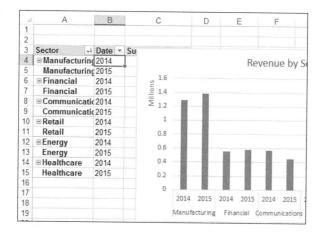

6. Select the Chart. The PivotChart Fields pane returns.

7. Drag the Date field from the Axis drop zone to the Legend drop zone.

The resulting chart (see Figure 8.9) now shows a legend comparing 2014 to 2015. The horizontal axis shows only the Sector values.

Figure 8.9
Pivot the Date field to the Legend drop zone.

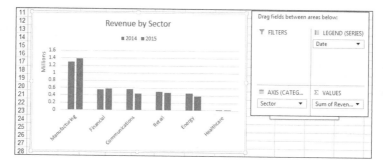

> **NOTE** Why is the chart in Figure 8.9 better than the chart in Figure 8.8? In Figure 8.9, you could use the Change Chart Type icon in the Design tab to change the chart to a stacked chart instead of a clustered column chart. This doesn't particularly make sense in this case, but in other cases it might.

Filtering Pivot Charts Using the Filter Fly-out Menu

You might have noticed that the Filter icon is missing from the right side of the pivot chart. Although you cannot filter using the Filter icon, there are more powerful ways to filter a pivot chart.

For fields in the pivot table, you can use the Filter fly-out menus available in the pivot table.

For example, the Top Ten filter enables you to limit a pivot chart to show the top or bottom values. Change the pivot chart from Figure 8.9 to show all customers instead of sectors. Follow these steps:

1. Uncheck Sector from the PivotChart Fields.
2. Check Customer from the PivotChart Fields.
3. Open the Customer drop-down in the pivot table. Choose More Sort Options. Sort Descending by Sum of Revenue.

You now have a chart with too many customers to be useful. You want to filter the chart to show only the top customers.

1. Open the Customer drop-down in the pivot table.
2. Choose Value Filters.
3. From the Value Filter fly-out menu, Choose Top 10. Excel displays the Top 10 Filter dialog.
4. In the Top 10 Filter, choose Top, 5, Items, by Sum of Revenue. Click OK.

You now have a report and chart showing the top five customers.

Filtering Pivot Charts Using Slicers

Excel 2010 introduced a new visual filter called a Slicer. These new filters are highly visual. They beckon the person reading your workbook to click the filter to do ad hoc analyses on the report.

The best part is that a single slicer can filter multiple pivot tables and pivot charts. Here is how to set up a slicer for the Sector field:

1. With the pivot table selected, choose Insert Slicer from the Analyze tab.
2. Choose Sector and click OK.
3. Excel draws a default one-column slicer in the middle of your screen.
4. Click the slicer to select it. A Slicer Tools Option tab appears in the ribbon.

5. In the Slicer Tools Options, change the Columns to 3. Resize the slicer to allow all the sector names to appear in a three row by two column arrangement.

Figure 8.10 shows the slicer and the chart. To see the customers for a single sector, choose that sector. To see the customers for a contiguous range of sectors, click the first sector and drag to the last sector. For noncontiguous sectors, choose the first one and then Ctrl+click on the other sectors.

Figure 8.10
As you choose Sectors from the slicer, the chart and pivot table update.

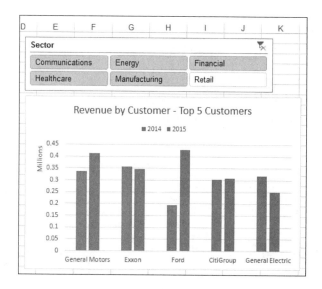

Connecting Multiple Pivot Charts to One Slicer

When you create a second pivot table from the same data set, Excel assumes that both pivot tables will share the same pivot cache in memory. Provided that multiple pivot tables use the same pivot cache, they can share the same set of slicers. This requires a few extra steps to set up.

1. Go back to the original data set.
2. Select a cell in that data set.
3. On the Insert tab, click the PivotChart icon. Excel displays the Create PivotChart dialog.
4. Change the location to an Existing Worksheet.
5. Click the RefEdit icon at the right side of the Location box. Click the worksheet where the first pivot chart is located. Choose a blank spot below the first pivot chart.
6. Build a new pivot chart.
7. Select a cell in the second pivot table.
8. From the Analyze tab, choose Filter Connections. Excel displays the Filter Connections dialog as shown in Figure 8.11.

9. In the Filter Connections dialog, choose the Sector filter. Click OK.

Figure 8.11
Connect the second pivot chart to the slicer.

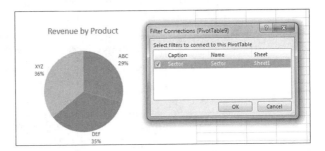

The one slicer now drives both pivot charts, as shown in Figure 8.12. You can continue creating new pivot charts from the same data set and hooking those pivot charts up to the slicer. This is a great way to build an impromptu dashboard.

Figure 8.12
Two pivot charts are now filtered by the same slicer.

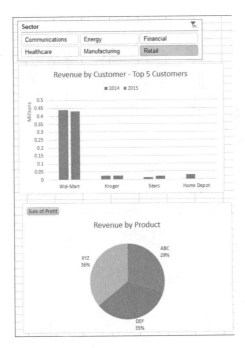

Using PowerPivot and Power View

Your version of Excel 2013 might not have the two features described in the rest of this chapter. Microsoft is competing with expensive Business Intelligence tools and introduced PowerPivot and Power View add-ins to provide amazing functionality. However, these add-ins are not included with Excel RT on the Surface, nor with Office 2013 Home & Student, nor with Excel 2013 Standard. To use these add-ins, you need Office 2013 Pro Plus or a subscription to Office 365.

In a nutshell, the new add-ins perform these functions:

- PowerPivot enables you to create a relational model, linking worksheets without doing VLOOKUP.
- Power View combines pivot tables, charting, mapping, product images, tables, slicers, filters, and a date animation in a single screen-sized canvas. The data source for Power View is the relational model stored in PowerPivot.

Enabling PowerPivot and Power View

If you have a qualifying version of Excel 2013, both add-ins were installed but not enabled. Follow these steps to enable the add-ins:

1. Select File, Options. In the Options dialog, choose Add-Ins from the left navigation.
2. At the bottom of the Options dialog is a drop-down for Manage Add-Ins. Choose COM Add-ins from the drop-down and click Go.
3. In the COM Add-Ins dialog, choose Microsoft Office PowerPivot for Excel 2013. Also choose Power View for Excel Add-In. (If you are missing either item, you have to upgrade to Excel 2013 Pro Plus.) Click OK.

When PowerPivot is successfully installed, you have a new PowerPivot tab in the ribbon. When Power View is installed, you see a Power View icon between Charts and Sparklines in the Insert tab.

Loading Your Excel Data to PowerPivot

You probably have data in the Excel grid. You need to load the data in the Excel grid into the PowerPivot grid and define relationships. This takes just a few minutes per table.

The data set used for the rest of this chapter is an ugly transactional data set with more than 400,000 records. The data covers 10 years of product sales. Typical of most data sets created by the I.T. department, each record has bizarre codes in fields, such as ProdID and GeoID instead of real product and region names.

You, however, have lookup tables that convert the ProdID code to a real product name, along with category and price information. Another lookup table converts the GeoID to a state and region, and maybe a regional manager. Figure 8.13 shows three worksheets in the workbook.

For each table, follow these steps to load the table to PowerPivot:

1. Select a cell in the data set.
2. Press Ctrl+T to declare the data as a Table. Confirm that the data has headers, confirm the range, and click OK. Excel applies some formatting to the table and a new Table Tools Design tab appears in the ribbon.

Figure 8.13
Your data includes a detailed data set and lookup tables for Product and Geography.

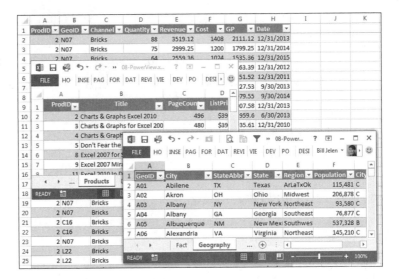

3. Each table is assigned a sequential name, such as Table1, Table2, Table3, and so on. Go to the Table Tools Design tab and type a meaningful name for each table. Your main table can be called Data or Fact. The lookup tables can be Geography and Products.

4. After naming the table, go to the PowerPivot tab in the Excel ribbon. Click the Add to Data Model icon. Excel prepares the PowerPivot window, and then you see the data in the PowerPivot grid.

5. You need to leave the PowerPivot grid and return to the Excel workbook. You can use the X to close the PowerPivot window. Or look in the top left of the PowerPivot window. The first little green icon is the PowerPivot icon. The second little green icon is the Return to Excel icon.

6. Continue loading the next table to PowerPivot.

Adding a Date Lookup Table

You should create one extra lookup table to convert the daily dates to years, quarters, and/or months. This step always seems extraneous because both the Excel grid and the PowerPivot DAX formula language offer functions to convert a daily date up to months and years.

However, using a lookup table for dates enables some cool time intelligence functions in the DAX formula language. DAX isn't covered here, but by the time you graduate to Rob Collie's *DAX Formulas for PowerPivot* (ISBN 978-1-61547-015-0; Holy Macro! Books), it is best if you have already built the models to include the date table.

Follow these steps to create the date lookup table:

1. Insert a new worksheet in your workbook to hold the date lookup.

2. Copy the date column from your main data table and paste to column A of the new worksheet.

3. Select column A in the new worksheet and use Data, Remove Duplicates, OK to get just one occurrence of each date.

4. Add a Year heading in B1. The formula in B2 is `=YEAR(A2)`. Copy the formula to all date records.

5. Add a Quarter heading in C1. One formula to create quarters is `=YEAR(A2)&"Q"&CHOOSE (MONTH(A2),1,1,1,2,2,2,3,3,3,4,4,4)`.

6. Normally, you would add a MonthNumber and MonthName column. MonthNumber is `=MONTH(A2)`. MonthName is `=TEXT(A2,"MMM")`. However, the 400K row data set in this example includes only one row per product per city per quarter. Thus, adding month names would not be useful for this particular data set.

7. Follow the steps in the previous section to convert the date lookup worksheet and add it as a table in PowerPivot.

Format Your Data in PowerPivot

Pivot table veterans have always complained that pivot tables ignore the numeric formatting of the underlying data. The Excel team continues to ignore this issue. However, the PowerPivot team respects the numeric formatting that you apply in the PowerPivot window.

From Excel, go to the PowerPivot tab and click the Manage icon. This takes you to the PowerPivot window. In the PowerPivot window is a new ribbon with tabs for Home, Design, Advanced, and Linked Table. At the bottom of the window are four worksheet tabs: one for Fact, DateTable, Geography, and Products.

Go through each worksheet, looking for numeric fields that you might include in your charts. Select a cell in the column. On the Home tab in the PowerPivot ribbon, use the Format drop-down to apply the proper format.

On the Advanced tab in PowerPivot is a Reporting Properties group with a Data Category drop-down. If you have columns that represent geography, product, web addresses, or image files, you should select that column and declare the Data Category as appropriate. In the Geography table, fields can be categorized for City, State, or Province. In the Products table, you can mark the Product Name category with a category of Product. Note that Product is not in the drop-down. You have to choose More Categories, All, and then choose Product.

Select the DateTable tab in PowerPivot. On the Design tab, open the Mark as Date Table drop-down and then choose the redundant Mark as Date Table command (see Figure 8.14). You have to specify which column contains a date field and contains only unique dates.

Figure 8.14
Declare the date lookup table as a date table.

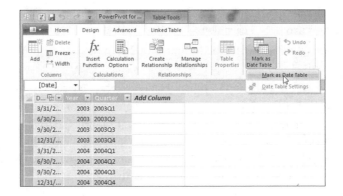

VLOOKUPs? Replacing VLOOKUPs with Relationships

If you are a VLOOKUP guru, you are ready to join all the tables using millions of VLOOKUP formulas, right? One of the benefits of PowerPivot is that you do not have to do millions of VLOOKUPs. Instead, you define a relationship for each lookup table.

Follow these steps to define a relationship from the main table to the lookup table.

1. You want to create a link from the GeoID column in the Fact table to the GeoID column in the Geography column. In the PowerPivot grid, go to the Fact table and select one cell in the GeoID column.

2. On the Design tab in the PowerPivot ribbon, choose Create Relationship. PowerPivot displays the Create Relationship dialog. There are four drop-downs, but because you selected the cell in step 1, the first two drop-downs are already filled in correctly.

3. Open the Related Lookup Table drop-down and choose the Geography table. PowerPivot automatically chooses GeoID as the Related Lookup Column.

Figure 8.15 shows the completed Create Relationship dialog.

Figure 8.15
Instead of VLOOKUP, create a relationship.

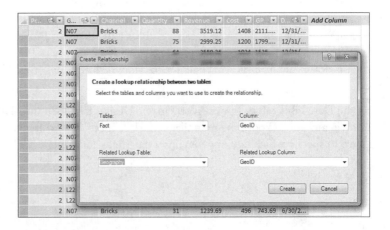

Repeat these steps to define a relationship from ProdID to the Product table. Also define a relationship from the Date field to the DateTable table.

> **TIP**
>
> Creating relationships is fast. There is no waiting for millions of cells to calculate. I love VLOOKUP, but even I have to admit that creating relationships is so much easier than millions of VLOOKUPs.

After you are done defining the relationships and the categories, close the PowerPivot window to return to Excel.

Creating a Power View Worksheet

A Power View dashboard is just another worksheet in your workbook. Go to the Insert tab in the ribbon and choose Power View (see Figure 8.16). A new worksheet is inserted to the left of the current worksheet. The worksheet is given a name, such as Power View1. You can right-click the sheet tab to delete it the same as a worksheet. You can drag to move it to a new location. It is just like a worksheet.

Figure 8.16
Choose Power View from the Insert tab.

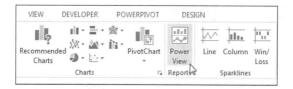

The Power View window contains a Power View Field List, sort of like the PivotTable Field List on the right side. A large blank canvas appears on the left. A collapsible Filters panel appears to the right of the canvas (see Figure 8.17). As you work with Power View, several ribbon tabs related to Power View will come and go. If you see a tab to the right of the Power View tab labeled Formatting, Text, or Analyze, it is related to Power View. These tabs are not labeled as Power View Tools Design like every other contextual tab.

Figure 8.17
A new Power View window.

Blank canvas   Filter pane   Field list

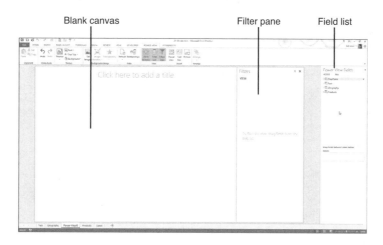

Every New Dashboard Element Starts as a Table

Expand one of the data tables in the Field List and choose any field. That field flies over to a new element on the canvas. Every new element starts as a table. You can change an element to something else, but it starts as a table.

The active element has four L-shaped gray corners. If you choose another field from the Field list, that field is added to the active element. Figure 8.18 shows the table created by choosing Year and Revenue.

Figure 8.18
The Field List shows settings for the active element.

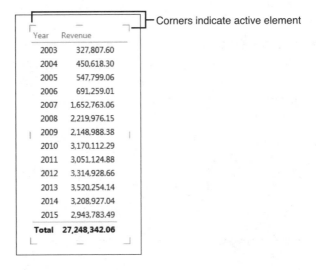

Corners indicate active element

Year	Revenue
2003	327,807.60
2004	450,618.30
2005	547,799.06
2006	691,259.01
2007	1,652,763.06
2008	2,219,976.15
2009	2,148,988.38
2010	3,170,112.29
2011	3,051,124.88
2012	3,314,928.66
2013	3,520,254.14
2014	3,208,927.04
2015	2,943,783.49
Total	**27,248,342.06**

Converting the Table to a Chart

With the first table selected, you see a Design tab in the ribbon. The left group in this tab is called Switch Visualization. There are 13 choices in four drop-downs and the Map icon. The Column Chart drop-down offers Stacked, 100% Stacked, and Clustered Column charts. The Other Chart drop-down offers Line, Scatter, and Pie charts (see Figure 8.19).

Figure 8.19
Convert the default table to a chart or a map.

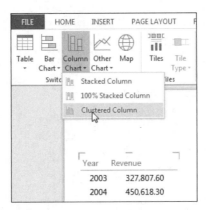

For now, choose a stacked column chart. The element stays the same size, and Power View tries to fit a chart in that small area. It doesn't fit, as you can see Figure 8.20.

Figure 8.20
The converted chart doesn't fit in the previous space.

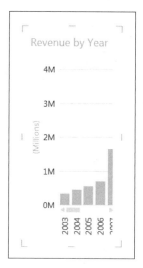

Click one of the eight resize handles and stretch the element frame until the chart looks good. At this view, shown in Figure 8.21, you see several interactive elements:

- A drop-down lets you choose how to sort the chart. In this case, sorting by ascending years is really the only way that makes sense, but you could sort by Revenue descending to have the highest years at the left.
- The Funnel icon takes you to the Filters panel. You could choose to show only years greater than $1.5 million to get rid of the start-up years of a product.
- The pop-out icon makes the element temporarily display at full screen. Suppose you have 10 small elements on the dashboard. You can click the pop-out icon to make one of the small elements full screen. After the element is full screen, a pop-in icon returns the element to the original size.

In the Field List, drag the Channel field to the Legend area. The chart becomes a stacked chart showing book sales by Online, eBook, and Brick and Mortar stores (see Figure 8.22). Notice that the legend starts on the right, which takes up some space. Power View automatically staggers the years along the horizontal axis to get them to fit.

Although a chart is selected, a Layout tab appears in the ribbon. Using the Layout tab, you can move the legend to the top, add data labels, or change the type of horizontal axis.

Figure 8.21
Several subtle controls appear to add interactivity.

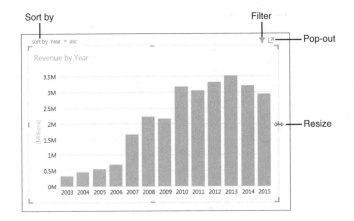

Figure 8.22
Add a field to the Legend area in the Field List to create a stacked column chart.

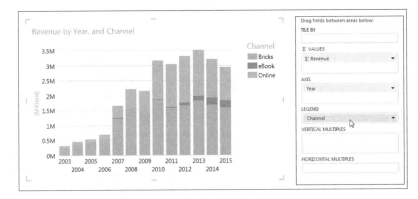

Creating a New Element by Dragging

To add a new element to the dashboard, you drag a field from the Field List and drop it in a blank portion of the canvas. Just as with the first element, this element starts as a small table. You can switch it to a chart, resize it, and add more fields. Keep adding new elements as necessary.

You can also create a new element by copying and pasting an existing element. If you have designed one chart, right-click that chart and choose Copy. Click in a blank area of the canvas and paste. You can now change the fields in the Field List to change the chart.

The next bit is magic.

Every Chart Point Is a Slicer for Every Other Element

In Figure 8.23, three charts appear on the canvas. The top-left chart shows revenue by year by channel. The bottom-left chart shows revenue by year by version. The top-right chart is a pie chart showing total revenue by version.

If you click any part of any chart, all the other charts are filtered to the same element. The mouse pointer is clicking the Excel 2010 version in the pie chart. The other two charts instantly update. All the non-2010 portions of the columns are faded, leaving only the colored portions as bright.

You can select the original chart element again to turn the filter off.

Figure 8.23
All elements are connected. Click a pie wedge, and the other charts highlight the corresponding data.

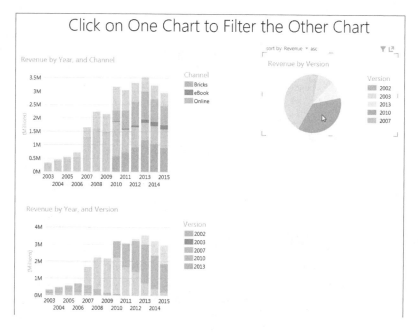

Adding a Real Slicer

The slicers in Power View look different from regular slicers, but they act the same way. To create a slicer, drag a field to a blank area of the canvas. That field starts out as a new table. Go to the Design tab of the ribbon and choose Slicer. The table is converted to a Power View slicer (see Figure 8.24).

Notice these differences from a regular slicer:

■ A colored square next to an item means the item is selected.

■ You can click one item to select that one item.

■ To select multiple items, you have to Ctrl+click the other items.

■ The slicer is always one column. You cannot rearrange slicers in Power View the way you can in a regular pivot table.

■ An eraser icon appears in the top right of the slicer. This is the Clear Filter icon. It is equivalent to the Funnel with X icon in a regular slicer.

Figure 8.24
A slicer on the canvas controls all elements on the canvas.

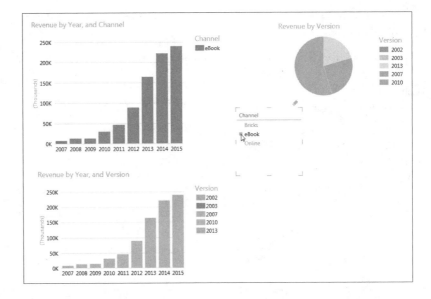

The Filter Pane Can Be Confusing

The last two sections show you how to filter the canvas. There is also a filter pane. The Filter pane includes a category for View, Chart, or Table. The Chart or Table category appears only when an individual chart or table element is active.

> **CAUTION**
>
> There are two really important distinctions when working with the Filter pane. The first involves how Power View calculates the filter:
>
> - When you are working with a Chart filter, you are filtering at the summary level. Ask for years greater than $1.5 million and you get only the years with a total yearly revenue over $1.5 million.
>
> - When you are working with the View filter, you are filtering at the detail row level. Apply a filter where Revenue is greater than $100 and Power View goes back to the original 411,000 records and rolls up only the records greater than $100.

The other distinction is not as confusing. Filters applied to the view affect all elements in the view. Filters applied to a chart affect only the active chart.

The Filter pane for Chart or Table starts with the fields in the chart or table. The Filter pane for View is always an empty canvas. You have to drag fields from the top of the Field List to the Filter pane.

Use Tile Boxes to Filter One or a Group of Charts

The Power View Field List offers a field called Tile By that provides another way to filter an element on the dashboard.

Select a chart or table that you want to filter. In the Field List, hover over the filter field. A drop-down menu appears. Open the drop-down and choose Add as Tile By.

The filter appears as a category list across the top of the chart. Notice the thick blue lines above and below the chart. These lines tell you that only the one chart between the lines is affected by the Tile categories (see Figure 8.25).

Figure 8.25
Only the elements between the tile boundary lines are filtered by the Tile category filters.

Title categories

Title boundaries

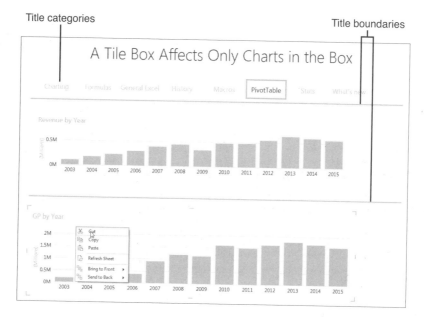

Tiles are good. They provide a way to filter one chart and not the other charts. But I can already sense that you will want to have two charts controlled by a single Tile. Fortunately, this can be done.

In Figure 8.25, right-click the element that is outside of the boundary and choose Cut. Click anywhere inside the Tile boundary lines, right-click, and paste. The result will inevitably be two charts right on top of each other. Drag the bottom boundary line to add some room. Then individually move the two charts so they fit. The result is shown in Figure 8.26. Both of these charts are within the boundary lines, so they are both controlled by the category filters at the top.

Figure 8.26
Both elements are within the boundary lines and they are filtered together.

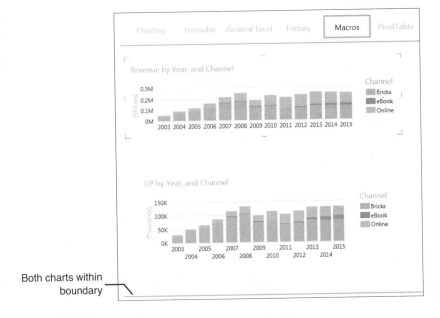

Both charts within boundary

Replicating Charts Using Multiples

Suppose you have a chart element that shows revenue by year. You could add a new field to the Legend area to create a stacked or clustered column chart.

Alternatively, you can drag the new field to the Vertical Multiples or Horizontal Multiples field. This causes Power View to replicate the chart for each value in that field. In Figure 8.27, the revenue chart appears as three charts based on the Channel field dropped in the Vertical Multiples field.

Figure 8.27
Add a field to the Vertical Multiples field to replicate the chart.

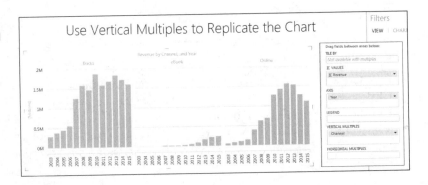

> **NOTE** It seems that in many cases, there is no difference between dropping a field in Vertical Multiples and Horizontal Multiples. Power View chooses the best arrangement to make the charts fit inside the element.

Animating a Scatter Chart Over Time

My world changed the day I saw Hans Rosling talk about religions and babies on the Internet. One of my fellow MVPs alerted me to the video. Although the 13-minute talk is interesting, it is not life changing. The life-changing feature of the video comes at the 4:46 mark in the video, when Mr. Rosling presses the Play button and his scatter chart animates to show the changes over the past 50 years. At the 5:15 mark in the video, the animation is done. Listen to the video carefully. The live studio audience applauded the chart. Check it out at http://www.ted.com/talks/hans_rosling_religions_and_babies.html.

Power View enables you to do the same trick. To create a great scatter chart, you need three or four numeric fields that are related. Drag the first field to a blank section of the canvas. Choose Design, Switch Visualizations, Other Charts, Scatter. Figure 8.28 shows the detail of the choices available in the Field List when you are creating a scatter chart:

- Any numeric field for the X axis.
- Any numeric field for the Y axis.
- Optionally, a field to control the size of the data point.
- A Details field. For every unique value in the Details field, you get one point in the scatter chart.
- Optionally, a color field. Each point will be colored according to values in this field.
- A time field for the Play axis.

Figure 8.28
The scatter chart offers the most choices for drop zones.

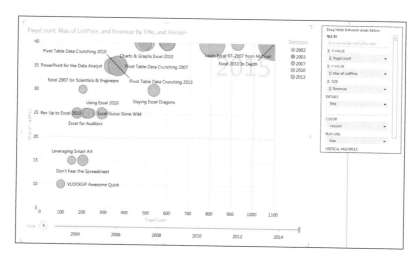

Note that you can change the calculation for any field after you drop it in the area. Choose the drop-down to the right of the field. Each field can use Sum, Average, Max, and Min. Also, you can choose to count the nonblanks or to provide a distinct count. In the chart shown in Figure 8.29, the Y-axis initially summed the list price for all books sold, which is not meaningful. Changing the calculation to Min, Max, Average would all present the actual list price for the title in the bubble.

A scrubber control appears along the bottom of the chart. You can drag the marker left or right to see the chart at various points in time, or you can click the Play button to watch the chart animate.

Figure 8.29
Add a field to the Play axis, and you can animate the chart over time.

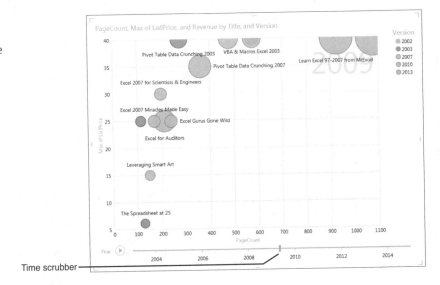

Time scrubber

The Play dimension is the key to having the chart animate. Unfortunately, at this time, only the scatter chart offers a Play field. You cannot animate column charts, bar charts, pie charts, or tables.

Some Closing Tips on Power View

As you experiment with Power View, keep these tips in mind:

- Be careful when clicking charts. Click in the whitespace to select a chart. If you advertently click one of the chart columns, you've just filtered everything else on the canvas.

- The Field List has headings for Active and All. If you just created a little chart with two fields, it is likely that the Field List is now in Active mode, which means you see only the tables used in that chart. This is alarming, because all your other tables and fields are missing. Don't be alarmed. Click All at the top of the field list, and they all come back.

■ Don't be afraid to try new charts or tables. Create something. If it doesn't look good, right-click and cut it. No harm. After using Power View, I am surprised how snappy and efficient it is. I have been dealing with 411,000 records in five charts and animating over time and have not had one crash.

Next Steps

Pivot charts are about as high tech as you can get. In some cases, you do not need a chart to present your data. Chapter 9, "Using Sparklines, Data Visualizations, and Other Nonchart Methods," goes low tech, showing you how to use the new sparkline feature or various formula tricks to build graphic displays of information right in your spreadsheet cells.

Using Sparklines, Data Visualizations, and Other Nonchart Methods

IN THIS CHAPTER

Fitting a Chart Into the Size of a Cell with Sparklines..250

Using Data Bars to Create In-Cell Bar Charts...259

Using Color Scales to Highlight Extremes 263

Using Icon Sets to Segregate Data 265

Creating a Chart Using Conditional Formatting in Worksheet Cells....................271

Creating a Chart Using the REPT Function ..273

Next Steps 274

Edward Tufte wrote about small, intense, simple data words in his 2006 book, *Beautiful Evidence*. Tufte called them sparklines and produced several examples where you could fit dozens of points of data in the space of a word. Six months later, the Excel team began planning for Excel 2010 and Tufte's concepts made it into Excel 2010.

Sparklines appear on the special drawing layer added in Excel 2007 to hold these visualizations:

- **Data bars**—This tool offers a tiny, in-cell bar chart for each number in a range. The reader's eye is drawn to the largest numbers because of the size of the bars.

- **Color scales**—Color scales, also called heat maps, are color cells in a range of colors. You can use one of nine built-in schemes where red is high and blue is low, or green is high and red is low, or you can define your own color scheme.

- **Icon sets**—You can now add a tiny icon next to each number in a range. Icons can use a traffic light metaphor, a power bar metaphor, or arrow metaphors to show which data points are the best performers in a data set.

With each of these new data visualizations, Excel requires only three clicks to get a result. However, each visualization offers advanced settings that give you finer control.

This chapter starts by discussing the new sparklines, then data visualizations, and finally some of the legacy data visualizations, such as using the REPT function to build bar charts in cells.

9

Fitting a Chart into the Size of a Cell with Sparklines

Excel's implementation of sparklines offers line charts, column charts, and a win/loss chart. See Figure 9.1 for an example of each.

- **Win/Loss**—The 1951 Pennant Race in rows 7 and 8 show two examples of a win/loss chart. In this case, each event in a baseball game is represented by either an upward-facing marker to indicate a win, or a downward-facing marker to indicate a loss. This type of chart shows winning streaks. The final three games were the playoff between the Dodgers and the Giants, with the Giants winning 2 games to 1.

- **Sparkline**—The sparkline in row 12 shows 120 monthly points of the Dow Jones Industrial Index showing the closing price for each month in one decade.

- **Sparkcolumns**—Rows 16 through 21 compare monthly high temperatures for various cities. The minimum and maximum values for each city are marked in a contrasting color. Curitiba, in the southern hemisphere, has its warmest month in February.

Figure 9.1
Excel 2013 offers three types of sparklines.

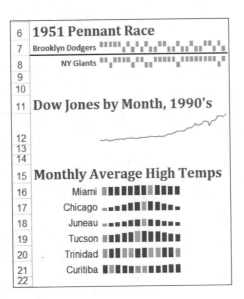

Sparklines can exist as a single cell, such as the Dow Jones example, or as a group of sparklines, such as the temperature example. When sparklines are created as a group, you can specify that all the sparklines should have the same scale or that they should be independent. There are times when each is appropriate.

The sparkline feature offers the capability to mark the high point, the low point, the first point, the last point, and/or all negative points.

There is no built-in way to label sparklines. However, sparklines are drawn on a special drawing layer that was added to Excel 2007 to accommodate the data visualizations discussed later in this chapter. This layer is transparent, so with some clever formatting, you can add some label information in the cell behind the sparkline.

Creating a Group of Sparklines

The worksheet in Figure 9.2 includes a decade of leading economic indicators.

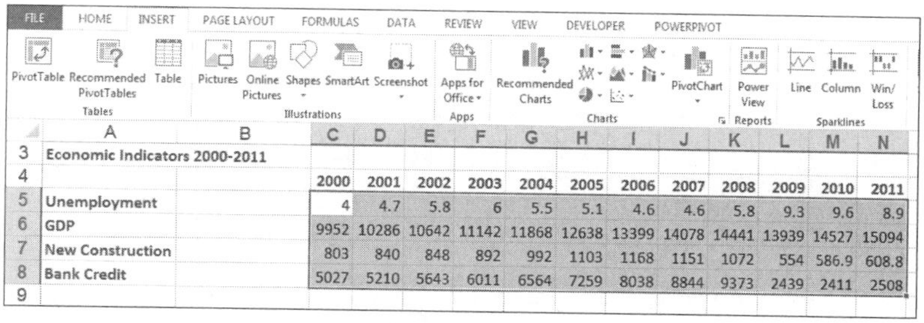

Figure 9.2
Add space in your table for the sparklines.

To add sparklines to the table, follow these steps:

1. Insert a blank column between columns A and B. This provides room for the sparklines to appear next to the labels in column A. You might find that you do not need to print the table of numbers, just the labels and sparklines suffice.

2. Select the data in C5:N8. Note that you do not include any headings in this selection.

3. On the Insert tab, select Column from the Sparkline group. Excel displays the Create Sparklines dialog.

> **NOTE** This dialog is the same for all three types of sparklines. You have to specify the location of the data and the location where you want the sparklines. Because your data is 4 rows by 12 columns, the Location Range must be a 4-cell vector. You can either specify 1 row × 4 columns or 4 rows × 1 column.

4. Select B5:B8 as the location range, as shown in Figure 9.3.

5. Click OK to create the default sparklines.

As shown in Figure 9.4, the sparklines have no markers. They are scaled independently of each other. The unemployment max of 9.3 reaches nearly to the top of cell B5, indicating the maximum for unemployment is probably about 10. By contrast, the maximum for GDP in B6 is closer to 15,000.

The Show group of the Sparkline toolbar enables you to mark certain points on the line. In Figure 9.5, the high point is marked with a dot. This one change adds a lot of information to the sparklines. New Construction peaked in 2006. GDP and Bank Credit peaked in 2008. Unemployment peaked in 2009. Did the drop in new construction in 2007 foretell the other items?

9

Figure 9.3
Preselect the data range and then specify the location range.

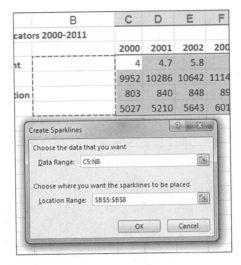

Figure 9.4
Default sparklines have no markers and are autoscaled to fit the cell.

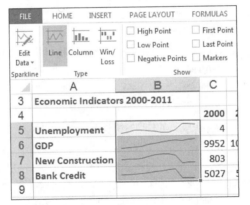

Figure 9.5
Adding a marker at the high point adds key information to the sparkline.

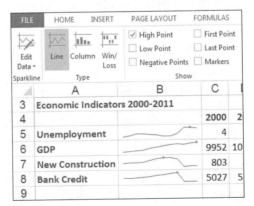

Built-in Choices for Customizing Sparklines

The Sparkline Tools Design tab offers several built-in choices for customizing sparklines:

- The **Edit Data** drop-down enables you to revise the data range for the source data and the location. If you have to add new data to existing sparklines, you can do so here. Generally, you would edit the location for the whole group, but the drop-down menu enables you to edit data for a single sparkline.

- The **Type** group enables you to switch between line, column, and win/loss charts.

- The **Show** group offers the second-most useful settings in the tab. Here you can choose to highlight the High Point, Low Point, First Point, or Last Point. Note that if there is a tie for High or Low Point, both points in the tie are marked. You can also choose to highlight all points and/or the negative points.

- For sparklines, any item that you choose in the Show group is drawn as a marker on the line. You can control the color for each of the six options using the Marker Color drop-down, discussed in the following section.

- For sparkcolumns, the markers are always shown. Choosing any of the five other choices causes those particular columns to be drawn in a different color.

- For Win/Loss, you generally always select Markers and Negative. This is how the losses show in a contrasting color from the wins.

Figure 9.6 shows examples of the various options:

- In cell B3, the high, low, first, and last points are shown.

- In cell B5, all markers are shown in the same color.

- When you select Markers and Negative, all points appear, but you can change the negative points to another color, as shown in cell B7.

- In cells B11 and B13, the chosen markers are shown in a contrasting color.

- Cell B9 and B15 show examples where the horizontal axis is shown. This helps to differentiate positive from negative. Note that the axis always appears at a zero location.

The Style gallery seems to be a huge waste of real estate. In the Office theme, it offers 36 ugly alternatives for sparkline color. This group also offers the Sparkline Color drop-down, which is the standard Excel 2013 color chooser. The color chosen here controls the line in a sparkline. In the Marker Color drop-down, you can control the color of the High, Low, First, Last, Negative points, as well as the default color for regular markers. Figure 9.7 shows the Marker Color drop-down.

Use the Group group to logically unlink a set of sparklines.

Figure 9.6
Use the Show Group to
highlight certain points.

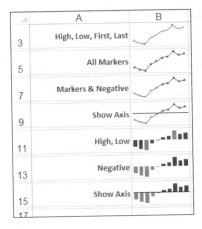

Figure 9.7
Control the color of the
chosen markers in this
drop-down.

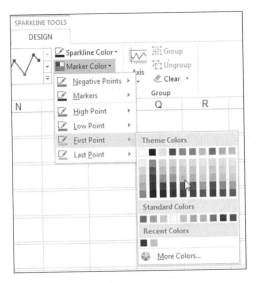

Any changes that you make on the Design tab apply to all the sparklines in the group. This
is usually a desired outcome. However, if you need to mark the High point in one line and
the Low Point in another line, you must ungroup the sparklines. You can also group sparklines or clear sparklines using icons in the Group group. The Axis drop-down appears in
this group and contains the most important settings for sparklines. You find out how to use
the Axis drop-down in the next example.

Controlling Axis Values for Sparklines

Figure 9.8 shows a group of sparkcolumns showing the average high temperature for several cities. These cities are a mix of tropical and frigid cities.

Figure 9.8
The automatic vertical scale assigned to each sparkline does not work in this example.

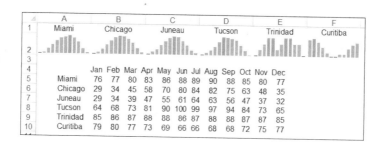

	Jan	Feb	Mar	Apr	May	Jun	Jul	Aug	Sep	Oct	Nov	Dec
Miami	76	77	80	83	86	88	89	90	88	85	80	77
Chicago	29	34	45	58	70	80	84	82	75	63	48	35
Juneau	29	34	39	47	55	61	64	63	56	47	37	32
Tucson	64	68	73	81	90	100	99	97	94	84	73	65
Trinidad	85	86	87	88	88	86	87	88	88	87	87	85
Curitiba	79	80	77	73	69	66	66	68	68	72	75	77

The default behavior of sparklines is that each sparkline in the group gets its own scale. This worked for the varying economic indicators shown previously in Figure 9.1. However, it does not work here.

When the vertical axis scale is set to Automatic, you can never really know the high and low of the scale in use. If you study the data and the sparkline for Trinidad, it appears as if Excel has chosen a min point of 84.8 and a max point of 89. Without any scale, you might think that Trinidad in January is as cold as Chicago in January.

Figure 9.9 shows the options available in the Axis drop-down on the right end of the Sparkline Tools Design tab. The important settings here are the choices for the Minimum value and Maximum value.

Figure 9.9
Control the vertical axis using this drop-down.

If you change the min and max to the setting of Same for All Sparklines, all six sparklines in this group have the same min and max scale. The sparklines in Figure 9.10 initially look better. Juneau is never as warm as Tucson. However, you still do not know what the max and min values are. Take a close look at Chicago. It appears that the January high temperature is about zero, but the data table shows that the average high temperature in January is 29. You can estimate that these columns run from a min of 28 to a max of 101, based on looking through the data.

Figure 9.10
Force all sparklines to have the same vertical scale.

January appears to be near 0

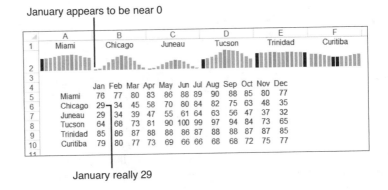

January really 29

My suggestion is to always visit the axis drop-down and set a custom min value and a custom max value. In Figure 9.11, the minimum is 0 and the maximum is 100.

Figure 9.11
For absolute control, define a custom min and max value.

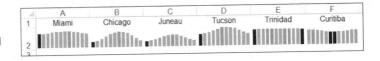

Setting Up Win/Loss Sparklines

The data for a Win/Loss sparkline is simple: Put a 1 (or any positive number) for a win. Put a –1 (or any negative number) for a loss. Put a zero to have no marker.

In Figure 9.12, you can see the data for a pair of Win/Loss sparklines. The 2 in Cell F3 does not cause the marker to appear any taller than any of the 1s in the other cells. It does cause the marker to appear as a different color if you choose to mark the high point. Maybe you can think of a use where you need to show two different colors among the wins or losses.

Figure 9.12
Data sets for wins and losses consist of 1s and –1s.

	A	B	C	D	E	F	G	H	I	J
1	1	-1	1	1	-1	-1	0	1	1	
2										
3	1	1	1	-1	1	2	1	1	1	

Showing Detail by Enlarging the Sparkline

Professor Tufte's definition of sparklines included the word *small*. If you show the sparklines on a computer screen, there is no reason that the sparklines have to stay small.

When you increase the height and width of the cell, the sparkline automatically grows to fill the cell. If you merge cells, the sparkline fills the complete range of merged cells.

In Figure 9.13, the 279-game season of the Harlem Globetrotters seemed as if it needed more than just one cell, so cells B2 and C2 were merged. In cell B4, the row height was increased to 30 to show more detail.

Figure 9.13

Increase cell size or merge cells to increase the detail in the sparkline.

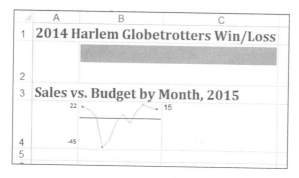

Labeling a Sparkline

The examples of sparklines created by Tufte in *Beautiful Evidence* almost always labeled the final point. Some examples included min and max values or a gray box to indicate the normal range of values.

Figure 9.13 shows labels for Min and Max to the left of the sparkline and a label for the final point to the right of the sparkline. Those labels are cell values. To create the label on the left, follow these steps:

1. Type the high value. Press Alt+Enter four times to move to the fifth line of text in the cell. Type the low value. Press Ctrl+Enter.

2. Format the cell as 8 point or smaller.

3. Use the Right Align and Top Align icons on the Home tab to position the labels at the right edge of the cell.

To label the final point, you can precede the value with the appropriate number of Alt+Enter keystrokes to vertically position the label close to the correct place.

If you set a row height equal to 110, you can fit 10 lines of text in the cell using Alt+Enter. Even with a height of 55, you can fit 5 lines of text. This makes it possible for the label for the final point to get near to the final point.

In Figure 9.14, the city labels are values typed in the same cell as the sparkcolumns. The max scale was set to 120 to make sure that there was room for the city name to appear. The Month abbreviations below the charts are "J F M A M J J A S O N D" in 6.5-point Courier New font. After trying both 6 point and 7 point and not having the labels line up with the columns, I ended up using 6.5 point and adjusted the column widths until the columns lined up with the labels.

Figure 9.14
Labels are created by
typing in a small font in
the cell.

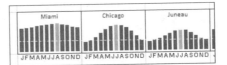

In Figure 9.15, a semitransparent gray box indicates the acceptable limits for a measurement. In this case, anything outside of 95 percent to 105 percent is sent for review. Those gray boxes are simply Shapes from the Insert tab.

Figure 9.15
A gray box shows the
acceptable range to help
the reader locate items
outside of the acceptable
range.

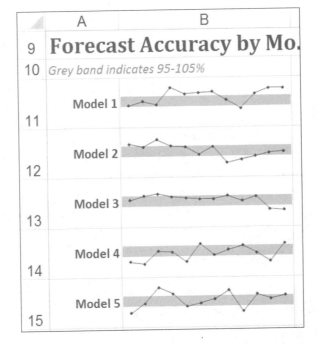

Here are some tips for setting up the box:

1. Temporarily change the first two points in the first cell to be at the min and max for the box.
2. Increase the zoom to 400 percent.
3. Draw a rectangle in the cell.
4. Use the Drawing Tools Format tab to set the outline to None.
5. Under Shape Fill, select More Fill Colors. Select a gray color. Because shapes are drawn on top of the sparkline layer, drag the transparency slider up to about 70 percent transparent.
6. Use the resize handles to make sure the top and bottom of the box go through the first and second points of the line.

7. After getting the box sized appropriately, reset the first two data points back to their original values.

8. Copy the cell that contains the first box. Paste onto the other sparkline cells. Because the sparklines are not copied, only the box will be pasted.

> **TIP**
>
> It is possible to copy sparklines. You have to copy both the sparkline and the data source in a single copy. If your copy range includes both elements, the sparkline gets pasted.

Using Data Bars to Create In-Cell Bar Charts

A data bar is a swath of color that starts at the side of a cell and extends into the cell based on the value of the cell. Small numbers get less color. The largest numbers might be 100% filled with color. This creates a visual effect that enables you to visually pick out the larger and smaller values. Figure 9.16 shows many examples of data bars.

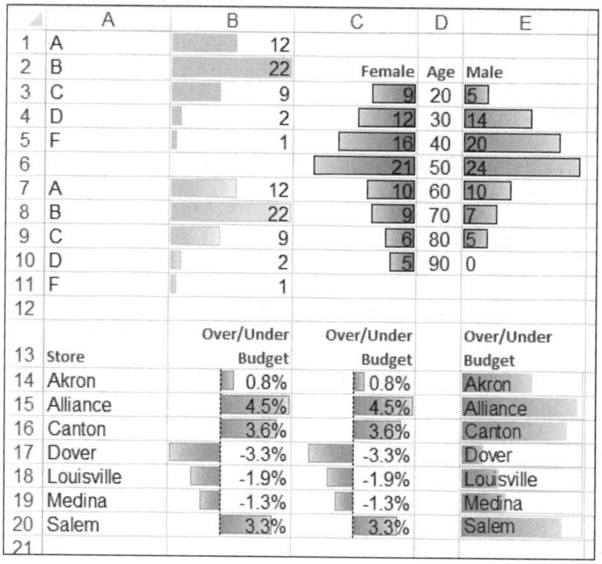

Figure 9.16
The data bars illustrate many of the new properties in Excel 2013 data bars.

As of Excel 2010, many new options were available in data bars:

- Data bars can be solid or a gradient. In Excel 2013, the default gradient bar has a border. Tufte and others complained that the gradient in E14:E20 were misleading. The gradient is useful for helping to see the numbers behind the data bar. Contrast the solid bar in B2 and the gradient in B8. By adding the border around the gradient, Microsoft leaves no doubt where the data bar ends, but allows the numbers to show through.

- Values of zero now get no data bar, as shown in cell E10. Previously, the smallest value would get 4 pixels of color.

- Data bars can now be negative. Negative bars are shown in a different color and usually extend to the left of a central axis. You have three choices in where to place the zero axis. In cells B14:B20, the setting is Automatic. Because the largest positive number is further from zero than the smallest negative number, the axis appears slightly to the left of center. This allows the bar for 4.5 percent in B15 to appear larger than the bar for –3.3 percent in B17. You can also force the axis to appear in the center, as in cells C14:C20. Alternatively, in a bizarre setting, you can force the negative bars to extend in the same direction as the positive values, but with a different color.

There are two philosophical ways to show the negative bars. You can assign –3.3 percent the most color because it is farthest from zero, or you can assign –1.3 percent the most color because it is the mathematically the largest of the negative numbers (–1.3% > –3.3%).

- You can control the color of the positive bar, positive bar border, negative bar, negative bar border, and axis color.

- With Excel 2013, bars can now extend right to left, as shown in cells C3:C10. This allows comparative histograms as in C2:E10.

The following options are not new in Excel 2013, but still remain from Excel 2007:

- You can specify the scale of the data bars. Although the scale is initially set to automatic, you can specify that the min/max are set to a certain number or to the lowest value, a percentage, a percentile, or a formula.

- You can choose to show only the data bar and to hide the number in the cell. This is how words were included in cells E14:E20. The numbers are hidden by the conditional formatting dialog, and then a linked picture of the words is pasted over the cells. Because the data bars are on a drawing layer above the regular drawing layer, this works.

- You can format the number in the cell with a custom number format of specific text. For example, a custom number format of "Akron" in cell E14 always shows the word "Akron" in the cell, no matter what number is typed in the cell.

- All data bars in a group have the same scale. This is unlike sparklines where the scale is allowed to change from graphic to graphic.

Creating Data Bars

Creating data bars requires just a few clicks. Follow these steps:

1. Select a range of numeric data. Do not include the total in this selection. If the data is in noncontiguous ranges, hold down the Ctrl key while selecting additional areas. This range should be numbers of similar scale. For example, you can select a column of sales data or a column of profit data. If you attempt to select a range that contains both units

sold and revenue dollars, the size of the revenue numbers overpowers the units sold numbers, and no color appears in the units sold cells.

2. From the Home tab, select Conditional Formatting, Data Bars. You see six built-in colors for the data bars: blue, green, red, orange, bright blue, and pink. The colors appear both in solid and gradient forms. Select one of them.

> **NOTE**
> If you do not like the six basic colors Excel offers for data bars, you can choose any other color, as described in the next section.

The result is a swath of color in each cell in the selection, as shown in Figure 9.17.

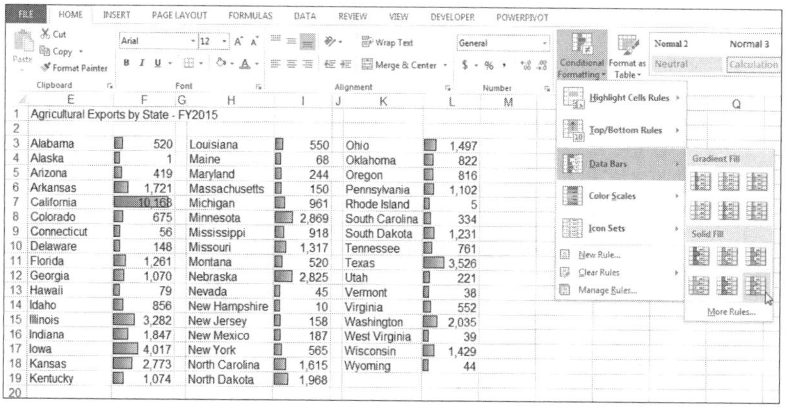

Figure 9.17
After applying a data bar, you can see that California is a leading exporter of agriculture products.

Customizing Data Bars

By default, Excel assigns the largest data bar to the cell with the largest value and the smallest data bar to the cell with the smallest value. You can customize this behavior by following these steps:

1. From the Conditional Formatting drop-down on the Home tab, select Manage Rules.

2. From the Show Formatting Rules drop-down, select This Worksheet. You now see a list of all rules applied to the sheet.

3. Click the Data Bar rule.

4. Click the Edit Rule button. You see the Edit Formatting Rule dialog, as shown in Figure 9.18.

There are a number of customizations available in this dialog:

■ Select the Show Bar Only setting to hide the numbers in the cells and to show only the data bar.

■ For the Minimum and Maximum values, you can choose from Automatic, Number, Percent, Percentile, Formula, or Smallest/Largest Number. If you choose Automatic, Excel chooses a minimum and maximum value. You can override this by setting one value to a specific number.

■ In the Bar Appearance section, you can specify gradient or solid fill for the bar. You can specify a solid border or no border. Two color-chooser drop-downs enable you to change the color of the bar and the border.

■ The Bar Direction drop-down enables you to choose Context, Left to Right, or Right to Left. The default choice of Context is always left to right, unless you are in an international edition of Excel where the language reading order is right to left.

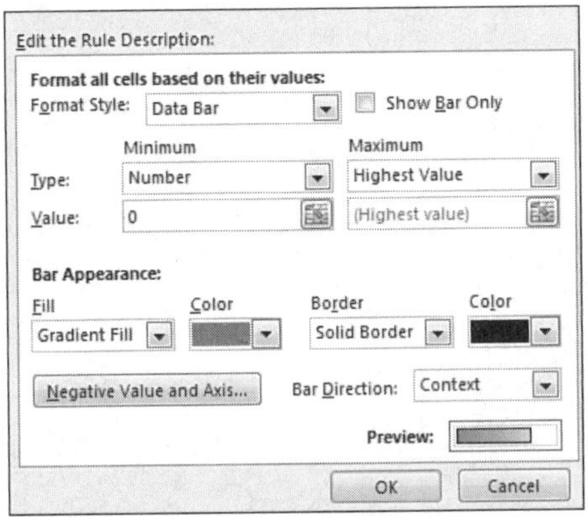

Figure 9.18
You customize data bars by using the Edit the Rule Description dialog.

When you choose Negative Values and Axis, you have new settings to adjust the color of the bar and the border for negative bars. You can also control whether the zero axis is shown at the cell midpoint or at an automatic location based on the relative size of the negative and positive numbers. If the axis is shown, you can adjust the color, too.

> **CAUTION**
>
> One frustrating feature with data bars is that you cannot reverse their size, using the smallest bar for the highest number and vice versa. Although in some scenarios, such as top 100 rankings, the lowest score might deserve the largest bar, there is no way to make this happen with data bars. If you need to do this, you could consider using color scales or formulas to reverse the values.

Showing Data Bars for a Subset of Cells

In the data bar examples given in the previous sections, every cell in the range receives a data bar. However, what if you just want some of the values, such as the top 20% or the top 10, to have data bars? The process for making this happen is not intuitive, but it is possible. Basically, you apply the data bar to the entire range. Then you add a new conditional format (a very boring format) to all the cells that you do not want to have data bars. For example, you might tell Excel to use a white background on all cells with values outside of the top 10.

The final important step is to manage the rules and tell Excel to stop processing more rules if the white background rule is met. This requires clever thinking. If you want to apply data bars to cells in the top 10, you first tell Excel to make all the cells in the bottom 40 look like every other cell in Excel. Turning on Stop If True in the Conditional Formatting Rules Manager dialog is the key to getting Excel to not apply the data bar to cells with values outside of the top 10.

Figure 9.19 shows data bars applied to only the top 10 states.

Figure 9.19
Using Stop If True after formatting the lower 21 with no special formatting allows the data bars to appear only on the top states.

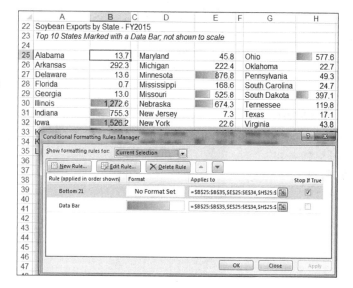

Using Color Scales to Highlight Extremes

Color scales are similar to data bars. However, instead of having a variable-size bar in each cell, color scales use gradients of two or three different colors to communicate the relative size of each cell. Here's how you apply color scales:

1. Select a range that contains numbers. Be sure not to include headings or total cells in the selection.

2. Select Conditional Formatting, Color Scales from the Home tab.

3. From the Color Scales fly-out menu, select one of the 12 styles to apply the color scale to the range. Note that the fly-out menu offers subtle differences to which you should pay attention. For example, the first six options are scales that use three colors. These are great onscreen or with color printers. The last six options are scales that use two colors. These are better with monochrome printers.

9

In a two-color red-white color scale, the largest number is formatted with a dark red fill. The smallest number has a white fill. All of the numbers in between receive a lighter or darker shade of pink based on their position within the range (see Figure 9.20).

Figure 9.20
Excel provides a range of shading, depending on the value. You can see that Carole and John's receivables have been increasing throughout the year.

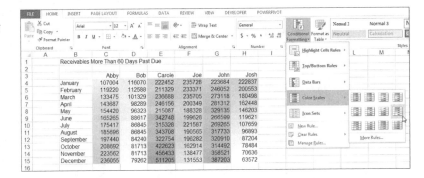

Customizing Color Scales

You are not limited to the color scales shown in the fly-out menu. If you select Home, Conditional Formatting, Manage Rules, Edit Rule, you can choose any two or three colors for the color scale.

You also have choices of where to assign the smallest, largest, and midpoint values (see Figure 9.21).

You should be aware of one strange situation. Normally, Excel lets you mix conditional formatting in the same range. You might apply both a color scale and an icon set.

Figure 9.21
You can choose any colors to use in the color scale.

Edit Formatting Rule		
Select a Rule Type:		

- Format all cells based on their values
- Format only cells that contain
- Format only top or bottom ranked values
- Format only values that are above or below average
- Format only unique or duplicate values
- Use a formula to determine which cells to format

Edit the Rule Description:

Format all cells based on their values:
Format Style: 3-Color Scale

	Minimum	Midpoint	Maximum
Type:	Lowest Value	Percentile	Highest Value
Value:	(Lowest value)	50	(Highest value)
Color:			

Preview:

OK   Cancel

If you have a three-color scale applied to some cells and choose a different three-color scale from the fly-out menu, the latter choice overwrites the first choice.

However, Excel treats two-color scales as a different visualization than three-color scales. If you have a three-color scale applied and you then try to switch it to a two-color scale using the fly-out menu, Excel creates two rules for those cells. The latter two-color scale is the only one to appear in Excel 2013, but you might be confused when you go to the Manage Rules dialog to see two different rules applied to the cells.

Using Icon Sets to Segregate Data

Icon sets, which were popular with expensive management reporting software in the late 1990s, have now been added to Excel. An icon set might include green, yellow, and red traffic lights or another set of icons to show positive, neutral, and negative meanings. With icon sets, Excel automatically applies an icon to a cell, based on the relative size of the value in the cell compared to other values in the range.

Excel 2013 ships with 20 icon sets that contain three, four, or five icons. The icons are always left-justified in the cell. Excel applies rules to add an icon to every cell in the range:

- **Three-icon sets**—For the three-icon sets, you have a choice between arrows, flags, two varieties of traffic lights, signs, stars, triangles, and two varieties of what Excel calls *3 Symbols*. This last group consists of a green check mark for the good cells, a yellow exclamation point for the middle cells, and a red X for the bad cells. You can either get the symbols in a circle (that is, 3 Symbols [Circled]) or alone on a white background (that is, 3 Symbols). One version of the arrows is available in gray. All the other icon sets use red, yellow, and green.

- **Four-icon sets**—The four-icon sets have two varieties of arrows: a black-to-red circle set, a set of cell phone power bars, and a set of four traffic lights. In the traffic light option, a black light indicates an option that is even worse than the red light.

- **Five-icon sets**—The five-icon sets have two varieties of arrows, boxes, a five-power bar set, and an interesting set called *5 Quarters*. This last set is a monochromatic circle that is completely empty for the lowest values, 25 percent filled, 50 percent filled, 75 percent filled, and completely filled for the highest values.

The power bars icons seem to work well on both color displays and monochromatic printouts.

Three of these sets were new in Excel 2010. If you choose Three Triangles, Three Stars, or Five Boxes, those icon sets will not appear if the workbook is opened in Excel 2007.

Setting Up an Icon Set

Icon sets require a bit more thought than the other data visualization offerings. Before you use icon sets, you should consider whether they will be printed in monochrome or displayed in color. Several of the 20 icon sets rely on color for differentiation and look horrible in a black-and-white report.

To set up an icon set, you follow these steps:

1. Select a range of numeric data of a similar scale. Do not include the headers or total rows in this selection.

2. From the Home tab, select Conditional Formatting, Icon Sets. Select 1 of the 20 icon sets. Figure 9.22 shows the 3 Stars choice selected.

Figure 9.22
You can choose from the 20 icon sets.

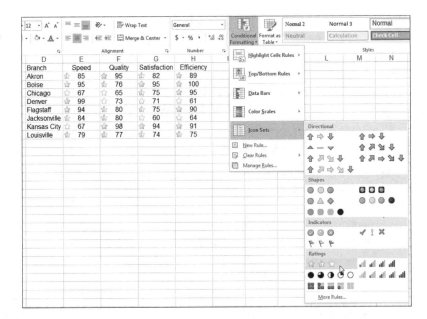

Moving Numbers Closer to Icons

In the top rows of Figure 9.23, the icon set has been applied to a rectangular range of data. The icons are always left-justified. Numbers are typically right-justified. This can be problematic. Someone might think that the icon at the left side of cell G3 is really referring to the right-aligned number in F3.

You might try centering the numbers to get the numbers closer to the icons in Rows 7 through 9. This will drive purists crazy because the final digit of the 100 in cell H8 does not line up with the final digits of cells H7 and H9.

A better solution is to use the Alignment tab of the Format Cells dialog. Select Right (Indent) for the horizontal alignment. Bump the indent figure up to move the numbers closer to the icon. In Rows 12 through 14, the indent is set at four characters.

If you do not want to show numbers at all, you can edit the conditional formatting rule and select Show Icon Only. Rows 17 through 19 show this solution. Ironically, when the numbers are no longer displayed, you can position the icons by using the Left Align, Center Align, and Right Align icons.

Figure 9.23
Changing the alignment of the numbers moves them closer to the icon.

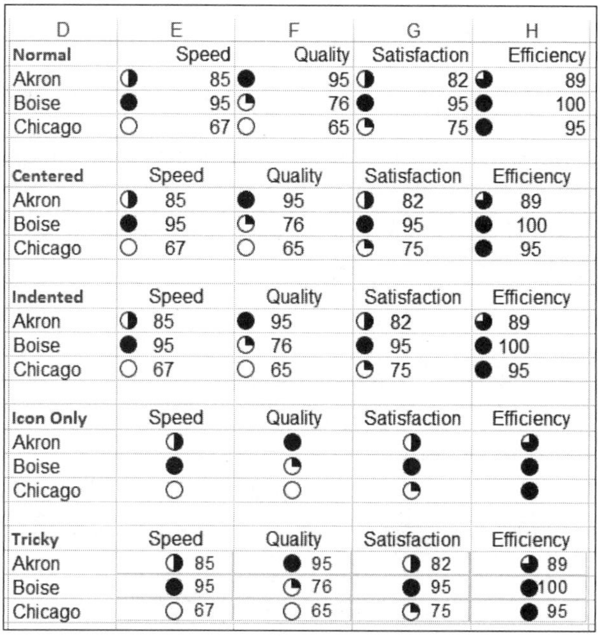

The over-the-top solution in rows 22 through 24 involve using Show Icon Only and then pasting a linked picture of the numbers from other cells.

Here are the steps to create rows 22 through 24:

1. Select one of the cells with the icon set formatting.

2. From the Home tab, select Conditional Formatting, Manage Rules.

3. In the Conditional Formatting Rules Manager dialog, click the Icon Set rule and then click Edit Rule.

4. In the middle of the Edit Formatting Rule dialog, select Show Icon Only. Click OK twice to close the two dialog boxes.

5. Select all the cells that contain icons and click the Align Center button on the Home tab.

6. Page down so that you are outside of the printed range. Stay in the same column. Set up a formula to point to the number in the top-left corner of the icon set range. Copy this formula down and over to be the same size as your icon set range. This gives you a range of just the numbers.

7. Format this range of numbers to be right-aligned with an indent of 1. Choose the range and press Ctrl+1 to display Format Cells. On the Alignment tab, open the Horizontal drop-down and choose Right (Indent). Increase the Indent spin button to 1.

8. Copy this range of numbers.

9. Go back to the original set of icons and Paste, Picture Link. A picture of the original numbers appears behind the icons.

CASE STUDY: REVERSING THE SEQUENCE OF ICONS

Suppose you have data to track reject rates for several manufacturing lines. You apply an icon set that offers green check marks, yellow exclamation points, and red X icons.

In the default view of the data, Excel always assumes that higher numbers are better. However, that is not the case in this situation, where higher reject rates are bad.

Unlike with color scales or data bars, with icon sets, you can reverse the order. To do so, you follow these steps:

1. Select one cell in your data.

2. From the Conditional Formatting drop-down on the Home tab, select Manage Rules.

3. Click Icon Set to select this rule. The rule color changes from gray to blue.

4. Click the Edit Rule button. The Edit Formatting Rule dialog appears.

5. In the Edit Formatting Rule dialog, select the Reverse Icon Order button. Click OK twice to close both open dialog boxes.

Showing an Icon for Only the Best Cells

Previous versions of this book used to contain a really complicated method for showing an icon for only the best cells. Thankfully, the process was simplified as of Excel 2010. Figure 9.24 shows a data set where only values greater than 95 are marked with a check mark. The other icons from the set never appear.

Follow these steps to set it up:

1. Apply any icon set to a range.

2. Choose Home, Manage Rules, Edit Rule.

3. The first icon is initially set up to be displayed when the value is >=67 Percent. Open the Type drop-down and change from Percent to Number. You can now specify that the first icon appears for values >= 96.

4. There is a drop-down for each of the three icons. Open the drop-down for the second icon and choose No Icon. Repeat for the third icon. Click OK.

Any scores of 96 or higher get the first icon. All the remaining values do not get an icon.

Figure 9.24
Show an icon only for the top cells.

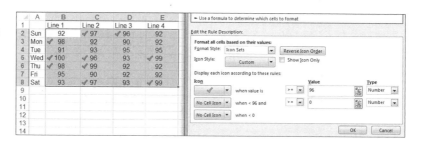

Creating a 10-Icon Set Using a Formula

This trick is one of my favorites and has far-reaching implications, more than just doing a 10-icon visualization. The tip was posted by David Gainer in the Excel team blog on February 24, 2006. The trick never caught on. You will be one of the few who are using it. For reference, that original post is hanging on at `http://tinyurl.com/asfbot8`.

Currently, only one of each type of conditional formatting can appear in a range. If you apply two icon set rules, only the one on top in the Conditional Formatting Rules Manager appears in the worksheet.

This trick uses a Formula property that you can apply to a conditional formatting rule. There is no place to actually enter this formula in the Excel interface. You have to apply the formula in the VBA window. After the formula is applied, Excel decides on a cell-by-cell basis if the visualization should appear. If the formula turns off Icon Set Rule 1 for several cells, Icon Set Rule 2 is allowed to show through!

Here is how to set it up:

1. Select a range of cells. Use the Home, Conditional Formatting menu to apply an icon set with five icons.

2. Choose Home, Conditional Formatting, Manage Rules to display the Conditional Formatting Rules Manager dialog.

3. Edit the Icon Set rule. Edit the Type, the Value, and the Icon for all five icons in this set. (See Figure 9.25.) Click OK.

Figure 9.25
Choose five different icons for the top half of the values.

Edit the Rule Description:

Format all cells based on their values:

Format Style:	Icon Sets	Reverse Icon Order
Icon Style:	Custom	☐ Show Icon Only

Display each icon according to these rules:

Icon				Value		Type	
☆	▼	when value is	>= ▼	90	🔢	Number	▼
✓	▼	when < 90 and	>= ▼	80	🔢	Number	▼
⚑	▼	when < 80 and	>= ▼	70	🔢	Number	▼
△	▼	when < 70 and	>= ▼	60	🔢	Number	▼
△	▼	when < 60					

OK   Cancel

4. Click New Rule.

5. A new rule starts out with Format All Cells Based on Their Values selected. Keep this setting, but open the Format Style and change from 2-Color Scale to Icon Sets.

6. Choose a different icon set with five icons.

7. As you did in step 3, you need to edit the Type, the Value, and the Icon for all five icons in this set. Click OK.

You now have two rules set up as shown in Figure 9.26. The second rule does not show in the cells.

Figure 9.26
You've now created two rules, but that does not mean it works yet.

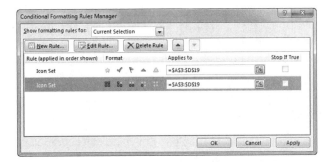

Before you do the next step, you need to look at the data and note several things.

- The top-left corner cell of your selection is in cell A3.

- The first rule is for cells of 50 and above. If the cell contains 50 or more, you want the first rule to show up in the worksheet. If not, you want Excel to move on to the second rule.

You achieve this by setting up a formula to specify when the first rule is allowed to be used. The formula has to be written as if it is referring to the first cell in the selection, which is cell A3. You want the first icon set to be used when the value is greater than or equal to 50. The formula is "=if(a3>=50, true, false)". Follow these steps to apply this formula to the first conditional formatting rule.

1. Press Alt+F11 to open the VBA editor.

2. Press Ctrl+G to display the Immediate pane.

3. Type **Selection.FormatConditions(1).Formula = "=if(a3>=50, true, false)"** and press Enter. (See Figure 9.27.) You have to do this step only once—the range continues to work.

4. Press Alt+Q to close the VBA editor and return to Excel.

Figure 9.27
This is currently the only way to apply a formula to the conditional formatting.

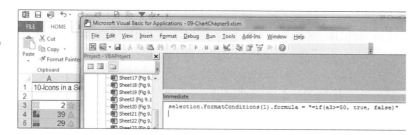

The range now displays 10 different icons. It is admittedly difficult to track 10 different icons, so you can easily build a key to the right of your data. Select any 10-cell range from the data set and copy it to a blank section of the worksheet. Type the numbers 0, 10, 20, ... 90 in the 10 cells. If desired, you can edit the conditional formatting rules for the key and change to Show Icon Only. Column F in Figure 9.28 is a formula to combine =G3&"-"&G4-1.

Figure 9.28
This is currently the only way to apply a formula to the conditional formatting.

	A	B	C	D	E	F	G
1	10-Icons in a Set!						
2							Key
3	2	96	3	89		1-9	
4	39	57	76	66		10-19	
5	29	51	97	18		20-29	
6	25	53	13	76		30-39	
7	45	28	68	25		40-49	
8	16	62	71	82		50-59	
9	87	58	57	75		60-69	
10	69	89	74	53		70-79	
11	76	70	67	66		80-89	
12	18	41	69	43		90-100	
13	100	69	23	44			
14	45	18	92	28			
15	50	37	15	80			
16	31	3	68	50			
17	96	44	40	68			
18	59	92	8	15			
19	19	82	37	31			
20							

The formula concept could be extended or applied to any conditional formatting. You could apply green color bars to values above 80 and red color bars to values below. You could create six rules with icon sets and have a 30-icon set.

Creating a Chart Using Conditional Formatting in Worksheet Cells

In the old days, charts were drawn by hand, using a sheet of graph paper and a pencil. Think about the Excel worksheets on your computer. Basically, an Excel worksheet is a very large sheet of graph paper, with 17 billion tiny boxes.

You can create plenty of charts right on a worksheet, without ever invoking the Excel charting engine. Figure 9.29 shows such a chart. The gray bars in D2:R6 are drawn based on conditional formatting rules in response to data entered in B2:C6. Note how the bars have expanded or contracted in the bottom image when starting or ending years are adjusted.

I created this worksheet for a friend who was trying to visualize the years of production for various models of Mullins Steel Boats. The years stretch from cell D1 and extend as far right as necessary. To make the chart narrow, you can select Vertical Text from the Orientation drop-down in the Home tab. You can then resize the columns to a column width of 2.

The logic for creating the bars is as follows:

- If the start and end year are equal and they match the year in row 1, color the cell gray, with borders on all four sides.

- If the start year in column B matches the year in row 1, color the cell gray. Include left, top, and bottom borders.

- If the end year in column C matches the year in row 1, color the cell gray. Include right, top, and bottom borders.

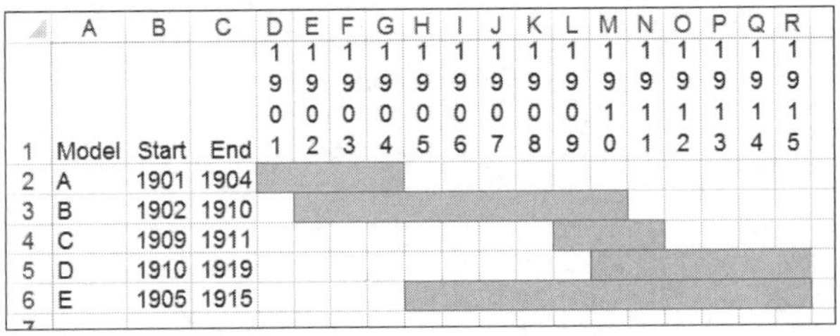

Figure 9.29

The gray bars are created through a series of conditional formatting rules.

- If the year in row 1 is greater than the start year and less than the end year, color the cell gray, with top and bottom borders but no side borders.

You follow these steps to create the conditional formatting rules for this logic:

1. Select the range D2:R6. Although you have selected many cells, you write the conditional formatting rules as if they applied to the top-left cell, which is D2.

2. From the Home tab, select Conditional Formatting, Manage Rules. Excel displays the Conditional Formatting Rules Manager dialog.

3. Click the New Rule button. Excel displays the New Formatting Rule dialog.

4. In the top half of the dialog, select Use a Formula to Determine Which Cells to Format. The bottom half of the dialog box redraws to show Format Values Where This Formula Is True.

5. Enter the formula =$B2=D$1 for the first condition. This formula checks whether the start year in column B of the current row is equal to row 1 of the current column. It is crucial that you enter dollar signs before the B and 1 but not before the 2 and D.

6. Click the Format button in the dialog. On the Fill tab, choose a fill color for the cell.

On the Border tab, click None and then click the Top, Bottom, and Left. Click OK to close the Format Cells dialog. Click OK to close the New Formatting Rule dialog. If you click the Apply button, you should see that the first cell for each bar is drawn in the worksheet.

7. Repeat steps 3 and 4, and then enter the formula =$C2=D$1 for the second rule; this is the formula to format the last cell of the bar. The Format selection is the same color fill as in step 6. On the Border tab, select None, Top, Bottom, and Right.

8. Repeat step 7 and then enter the formula =AND($B2<D$1,$C2>D$1) for the third rule; this is the formula to format center cells in the bar. The Format selection is the same fill as in step 6. On the Border tab, select None, Top, and Bottom.

9. Repeat step 7 and then enter the formula =AND($B2=$C2,$B2=D$1) for the last rule; this is the formula to find where the model was only available for a single year. The Format selection is the same fill color as in step 6. On the Border tab, select Outline. Rules are added to the beginning of the rule list. By entering this rule last, you ensure that it is evaluated first.

At this point, your Conditional Formatting Rules Manager dialog should look similar to the one in Figure 9.30.

This example is complicated by the fact that you draw borders on the appropriate edges of each cell. If you instead used a solid black fill, you could create the effect with a single rule, using the formula =AND($B2<=D$1,$C2>=D$1).

Figure 9.30
Four rules create the chart.

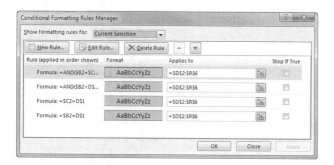

Creating a Chart Using the REPT Function

The REPT function, which has been around since Excel 5, takes two arguments. The first argument is the text to repeat. The second argument is the number of times to repeat the text.

In Figure 9.31, column B shows cotton exports. The numbers range from 1,337 down to 13. You create the bar charts in column C by repeating the | character numerous times. However, instead of showing a line of 1,337 pipe characters in cell C4, the repeat argument in cell B4 is 1,337 divided by 10. Therefore, cell C4 contains 133 vertical bars. Cell C20 contains one vertical bar. Even though 13.7 divided by 10 is 1.37, Excel shows only whole bars.

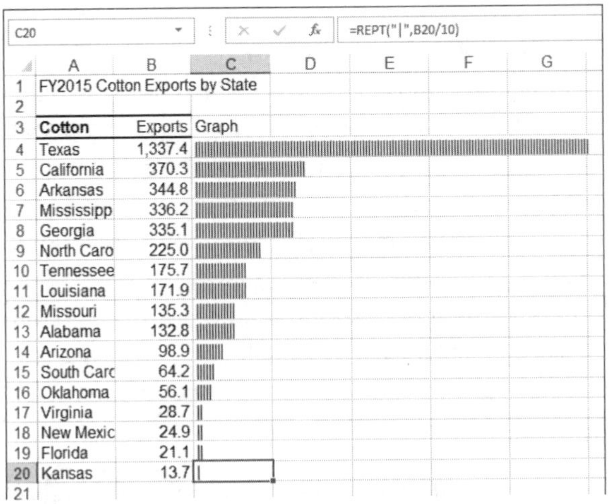

Figure 9.31
Using the REPT function is a quick way to produce a bar chart right in a worksheet. The trick is to use the proper scaling factor.

The result of the REPT function can be left- or right-justified. In Figure 9.32, the results in column E are right-justified, and the results in column G are left-justified to create a comparative histogram. The formulas on the right side of the chart use a REPT function concatenated with a space and then the value. The formulas on the left side of the chart concatenate the value, a space, and the REPT function.

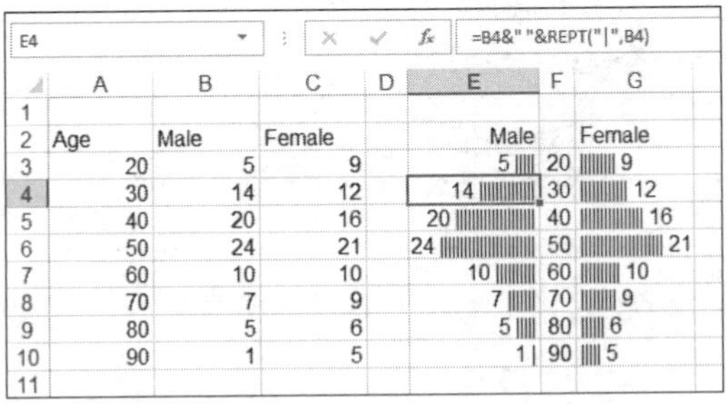

Figure 9.32
Here, pairs of REPT functions create a comparative histogram.

Next Steps

In Chapter 10, "Presenting Excel Data on a Map," you find out how to combine Microsoft Excel with Microsoft MapPoint to visually show geographic data. Several of the examples included in this chapter show tables of data by state. Think how these examples would take on a new meaning if they were plotted on a map. Microsoft MapPoint adds this functionality to Excel.

Presenting Excel Data on a Map

10

Plotting Data Geographically

In many cases, the best way to present data is to plot it on a geographic map. Mapping software used to cost thousands of dollars. There are now three viable alternatives for mapping your data.

Plotting Data Geographically.....................275

Importing Data to MapPoint.....................275

Creating a Map in PowerView.....................279

Creating a Map in GeoFlow.....................284

Next Steps.....................286

- Microsoft offers a product called Microsoft MapPoint. MapPoint is available in editions for North America and Europe. MapPoint can import data from Excel and display it on a map. MapPoint retails for $299.

- Power View is an add-in for Excel 2013 Pro Plus. Power View uses Bing Maps to display records on a map. Power View is included in the installation DVD if you have the Pro Plus version of Excel 2013 or higher. You might have to visit File, Options, Add-Ins, Manage COM Add-ins to enable Power View.

- GeoFlow is an add-in for Excel 2013 Pro Plus. GeoFlow enables you to plot Excel data on a map and create virtual tours through the map. GeoFlow is available to people with Excel 2013 Pro Plus, and as a separate download starting in January 2013.

Each mapping program expects there to be one or more geographic columns in your data. If your data has City, State, ZIP Code, Latitude, and Longitude, you are ready to go. MapPoint even uses the street address to allow you to analyze data down to the city block level.

Importing Data to MapPoint

For some strange reason, MapPoint cannot import data stored in XLSM files. If your data currently is stored as XLSM, you should use File, Save As to save the file as XLSX.

The example in this section is an Excel file showing all the Dairy Queen and Starbucks locations in Florida. You want to plot the data to show the distribution of these two chain restaurants.

Follow these steps to plot your Excel data in MapPoint:

1. Save your data in an Excel workbook. Close the workbook.

2. Open Microsoft MapPoint.

3. From the MapPoint menu, choose Data, Import Data Wizard.

4. Browse to and select your Excel file.

5. In the Import Data Wizard dialog, choose the proper data type for each column. (See Figure 10.1.) Click Next.

6. If your data has only one type of data (for example, all Starbucks), choose Pushpin for the MapType. But because this data has Starbucks and Dairy Queen, choose Multiple Symbol so you can differentiate between the chains (see Figure 10.2). Click Next.

7. For the Data Fields, choose Name. Each different value in the Name field will appear as a different symbol in the map. (See Figure 10.3.)

8. In the Legend, choose the symbols to use for Dairy Queen and Starbucks. A variety of shapes and colors are available. In Figure 10.4, red circles are used for Dairy Queen and green triangles for Starbucks.

Figure 10.1
While importing to MapPoint, verify the data type of each geography field.

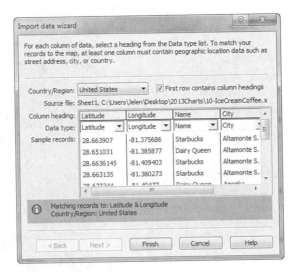

Figure 10.2
Choose Multiple Symbol to differentiate one category from another.

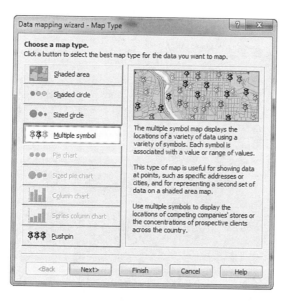

Figure 10.3
Because the Name field identifies Dairy Queen versus Starbucks, choose Name as the Data Field.

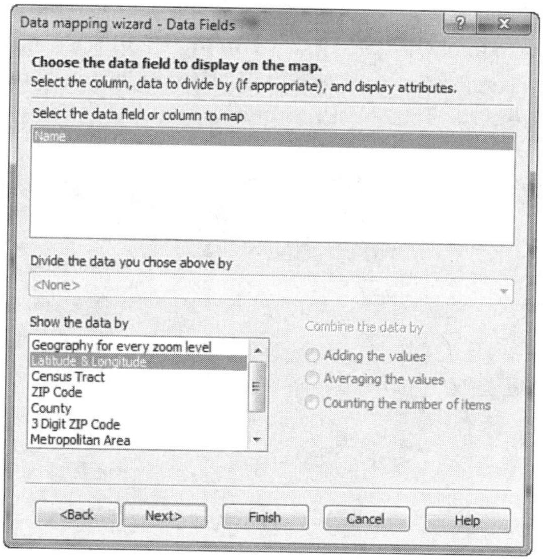

10

Figure 10.4
Choose a different symbol for each category.

MapPoint plots your Excel data on the map. The map window automatically zooms in to show the extent of geography in the database. In Figure 10.5, the map is zoomed in to Florida. If, somehow, a single Starbucks from Alaska was erroneously in the database, the map would zoom out to show from Alaska to Florida.

Figure 10.5
Initially, the map zooms out to show all the data points.

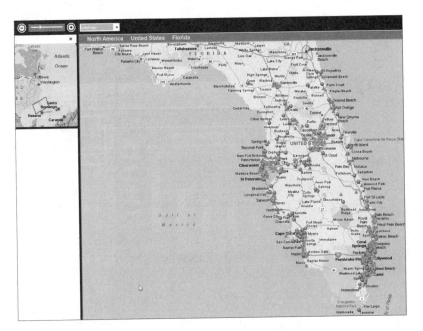

MapPoint offers a zoom slider above the map. You can use the Zoom Slider or Ctrl+wheel mouse to zoom. You can click and drag to recenter the map. If you click near the edge of the map, MapPoint scrolls in that direction.

After importing data, the default view is a Road and Data Map. This map shows the roads as well as the data points. The drop-down just above the map lets you change to a data map, which hides the roads.

In Figure 10.6, the map is zoomed in to show Orlando and central Florida. You could continue zooming in down to the city block level.

Figure 10.6
You can zoom in to show a region or even a neighborhood.

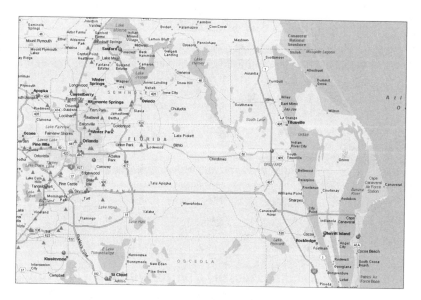

As the dedicated mapping tool, MapPoint provides the most geographic accuracy of the three tools discussed in this chapter. It comes packaged with socioeconomic data, so you could overlay crime, income, and median age data on your map. You can choose to have the Route Planner organize driving directions between all of the points on the map.

Earlier versions of MapPoint were tightly integrated with Excel. You could add the MapPoint COM add-in in Excel and build the maps in Excel. For Excel 2013, this feature does not work with the 64-bit versions of Excel.

Creating a Map in Power View

Power View is a new tool in Excel 2013. As described in Chapter 8, "Creating Pivot Charts and Power View Dashboards," the Power View add-in creates an interactive dashboard worksheet in your Excel workbook. One of the dashboard elements available is a map.

Power View works with data that has been stored in the PowerPivot engine.

Power View and PowerPivot are part of Excel 2013 Pro Plus and higher. They are not a part of the Office Home and Student or Office Standard offerings. If you have an eligible version of Excel 2013, you still have to enable the add-ins. Follow these steps:

1. In Excel 2013, choose File, Options.

2. In the Options dialog, choose Add-Ins from the left navigation panel.

3. At the bottom of the Options dialog is a Manage drop-down. Open the drop-down and choose COM Add-ins. Click Go. Excel displays the COM Add-ins dialog.

4. You must choose Microsoft Office PowerPivot for Excel 2013 and Power View for Excel Add-In as shown in Figure 10.7. You can optionally choose GeoFlow for Microsoft Excel or Microsoft MapPoint if those choices are present.

5. Click OK. You should see a new PowerPivot tab appear in the ribbon. A new Power View icon displays on the Insert tab. A new 3D Map appears in the Data tab if you have GeoFlow. A new MapPoint icon appears in the Add-Ins tab if you have the 32-bit version of Excel and MapPoint.

Figure 10.7
You have to enable the add-ins one time before using them.

Power View is designed to work with data that is stored in the Data Model. To load the data shown in Figure 10.8 into the Data Model, follow these steps:

Figure 10.8
You want to map this data in Power View.

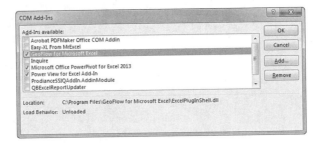

	Latitude	Longitude	Name	City	ST
1	Latitude	Longitude	Name	City	ST
2	28.663907	-81.375686	Starbucks	Altamonte Spring	FL
3	28.651031	-81.385877	Dairy Queen	Altamonte Springs	FL
4	28.6636145	-81.409403	Starbucks	Altamonte Springs	FL
5	28.663135	-81.380273	Starbucks	Altamonte Springs	FL
6	28.673244	-81.49477	Dairy Queen	Apopka	FL
7	28.652337	-81.468037	Starbucks	Apopka	FL
8	25.943955	-80.147145	Starbucks	Aventura	FL
9	25.955973	-80.146649	Starbucks	Aventura	FL
10	25.9566365	-80.1468004	Starbucks	Aventura	FL
11	25.95267	-80.146225	Starbucks	Aventura	FL
12	27.912579	-81.844205	Dairy Queen	Bartow	FL
13	28.482573	-81.3308039	Starbucks	Belle Isle	FL
14	27.9168497	-82.8169114	Starbucks	Belleair Bluffs	FL

1. Select one cell in your data set.

2. Press Ctrl+T to define the range as a table.

3. On the Table Tools Design tab, Excel shows you that the table has a default name, such as Table1. Type a new useful name, such as Locations.

4. On the PowerPivot tab in Excel, click the Add to Data Model icon. (See Figure 10.8.) Excel pauses briefly as the PowerPivot engine prepares a new model. Soon you will be taken to the PowerPivot window. The grid changes color and you have different tabs available.

5. Go to the Advanced tab in the PowerPivot window. Check the Data Category for each of the geographic fields. In this particular data set, Excel guessed correctly for each column except the State column. Apparently, the "ST" abbreviation is not recognized by PowerPivot. For the ST column, open the Data Category drop-down and choose State or Province. (See Figure 10.9.)

6. To return to Excel, use the second icon in the Quick Access toolbar.

10

Figure 10.9
Specify a category for all the geographic columns.

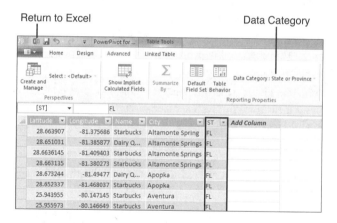

Now that your data is loaded in the Data Model, you can create a Power View worksheet. From the Insert tab, select the Power View icon. Excel inserts a new worksheet. By default, that sheet has a single element and the element is a table, as shown in Figure 10.10.

Look in the Excel 2013 ribbon. All tabs from Power View up to the PowerPivot tab are actually Power View tabs. It is strange that these tabs are not labeled as Power View Design. The various tabs come and go, depending on what element is selected. The icon that you need is on the Design tab.

Click the Map icon in the Design tab. The table element changes to a map element.

Figure 10.10
The default Power View sheet shows your data as a table.

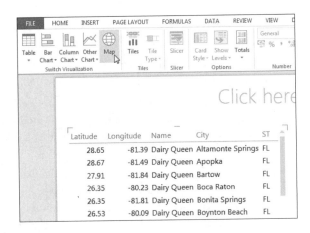

Figure 10.11 shows the various parts of the PowerView window.

■ The Power View canvas holds one or more dashboard elements. Presently, you have a single map, so you can use the resize handles to make the map larger.

■ The Filter pane enables you to filter the information in the dashboard. Drag the Name field from the Power View Fields pane to add a filter where you can choose Starbucks, Dairy Queen, or both.

■ The Power View Fields pane offers a list of all fields and tables stored in the model. Drop zones appear for Tile By, Size, Locations, Longitude, Latitude, Color, Vertical Multiples, and Horizontal Multiples.

In Figure 10.11, the Name field is in the Color drop zone. This causes Dairy Queen to appear in blue, and Starbucks in red. Cities that contain both chains appear with a split circle.

Drag the Name field to the Vertical Multiples field and the map splits to show one map for each Name. The left map is Dairy Queen locations. The right map is Starbucks. (See Figure 10.12.)

Figure 10.11
The map shows cities with one or both chains.

Figure 10.12
Use the Vertical Multiples drop zone to replicate the map for each item.

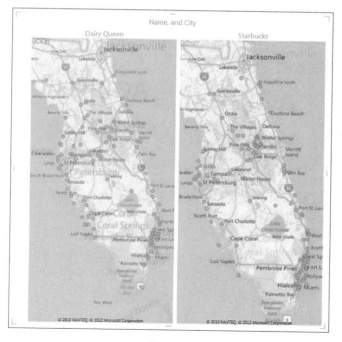

Click the map to reveal Zoom In and Zoom Out controls. Figure 10.13 shows the map zoomed in to the equivalent area as in Figure 10.6.

Figure 10.13
You can zoom in or out in the map.

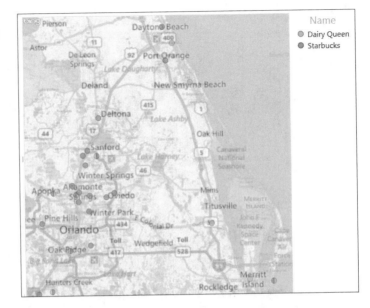

Creating a Map in GeoFlow

GeoFlow is an add-in from the Excel team at Microsoft. Using GeoFlow, you can explore your map in 3D. You can watch a map populate over time, much the same way that Power View shows a scatter chart over time. You can also create a video tour where the map populates over time, and then you fly from region to region in the map.

GeoFlow requires the PowerPivot and GeoFlow add-ins to be enabled in Excel 2013 Pro Plus. PowerPivot is already installed if you have the correct edition of Excel 2013. You will have to download GeoFlow from Microsoft. The final URL has not been published because the product will not release until January 2013. You could do an Internet search for Microsoft GeoFlow to find the download site.

Follow the steps in the Power View section to enable the COM Add-Ins for PowerPivot and GeoFlow. Also, load your data to PowerPivot before creating the GeoFlow map.

From Excel, choose Data, 3D Map, Explore in 3D.

Excel switches to the GeoFlow window (see Figure 10.14). You see a large globe in the center of the screen. A list of fields is available on the right side. Choose the geographic fields and click the Map It button at the bottom right.

Figure 10.14
Choose the geography fields and click Map It.

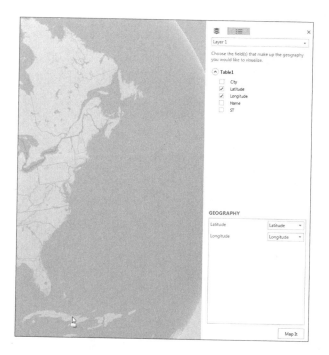

The process of locating each record in the map is called *geocoding*. This data set of roughly 600 points that contain latitude and longitude will be mapped nearly instantly. A data set of 15,000 points with street address, city, and state will take a couple of minutes to geocode.

GeoFlow maps the data. Drag the Name field to the Category drop-zone to use a different color for Starbucks compared to Dairy Queen. (See Figure 10.15.)

GeoFlow allows for more interesting panning and zooming.

- Click and drag the map to change the center position of the map.
- Roll the mouse wheel to zoom in or out.
- Use Ctrl+wheel to change the altitude of the camera.
- Hold down Alt while dragging to rotate the map.

Figure 10.16 shows a GeoFlow map where median income controls the height of the marker. Using the navigation controls mentioned in the preceding list, this map shows the Orlando and Central Florida area looking from the east. You can see Cocoa Beach in the foreground, and Tampa and St. Petersburg in the background. From here, you could arrange a tour that flies in for a close-up look at Orlando by neighborhood.

Figure 10.15
Drag the Name field to the Category. Each point is color coded based on Starbucks or Dairy Queen.

Figure 10.16
You can fly through the map.

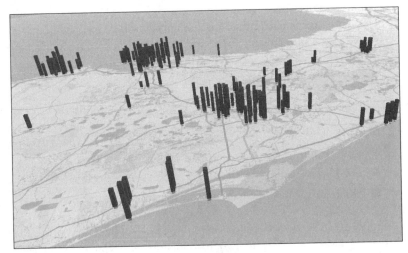

Next Steps

In Chapter 11, "Using SmartArt Diagrams and Shapes," you learn how to use Excel's business diagramming tools to communicate relationships and organization charts.

Using SmartArt Diagrams and Shapes

Images and artwork provide an interesting visual break from tables of numbers. Excel 2007 introduced a new array of business diagrams called SmartArt. Whereas Excel 2003 offered 6 types of business diagrams, SmartArt in Excel 2013 offers 200 types. These diagrams communicate messages about your organization and processes.

The Office team envisioned that SmartArt would be most popular in PowerPoint presentations, so SmartArt is designed for static messages. Later in this chapter, you find out how to convert SmartArt to shapes, allowing the words in the diagram to come from calculations in the cells.

This chapter covers the following:

- **SmartArt**—SmartArt is a collection of similar shapes, arranged to imply a process, groups, or a hierarchy. In legacy versions of Excel, SmartArt was known as diagrams. As in legacy versions, with Excel 2013 it is easy to add new shapes, reverse the order of shapes, and change the color of shapes. Office 2013 includes a text editor that allows for Level 1 and Level 2 text for each shape in a diagram. Many styles of SmartArt include the capability to add a small picture or logo to each shape.

- **Shapes**—You can add interesting shapes to a document. A shape can contain words; it is the only art object in which the words can come from a cell on the worksheet. You can add glow, bevel, and 3D effects to shapes. In legacy versions of Excel, shapes were known as AutoShapes. Microsoft added some new shapes, starting in Excel 2007, and several formatting properties.

- **WordArt**—You use WordArt to present ordinary text in a stylized manner. You can use it to bend, rotate, and twist the characters in text. In

IN THIS CHAPTER

Using SmartArt 288

Choosing the Right Layout for Your Message 302

Exploring Business Charts That Use SmartArt Graphics 303

Using Shapes to Display Cell Contents 309

Using WordArt for Interesting Titles and Headlines 312

Next Steps 315

Excel 2013, you can add glow, bevel, and material effects. WordArt has been completely redesigned from legacy versions of Excel. A limited version of WordArt is available for formatting titles and labels in Excel charts.

Using SmartArt

You use SmartArt to show a series of similar shapes, where each shape represents a related step, concept, idea, or grouping. SmartArt in Excel 2013 is an enhanced version of business diagrams from legacy versions of Excel. In Excel 2013, Microsoft has addressed many of the shortcomings of business diagrams, including the following:

- Each shape has an associated text editor.
- Shapes can contain Level 1 text for headlines and Level 2 text for body copy.
- Forty styles now allow shapes to include an image.
- Automatic settings in SmartArt can automatically resize the text in all shapes to allow the longest text to fit.
- SmartArt styles enable you to apply glow and bevels to an entire SmartArt diagram.

The goal of SmartArt is to enable you to create a great-looking graphic with minimal effort. After you define a SmartArt image for your text, you can quickly change to any of the other 200+ styles by clicking the desired style in the gallery. Figure 11.1 shows four different SmartArt layouts:

- **Basic Process**—In this style, all text is typed as Level 1.
- **Accent Process**—This style puts the Level 1 text in the background and highlights the Level 2 text in the foreground boxes.
- **Picture Accent Process**—This style gives equal weight to the Level 1 and Level 2 text. Pictures are added behind each shape.
- **Picture Accent List**—Unlike the process charts, a list chart does not include arrows to indicate a process.

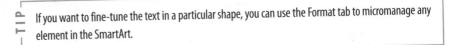

TIP: If you want to fine-tune the text in a particular shape, you can use the Format tab to micromanage any element in the SmartArt.

Figure 11.1
Subtle differences in four of the 200+ possible SmartArt styles give more weight to either Level 1 or Level 2 text. Notice that the Level 1 text is prominent (top), in the background (second), small (third), or vertical (bottom).

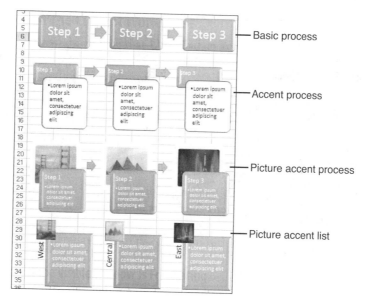

Elements Common Across Most SmartArt

A SmartArt style is a collection of related shapes. In most styles, you can add additional shapes to illustrate a longer process. A few styles are limited to only *n* items. Each shape can contain a headline (Level 1 text), body copy (Level 2 text), and sometimes a graphic. Some of the 200 styles show only Level 1 text. If you switch to a style that does not display Level 2 text and then switch back before closing the workbook, the shape remembers the Level 2 text it originally had. Starting in Excel 2010, any text that is not visible in the SmartArt diagram is discarded when the file is saved and closed. This prevents you from accidentally sending out text that you forgot to delete.

While you're editing SmartArt, a text pane that is slightly reminiscent of PowerPoint appears. You can type some bullet points in the text pane. If you demote a bullet point by pressing the Tab key, the text changes from Level 1 text to Level 2 text. If you add a new Level 1 bullet point, Excel adds a new shape to the SmartArt.

A Tour of the SmartArt Categories

The SmartArt gallery groups the 200 SmartArt layouts into nine broad categories:

- **List**—This category is designed to show a nonsequential list of information. Variations include horizontal, vertical, and bending lists. Some lists include chevrons, and some include pictures. In general, these styles do not include arrows between shapes.

- **Process**—This category is designed to show a sequential list of steps. Variations include horizontal, vertical, bending, equations, funnels, gears, and several varieties of arrows. Some process charts allow the inclusion of images. Most styles include arrows or other connectors to convey a sequence.

- **Cycle**—This category is designed to show a series of steps that repeat. It includes cycle charts, radial charts, a gear chart, and a pie chart.
- **Hierarchy**—This category is designed to show organization charts, decision trees, and other hierarchical relationships. Variations include horizontal and vertical charts and charts with and without connecting lines.
- **Relationship**—This category is designed to show a relationship between items. Many of the layouts in this category are duplicated from the other seven categories. This category includes examples of arrow, chart, cycle, equation, funnel, gear, hierarchy, list, process, pyramid, radial, target, and Venn chart layouts.
- **Matrix**—This category is designed to show four quadrants of a list. The Titled Matrix layout offers a fifth block for an overall title. The new Cycle Matrix allows for Level 2 text outside the main blocks.
- **Pyramid**—This category is designed to show containment, overlapping, proportional, or interconnected relationships.
- **Picture**—All the layouts that contain pictures are repeated in this category. Some of the styles appear only in this category. Some of these picture layouts are appropriate only for pictures with little or no text.
- **Office.com**—In addition to the built-in SmartArt layouts, another 17 layouts (or more by the time you read this) are available for download from Office.com. You will find some badly needed layouts, such as an org chart with space for pictures of each person.

Figure 11.2 shows one version of each of the nine categories.

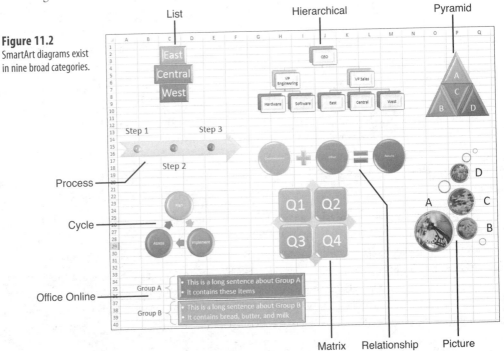

Figure 11.2
SmartArt diagrams exist in nine broad categories.

Inserting SmartArt

Although there are 200 different layouts of SmartArt, you follow the same basic steps to insert any SmartArt layout:

1. Select a cell in a blank section of the workbook.
2. From the Insert tab, select SmartArt from the Illustrations group. The Choose a SmartArt Graphic dialog appears.
3. From the left side of the Choose a SmartArt Graphic dialog, choose a category.
4. Click a SmartArt type in the center of the Choose a SmartArt Graphic dialog.
5. Read the description on the right side. This description tells you whether the layout is good for Level 1 text, Level 2 text, or both. In Figure 11.3, you can see that the Vertical Block List layout is good for large amounts of Level 2 text.
6. Repeat steps 4 and 5 until you find a style suitable for your content. Then click OK. As shown in Figure 11.4, an outline of the SmartArt is drawn on the worksheet. The flashing insertion cursor is in the first item of the text pane. One element of the SmartArt is selected. When you type text at the flashing insertion point, it is added to the selected shape.

Figure 11.3
The information for each style provides information about whether a particular style is appropriate for more Level 1 or Level 2 text.

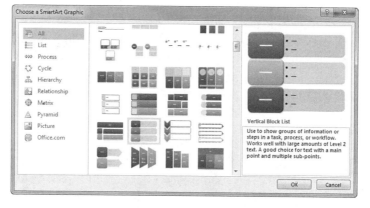

Figure 11.4
When you type in the text pane, the text is added to the selected element of the SmartArt.

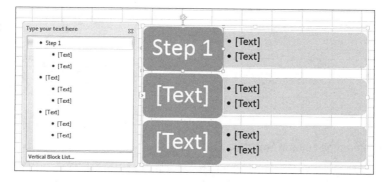

7. Fill in the text pane with text for your SmartArt. You can add, delete, promote, or demote items by using icons in the SmartArt Tools, Design, Create Graphic group. The SmartArt updates as you type more text.

> **NOTE** In many cases, adding a new Level 1 item adds a new shape element to the SmartArt. If you add longer text to the SmartArt, Excel shrinks all the elements to make the text fit.

8. Make the entire SmartArt graphic larger, if needed, by grabbing the resizing handles in the corners of the SmartArt and dragging to a new size. After you resize the graphic, Excel resizes the text to make it fit in the SmartArt at the largest size possible.

9. If you like, change the color scheme of the SmartArt, which initially appears in one color. To do so, from the SmartArt Tools Design tab, select Change Colors from the SmartArt Styles group. Excel offers several versions of monochromatic styles and five styles of color variations for each shape.

10. Choose a 2D or 3D style from the SmartArt Styles gallery on the Design tab. The Inset and Polished styles have a suitable mix of effects but are readable.

11. Move the SmartArt to the proper location. Position the mouse over the border of the SmartArt, avoiding the eight resizing areas. The cursor changes to a four-headed arrow. Click and drag the SmartArt to a new location. If you drag the SmartArt to the left side of the worksheet, the text pane moves to the right of the SmartArt.

12. Click outside the SmartArt. Excel embeds the SmartArt graphic in the worksheet and hides the SmartArt tabs. Figure 11.5 shows some completed SmartArt.

Figure 11.5
You click outside the SmartArt boundary to embed the completed SmartArt.

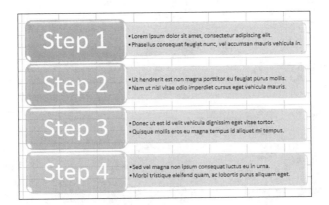

Changing the Color of SmartArt Graphics

The Design tab's Change Colors drop-down offers 38 color schemes for each theme. Five options in the Colorful category offer to mix up the colors used for each shape. Thirty other options offer five varying shades of each of six accent colors.

Changing the Theme colors on the Page Layout tab affects the colors offered in the Change Colors drop-down.

Applying a SmartArt Style

The Design tab offers a large gallery of 14 SmartArt styles. There are 5 2D styles in a section labeled Best Fit for Document. There are also 9 3D styles.

Choosing a style from the gallery applies a different mix of bevel, shadow, transparency, gradient, reflection, and glow to all shapes. The built-in styles range from subtle to outlandish. Some of the later 3D styles, such as Bird's Eye Scene and Brick Scene, are very hard to read. If you are trying to present bad news that no one can read, you might want to choose the later 3D styles. Otherwise, the second and third 3D styles, known as Inset and Cartoon, seem to offer a great mix of effects and readability. Figure 11.6 shows a Continuous Arrow Process graphic with the 14 styles applied.

Figure 11.6
The SmartArt styles range from simple to over-the-top. The Inset and Polished styles offer a mix of style and readability.

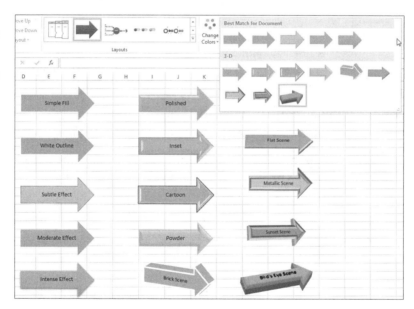

11

Changing Existing SmartArt to a New Style

You can use a couple of ways to change SmartArt to a new style:

■ You can left-click the SmartArt, and then select the SmartArt Tools, Layouts from the Design tab to choose a new layout. As shown in Figure 11.7, the Layouts drop-down initially shows only the styles that Excel thinks are a close fit to the current style. If you want to access the complete list of styles, you have to select More Layouts. The advantage of this method is that Live Preview shows you the changes before you commit to a style.

Figure 11.7
Browse other layouts.

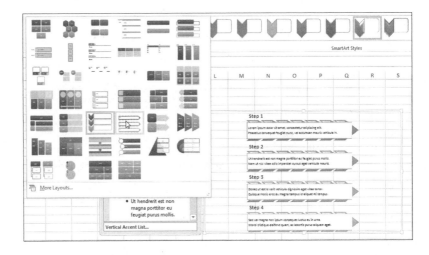

■ A faster way to access the complete list of styles is to right-click between two shapes in the SmartArt and select Change Layout from the context menu. This step is a little tricky because you cannot click an existing shape; you must click inside the SmartArt border—but on a section of the SmartArt that contains nothing.

Micromanaging SmartArt Elements

There are two tabs on the Ribbon for SmartArt tools: the Design and Format tabs.

The Design tab enables you to change the overall design of the SmartArt. If you stay on the Design tab, Microsoft makes sure that your SmartArt looks good. It keeps the font for all Level 2 text consistent for all shapes. It keeps all the shapes proportional. If you have a particular need to override some aspect of one shape, however, you can do so on the Format tab.

> ┌ C A U T I O N ─────
> When you change any setting on the Format tab, Microsoft turns off the automatic formatting for the other elements. Changing a setting on the Format tab is a great way to make horrible-looking SmartArt. If you absolutely have to use the Format tab, you should first get your SmartArt as close as possible to the final version by using the Design tab.

Changing Text Formatting in One Element

In Automatic mode, Excel chooses a font size that is small enough to show the longest text completely. This can cause problems if you have one shape with long text and all the other shapes have short text. In this case, Excel chooses a small font size for the long text and then forces all the other items to have the same tiny text, too. In such a situation, you might want to override the text size for the shape that has the longest text. Excel then automatically resizes the font size in the remaining automatic shapes to be larger.

> **TIP** New in Excel 2013, the Varying Width List breaks the just-mentioned rule. As you type more text in this layout, the size of the box increases. Find this layout in the Office.com section of the Choose a SmartArt Graphic dialog.

The mini toolbar is useful for making these types of changes. You select the text either directly in the shape or in the text pane. Immediately after you complete the selection, a floating formatting box appears. You can then change the font size by using the drop-down in the mini toolbar. If the mini toolbar disappears before you use it to make your changes, you can use the formatting tools on the Home tab to change the font size.

In Figure 11.8, the long Level 2 text in step 4 was resized. Excel then calculated the proper text size for steps 1 through 3, resulting in the text in the top three shapes automatically growing to a larger font size.

Figure 11.8
When you manually override the font size in the fourth shape, the text in the remaining three shapes automatically becomes larger.

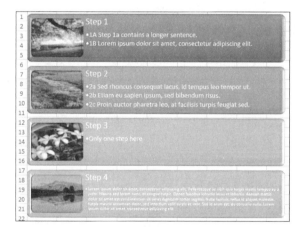

Changing One Shape

You can edit many items for a SmartArt shape. To see how this works, you can click any shape in the SmartArt and then try the following:

- Use the green handle to rotate the shape.
- Use the resize handles to resize the shape.
- Use the move handle to nudge the shape.
- Select Change Shape from the Format tab to change the outline to a different shape.

■ Select settings from the Shape Styles group to change fill, outline, and effects for the shape.

■ Select settings from the WordArt Styles group to change the text inside the shape.

■ Right-click the shape and select Format Shape to have complete control over the shape.

In general, SmartArt created on the Design tab looks uniform and neat. When you move to the Format tab, the possibility for chaos arises. For example, the SmartArt in Figure 11.9 contains mixed effects, font sizes, and rotation; it was created in the Format tab.

Figure 11.9
After experimenting with the Format tab, you can select Reset Graphic on the Design tab to turn the SmartArt back into something more uniform.

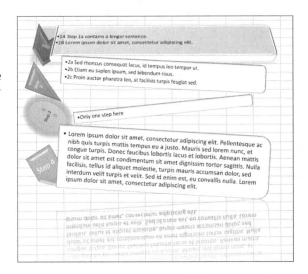

Controlling SmartArt Shapes from the Text Pane

The text pane represents a fantastic improvement over business diagrams in Excel 2003. By using only the keyboard, you can add or delete shapes and promote or demote items. Further, the text pane includes proofing tools such as spell check. Using the text pane is similar to creating bullet points in a PowerPoint slide.

Figure 11.10 shows a newly inserted pyramid SmartArt in Excel. By default, most new SmartArt diagrams have three shapes, but you can change that number by using the text pane.

The following rules apply to the text pane for SmartArt:

■ Press the up-arrow and down-arrow keys to move from one line to another.

■ Press the Enter key to insert a new line below the current line. The new line will be at the same level as the current line. Adding a new Level 1 line inserts a new shape in the SmartArt.

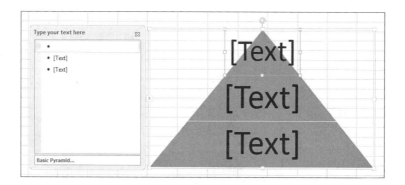

Figure 11.10
A default SmartArt includes three shapes. You can edit the number of shapes by using the text pane.

- Press the Tab key to demote Level 1 text to Level 2 text.
- Press Shift+Tab to promote Level 2 text to Level 1 text.
- Press the Backspace key on an empty line to delete the line.
- Press Delete at the end of any line to combine text from the next line with this line.
- Press End to move to the end of the current line.
- Press Home to move to the beginning of the current line.

As you add shapes, Excel continues to attempt to squeeze them into the default size. You can resize an entire piece of SmartArt by using the resizing handles around the SmartArt.

As an example of how the text pane works, you can use the following steps to customize the inverted pyramid graphic shown in Figure 11.10 into the one shown in Figure 11.1. This example illustrates how quickly and simply you can change from the default SmartArt with three shapes to any number of shapes:

1. Type **Shape 1** and then press Enter.
2. Type **Subtext** and then press Tab to demote the item. Then press the down-arrow key to move to text 2.
3. Type **Shape 2** and then press Enter.
4. Type **Point 1** and then press Tab and Enter.
5. Type **Point 2** and then press the down-arrow key.
6. Type **Shape 3** and then press Enter.
7. Type **Point 3** and then press Tab and Enter.
8. Excel wants the next item to be Level 2 text, so press Shift+Tab to promote this item.
9. Type **Shape 4** and then press Enter; type **Shape 5** and then press Enter; type **Shape 6** and then press Enter.
10. Type **Point 4** and then press Tab.
11. Using the mouse, resize the SmartArt so that it is larger.
12. From the SmartArt Styles gallery on the Design ribbon tab, choose a color scheme.

11

The result is shown in Figure 11.11. As this example shows, by using only the keyboard and the text pane, you can quickly expand SmartArt and add Level 2 subpoints.

Figure 11.11
You can add additional shapes and subpoints simply by using the text pane.

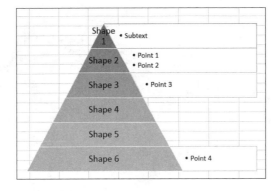

Adding Images to SmartArt

In the Picture category, 36 SmartArt layouts are designed to hold small images in addition to text. In some of these styles, the picture is emphasized; in others, the focus is on the text, and the picture is an accent.

When you select one of these styles, you add text with the text pane and then specify pictures by clicking the picture icon inside each Level 1 shape. The SmartArt shows a picture icon next to bullet points in the text pane and also in each shape (see Figure 11.12).

Figure 11.12
Each Level 1 bullet includes a picture placeholder.

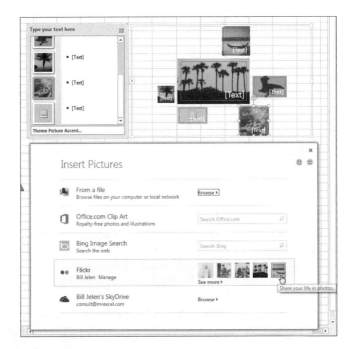

You can click a picture icon to display the Insert Picture dialog. You can then choose a picture and click Insert. You repeat this process to add each additional picture. The pictures are automatically cropped to fit the allotted area, as shown in Figure 11.13.

Figure 11.13
Pictures have been added to each shape.

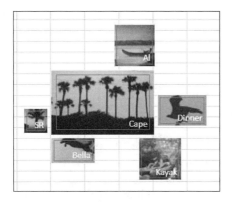

Special Considerations for Organization Charts

Hierarchical SmartArt can contain more than two text levels. As you add more levels to the SmartArt, Excel continues to intelligently add boxes and resize them to fit.

Figure 11.14 shows a diagram created in the Hierarchy style. In this style, each level is assigned a different color.

Figure 11.14
Hierarchical SmartArt can contain more than two levels.

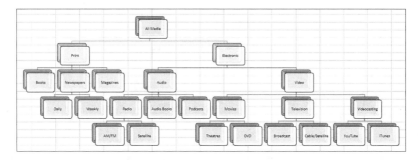

Using Assistant Shapes in Organization Charts

The first style available in the Hierarchy category is the Organization Chart style. You use this style to describe reporting relationships in an organization. There are a few extra options in the ribbon for organization charts. For example, select one manager shape in your organizational chart diagram. The Add Shape drop-down on the Design tab includes the Add Assistant option, as shown in Figure 11.15. You can select this option to add an extra shape immediately below the selected level.

11

Figure 11.15
The Add Assistant selection adds a box for an assistant below the selected shape.

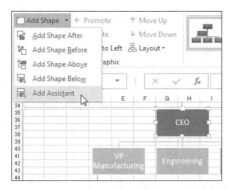

Arranging Subordinates on an Organization Chart

In the Create Graphic group of the Design tab, the Layout drop-down offers four options for showing the boxes within a group. First, you select the manager for the group. Then you select the appropriate type from the drop-down to affect all direct reports for the manager. Figure 11.16 illustrates the four options for the Layout drop-down:

- **VP of Sales**—This option shows a standard organization chart. The regions are arranged side by side.
- **VP of Manufacturing**—This option has a right-hanging group. The departments are arranged vertically to the right of the line.
- **VP of Engineering**—This option has a left hanging group. The departments are arranged vertically to the left of the line.
- **CFO**—This option has a Both group. The direct reports are listed in two columns under the manager, on both sides of the vertical line.

In each group, the assistant box is arranged to the left of the vertical line.

Figure 11.16
Organization charts include options to control the arrangement of direct reports.

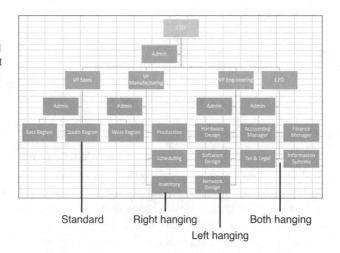

Showing Dotted-Line Reporting Relationships

The SmartArt graphics engine cannot automatically create dotted-line reporting relationships. However, you can manually add a line to a diagram (see Figure 11.17).

To add a dotted line, follow these steps:

1. Prepare the organization chart, using the SmartArt tools.

2. From the Insert tab, select the Shapes drop-down.

3. Click the elbow connector.

4. Draw a line that connects the appropriate two boxes on the organization chart. Grab the yellow diamond handle to lower the horizontal portion of the line to be at the same height as the lower box. Don't worry that the line is the wrong weight and style.

5. Click the line to select it.

6. In the Drawing Tools, Format tab, select the Shape Outline drop-down. From the Weight fly-out menu, choose a thicker line style, such as 3 pt.

7. Access the Shape Outline drop-down again. From the Dashes fly-out menu, choose one of the dotted-line styles.

Figure 11.17
Add the shape, drag the yellow diamond into position, and then format the line as dotted.

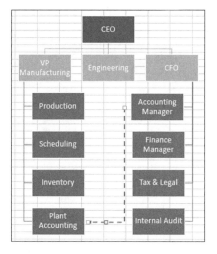

> **NOTE** You should get your graphic as close to being done as possible before adding manual shapes. Any subsequent changes to the text pane require manual repositioning of the lines.

Using Limited SmartArt

Most of the SmartArt examples described so far are expandable: As you add Level 1 text, new shapes are added to the SmartArt. However, the SmartArt styles in the following list cannot be expanded (see Figure 11.18).

■ Both gear and funnel charts are limited to three items. If you add additional items to the text pane, each appears with a red X. These items do not display in the SmartArt, but they are stored until the file is saved and closed in case you later change to another SmartArt layout. For privacy reasons, the extra text is discarded when you save and close the file.

■ Many of the arrow layouts in the Relationship category are limited to two shapes.

■ The Matrix layouts are limited to four quadrants. Grid Matrix offers four quadrants plus a title, as shown in the center of Figure 11.18.

■ The Segmented Pyramid style can be expanded, but it must contain 1, 4, 9, or 16 shapes. As soon as you add a fifth style to the SmartArt in the upper-left corner of the display, an entire row is added to the bottom of the pyramid, resulting in the SmartArt shown in the lower right of Figure 11.18.

■ The Equation style can be expanded, but the answer is always the last Level 1 item in the text pane.

Figure 11.18
Arrows, gears, funnels, and matrix shapes have certain limitations on the number of shapes they can contain.

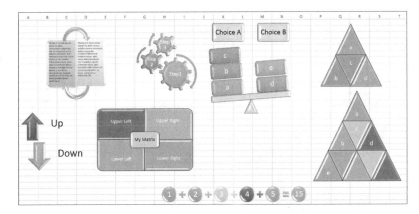

Choosing the Right Layout for Your Message

With 200 built-in layouts of SmartArt graphics, choosing the right layout can be daunting.

The following questions are designed to help you narrow your choices, assuming that you do not want to further customize the look of a graphic:

■ Do you need accent images in the shape? If so, select Bending Picture Accent List, Picture Caption List, Horizontal Picture List, Picture Accent List, Continuous Picture List, Vertical Picture Accent List, Vertical Picture List, Picture Accent Process, or Radial List.

■ Do you have extremely long sentences of Level 2 text? If so, choose Vertical Box List or Vertical Bullet List.

- Do you need to show a continuous process? If so, choose one of the cycle charts: Text Cycle, Basic Cycle, Continuous Cycle, Block Cycle, or Segmented Cycle.

- Do you need to show a circular process that can travel both ways? If so, select Multidirectional Cycle.

- Do you need to show a process that progresses from left to right? If so, choose Basic Process, Accent Process, Continuous Arrow Process, Alternating Flow, Process Arrows, Detailed Process, Continuous Block Process, Picture Accent Process, Basic Chevron Process, or Closed Chevron Process.

- Do you need to show many processes that progress from left to right? If so, select Chevron List.

- Do you need to show a process that progresses from top to bottom? If so, choose Vertical Process, Segmented Process, Vertical Chevron List, or Staggered Process.

- Do you need to show a one-way process and need to fit many shapes into a small area? If so, choose Basic Bending Process, Circular Bending Process, Repeating Bending Process, or Vertical Bending Process.

- Do you need to show an organization? If so, select Organization Chart.

- Do you need to show a hierarchy? If so, choose one of the pyramid, radial, matrix, target, or hierarchy layouts.

- Do you need to make a decision between two choices? If so, select Balance.

- Do you need to show how parts add together to create an output? If so, choose an Equation or a Funnel layout.

- Do you need to illustrate two opposing forces? If so, choose Diverging Arrows, Counterbalance Arrows, Opposing Arrows, Converging Arrows, or Arrow Ribbon.

- Do you need to illustrate a containment chart? If so, choose Nested Target or Stacked Venn.

Exploring Business Charts That Use SmartArt Graphics

The examples in this section show off a few of the 200 SmartArt graphics that might be suitable for your business presentations.

In particular, a few of the examples in this section show layouts that are a bit more difficult than average to utilize.

> **NOTE** To see more examples of SmartArt, take a look at *Leveraging SmartArt Graphics in the 2007 Microsoft Office System*, an e-book published by Que (ISBN 0-7686-6833-6).

Illustrating a Pro/Con Decision by Using a Balance Chart

The Balance layout is used to illustrate weighing two alternatives, as shown in Figure 11.19.

The layout requires two Level 1 text entries to represent the boxes at the top of the graphic. You can then have up to three Level 2 entries for each Level 1 entry. The scale tips in the direction of the side that has more boxes.

Figure 11.19
This graphic leans either left or right, depending on which side has more Level 2 text entries.

Illustrating Growth by Using an Upward Arrow

Microsoft had to create a new shape, called a swoosh arrow, to add the Upward Arrow layout. This layout holds up to five bullets of Level 1 text. Any Level 2 text is shown below the Level 1 text. This makes it very difficult to fit any Level 2 text beneath the first bullet point of Level 1 text.

In Figure 11.20, a few bullet points of Level 2 text are placed beneath the final Level 1 text entry to provide a caption for the whole chart.

Figure 11.20
The swoosh arrow shows up to five bullets of Level 1 text.

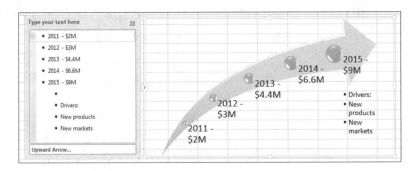

Showing an Iterative Process by Using a Basic Cycle Layout

Several cycle process charts are available in the SmartArt gallery. In some layouts, the arrows are too small to be seen. The Basic Cycle layout offers a good balance between text-holding shapes and arrows (see Figure 11.21).

Figure 11.21
The Basic Cycle layout offers a balance between text and arrows.

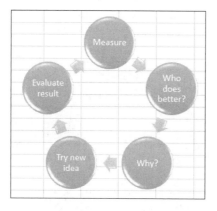

Showing a Company's Relationship to External Entities by Using a Diverging Radial Diagram

The radial layouts show the relationship of one center entity to several entities around the perimeter of the diagram, as shown in Figure 11.22. Whereas many layouts offer a hub-and-spokes arrangement, the Diverging Radial layout adds arrows that point outward from the central diagram to each external shape.

Figure 11.22
The Diverging Radial layout shows how a central organization supports many other organizations.

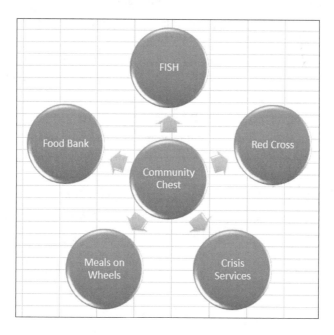

11

The text for the central circle should be entered as a single bullet of Level 1 text. You build the remaining shapes around the perimeter by adding Level 2 bullets.

Illustrating Departments Within a Company by Using a Table List Diagram

The Table List layout holds a single entry of Level 1 text as a title across the top of the diagram. Each Level 2 entry causes the diagram to be vertically split. You could show additional bullets in each box by adding Level 3 text (see Figure 11.23).

Figure 11.23
You can illustrate groups within a whole by using the Table List layout.

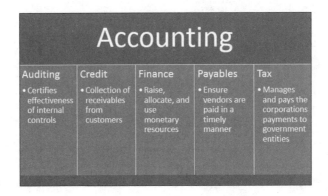

11

Adjusting Venn Diagrams to Show Relationships

The Basic Venn layout illustrates two to seven overlapping circles. Unfortunately, all the Venn diagrams created by the SmartArt engine show circles that are perfectly overlapping, as shown on the left side of Figure 11.24. This is not how relationships usually happen.

To create Venn diagrams that represent relationships, you can usually adjust the size of each circle and the percentage of overlap in the circles. For example, on the right side of Figure 11.24, the diagram indicates that whereas 80 percent of the bowling team is made up of people from the accounting department, fewer than one-fifth of the accountants are on the bowling team. To create this chart, you follow these steps:

1. Add a SmartArt diagram with a Basic Venn layout.
2. Enter two Level 1 text entries and name them Accounting and Bowling Team.
3. Click the Accounting circle. Excel displays resizing handles. Drag a resizing handle out from the center of the circle to make the circle larger.
4. Click the Bowling circle. Drag a resizing handle inward to make the circle smaller.
5. While the resizing handles are displayed, drag the Bowling circle so that about 80 percent of that circle is inside the larger circle.

Figure 11.24
Venn diagrams require adjustment to show the real size and proportion of overlap.

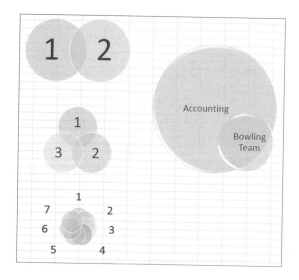

Understanding Labeled Hierarchy Charts

To figure out two of Excel 2013's hierarchy charts—Labeled Hierarchy and Horizontal Labeled Hierarchy—you almost need a Ph.D. However, when you figure out the bizarre layouts required in the text pane, these are handy hierarchy charts.

The Horizontal Labeled Hierarchy (see Figure 11.25) offers a horizontal hierarchy chart that progresses from left to right. Each level of the chart lies in a colored band with a title. To create this chart, follow these steps:

1. Create a single Level 1 item.

2. Beneath the first Level 1 item, build the complete hierarchy of Level 2, Level 3, and so on.

3. Count the number of levels in the hierarchy, including the first level. The chart in Figure 11.25 includes three levels. Remember this number for step 4.

4. At the bottom of the text pane, add new Level 1 entries. The first new Level 1 entry should include the title for the leftmost level of the hierarchy. The second new Level 1 entry should include the title for the second level of the hierarchy. Do not add any Level 2 text to these Level 1 entries.

When the number of bottom Level 1 entries exactly matches the number of levels in the hierarchy, the diagram snaps into place, with the titles lining up in the colored bands.

11

Figure 11.25
Getting the titles at the top of each band requires Level 1 shapes at the end of the text pane.

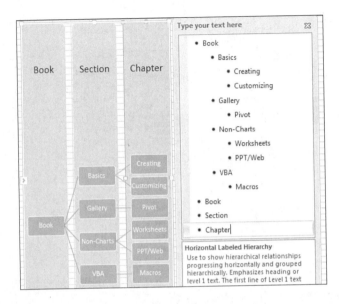

Using Other SmartArt Layouts

With Excel's 200 built-in layouts, you can use SmartArt graphics in a variety of ways. During Power Excel seminars that I conduct, I often show a slide with a few of the new graphics, such as the funnel or gear charts. A clever accountant in one of my audiences wryly pointed out that the funnel chart would be perfect for illustrating the ingredients in a martini (see Figure 11.26).

Figure 11.26
Your use of SmartArt diagrams for illustrating business concepts is limited only by your imagination.

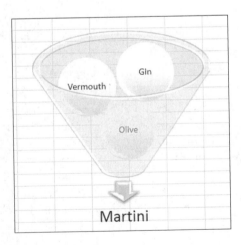

Although Microsoft does not currently allow SmartArt to be created using VBA, it does allow someone with an understanding of XML to create brand-new SmartArt layouts. *Leveraging SmartArt Graphics in the 2007 Microsoft Office System*, an e-book published by

Que (ISBN 0-7686-6833-6), includes several examples that illustrate how to create new layouts that use different shapes, such as pentagons instead of circles, or change the default proportions of the SmartArt layouts.

Overall, SmartArt is a great addition to the Office family. The one real drawback related to SmartArt in Excel 2013 is the inability to link cell content to the text in SmartArt. To do that, you have to use shapes, as described in the following section.

Using Shapes to Display Cell Contents

Shapes were known in legacy versions of Excel as AutoShapes. Microsoft has added new shapes to the already long list of shapes available in AutoShapes. In addition, as of Excel 2010, shapes have some new formatting options, such as shadow, glow, and bevel.

Perhaps the best part of shapes is that you can tie the text on a shape to a worksheet cell. In Figure 11.27, for example, the shape is set to display the current value of Cell B26. Every time the worksheet is calculated, the text on the shape is updated.

Figure 11.27
Shapes can be set to display the current value of a cell.

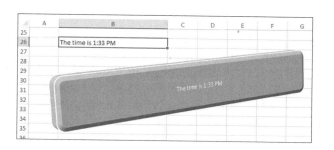

You follow these steps to insert a shape into a worksheet:

1. Select a blank area of the worksheet.
2. From the Insert tab, open the Shapes drop-down.
3. Select 1 of the 159 basic shapes, as shown in Figure 11.28.
4. When the mouse pointer changes to a small crosshair, click and drag in the worksheet to draw the shape.
5. Choose a color scheme from the Shapes Styles drop-down.
6. Select Shape Effects, Preset, and select an effect.
7. Look for a yellow diamond on the shape. Change the inflection point for the shape, if necessary. On the rounded rectangle, for example, sliding the yellow diamond controls how wide the rounded corners are.
8. Look for a green circle on the outside of the shape. Drag this circle to rotate the shape, if necessary.

Figure 11.28
Choose from these shapes.

9. To include static text in the shape, click in the middle of the shape and type the text. You can control the style by using the WordArt Styles drop-down. You can control text size and color by using the formatting buttons on the Home tab. The shape can include text from any cell, but it cannot perform a calculation. If you want the shape to include a calculated value, skip this step and follow steps 10 through 12.

10. If desired, add a new cell that formats a message for the Shape. As shown in Figure 11.29, you can add the formula ="We are at "&TEXT(B13,"0%")&" of our goal!" to an empty cell to convert the calculation in cell B13 to a suitable message.

Figure 11.29
This shape picks up the formula from cell B14 to show a message that changes with the worksheet.

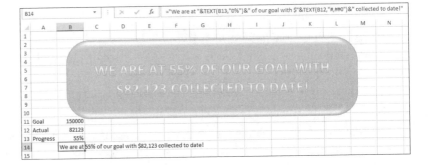

11. Click the middle of the text box as if you were about to type some text.

12. Click in the Formula Bar, type =B14, and then press Enter. As shown in Figure 11.29, the shape displays the results from the selected cell.

13. To increase the size of the text, use the Font group on the Home tab.

14. To add effects to the text, use the WordArt group on the Drawing Tools Format tab.

Working with Shapes

The Drawing Tools Format tab contains options to change the shape style, fill, outline, effects, and WordArt effects.

In the Insert Shapes group of the Format tab, choose Edit Shape and then Change Shape to change from one shape to another.

If you right-click a shape and select Format Shape, Excel displays the Format Shape dialog, with the fine-tuning settings Fill, Line, Line Style, Shadow, 3D Format, 3D Rotation, and Text Placement.

Using the Freeform Shape to Create a Custom Shape

Despite my friendly relationship with Microsoft, I have not convinced them to add the MrExcel logo to the Shapes gallery (yet). However, you can build any shape by using the Freeform line tools in the Shapes gallery.

After you create a shape, you can add 3D effects, glow, and so on to make a cool-looking version of your company logo, as shown in Figure 11.30.

Figure 11.30
This shape was created with the Freeform shape tool and then enhanced using the Drawing Tools section of the Format tab.

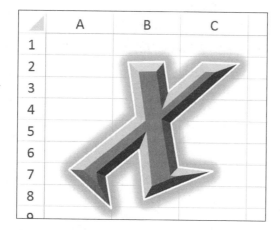

To create a custom shape, follow these steps:

1. Insert a picture of the shape that you can use as a guide to trace.

2. From the Insert tab, select the Shapes drop-down. In the Lines section, the last two shapes are Freeform and Scribble. Select the Freeform shape.

3. Click one corner of your logo.

4. Move the mouse to the adjacent corner of the logo and click again.

5. Repeat step 4 for each corner. If your logo has a curve, click several times around the perimeter of the curve. The more often you click, the better the curve will be.

6. When you arrive back at the original corner, click one final time to close the shape and complete the drawing.

7. Use the effect and fill settings to color and stylize the logo.

Using WordArt for Interesting Titles and Headlines

WordArt was rewritten for Excel 2007. As in legacy versions, WordArt is best used sparingly—possibly for a headline or title at the top of a page. It is best used for impressive display fonts to add interest to a report. You would probably not want to create an entire 20-page document in WordArt.

To use WordArt, follow these steps:

1. Select a blank section of a worksheet.

2. From the Insert tab, select the WordArt drop-down.

3. As shown in Figure 11.31, select from the 20 WordArt presets in the drop-down. Don't worry that these presets seem less exciting than the WordArt in prior versions of Excel. You will be able to customize the WordArt later.

4. Excel adds the generic Your Text Here in the preset WordArt you chose. Select this default text and then type your own text.

5. Select the text. Choose a new font style by using either the mini toolbar that appears or the Home tab.

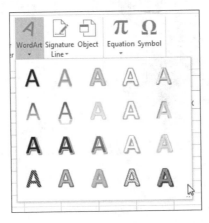

Figure 11.31
Excel offers 30 WordArt presets.

6. Use the WordArt Styles group on the Drawing Tools Format tab to color the WordArt. To the right of the Styles drop-down are icons for text color and line color and a

drop-down for effects. The Effects drop-down includes the fly-out menus Shadow, Reflection, Glow, Bevel, and 3D Rotation.

7. To achieve the old-style WordArt effects, from the Format tab, select Drawing Tools, WordArt Styles, Text Effects, Transform, and then select a shape for the text. Figure 11.32 shows the WordArt with a Wave 1 transformation.

Figure 11.32
WordArt includes the Transform menu to bend and twist type.

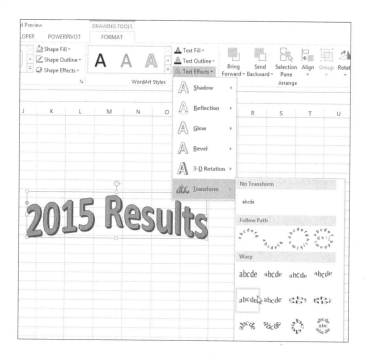

11

CASE STUDY: CONVERTING SMARTART TO SHAPES TO ALLOW DYNAMIC DIAGRAMS

Microsoft's official position is that you cannot use formulas to populate the text pane in SmartArt diagrams. However, using the steps in this section, you can simulate this effect.

The diagram in Figure 11.33 looks like a SmartArt Table Hierarchy layout, yet the values in all the shapes are fed from formulas on the Excel worksheet.

> ┌ C A U T I O N ─────────────────────────────────
>
> This solution does not work when the number of shapes needs to change in response to the values in the Excel worksheet. The number of shapes has to remain the same. Only the text in the shapes is based on live formulas.

Figure 11.33
This looks like a SmartArt diagram, but the values come from formulas on the worksheet. Although using formulas this way sounds simple, the feature is not hooked up in Excel 2013.

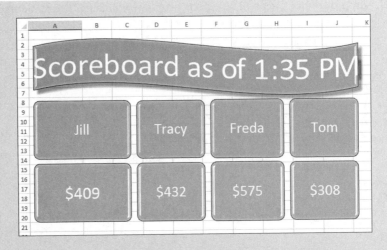

You achieve the live formulas in the SmartArt diagram by cheating slightly. In the steps that follow, you first use the SmartArt diagram engine and then convert the SmartArt diagram to a collection of shapes.

To build the workbook shown in Figure 11.33, follow these steps:

1. Select Insert, SmartArt, and choose a Table Hierarchy from the relationship group.

2. Build a static SmartArt diagram with a single Level 1 item, four Level 2 items, and a Level 3 item for each Level 2 item. Type sample values in the text pane. The sample values should be about the same size as the real values that you expect to have in the final diagram.

3. On the Page Layout tab, change the Theme to Opulent.

4. On the SmartArt Tools Design tab, change the SmartArt Styles to Cartoon.

5. Use the Change Colors tab to select Colorful, Accent Colors.

6. Click the Level 1 shape. On the Format tab, use the Change Shape drop-down to select a wave shape.

7. Also on the Format tab, select Shape Styles, Shape Effects, Shadow, Offset Diagonal Bottom Right.

8. Select Shape Styles, Shape Effects, Shadow, Shadow Options.

9. In the Format Shape dialog box, change the distance from 4 points to 9 points.

10. Select the text within the Level 1 shape. On the Format tab, select WordArt Styles, Text Effects, Transform, Wave1.

11. On the SmartArt Tools Design ribbon tab, click Convert to Shapes. This converts the SmartArt diagram to a collection of shapes. You no longer have access to the SmartArt tools or the text pane. You should do this step only after you have the diagram in its final appearance.

12. Create an external query in row 30 to retrieve TicketID, Associate, and SaleTotal from a point-of-sale system. Set up the query properties to refresh every minute.

13. In cell A24, enter the formula =`"Scoreboard as of "&TEXT(NOW(),"H:MM AM/PM")`.

14. In cells A25:D25, type the names of the four associates working in the store today.

15. In cell A26, enter the formula =TEXT(SUMIF($B$31:$B$300,A25,$C$31:$C$300),"$#,##0").
16. Copy the formula from cell A26 to B26:D26.
17. Select the text in one shape. Click in the Formula Bar and type a formula, such as =A24.
18. Use the mini toolbar to center the text and select the same size as used for similar shapes in the diagram.
19. Repeat steps 17 and 18 for the other eight shapes.

Throughout the day, the external query brings new data into the worksheet, and it is presented in the scoreboard diagram (refer to Figure 11.33).

Although this is a tedious process, it is a way to use the SmartArt engine to create a great-looking scoreboard in Excel. It is unfortunate that Microsoft did not have time to hook up the decade-old Shapes formula functionality for SmartArt graphics. Although I had hoped this would come in Excel 2010, the one addition in Excel 2010 was the Convert to Shapes command, which shortened this case study by four steps.

Next Steps

In Chapter 12, "Exporting Charts for Use Outside of Excel," you find out how to share your charts and graphics with others through either PowerPoint or by publishing to the Web.

11

Exporting Charts for Use Outside of Excel

12

Presenting Excel Charts in PowerPoint or Word

IN THIS CHAPTER

Presenting Excel Charts in PowerPoint
or Word..317

Presenting Charts on the Web 328

Exporting Charts to Graphics Using VBA 331

Converting to XPS or PDF............................332

Next Steps 332

Although Excel is a great place for you to create charts, you might need to share charts with others, either in PowerPoint, as Word documents, as web pages, as PDF documents, or as graphic files.

Excel 2013, Word 2013, and PowerPoint 2013 share the same charting engines. This makes it possible to copy and paste charts from one application to the other without the unpredictability that often happened when moving charts from Excel 2003 to PowerPoint 2003.

There is a dizzying array of options for how to paste the chart in PowerPoint or Word. Each option offers different advantages and potential disadvantages.

The new Paste Options menu in PowerPoint 2013 and Word 2013 offers five paste alternatives in addition to the regular paste. Paste Special offers 9 more choices, bringing the total paste choices to 15. Further, some of those 15 choices behave differently if you are saving to a document that will be saved in compatibility mode.

When you are trying to decide which paste method to use, consider some of these questions:

Do you want the PowerPoint or Word chart to respond to data changes in the Excel file?

If this is important to you, use Paste, Paste Special, Paste Link, Microsoft Excel Chart Object. Every time you open the PowerPoint presentation, you will be given the opportunity to update the charts with data from the source Excel file.

If you want to have the capability to refresh the chart to get new data, select the default Paste option.

The chart keeps the data at the time of the paste, but you can use Chart Tools Design, Refresh to retrieve the current data from Excel.

If you absolutely do not want the chart in PowerPoint to change when the underlying data changes, you can use one of the Embed options from the Paste Options menu or Paste as Picture. Alternatively, use the new Insert, Screenshot, Screen Clipping feature from PowerPoint or Word.

Do you love the formatting in Excel, or do you want the chart to take on the look and feel of the Word or PowerPoint document?

A default paste allows your chart to change in response to theme changes in the PowerPoint or Word document. This is probably the best choice because the chart will look like it is part of the other document.

However, you might want to keep those custom colors that you lovingly created in Excel. In those cases, use the K or F choices in the Paste Options menu. K will Keep Source Formatting and Embed Workbook. F will keep Source Formatting and Link Workbook.

If you really want the PowerPoint chart to keep up with formatting changes in the Excel chart, the only option is to select Paste, Paste Special, Paste Link, Microsoft Excel Chart Object. With this option, you will not be able to edit the chart in PowerPoint or Word. Your only choice is to update the link. This is the only option that will bring formatting changes from Excel to the Word or PowerPoint document.

Will the PowerPoint file and the Excel file stay in the same locations?

Suppose you are creating a PowerPoint presentation. When you are making the presentation, will PowerPoint still have access to your Excel file? Alternatively, are you sending the PowerPoint presentation to your boss, who will be presenting from another computer?

If the PowerPoint presentation has access to the original Excel file, all your options are available and can be used.

But if the PowerPoint file will be used on a different computer, you might want to consider choosing the K or H options from the Paste Options menu. H uses the PowerPoint theme and embeds the workbook. K keeps the Excel theme and embeds the workbook.

As you can imagine, there are disadvantages to this, including the following:

- The PowerPoint file size increases by the size of the Excel file.
- There are privacy concerns. Even if your chart is based on one tiny 40-cell range on Sheet1, your boss can double-click the chart and access all the data anywhere in the workbook.
- When you embed the workbook, any changes made to the original workbook will not update the chart.

If you are concerned about privacy and the workbook contains sensitive data, you should paste the chart as a picture or as a screen clipping. This shows a snapshot of the current chart, but the person using the PowerPoint or Word document is not able to see any other data in the workbook.

In addition, if you are concerned about privacy and you want the chart to keep the formatting of the target PowerPoint document, you should consider re-creating the chart in PowerPoint.

Do you want to have access to the Office 2013 charting tools in the target document?

When you use Paste as Picture or Paste as Link, you lose the ability to edit and format the chart in Word or PowerPoint. If you paste as picture, you do have access to the Picture Tools Format tab, so you can add a fancy border. You do not have access to the Charting Tools Format, Layout, and Design tabs.

The following sections compare the various methods for getting a chart from Excel to PowerPoint.

Copying a Document from Excel and Pasting to PowerPoint Sets Up an As-Needed Link

Copying a chart as a live chart linked to the original workbook is the easiest method of getting a chart from Excel to PowerPoint. You basically copy the chart from Excel and paste it to PowerPoint.

With this method, you have full access to all the Charting Tools tabs in PowerPoint. You can customize the chart to match the theme of the PowerPoint presentation, and you can choose new layouts, styles, and so on.

The data remains linked to the original workbook. If you change the workbook and later open the PowerPoint presentation, the chart reflects the new numbers from the Excel workbook.

12

> **NOTE** This feature works only if the PowerPoint presentation still has access to the original Excel file. Otherwise, PowerPoint shows a static version of the last-known numbers in the chart.

The simplest method is to copy the chart from Excel and paste the chart into PowerPoint. Excel then sets up what I call a weak link between the presentation and the Excel workbook.

This method has the following pros and cons:

Pro: If you want to change the formatting of the chart in PowerPoint, you have full access to the charting tabs.

Pro: By default, the chart responds to changes in the theme of the PowerPoint presentation. You have a chart that has the same look and feel of the rest of the presentation.

Con: By default, you lose your original colors from the Excel chart. To overcome this, use the F option from the Paste Options menu—Keep Source Formatting and Link Data.

Con: Any subsequent changes to the formatting of the Excel chart never appear in the PowerPoint chart. You can force PowerPoint to get data changes, but you never get the formatting changes.

Con: This method does not work perfectly with documents stored in compatibility mode. Changes to the theme do not affect the linked chart.

Pro: The PowerPoint file size remains small. Excel does not embed the entire workbook in the PowerPoint file.

Pro: You have icons on the Charting Tools Design tab to either refresh the data or edit the data. Provided that the original Excel file is still available in the original folder, the workbook is opened and current data is used to redraw the chart. If the Excel workbook has been moved or renamed, you can use the File, Information, Related Files to change the linked location.

Con: If the original workbook is not available, you cannot refresh data in the chart. However, this becomes an issue only if someone clicks the Refresh icon in the Charting Tools Design tab. If you are doing a presentation and stay away from that icon, you will successfully present using a cached version of the Excel chart.

Pro: Although there is a link between the PowerPoint document and the Excel workbook, you will not be nagged with Information Bar warnings that links exist in the document.

Neutral: If data in the underlying Excel workbook changes, the new data does not automatically appear in the PowerPoint presentation. You have to explicitly click Charting Tools Design, Refresh Data.

To copy the chart, follow these steps:

1. Open both PowerPoint and Excel.
2. In Excel, select the chart.
3. Press Ctrl+C or click the Copy icon on the Home tab.
4. Switch to PowerPoint by pressing Alt+Tab.
5. Paste by pressing Ctrl+V or by clicking the Paste icon on the Home tab to perform a default paste.

The chart fills the text area of the slide. The data stays the same, but the theme colors and effects are changed to reflect the active theme in the destination slide show. The Chart Tools ribbon icons are available, as well as the three icons to the right of the chart (see Figure 12.1).

By using the default paste, you have set up a weak link between the Excel workbook and the PowerPoint slide. With this link, you have the best of both worlds; you can keep the original data in the PowerPoint chart, or you can get new data from Excel.

Figure 12.1
Copying and pasting is the simplest method for getting a chart from Excel to PowerPoint.

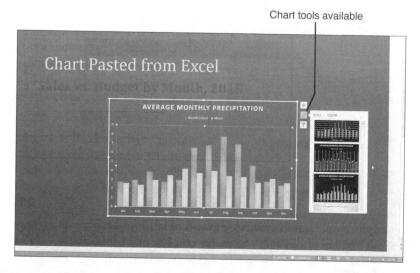

Chart tools available

To illustrate, consider this example:

1. Close the PowerPoint presentation.
2. In the Excel workbook, change the data in the chart. In Figure 12.2, the Akron precipitation for January is increased to 8.
3. In the Excel workbook, use the Paintbrush icon to choose a new color and style.
4. In the Excel workbook, change some other aspect of the chart, such as applying a bevel and a color to one point (see Figure 12.2).
5. Save the Excel workbook.
6. Close the Excel workbook.
7. Open the PowerPoint presentation. No warning appears in the information bar that a link is present. You are not asked to update the links. The original chart is presented with the original data. Even though a link appears, you can run the slideshow without ever needing the original Excel file.
8. Click the chart in PowerPoint. The Chart Tools tabs appear.
9. On the Chart Tools Design tab, select Refresh Data. As shown in Figure 12.3, the chart is updated to show the new value for Akron. Although the data is updated, none of the other formatting changes appear in the chart. The new colors do not appear.
10. In PowerPoint, choose a new theme from the Design tab. The colors, fonts, and effects used in the chart are updated to match the theme in PowerPoint.

12

Figure 12.2
Change the chart in Excel.

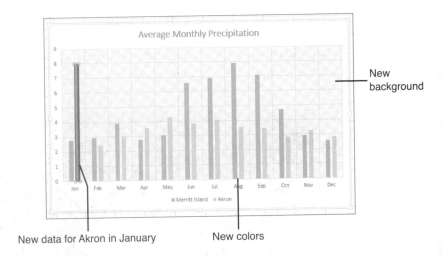

New background

New data for Akron in January

New colors

Figure 12.3
Use Refresh Data to bring in new data from Excel without changing the formatting.

Refresh Data

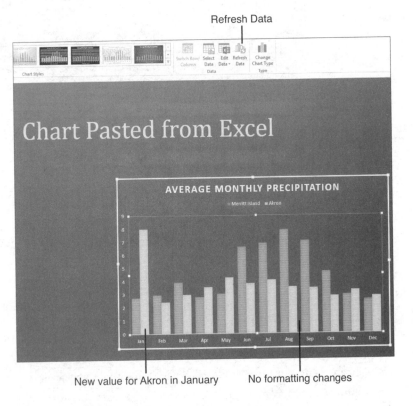

New value for Akron in January

No formatting changes

As you can see, the default is pretty cool: You have the ability to get new data from Excel, but the formatting matches the destination PowerPoint presentation.

Copying and Pasting While Keeping Original Formatting

The previous method sets up a link to the data stored in the Excel workbook. However, all of the colors and effects used in the original chart were lost when you pasted to PowerPoint or Word.

At times you might want to keep the colors from the original workbook. The Paste Options menu offers the F shortcut—to Keep Source Formatting and Link Data.

Like the previous method, you have the ability to keep the original data or to refresh the chart and get the new data.

Unlike the previous method, the original colors and effects stay with the chart in PowerPoint. The chart does not respond to theme changes in PowerPoint.

You still have access to Chart Tools tabs in PowerPoint to change the colors in the chart.

To copy the chart while keeping the original formatting, follow these steps:

1. Open both PowerPoint and Excel.
2. In Excel, select the chart.
3. Press Ctrl+C or click the Copy icon on the Home tab.
4. Switch to PowerPoint by pressing Alt+Tab.
5. Open the Paste drop-down on the Home tab. Select the third icon for Keep Source Formatting and Link Data (F). Alternatively, you can press Ctrl+V, then Ctrl alone, then the letter F. The chart is pasted with the original formatting (see Figure 12.4).

> **CAUTION**
>
> The source formatting options copy the chart formatting at the time of the paste. If you later change formatting in the Excel file, those formatting changes never show up in the PowerPoint version of the chart. If you need the PowerPoint chart to show formatting changes made in Excel, you should use the steps in Pasting as a Link to Capture Future Excel Formatting Changes.

12

Figure 12.4
Set up a refreshable link to the data, but keep the formatting at the time of the paste.

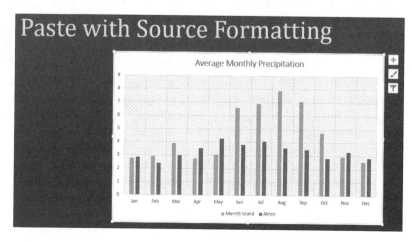

Pasting as Link to Capture Future Excel Formatting Changes

The default methods for pasting in Excel do not set up a link to the current formatting in the Excel workbook. If you want to be able to change formatting in Excel and have those formats carry through to PowerPoint or Word, you can use Paste Special and set up a Paste Link.

This method has the following pros and cons:

- Con: You need to have access to the Excel file if you want to show the current formatting.
- Con: You will be nagged about updating links every time you open the PowerPoint file.
- Pro: This method also works with files stored in compatibility mode.
- Pro: Formatting changes to the original Excel file show up in the PowerPoint file.
- Con: If you change the theme in the PowerPoint presentation, the formatting of the linked chart does not change.

To set up a linked chart, follow these steps:

1. Open both PowerPoint and Excel.
2. In Excel, select the chart.
3. Press Ctrl+C or click the Copy icon on the Home tab.
4. Switch to PowerPoint by pressing Alt+Tab.
5. On the Home tab, open the Paste drop-down. Select Paste Special. PowerPoint displays the Paste Special dialog.
6. On the left side of the dialog, select Paste Link. You now have only one option—Microsoft Excel Chart Object (see Figure 12.5). Click OK.

A copy of the original chart appears in PowerPoint. You do not have access to the Chart Tools, but you do have access to the Drawing Tools Format tab. You can use this tab to add a border around the chart.

The link set up with this option is the strongest link of any in this chapter. You can switch to Excel, change some data, and change some formatting. When you come back to PowerPoint, right-click the chart and choose Update Link. The data and formatting changes appear in the chart.

If you make changes to the Excel file while the PowerPoint workbook is closed, you are prompted to update the links when you later open the PowerPoint presentation.

12

Figure 12.5
Bypass the Paste Options menu and go to Paste Special to set up the only link that can capture future formatting changes to the Excel chart.

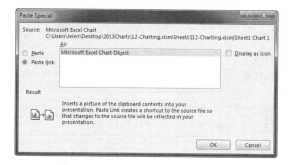

Embedding the Chart and Workbook in PowerPoint

The problem with a straight copy and paste is that the PowerPoint slide and the original Excel workbook must remain on the same computer to maintain the link. If you plan to distribute the PowerPoint file to others, you can copy the chart along with the entire workbook.

To copy the chart, follow these steps:

1. Open both PowerPoint and Excel.
2. In Excel, click the chart.
3. Press Ctrl+C or click the Copy icon on the Home tab.
4. Switch to PowerPoint by pressing Alt+Tab.
5. Paste by pressing Ctrl+V.
6. An icon appears at the lower-right corner of the pasted chart. Hover over the icon, and a drop-down arrow appears. Choose either the first icon for Keep Source Formatting and Embed Workbook or the second icon for Use Destination Theme and Embed Workbook.

One advantage of this method is that you can send the PowerPoint presentation to any recipient whose computer has Office 2007 or newer. The recipient can right-click the chart, select Edit, and see the entire Excel workbook. If that person makes changes to the assumptions in the workbook, the chart updates. The recipient also has full access to the Charting Tools tabs in PowerPoint.

However, the main advantage of this method is also a disadvantage. Even though you paste a single chart, Office 2013 embeds the entire workbook. This can create privacy concerns if the workbook contains sensitive data on other worksheets or create file size concerns if you have millions of cells on other worksheets in the workbook.

Copying a Chart as a Picture

You can paste a picture of a chart in a PowerPoint slide. The picture is initially the same size as the chart in the Excel worksheet. Instead of having access to the Charting Tools tab, you only have access to the Picture Tools tab. The Picture Tools tab might allow you to change the chart to grayscale or a monochrome color, but you do not have access to the rich chart formatting tools.

As of Excel 2010, this process became simpler. You can use the PowerPoint Screen Clipping tool to capture the picture from Excel. Here is a little prework before taking the screenshot: If you have two monitors, put Excel on one monitor and PowerPoint on the other monitor. If you have only one monitor, minimize PowerPoint and get the Excel chart visible in your monitor. Switch directly to PowerPoint.

In PowerPoint, the Insert tab has a new Screenshot drop-down. The drop-down shows that Excel has one of the available screenshots. Do not select Excel from this list. Instead, go to the bottom of the drop-down and choose Screen Clipping.

In a moment, PowerPoint disappears. The entire monitor grays out. Using the mouse, drag a box around your chart. As you drag, the chart comes back to the original color. After you finish drawing the box, release the mouse. A snapshot of the current chart is pasted to your PowerPoint slide.

At this point, you can use any of the tools on the Picture Tools Format tab to apply effects, adjust color, and so on. The chart in Figure 12.6 shows the Bevel Perspective Picture Style.

Figure 12.6
Use the Screen Clipping tool to get a static snapshot of an Excel chart (or any other application).

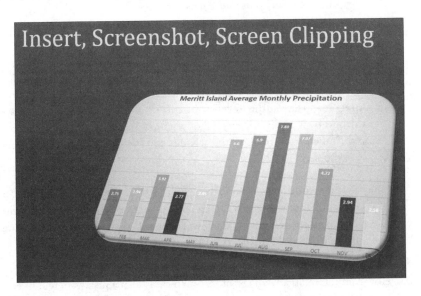

The screen clipping tool works as well as pictures for 99% of the things you do with PowerPoint. I once had a situation where I uploaded a file to SharePoint and viewed it in the browser. Regular pictures rendered fine, but the screenshots did not. If this happens to you, try the old method: Copy the chart in Excel. In PowerPoint, use Paste Special and Paste as Picture.

Creating a Chart in PowerPoint with Data Pasted from Excel

Creating a chart in PowerPoint and copying data from Excel might seem to be the most tedious method, but it has the advantage of getting a completely editable chart into PowerPoint without the need to copy an entire workbook into the PowerPoint file.

Follow these steps to create the chart:

1. In Excel, copy the data that will go on the chart.
2. In PowerPoint, select New Slide from the Home tab. A new slide appears, with six icons in the center of the slide (see Figure 12.7).
3. Click the Chart icon in the center of the slide.
4. Choose a chart type and click OK. You see your PowerPoint slide and a new Excel worksheet on the right. PowerPoint has inserted a three-series by four-category place-holder data set. (See Figure 12.8.)

Figure 12.7
When you insert a new slide in PowerPoint, six icons appear in the center of the slide.

Figure 12.8
PowerPoint creates a new tiny worksheet window with default data.

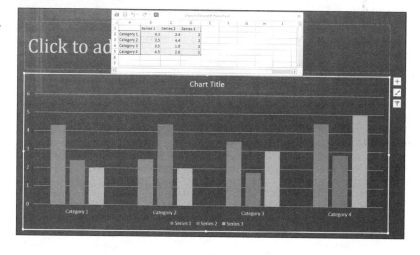

5. Paste your Excel data from step 1 into this mini Excel worksheet. Use the handles to resize the chart series outline to fit the new data. If necessary, use the Switch Row/Column icon in the ribbon (see Figure 12.9).
6. Click the X in the Excel pane to close the Excel view and return to PowerPoint.

12

Figure 12.9
Paste your Excel data
and adjust the handles
around the chart data to
fit the new data.

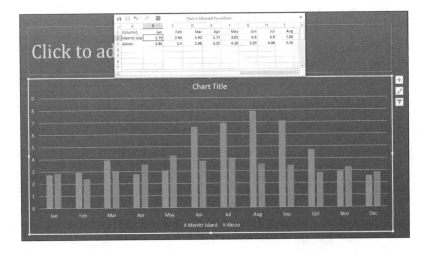

You've now created a new chart in PowerPoint. You can edit the chart using the Chart
Tools tabs. You've also minimized the size of the Excel data that must travel with the
PowerPoint file.

Presenting Charts on the Web

You can export a workbook, including charts and slicers, to the Web. Share the workbook
with others and they can interact with the chart.

To set up an interactive web page, follow these steps:

1. Define the worksheets that should be viewable on the Web. Go to File, Info. At the
   bottom of the center panel is a Browser View Options icon. When you click the icon,
   you see the Browser View Options as shown in Figure 12.10. You can choose which
   sheets will be visible on the Web.

Figure 12.10
Choose which
worksheet(s) to share.

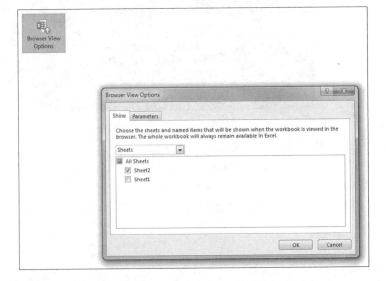

12

2. Save the workbook to your SkyDrive.

3. Use File, Share, Post to Social Networks. You can choose your Facebook, Twitter, or LinkedIn account. Choose Can Edit from the drop-down. Add a few words to describe the post. Click the Post icon. (See Figure 12.11.)

Figure 12.11
Post to Facebook or Twitter.

4. A few seconds later, a post appears on your profile with a link to the chart. (See Figure 12.12.)

Figure 12.12
Your Facebook friends can view the chart.

5. When users follow the link, they are able to interact with the slicers and see the charts update. (See Figure 12.13.)

6. In Figure 12.13, choose Share, Embed Workbook. You can define a range to share, hide gridlines, and allow people to Sort & Filter. I always turn off the check box to Include Download Link, although someone clever with JavaScript skills can later turn it back on. Copy the Embed Code from the workbook (see Figure 12.14).

12

Figure 12.13
The chart and slicers work in the browser.

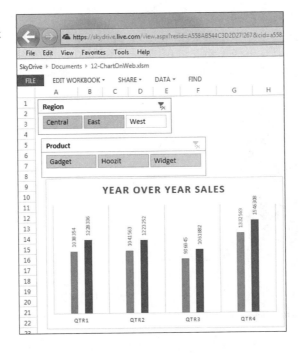

Figure 12.14
Get code to embed the chart in a blog post or web page.

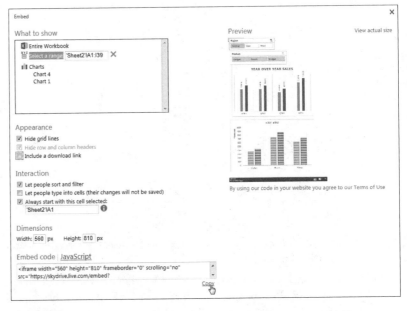

7. Add this code to a web page or a blog post. People who visit the page are able to interact with the slicers and see the charts update (see Figure 12.15).

Figure 12.15
Your Excel workbook is now an interactive web app.

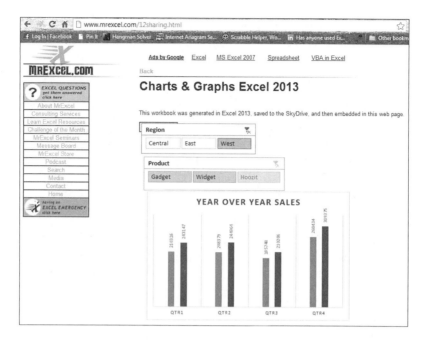

Exporting Charts to Graphics Using VBA

The steps in the preceding section are a convoluted way of creating a PNG version of a chart. If you don't mind typing a bit of VBA code, you can export the active chart quickly.

VBA is the macro language behind Excel. Although Chapter 13, "Using Excel VBA to Create Charts," takes a more in-depth look at VBA, this section takes a quick peek into using VBA to convert charts to graphics files.

If you want to display the VBA Editor, try pressing Alt+F11. A few modern keyboards have repurposed the Function keys for other purposes, so Alt+F11 might not work for you.

If Alt+F11 doesn't get you to the VBA editor, you need to display the Developer tab in the ribbon. If this tab is not on your computer, select the File menu to open the backstage view. Select Options from the left navigation. In the Excel Options dialog, select Customize Ribbon from the left navigation. In the right list box, select the Developer box. When the Developer tab is available, you can display the Visual Basic Editor using the Visual Basic icon on the Developer tab.

1. Switch to Excel.
2. Select a chart.
3. Switch back to Visual Basic.
4. Press Ctrl+G to display the Immediate window.
5. Type the following line of code and then press Enter: `ActiveChart.Export "C:\MyChart.JPG", "JPG"`.

Of course, you can specify any path and filename instead of the name shown in the preceding code snippet. The file type can be GIF, JPG, or any other graphics filter installed on your computer's copy of Office.

Converting to XPS or PDF

PDF is the ubiquitous Portable Document Format from Adobe. XML Paper Specification (XPS) is the newer open-source competitor from Microsoft.

To save a chart as a PDF file, follow these steps:

1. Select a chart in Excel.
2. Select the File menu to open Backstage View.
3. In the left navigation, select Export.
4. In the left panel of the Share Backstage View, select Create PDF/XPS Document.
5. In the right panel of the Backstage View, select Create a PDF/XPS.
6. In the Publish and PDF or XPS dialog, select PDF from the Save as Type list box.
7. Specify a filename.
8. Click Publish. The selected chart is created as a single-page PDF file.

Next Steps

In Chapter 13, you find out how to use VBA macros to automate the creation and formatting of charts. VBA is a macro language that has been in Excel for more than a decade; you can use it to automate repetitive tasks.

12

Using Excel VBA to Create Charts

13

Introducing VBA

Version 5 of Excel introduced a powerful new macro language called Visual Basic for Applications (VBA). Every copy of Excel shipped since 1993 has had a copy of the powerful VBA language hiding behind the worksheets. VBA enables you to perform steps that you normally perform in Excel, but perform them very quickly and flawlessly. A VBA program can turn a process that used to take days each month into a single button click and a minute of processing time. If you have a lot of charts to create, you can set up a macro to automatically produce a series of charts. This is appropriate if you regularly have to produce a similar set of charts every day, week, or month.

You shouldn't be intimidated by VBA. The VBA macro recorder tool gets you 80% of the way to a useful macro, and the examples in this chapter get you the rest of the way there.

Every example in this chapter is available for download from http://www.mrexcel.com/chart2013data.html.

IN THIS CHAPTER

Introducing VBA 333

Learning Tricks of the VBA Trade 337

Understanding Backward Compatibility 341

Referencing Charts and Chart Objects in VBA Code 342

Understanding the Global Settings 342

Creating a Chart in Various Excel Versions ... 346

Customizing a Chart 350

Using `SetElement` to Emulate Changes on the Layout Tab 358

Formatting a Data Series 367

Creating Advanced Charts 381

Exporting a Chart as a Graphic 389

Creating Pivot Charts 390

Creating Data Bars with VBA 392

Creating Sparklines with VBA 395

Next Steps 399

Enabling VBA in Your Copy of Excel

By default, VBA is disabled in Office 2013. Before you can start using VBA, you need to enable macros in the Trust Center. Follow these steps:

1. From the File menu, select Options.

2. In the left navigation, select Trust Center.

3. On the right side of the Options dialog, click Trust Center Settings.

4. In the Trust Center left navigation, select Macro Settings.

5. Select Disable All Macros with Notification.

This allows macros to run after you verify that you are expecting the macros to be in the file. For files stored on the local hard drive, you need to confirm that you trust the macros only once per workbook.

Further, when you save your files, you have to save the files as macro-enabled workbooks, with the .xlsm extension.

> **TIP** If you have previously displayed the Developer tab of the ribbon, you can use the Macro Security icon on the Developer tab to jump quickly to the Trust Center dialog box.

Enabling the Developer Tab

Most of the VBA tools are located on the Developer tab of the Excel 2013 ribbon. By default, this tab is not displayed. To enable it, go to File, Options, Customize Ribbon. In the right list box, the Developer tab is unchecked. Click to add a check mark and then click OK.

As shown in Figure 13.1, the Code group on the Developer tab of the ribbon offers icons for accessing the Visual Basic Editor, the Macros dialog box, macro recording tools, and the Macro Security setting.

Figure 13.1
You need to enable the Developer tab to access the VBA tools.

Macro recording tools
Macros dialog box

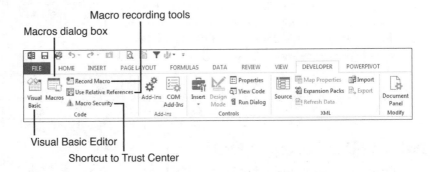

Visual Basic Editor
Shortcut to Trust Center

The Visual Basic Editor

From Excel, you press Alt+F11 or, from the Developer tab, select Visual Basic to open the Visual Basic Editor. The VBA Editor, shown in Figure 13.2, has three main sections:

> **NOTE** If this is your first time using VBA, some of these items might be disabled. Follow the instructions given in the following list to make sure each is enabled.

- **Project Explorer**—This pane displays all open workbooks in an expandable list. Click the plus (+) sign next to any workbook to see worksheets, code modules, user forms, and class modules. Press Ctrl+R to display the Project Explorer.

- **Properties window**—The Properties window is important when you begin to program user forms. It is also useful when you're writing normal code. You enable it by pressing F4.

- **Code pane**—This is the area where you write your code. Code is stored in one or more code modules attached to the workbook. To add a code module to a workbook, you select Insert, Module from the application menu.

Figure 13.2
The Visual Basic Editor window is lurking behind every copy of Excel shipped since 1993.

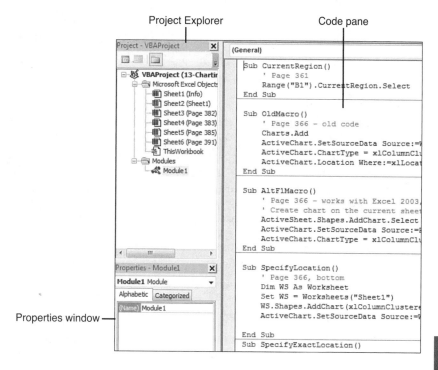

Visual Basic Tools

Visual Basic is a powerful development environment. Although this chapter cannot offer a complete course on VBA, if you are new to VBA, you should take advantage of the following:

- As you begin to type code, Excel usually offers a drop-down with valid choices. This feature, known as AutoComplete, enables you to type code faster and eliminate typing mistakes.

- For assistance with any keyword, you can put the cursor in the keyword and press F1. Online Excel VBA Help displays information about the keyword.

13

■ Excel checks each line of code as you finish it. Lines in error appear in red. Comments appear in green. You can add a comment by typing a single apostrophe. You should use lots of comments so you can remember what each section of code is doing.

■ Despite the aforementioned error checking, Excel might still encounter errors at run-time. If this happens, you can click the Debug button. The line that caused the error is highlighted in yellow. You can then hover your mouse cursor over any variable to see the current value of the variable.

■ When you are in Debug mode, you can use the Debug menu to step through code line-by-line. You can toggle back and forth between Excel and VBA to see the effect of running a line of code on the worksheet.

■ Other great debugging tools are breakpoints, the Watch window, the Object Browser, and the Immediate window. You can read about these tools in the Excel VBA Help menu.

The Macro Recorder

Excel offers a macro recorder that is about 80% perfect for charts. Code that you record to work with one data set is hard-coded to work only with that data set. This behavior might work fine if your chart data occupies cells A1:E7 every single day, but if you have a different number of customers each day, it is unlikely that you will have the same number of rows each day. Given that you might need to work with other data, it would be a lot better if Excel could record your actions of selecting cells when you use the End key. This is one of the shortcomings of the macro recorder.

Excel pros often use the macro recorder to record code and expect to have to then clean up the recorded code. Although the macro recorder in Excel 2007 was not finished for chart-ing, it is now working well in Excel 2013.

Understanding Object-Oriented Code

If you took a class in BASIC a long time ago, the recorded code in VBA is going to appear rather foreign to you. Whereas BASIC is a procedural language, VBA is an object-oriented language. Most lines of VBA code follow the Noun.Verb or Object.Method syntax. Objects can be workbooks, worksheets, charts, cells, ranges of cells, among others. Methods can be typical Excel actions, such as Copy, Paste, and PasteSpecial.

Many methods allow adverbs—that is, parameters you use to specify how to perform a method. If you see a construction that includes a colon and an equal sign, it is an adverb, and you know that the macro recorder is describing how the method should work. For example, in this line of code, ActiveChart is the object, SetSourceData is the method, and Source is a parameter: `ActiveChart.SetSourceData Source:=Range("A1:E4")`.

You might also see adjectives, or properties. If you set `ActiveCell.Font.ColorIndex = 3`, you are setting the font color (the property) of the active cell to red (the value).

13

Learning Tricks of the VBA Trade

You need to master a few simple techniques to be able to write efficient VBA code. These techniques will help you make the jump to writing effective code.

Writing Code to Handle a Data Range of Any Size

The macro recorder hard-codes the fact that your data is in a range, such as A1:E7. Although this hard-coding works for today's data set, it might not work as you get new data sets. You need to write code that can deal with different sizes of data sets.

One method is to use the `CurrentRegion` property. If you specify one nonblank cell and ask for the current region, Excel extends the selection in each direction until it encounters the edge of the worksheet, a blank row, or a blank column. In Figure 13.3, for example, the following line of code selected A1:E4:

```
Range("B1").CurrentRegion.Select
```

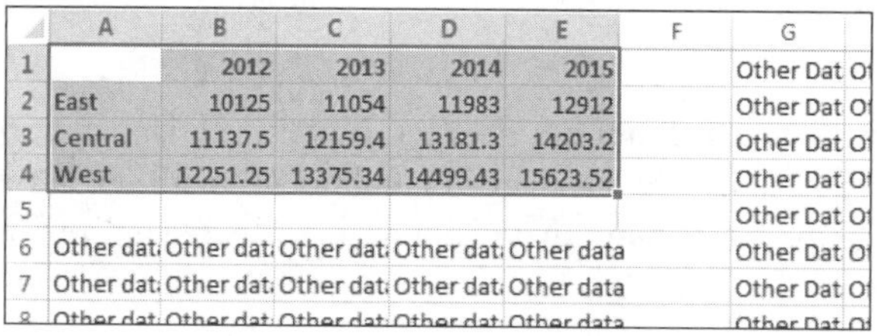

Figure 13.3
Selecting the current region extends the selection out until a blank row/column is encountered.

⊿	A	B	C	D	E	F	G
1		2012	2013	2014	2015		Other Dat O
2	East	10125	11054	11983	12912		Other Dat O
3	Central	11137.5	12159.4	13181.3	14203.2		Other Dat O
4	West	12251.25	13375.34	14499.43	15623.52		Other Dat O
5							Other Dat O
6	Other dat	Other dat	Other dat	Other dat	Other data		Other Dat O
7	Other dat	Other dat	Other dat	Other dat	Other data		Other Dat O
8	Other dat	Other dat	Other dat	Other dat	Other data		Other Dat O

If you are absolutely sure that cell B1 is nonblank and that no other data touches your chart data, you could use the `CurrentRegion` approach to specify the data for a chart.

The macro recorder uses syntax such as `Range("H12")` to refer to a cell. However, it is more flexible to use `Cells(12, 8)` to refer to H12. Why (12, 8)? Because H12 is in row 12, column 8. Similarly, the macro recorder refers to a rectangular range using syntax such as `Range("A1:K415501")`. However, it is better to use the `Cells` syntax to refer to the upper-left corner of the range and then use the `Resize()` syntax to refer to the number of rows and columns in the range:

```
Cells(1, 1).Resize(415501,11)
```

This approach is more flexible than using `Range("A1:K415501")` because you can replace any of the numbers with a variable. Rather than hard-coding cells(12,8), you will frequently replace the numbers with variables, such as cells(i, j).

13

In the Excel user interface, you can use the End key on the keyboard to jump to the end of a range of data. If you move the cell pointer to the final row on the worksheet and press the End key and then the up-arrow key, the cell pointer jumps to the last row that contains data. The equivalent of doing this in VBA is to use the following code:

```
Range("A1048576").End(xlUp).Select
```

You don't need to select this cell; you just need to find the row number that contains the last row. The following code locates this row and saves the row number to a variable named `FinalRow`:

```
FinalRow = Range("A1048576").End(xlUp).Row
```

There is nothing magical about the variable name `FinalRow`. You could call this variable *x* or *y*, or even give it your dog's name. However, because VBA allows you to use meaningful variable names, you should use something such as `FinalRow` to describe the final row.

> **TIP**
>
> Excel 2007–2013 offers 1,048,576 rows and 16,384 columns. Excel 97 through Excel 2003 offered 65,536 rows and 256 columns. Even Excel 2013 will sometimes have only 65,536 rows if you open a legacy .xls file. To make your code handle either worksheet size, you can use Rows.Count to learn the total number of rows available in the active workbook. The preceding code could then be generalized like so:
>
> ```
> FinalRow = Cells(Rows.Count, 1).End(xlUp).Row
> ```

You can also find the final column in a data set. If you are relatively sure that the data set begins in row 1, you can use the End key in combination with the left-arrow key to jump from cell XFD1 to the last column that contains data. To generalize for the possibility that the code is running on a legacy .xls file in compatibility mode, you can use the following code:

```
FinalCol = Cells(1, Columns.Count).End(xlToLeft).Column
```

End+Down Arrow Versus End+Up Arrow

You might be tempted to find the final row by starting in cell A1 and using the End key in conjunction with the down-arrow key. You should avoid this approach. Data coming from another system is imperfect. If your program will import 500,000 rows from a legacy computer system every day for the next five years, a day will come when someone manages to key a null value into the data set. This value will cause a blank cell or even a blank row to appear in the middle of your data set. The formula `Range("A1").End(xlDown)` will then stop prematurely just before the blank cell instead of including all your data. This blank cell will cause that day's report to miss thousands of rows of data, a potential disaster that will call into question the credibility of your report. You should take the extra step of starting at the last row in the worksheet to greatly reduce the risk of problems.

Using Super-Variables: Object Variables

In typical programming languages, a variable holds a single value. You might use $x = 4$ to assign a value of 4 to the variable x.

Many properties describe a single cell in Excel. A cell might contain a value such as 4, and the cell also has a font size, a font color, a row, a column, possibly a formula, possibly a comment, a list of precedents, and more. It is possible to use VBA to create a super-variable that contains all the information about a cell or any other object. A statement to create a typical variable such as x = Range("A1") assigns the current value of Cell A1 to the variable x.

You can use the Set keyword to create an object variable:

```
Set x = Range("A1")
```

This formula creates a super-variable that contains all the properties of the cell. Instead of having a variable with only one value, you now have a variable in which you can access the value of many properties associated with that variable. You can reference x.Formula to learn the formula in cell A1 or x.Font.Color to learn the color of the cell.

Using object variables can make it easier to write code. Instead of continuously referring to ThisWorkbook.Worksheets("Income Statement"), you can define an object variable and use that as shorthand. For example, the following code repeatedly refers to the same workbook:

```
ThisWorkbook.Worksheets("Income Statement").Shape("Chart1").Chart _
    .SetSourceData Source:= ThisWorkbook.Worksheets("Income Statement") _
    .Range("A1:E4")
ThisWorkbook.Worksheets("Income Statement").Shape("Chart1").Left = 10
ThisWorkbook.Worksheets("Income Statement").Shape("Chart1").Top = 30
ThisWorkbook.Worksheets("Income Statement").Shape("Chart1").Width = 300
ThisWorkbook.Worksheets("Income Statement").Shape("Chart1").Height = 200
```

If you define an object variable first, the code becomes shorter and easier to write:

```
Dim WS as Worksheet
Set WS = ThisWorkbook.Worksheets("Income Statement")
WS.Shape("Chart1").Chart.SetSourceData Source:= WS.Range("A1:E4")
WS.Shape("Chart1").Left = 10
WS.Shape("Chart1").Top = 30
WS.Shape("Chart1").Width = 300
WS.Shape("Chart1").Height = 200
```

If you define two object variables, you can simplify the code even further:

```
Dim WS as Worksheet
Dim Ch as Chart
Set WS = ThisWorkbook.Worksheets("Income Statement")
Set Ch = WS.Shape("Chart 1").Chart
Ch.SetSourceData Source:= WS.Range("A1:E4")
Ch.Left = 10
Ch.Top = 30
Ch.Width = 300
Ch.Height = 200
```

13

Provided that you do not type Option Explicit in the code window, VBA does not require you to declare your variables with the Dim statement. I tend not to declare regular variables. However, there is a benefit if you use Dim to declare your object variables; Excel offers AutoComplete drop-downs showing all the methods and properties available for the object variable. For this reason, I take the extra time to declare the object variables at the top of each macro.

Using With and End With When Referring to an Object

In the previous code, several lines refer to the same chart. Rather than reference this object on every line of code, you could specify the chart object once in a `With` statement. In each subsequent line, you could leave off the name of the chart and begin the line with a period. You would end the block of code with an `End With` statement. This is faster to write than typing the complete object name multiple times, and it executes faster because Excel only has to figure out what `WS.Shape("Chart1").Chart` means once. The following code uses the `With` syntax while setting five properties:

```
Dim WS as Worksheet
Set WS = ThisWorkbook.Worksheets("Income Statement")
With WS.Shape("Chart1").Chart
    .SetSourceData Source:= WS.Range("A1:E4")
    .Left = 10
    .Top = 30
    .Width = 300
    .Height = 200
End With
```

Continuing a Line of Code

Some lines of code can get very long. To improve readability, you can break a line and continue it. To indicate that the current line is continued on the next line, you can type a space and then an underscore character. Typically, the convention is to then indent the continued line of code. This is not required by VBA, but improves readability. For example, the following two lines of code are really a single line of code:

```
FinalCol = Cells(1, Columns.Count). _
    End(xlToLeft).Column
```

You are likely to break a line only when you reach the right edge of the code window, but the physical limitations of this book require lines to be broken into much smaller segments. Feel free to rejoin continued lines into a single line of code in your project.

CAUTION
Be careful to note that the continuation symbol is a space plus an underscore. If you forget the space, VBA doesn't realize that you are trying to continue the line, and you get a compile error.

Adding Comments to Code

When you figure out an interesting technique in code, it's a good idea to add comments in the code. This helps you if you return to the code several months later, and it helps others who have to troubleshoot your code.

The comment character in VBA is a single apostrophe ('). You can use a single-line comment, a several-line comment, or a comment that takes up only the end of a line. The Visual Basic Editor changes the color of your comments to green to differentiate them from other code. The following macro has comments to document where you can turn to for more information:

```
Sub CommentsImproveReadability()
    Dim WS As Worksheet
    Dim ch As Chart
    Set WS = ActiveSheet

    ' Select the data for the chart
    Range("A1:E4").Select ' Sales data

    ' Define the chart,
    ' use style 202 for rotated data labels
    Set ch = WS.Shapes.AddChart2( _
        Style:=202, _
        XlChartType:=xlColumnClustered, _
        Left:=[A6].Left, _
        Top:=[A6].Top, _
        Width:=[A6:G6].Width, _
        Height:=[A6:A20].Height, _
        NewLayout:=True).Chart
    ' Adjust the title
    ch.ChartTitle.Text = "2015 Sales by Region"

End Sub
```

Understanding Backward Compatibility

New chart features debuted in Excel 2013. Data label callouts with their text coming from ranges in Excel is new. The color choices are new. The chart styles are improved, with 153 new values. Excel 2013 no longer creates a legend for a single-series chart. The concept of filtering the totals out of a chart is new. All these features have new properties or methods in Excel 2013 VBA. But if you use those features, the code does not run in Excel 2010 or earlier.

If you know your code will be running exclusively in Excel 2013, you can create a chart using the new AddChart2 method. If the code might be running in Excel 2007–2010, use the AddChart method. For code running in Excel 2003 or earlier, use the Charts.Add method. An example of each follows.

13

Referencing Charts and Chart Objects in VBA Code

If you go back far enough in Excel history, you find that all charts used to be created as their own chart sheets. VBA was less complex then. To reference a chart, you simply referred to the chart sheet name.

```
Sheets("Chart1").ChartArea.Interior.ColorIndex = 4
```

Then, in the mid-1990s, Excel added the amazing capability to embed a chart right onto an existing worksheet. This allowed a report to be created with tables of numbers and charts all on the same page, something we take for granted today.

Up through Excel 2003, a macro would use the .ChartObjects as a container for a chart. Here is code to change the color of the chart area in Excel 2003:

```
Worksheets("Jan").ChartObjects("Chart1"). _
    Chart.ChartArea.Interior.ColorIndex = 4
```

Starting in Excel 2007, a chart is also a member of the Shapes collection. The macro recorder now uses the Shapes collection instead of ChartObjects. The equivalent code for referencing a chart in Excel 2007 through 2013 is

```
Worksheets("Jan").Shapes("Chart 1"). _
    Chart.ChartArea.Interior.ColorIndex = 4
```

Although it is less common to see standalone chart sheets today, you need to understand that you will have a different way of referring to a chart, depending on whether the chart is embedded or standalone, and whether the code is running in a version of Excel before Excel 2007.

Understanding the Global Settings

Although the charting interface has changed in Excel 2007 and Excel 2013, a few major concepts have applied to every chart since Excel 97. It does not matter if you are writing code for Excel 2003, Excel 2007, or Excel 2013, you need to understand the 73 chart types, size, position, and how to refer to a chart.

Specifying a Built-in Chart Type

Although the charting interface has evolved over the years, Excel has offered the same 73 chart types ever since Excel 97. Each method for creating a chart includes a ChartType property. You will use one of the constant values shown in the second column of Table 13.1.

What if you need to mix a column chart and a line chart? This is more complicated. See the "Creating a Combo Chart" section later in this chapter.

Table 13.1 lists the 73 chart type constants that you can use to create various charts. The sequence of the table matches the sequence of the charts in the All Charts tab of the Insert Chart dialog.

13

Table 13.1   Chart Types for Use in VBA

Chart Type	Constant
Clustered Column	`xlColumnClustered`
Stacked Column	`xlColumnStacked`
100% Stacked Column	`xlColumnStacked100`
3D Clustered Column	`xl3DColumnClustered`
Stacked Column in 3D	`xl3DColumnStacked`
100% Stacked Column in 3D	`xl3DColumnStacked100`
3D Column	`xl3DColumn`
Clustered Cylinder	`xlCylinderColClustered`
Stacked Cylinder	`xlCylinderColStacked`
100% Stacked Cylinder	`xlCylinderColStacked100`
3D Cylinder	`xlCylinderCol`
Clustered Cone	`xlConeColClustered`
Stacked Cone	`xlConeColStacked`
100% Stacked Cone	`xlConeColStacked100`
3D Cone	`xlConeCol`
Clustered Pyramid	`xlPyramidColClustered`
Stacked Pyramid	`xlPyramidColStacked`
100% Stacked Pyramid	`xlPyramidColStacked100`
3D Pyramid	`xlPyramidCol`
Line	`xlLine`
Stacked Line	`xlLineStacked`
100% Stacked Line	`xlLineStacked100`
Line with Markers	`xlLineMarkers`
Stacked Line with Markers	`xlLineMarkersStacked`
100% Stacked Line with Markers	`xlLineMarkersStacked100`
3D Line	`xl3DLine`
Pie	`xlPie`
Pie in 3D	`xl3DPie`
Pie of Pie	`xlPieOfPie`
Exploded Pie	`xlPieExploded`
Exploded Pie in 3D	`xl3DPieExploded`
Bar of Pie	`xlBarOfPie`
Clustered Bar	`xlBarClustered`

13

Chart Type	Constant
Stacked Bar	xlBarStacked
100% Stacked Bar	xlBarStacked100
Clustered Bar in 3D	xl3DBarClustered
Stacked Bar in 3D	xl3DBarStacked
100% Stacked Bar in 3D	xl3DBarStacked100
Clustered Horizontal Cylinder	xlCylinderBarClustered
Stacked Horizontal Cylinder	xlCylinderBarStacked
100% Stacked Horizontal Cylinder	xlCylinderBarStacked100
Clustered Horizontal Cone	xlConeBarClustered
Stacked Horizontal Cone	xlConeBarStacked
100% Stacked Horizontal Cone	xlConeBarStacked100
Clustered Horizontal Pyramid	xlPyramidBarClustered
Stacked Horizontal Pyramid	xlPyramidBarStacked
100% Stacked Horizontal Pyramid	xlPyramidBarStacked100
Area	xlArea
Stacked Area	xlAreaStacked
100% Stacked Area	xlAreaStacked100
3D Area	xl3DArea
Stacked Area in 3D	xl3DAreaStacked
100% Stacked Area in 3D	xl3DAreaStacked100
Scatter with Only Markers	xlXYScatter
Scatter with Smooth Lines and Markers	xlXYScatterSmooth
Scatter with Smooth Lines	xlXYScatterSmoothNoMarkers
Scatter with Straight Lines and Markers	xlXYScatterLines
Scatter with Straight Lines	xlXYScatterLinesNoMarkers
High-Low-Close	xlStockHLC
Open-High-Low-Close	xlStockOHLC
Volume-High-Low-Close	xlStockVHLC
Volume-Open-High-Low-Close	xlStockVOHLC
3D Surface	xlSurface
Wireframe 3-D Surface	xlSurfaceWireframe
Contour	xlSurfaceTopView
Wireframe Contour	xlSurfaceTopViewWireframe
Doughnut	xlDoughnut

13

Chart Type	Constant
Exploded Doughnut	`xlDoughnutExploded`
Bubble	`xlBubble`
Bubble with a 3D Effect	`xlBubble3DEffect`
Radar	`xlRadar`
Radar with Markers	`xlRadarMarkers`
Filled Radar	`xlRadarFilled`

Specifying Location and Size of the Chart

For each method, you have an opportunity to specify the chart type, chart location, and size of the chart.

Chart location is specified by specifying the .Top and .Left of the top-left corner of the chart *in pixels*. This is admittedly a really strange measurement. I can look at a cell and guess inches, but I can never remember how many pixels per inch or the dot pitch. Plus, if I want the chart to appear in cell S17, how do I even begin estimating the number?

The solution is to set the .Top and .Left of the chart to the .Top and .Left of the cell where you want the chart to appear. If you want the chart to appear starting in cell S17, specify

```
.Top:= Range("S17").Top, .Left:= Range("S17").Left
```

You can shorten this code by using [S17] as a shorter way to refer to Range("S17").

```
.Top:= [S17].Top, .Left:= [S17].Left
```

How about the length and width of the chart? Again, you could guess for .Height and .Width, or you can set these properties to the .Height and .Width of a known range. If you want the chart to fill S17:Y32, you could use

```
.Height:= [A17:A32].Height,
.Width:= [S1:Y1].Left
```

Referring to a Specific Chart

The macro recorder has an unsatisfactory way of writing code for the chart creation. The macro recorder uses the .AddChart2 method and adds a .Select to the end of the line to select the chart. The rest of the chart settings then apply to the ActiveChart object. This approach is a bit frustrating because you are required to do all the chart formatting before you select anything else in the worksheet.

The macro recorder does this because chart names are unpredictable. The first time you run a macro, the chart might be called Chart 1. But if you run the macro on another day or on a different worksheet, the chart might be called Chart 3 or Chart 5.

For the most flexibility, you should assign each new chart to a Chart object. This is a bit strange to do. Remember that a chart exists inside a container. Starting in Excel 2007, that container is a Shape object. You cannot refer to Worksheets("Sheet1").Charts("Chart 1"). This results in an error.

Ignoring the specifics of the AddChart2 method for a moment, you could use this coding approach, which captures the Shape object in the SH object variable and then assigns the SH.Chart to the CH object variable:

```
Dim WS as Worksheet
Dim SH as Shape
Dim CH as Chart
Set WS = ActiveSheet
Set SH = WS.Shapes.AddChart2(...)
Set CH = SH.Chart
```

You can simplify the preceding code by appending .Chart to the end of the AddChart2 method. The following code has one less object variable:

```
Dim WS as Worksheet
Dim CH as Chart
Set WS = ActiveSheet
Set CH = WS.Shapes.AddChart2(...).Chart
```

If you need to modify a preexisting chart—such as a chart that you did not create—and only one shape is on the worksheet, you can use this line of code:

```
WS.Shapes(1).Chart.Interior.Color = RGB(0,0,255)
```

If there are many charts, and you need to find the one with the upper-left corner located in cell A4, you can loop through all the Shape objects until you find one in the correct location, like this:

```
For each Sh in ActiveSheet.Shapes
    If Sh.TopLeftCell.Address = "$A$4" then
        Sh.Chart.Interior.Color = RGB(0,255,0)
    End If
Next Sh
```

Creating a Chart in Various Excel Versions

The following sections show the code for creating a chart. All of the code samples work in Excel 2013. If your code needs to run in Excel 2010 or even Excel 2003, you need to change the method used for creating the chart.

Using the .AddChart2 Method in Excel 2013

The Chart Styles available from the Paintbrush icon to the right of a selected chart are new in Excel 2013. The Excel team introduced the new .AddChart2 method to enable you to specify a specific chart style as you are creating the chart.

The .AddChart2 method lets you specify a ChartStyle. The valid values for ChartStyle are from 201 through 353. Although only chart styles #201 through 215 were designed with the Clustered Column chart in mind, you can apply any of the 153 styles to any chart.

The easiest way to discover the correct chart style number is to turn on the macro recorder, select a chart, and then choose the desired style from the Paintbrush icon.

The .AddChart2 requires you to specify a .ChartStyle (201 through 353), a chart type from Table 13.1, the location and size for the chart, and then an interesting parameter called NewLayout.

People using Excel have long complained about this typical chart in Excel 2010. In prior versions of Excel, a default chart always had a legend. The default chart only has a title when there is a single data series. The title repeats the single legend entry as the title, leading to the redundant title and legend in a single-series chart. (See Figure 13.4.)

Figure 13.4
Do you think this chart is about the East region?

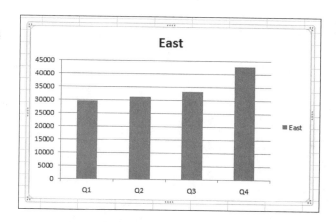

If you specify NewLayout:=False, you continue to get the chart with a legend and title for a single series chart. When you instead specify NewLayout:=True, your single-series chart does not have a legend. All charts have a title, even if that title is the useless "Chart Title." The theory is that when users sees "Chart Title," they are forced to click the title and change it. Of course, with VBA, you can change the chart title.

The following code produces the chart shown in Figure 13.5.

```
Sub CreateChartExcel2013()
    Dim WS As Worksheet
    Dim ch As Chart
    Set WS = ActiveSheet

    ' Select the data for the chart
    Range("A1:E4").Select

    ' Define the chart,
    ' use style 202 for rotated data labels
    Set ch = WS.Shapes.AddChart2( _
        Style:=202, _
        XlChartType:=xlColumnClustered, _
        Left:=[A6].Left, _
        Top:=[A6].Top, _
```

13

```
        Width:=[A6:G6].Width, _
        Height:=[A6:A20].Height, _
        NewLayout:=True).Chart
    ' Adjust the title
    ch.ChartTitle.Text = "2015 Sales by Region"

End Sub
```

Figure 13.5
Chart style 202 provides the rotated data labels in lieu of vertical axis labels.

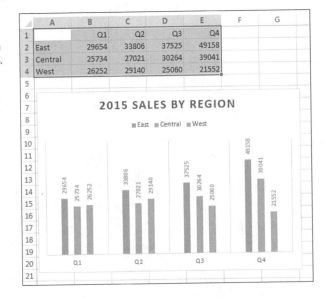

The preceding code required you to select the chart data before creating the chart. Good VBA code avoids selecting anything. You can avoid selecting the data by letting VBA create a blank chart and then specifying the source data with this code:

```
ch.SetSourceData Source:=Range("Data!$A$1:$E$4")
```

Two other features introduced in Excel 2013 are the 26 .ChartColor values and the capability to get chart data labels from a range of cells. These are discussed later.

Creating Charts in Excel 2007–2013

The AddChart2 method works only in Excel 2013. If you need to have your code work in Excel 2010 or Excel 2007, you have to use the AddChart method instead. This method enables you to specify a chart type, location, and size. You don't have access to chart styles or the NewLayout setting.

The following code works in Excel 2007 and later. It creates the bar chart shown in Figure 13.6.

```
Sub CreateChartExcel2007()
    ' Works in Excel 2007 & Newer
    Dim WS As Worksheet
```

```
     Dim ch As Chart
     Set WS = ActiveSheet

     ' Define the chart,
     Set ch = WS.Shapes.AddChart( _
         XlChartType:=xlBarClustered, _
         Left:=[A6].Left, _
         Top:=[A6].Top, _
         Width:=[A6:G6].Width, _
         Height:=[A6:A20].Height).Chart
     ch.SetSourceData Source:=Range("Data!$A$1:$E$4")

End Sub
```

Figure 13.6
After using the older .AddChart method, you usually have to customize the chart.

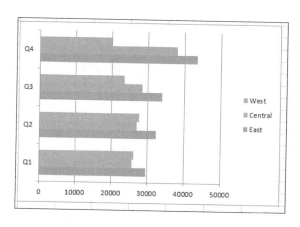

Creating Charts in Excel 2003–2013

Prior to Excel 2007, you needed to use Charts.Add to create a chart. This resulting chart is a new chart on a standalone Chart Sheet. Just as you can refer to the active worksheet with ActiveSheet, you can refer to the active chart sheet as ActiveChart. After specifying the chart type and source data, you move the ActiveChart to a worksheet, creating an embedded chart.

At this point, you cannot refer to ActiveChart anymore, but the newly created chart is still selected. The Excel 2003 code to assign the chart to an object variable requires you to Set CH = Selection.Parent.

Use this macro to create a chart if that chart has to be compatible with Excel 2003:

```
Sub Chart2003()
    Dim CH As Chart
    ' Add a chart as a ChartSheet
    Charts.Add
    ActiveChart.SetSourceData Source:=Worksheets("Sheet1").Range("A1:E4")
    ActiveChart.ChartType = xlColumnClustered
    ' Move the chart to a worksheet
    ActiveChart.Location Where:=xlLocationAsObject, Name:="Sheet1"
    ' You cannot refer to ActiveChart anymore
```

13

```
' The chart is still selected
Set CH = Selection.Parent
CH.Top = Range("B6").Top
CH.Left = Range("B6").Left
End Sub
```

Customizing a Chart

The AddChart or AddChart2 method enables you to specify a chart type, location, and size for your chart. You will probably need to customize additional items in the chart. The chart customizations fall into three broad categories:

- Global chart customizations, such as changing the chart style or color theme in the chart. In the Excel Interface, these are changes on the Design tab of the ribbon or in the Paintbrush icon to the right of the selected chart.

- Adding or moving a chart element, such as adding a chart title or moving the legend to a new location. In the Excel interface, the first- and second-level fly-out menus from the Plus icon to the right of the chart control the chart elements.

- Micromanaging the formatting for one specific series, point, or chart element. These are settings from the Format tab of the ribbon or the Format task pane.

However, given that the new charting interface is going to be creating a lot of charts with the unhelpful words "Chart Title" at the top of every chart, you should start with the code for changing the chart title to something useful.

Specifying a Chart Title

Every chart created with NewLayout:=True has a chart title. When the chart has two or more series, that title is the words "Chart Title." You are going to have to plan to change the chart title to something useful.

To specify a chart title in VBA, use this code:

```
ActiveChart.ChartTitle.Caption = "Sales by Region"
```

Assuming that you are changing the chart title of a newly created chart that is assigned to the CH object variable, you can use

```
CH.ChartTitle.Caption = "Sales by Region"
```

This code works assuming that your chart already has a title. If you are not sure that the selected Chart style has a title, you can ensure the title is present first with

```
CH.SetElement msoElementChartTitleAboveChart
```

Although it is relatively easy to add a chart title and specify the words in the title, it becomes increasing complex to change the formatting of the chart title. The following code changes the font, size, and color of the title:

```
With CH.ChartTitle.Format.TextFrame2.TextRange.Font
    .Name = "Rockwell"
    .Fill.ForeColor.ObjectThemeColor = msoThemeColorAccent2
```

```
    .Size = 14
End With
```

The two axis titles operate the same as the chart title. To change the words, use the .Caption property. To format the words, you have to use the Format property. The following code changes the axis title along the category axis:

```
CH.SetElement msoElementPrimaryCategoryAxisTitleHorizontal
CH.Axes(xlCategory, xlPrimary).AxisTitle.Caption = "Months"
CH.Axes(xlCategory, xlPrimary).AxisTitle. _
    Format.TextFrame2.TextRange.Font.Fill. _
    ForeColor.ObjectThemeColor = msoThemeColorAccent2
```

Quickly Formatting a Chart Using New Excel 2013 Features

Excel 2013 offers new chart styles, color settings, filtering, and the capability to create data labels as captions that come from selected cells. All these features are excellent additions, but the code works only in Excel 2013 and is not backward compatible with Excel 2010 or earlier.

Specifying a Chart Style

Excel 2013 introduces new chart styles that quickly apply professional formatting to a chart. You can see the chart styles in the large Chart Style gallery on the Design tab.

The chart style concept is not new in Excel 2013. Excel 2007 offered 48 chart styles. The difference is that the chart styles in Excel 2013 are interesting and offer variability between the styles. Back in Excel 2007–2010, the 48 chart styles were boring variations on four styles: monochrome, colorful, single-color, and dark background.

If you created your chart using the AddChart2 method, you can specify a chart style as the first parameter of that method. If you did not specify a chart style, or later want to change a start style, use this code:

```
ch.ClearToMatchStyle
ch.ChartStyle = 339
```

Valid chart styles are 201 through 353. The fastest way to learn the chart style is to select a chart, turn on the macro recorder, select a style from the gallery on the Design tab, and then stop recording.

> ┌ C A U T I O N ─────────────────────────────
>
> The ToolTip that appears in the Chart Styles gallery does not convert to the chart style value.
>
> As an experiment, create a clustered column chart. Copy that chart and paste it three times, changing the chart type to a line, stacked area, and stacked bar. Turn on the macro recorder. Select each chart and choose the last dark style from the Chart Styles gallery. You might notice that the ToolTip is different when you select the style. When you look at the recorded code, the .ChartStyle value is dramatically different for each chart. See the ToolTip and the ChartStyle value in the title of each chart in Figure 13.7.

Although the chart styles look alike in the various Chart Style galleries, they are different chart styles.

Using VBA, you can apply any of the 153 new chart styles to any type of chart. Although it works, it might not look as good as if you applied the style designed for that type of chart.

Rather than randomly selecting a chart style, use the macro recorder to learn the correct style.

Figure 13.7
The ToolTip says Style 8, but the .ChartStyle varies.

Style 8

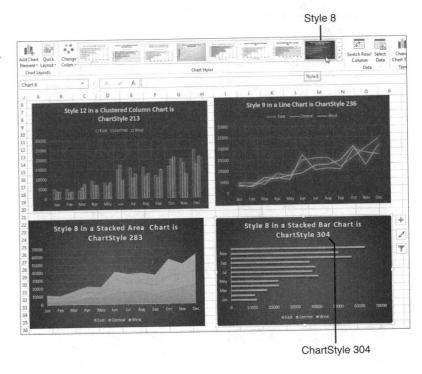

ChartStyle 304

TIP

Choose a chart type before choosing a chart style.

Suppose you create an area chart and apply Style 8 from the Chart Styles gallery. In the background, Excel applies .ChartStyle =283 to the chart. If you later change the chart type to a clustered column chart, Excel does not convert the .ChartStyle back to the correct value of 213. The chart style stays as 283.

Figure 13.8 shows the four charts from Figure 13.7 after they were converted back to a clustered column chart. Each chart looks a little different. Vertical gridlines do not appear on some charts. The legend moves from the top to the bottom. Glow, Fill, and Overlap are different in the various charts.

When you open the Chart Styles gallery, none of the thumbnails appear as the chosen style. This is because the current ChartStyle of 304 is no longer shown in the gallery.

Figure 13.8
If you change the chart type after choosing a style, you see subtle differences.

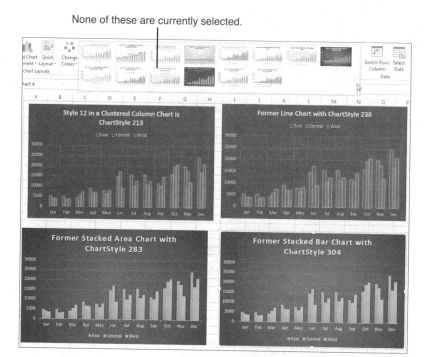

The old chart style values of 1 through 48 continue to work. Try 1 for Monochrome, 2 for colorful, 3 for shades of blue, and 42 for a dark background that works well with PowerPoint.

In the sample files for this book, open 13-TestAllStyles.xlsm to see a clustered column chart represented in all 153 styles.

Applying a Chart Color

Excel 2013 also introduces a ch.ChartColor property that assigns one of 26 color themes to a chart. Assign a value from 1 to 26, but be aware that the order of the colors in the Chart Styles fly-out menu (see Figure 13.9) has nothing to do with the 26 values.

To understand the ChartColor values, consider the color drop-down shown in Figure 13.10. This drop-down offers 10 columns of colors: Background 1, Text 1, Background 2, Text 2, and Theme 1 through Theme 6.

Following is a synopsis of the 26 values that you can use for ChartColor:

- ChartColors 1, 9, and 20 use grayscale colors from column 3. A value of 1 rotates from dark to light to medium. A value of 9 rotates light to medium to dark. A value of 20 starts with three medium grays, then black, very light gray, and medium gray.

- ChartColor 2 uses the six theme colors in the top row from left to right.

13

Figure 13.9
Colors schemes in the menu are called Color 1, Color 2, and so on, but have nothing to do with the VBA settings.

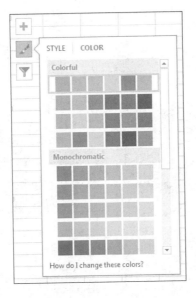

Figure 13.10
ChartColor combinations include a mix of colors from the current theme.

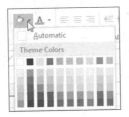

- ChartColors 3 through 8 use a single column of colors. For example, ChartColor = 3 uses the six colors in Theme 1, from dark to light. ChartColor values of 4 through 8 correspond to Themes 2 through 6.

- Value 10 repeats value 2 but adds a light border around the chart element.

- Values 11 through 13 are the most inventive. They use three theme colors from the top row combined with the same three theme colors from the bottom row. This produces light and dark versions of three different colors. ChartColor 11 uses the odd-numbered themes: 1, 3, 5. ChartColor 12 uses the even-numbered themes. ChartColor 13 uses Theme 6, 5, 4.

- Values 14 through 19 repeat values 3 through 8, but add a light border.

- Values 21 through 26 are similar to values 3 through 8, but the colors progress from light to dark.

The following code changes the chart to use varying shades of theme colors 6, 5, and 4:

```
ch.ChartColor = 13
```

In Excel 2007 and 2010, the ChartColor property causes an error. For backward compatibility, use a .ChartStyle value from 1 to 48. These correspond to the order of the colors in the old Chart Styles gallery in Excel 2007 and Excel 2010.

Filtering a Chart in Excel 2013

In real life, creating charts from tables of data is not always simple. Tables frequently have totals or subtotals. The table in Figure 13.11 has quarterly total columns intermixed with the monthly values. Rows 5, 9, and 10 contain totals of various regions. When you create a chart from this data, the total columns and rows create a bad chart. The scale of the chart is wrong because of the $5.3 million grand total cell.

Figure 13.11
The subtotals in this table cause a bad-looking chart.

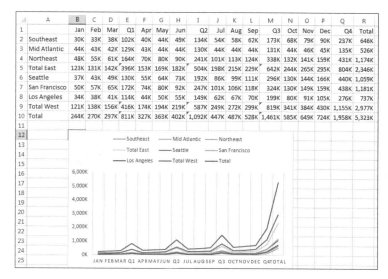

In previous versions of Excel, you could attempt to select the eight noncontiguous regions before creating the chart. For example, A1:D4, F1:H4, ..., N6:P8.

The new paradigm in Excel 2013 is to select the whole range, create the horrible looking chart, and then use the Funnel icon to the right of the chart to remove the total rows and total columns.

To filter a row or column in VBA, you set the new .IsFiltered property to True. The following code removes the total columns and total rows to produce the chart shown in Figure 13.12.

```
Sub FilterChart()
    Dim CH As Chart
    Dim WS As Worksheet
    Set WS = ActiveSheet

    Set CH = WS.Shapes.AddChart2(Style:=239, _
```

13

```
        XlChartType:=xlLine, _
        Left:=[B12].Left, _
        Top:=[B12].Top, _
        NewLayout:=False).Chart
CH.SetSourceData Source:=Range("Sheet1!$A$1:$R$10")
' Hide the rows containing totals from row 5, 9, 10
CH.FullSeriesCollection(4).IsFiltered = True
CH.FullSeriesCollection(8).IsFiltered = True
CH.FullSeriesCollection(9).IsFiltered = True
' Hide the columns containing quarters and total
CH.ChartGroups(1).FullCategoryCollection(4).IsFiltered = True
CH.ChartGroups(1).FullCategoryCollection(8).IsFiltered = True
CH.ChartGroups(1).FullCategoryCollection(12).IsFiltered = True
CH.ChartGroups(1).FullCategoryCollection(16).IsFiltered = True
CH.ChartGroups(1).FullCategoryCollection(17).IsFiltered = True
' Reapply style 239; it applies markers with <7 series
CH.ChartStyle = 239
```

End Sub

CAUTION ———————————————————————————————————————

The .IsFiltered property is not backward compatible with Excel 2010 or earlier.

Note: Chart Style 239 is supposed to include markers on the line. When the original chart contained nine series, the markers were deleted. Reapplying the chart style 239 at the end of the macro brings the markers back to the resulting six-series chart.

Figure 13.12
Filter the total rows and columns to have monthly data by region on the chart.

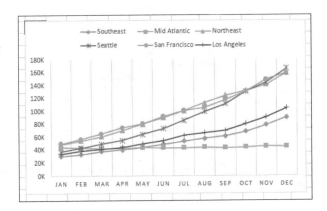

Using Cell Formulas as Data Label Captions in Excel 2013

Excel 2013 introduces the capability to caption a data point using a callout that is based on a cell in the worksheet. You now have the flexibility to calculate data captions on-the-fly.

In Figure 13.13, the sales figures in row 2 are random numbers that change every time the worksheet is calculated. You never know which month is going to be the best or the worst month.

Row 5 contains a somewhat complex formula to build a dynamic caption for the month. If the sales for the month match the maximum sales for all the months, the caption will read, "Best month with $x". If the sales match the minimum sales, the caption says it was the worst month. For all the other months, the caption is "". The formula in B5 is

```
=IF(B2=MAX($B2:$M2),"Best month with $"&B2,"")&
    IF(B2=MIN($B2:$M2),"Worst month with $"&B2,"")
```

Figure 13.13
A formula generates the caption that appears on the chart.

To specify that the data labels should appear as a callout, use this new argument in Excel 2013:

```
CH.SetElement (msoElementDataLabelCallout)
```

You can then specify the range that contains the labels for an individual series. The InsertChartField method is applied to the TextRange property of the TextFrame2.

```
' Specify a range for the data labels for Series 1
Dim Ser as Series
Dim TF as TextFrame2
Set Ser = CH.SeriesCollection(1)
Set TF = Ser.DataLabels.Format.TextFrame2
TF.TextRange.InsertChartField _
    ChartFieldType:=msoChartFieldFormula, _
    Formula:="=Sheet1!$B$5:$M$5", _
    Position:=xlLabelPositionAbove
Ser.DataLabels.ShowRange = True
```

The chart in Figure 13.14 is created with the following code:

```
Sub LabelCaptionsFromRange()
    Dim WS As Worksheet
    Dim CH As Chart
    Dim Ser As Series
    Dim TF As TextFrame2

    Set WS = ActiveSheet
    Set CH = WS.Shapes.AddChart2(Style:=201, _
        XlChartType:=xlColumnClustered, _
        Left:=[B7].Left, _
        Top:=[B7].Top, _
        NewLayout:=True).Chart
    CH.SetSourceData Source:=Range("Sheet1!$A$1:$M$2")
    ' Apply Labels as a Callout
    CH.SetElement (msoElementDataLabelCallout)
    ' Specify a range for the data labels for Series 1
```

```
    Set Ser = CH.SeriesCollection(1)
    Set TF = Ser.DataLabels.Format.TextFrame2
    TF.TextRange.InsertChartField _
        ChartFieldType:=msoChartFieldFormula, _
        Formula:="=Sheet1!$B$5:$M$5", _
        Position:=xlLabelPositionAbove
    ' New in Excel 2013
    Ser.DataLabels.ShowRange = True
    ' Turn off the category name and value
    ' This has to be done after ShowRange = True
    ' If you turn off all first, the label is deleted
    Ser.DataLabels.ShowValue = False
    Ser.DataLabels.ShowCategoryName = False
    ' Vary colors by points
    CH.ChartGroups(1).VaryByCategories = True
    ' Make columns wider by making gaps narrower
    CH.ChartGroups(1).GapWidth = 77
End Sub
```

Figure 13.14
The callouts dynamically appear on the largest and smallest points.

Using `SetElement` to Emulate Changes from the Plus Icon

When you select a chart, three icons appear to the right of the chart. The top icon is a plus sign. All the choices in the first and second-level fly-out menus use the SetElement method in VBA. Note that the Add Chart Element drop-down on the Design tab includes all these settings, plus Lines and Up/Down Bars.

> **NOTE**
> `SetElement` does not cover the choices in the Format task pane that often appears. See the "Using the Format Method to Micromanage Formatting Options" section later in this chapter to change those settings.

If you do not feel like looking up the proper constant in this book, you can always quickly record a macro.

The SetElement method is followed by a constant that specifies which menu item to select. For example, if you want to choose Show Legend at Left, you can use this code:

```
ActiveChart.SetElement msoElementLegendLeft
```

Table 13.2 shows all the available constants that you can use with the SetElement method. These constants are in roughly the same order as they appear in the Add Chart Element drop-down.

Table 13.2   Constants Available with SetElement

Element Group	Chart Element Constant
Axes	msoElementPrimaryCategoryAxisNone
Axes	msoElementPrimaryCategoryAxisShow
Axes	msoElementPrimaryCategoryAxisWithoutLabels
Axes	msoElementPrimaryCategoryAxisReverse
Axes	msoElementPrimaryCategoryAxisThousands
Axes	msoElementPrimaryCategoryAxisMillions
Axes	msoElementPrimaryCategoryAxisBillions
Axes	msoElementPrimaryCategoryAxisLogScale
Axes	msoElementSecondaryCategoryAxisNone
Axes	msoElementSecondaryCategoryAxisShow
Axes	msoElementSecondaryCategoryAxisWithoutLabels
Axes	msoElementSecondaryCategoryAxisReverse
Axes	msoElementSecondaryCategoryAxisThousands
Axes	msoElementSecondaryCategoryAxisMillions
Axes	msoElementSecondaryCategoryAxisBillions
Axes	msoElementSecondaryCategoryAxisLogScaIe
Axes	msoElementPrimaryValueAxisNone
Axes	msoElementPrimaryValueAxisShow
Axes	msoElementPrimaryValueAxisThousands
Axes	msoElementPrimaryValueAxisMillions
Axes	msoElementPrimaryValueAxisBillions
Axes	msoElementPrimaryValueAxisLogScale
Axes	msoElementSecondaryValueAxisNone
Axes	msoElementSecondaryValueAxisShow
Axes	msoElementSecondarValueAxisThousands
Axes	msoElementSecondaryValueAxisMillions

13

Element Group	Chart Element Constant
Axes	msoElementSecondaryValueAxisBillions
Axes	msoElementSecondaryValueAxisLogScale
Axes	msoElementSeriesAxisNone
Axes	msoElementSeriesAxisShow
Axes	msoElementSeriesAxisReverse
Axes	msoElementSeriesAxisWithoutLabeling
Axis Titles	msoElementPrimaryCategoryAxisTitleNone
Axis Titles	msoElementPrimaryCategoryAxisTitleBelowAxis
Axis Titles	msoElementPrimaryCategoryAxisTitleAdjacentToAxis
Axis Titles	msoElementPrimaryCategoryAxisTitleHorizontal
Axis Titles	msoElementPrimaryCategoryAxisTitleVertical
Axis Titles	msoElementPrimaryCategoryAxisTitleRotated
Axis Titles	msoElementSecondaryCategoryAxisTitleAdjacentToAxis
Axis Titles	msoElementSecondaryCategoryAxisTitleBelowAxis
Axis Titles	msoElementSecondaryCategoryAxisTitleHorizontal
Axis Titles	msoElementSecondaryCategoryAxisTitleNone
Axis Titles	msoElementSecondaryCategoryAxisTitleRotated
Axis Titles	msoElementSecondaryCategoryAxisTitleVertical
Axis Titles	msoElementPrimaryValueAxisTitleAdjacentToAxis
Axis Titles	msoElementPrimaryValueAxisTitleBelowAxis
Axis Titles	msoElementPrimaryValueAxisTitleHorizontal
Axis Titles	msoElementPrimaryValueAxisTitleNone
Axis Titles	msoElementPrimaryValueAxisTitleRotated
Axis Titles	msoElementPrimaryValueAxisTitleVertical
Axis Titles	msoElementSecondaryValueAxisTitleBelowAxis
Axis Titles	msoElementSecondaryValueAxisTitleHorizontal
Axis Titles	msoElementSecondaryValueAxisTitleNone
Axis Titles	msoElementSecondaryValueAxisTitleRotated
Axis Titles	msoElementSecondaryValueAxisTitleVertical
Axis Titles	msoElementSeriesAxisTitleHorizontal
Axis Titles	msoElementSeriesAxisTitleNone
Axis Titles	msoElementSeriesAxisTitleRotated
Axis Titles	msoElementSeriesAxisTitleVertical
Axis Titles	msoElementSecondaryValueAxisTitleAdjacentToAxis

13

Element Group	Chart Element Constant
Chart Title	msoElementChartTitleNone
Chart Title	msoElementChartTitleCenteredOverlay
Chart Title	msoElementChartTitleAboveChart
Data Labels	msoElementDataLabelCallout (new in Excel 2013)
Data Labels	msoElementDataLabelCenter
Data Labels	msoElementDataLabelInsideEnd
Data Labels	msoElementDataLabelNone
Data Labels	msoElementDataLabelInsideBase
Data Labels	msoElementDataLabelOutSideEnd
Data Labels	msoElementDataLabelTop
Data Labels	msoElementDataLabelBottom
Data Labels	msoElementDataLabelRight
Data Labels	msoElementDataLabelLeft
Data Labels	msoElementDataLabelShow
Data Labels	msoElementDataLabelBestFit
Data Table	msoElementDataTableNone
Data Table	msoElementDataTableShow
Data Table	msoElementDataTableWithLegendKeys
Error Bars	msoElementErrorBarNone
Error Bars	msoElementErrorBarStandardError
Error Bars	msoElementErrorBarPercentage
Error Bars	msoElementErrorBarStandardDeviation
GridLines	msoElementPrimaryCategoryGridLinesNone
GridLines	msoElementPrimaryCategoryGridLinesMajor
GridLines	msoElementPrimaryCategoryGridLinesMinor
GridLines	msoElementPrimaryCategoryGridLinesMinorMajor
GridLines	msoElementSecondaryCategoryGridLinesNone
GridLines	msoElementSecondaryCategoryGridLinesMajor
GridLines	msoElementSecondaryCategoryGridLinesMinor
GridLines	msoElementSecondaryCategoryGridLinesMinorMajor
GridLines	msoElementPrimaryValueGridLinesNone
GridLines	msoElementPrimaryValueGridLinesMajor
GridLines	msoElementPrimaryValueGridLinesMinor
GridLines	msoElementPrimaryValueGridLinesMinorMajor

13

Element Group	Chart Element Constant
GridLines	msoElementSecondaryValueGridLinesNone
GridLines	msoElementSecondaryValueGridLinesMajor
GridLines	msoElementSecondaryValueGridLinesMinor
GridLines	msoElementSecondaryValueGridLinesMinorMajor
GridLines	msoElementSeriesAxisGridLinesNone
GridLines	msoElementSeriesAxisGridLinesMajor
GridLines	msoElementSeriesAxisGridLinesMinor
GridLines	msoElementSeriesAxisGridLinesMinorMajor
Legend	msoElementLegendNone
Legend	msoElementLegendRight
Legend	msoElementLegendTop
Legend	msoElementLegendLeft
Legend	msoElementLegendBottom
Legend	msoElementLegendRightOverlay
Legend	msoElementLegendLeftOverlay
Lines	msoElementLineNone
Lines	msoElementLineDropLine
Lines	msoElementLineHiLoLine
Lines	msoElementLineDropHiLoLine
Lines	msoElementLineSeriesLine
Trendline	msoElementTrendlineNone
Trendline	msoElementTrendlineAddLinear
Trendline	msoElementTrendlineAddExponential
Trendline	msoElementTrendlineAddLinearForecast
Trendline	msoElementTrendlineAddTwoPeriodMovingAverage
Up/Down Bars	msoElementUpDownBarsNone
Up/Down Bars	msoElementUpDownBarsShow
Plot Area	msoElementPlotAreaNone
Plot Area	msoElementPlotAreaShow
Chart Wall	msoElementChartWallNone
Chart Wall	msoElementChartWallShow
Chart Floor	msoElementChartFloorNone
Chart Floor	msoElementChartFloorShow

13

Using SetElement enables you to change chart elements quickly. For example, charting gurus say that the legend should always appear to the left or above the chart. Few of the built-in styles show the legend above the chart. I also prefer to show the values along the axis in thousands or millions when appropriate. This is better than displaying three or six zeroes on every line.

Two lines of code handle these settings after creating the chart:

```
Sub UseSetElement()
    Dim WS As Worksheet
    Dim CH As Chart

    Set WS = ActiveSheet
    Set CH = WS.Shapes.AddChart2(Style:=201, _
        XlChartType:=xlColumnClustered, _
        Left:=[B6].Left, _
        Top:=[B6].Top, _
        NewLayout:=False).Chart
    CH.SetSourceData Source:=Range("Sheet1!$A$1:$M$4")

    ' Set value axis to display thousands
    CH.SetElement msoElementPrimaryValueAxisThousands

    ' Move the legend to the top
    CH.SetElement msoElementLegendTop
End Sub
```

Using the Format Method to Micromanage Formatting Options

The Format tab offers icons for changing colors and effects for individual chart elements. Although many people call the Shadow, Glow, Bevel, and Material settings "chart junk," there are ways in VBA to apply these formats.

Excel 2013 includes an object called the ChartFormat object that contains the settings for Fill, Glow, Line, PictureFormat, Shadow, SoftEdge, TextFrame2, and ThreeD. You can access the ChartFormat object by using the Format method on many chart elements. Table 13.3 lists a sampling of chart elements that you can format using the Format method.

13

Table 13.3   Chart Elements to Which Formatting Applies

Chart Element	VBA to Refer to This Chart
Chart Title	ChartTitle
Axis Title—Category	Axes(xlCategory, xlPrimary).AxisTitle
Axis Title—Value	Axes(xlValue, xlPrimary).AxisTitle

Chart Element	VBA to Refer to This Chart
Legend	Legend
Data Labels for Series 1	SeriesCollection(1).DataLabels
Data Labels for Point 2	SeriesCollection(1).DataLabels(2) or SeriesCollection(1).Points(2).DataLabel
Data Table	DataTable
Axes—Horizontal	Axes(xlCategory, xlPrimary)
Axes—Vertical	Axes(xlValue, xlPrimary)
Axis—Series (Surface Charts Only)	Axes(xlSeries, xlPrimary)
Major Gridlines	Axes(xlValue, xlPrimary).MajorGridlines
Minor Gridlines	Axes(xlValue, xlPrimary).MinorGridlines
Plot Area	PlotArea
Chart Area	ChartArea
Chart Wall	Walls
Chart Back Wall	BackWall
Chart Side Wall	SideWall
Chart Floor	Floor
Trendline for Series 1	SeriesCollection(1).TrendLines(1)
Droplines	ChartGroups(1).DropLines
Up/Down Bars	ChartGroups(1).UpBars
Error Bars	SeriesCollection(1).ErrorBars
Series(1)	SeriesCollection(1)
Series(1) DataPoint	SeriesCollection(1).Points(3)

The Format method is the gateway to settings for Fill, Glow, and so on. Each of those objects has different options. The following sections provide examples of how to set up each type of format.

Changing an Object's Fill

The Shape Fill drop-down on the Format tab enables you to choose a single color, a gradient, a picture, or a texture for the fill.

To apply a specific color, you can use the RGB (red, green, blue) setting. To create a color, you specify a value from 0 to 255 for levels of red, green, and blue. The following code applies a simple blue fill:

```
Dim cht As Chart
Dim upb As UpBars
Set cht = ActiveChart
```

```
Set upb = cht.ChartGroups(1).UpBars
upb.Format.Fill.ForeColor.RGB = RGB(0, 0, 255)
```

If you would like an object to pick up the color from a specific theme accent color, you use the `ObjectThemeColor` property. The following code changes the bar color of the first series to accent color 6, which is an orange color in the Office theme. However, this might be another color if the workbook is using a different theme.

```
Sub ApplyThemeColor()
    Dim cht As Chart
    Dim ser As Series
    Set cht = ActiveChart
    Set ser = cht.SeriesCollection(1)
    ser.Format.Fill.ForeColor.ObjectThemeColor = msoThemeColorAccent6
End Sub
```

To apply a built-in texture, you use the `PresetTextured` method. The following code applies a green marble texture to the second series. However, you can apply any of the 20 textures:

```
Sub ApplyTexture()
    Dim cht As Chart
    Dim ser As Series
    Set cht = ActiveChart
    Set ser = cht.SeriesCollection(2)
    ser.Format.Fill.PresetTextured msoTextureGreenMarble
End Sub
```

> **NOTE** When you type `PresetTextured` followed by a space, the VB Editor offers a complete list of possible texture values.

To fill the bars of a data series with a picture, you use the `UserPicture` method and specify the path and filename of an image on the computer, as in the following example:

```
Sub FormatWithPicture()
    Dim cht As Chart
    Dim ser As Series
    Set cht = ActiveChart
    Set ser = cht.SeriesCollection(1)
    MyPic = "C:\PodCastTitle1.jpg"
    ser.Format.Fill.UserPicture MyPic
End Sub
```

Microsoft removed patterns as fills from Excel 2007. However, this method was restored in Excel 2010 because of the outcry from customers who used patterns to differentiate columns printed on monochrome printers.

In Excel 2013, you can apply a pattern using the `.Patterned` method. Patterns have a type, such as `msoPatternPlain`, as well as a foreground and background color. The following code creates dark red vertical lines on a white background:

```
Sub FormatWithPicture()
    Dim cht As Chart
    Dim ser As Series
```

13

```
        Set cht = ActiveChart
        Set ser = cht.SeriesCollection(1)
        With ser.Format.Fill
            .Patterned msoPatternDarkVertical
            .BackColor.RGB = RGB(255,255,255)
            .ForeColor.RGB = RGB(255,0,0)
        End With
    End Sub
```

> **NOTE** Code that uses patterns works in every version of Excel except Excel 2007. Therefore, do not use this code if you will be sharing the macro with co-workers who use Excel 2007.

Gradients are more difficult to specify than fills. Excel 2013 provides three methods that help you set up the common gradients. The OneColorGradient and TwoColorGradient methods require that you specify a gradient direction, such as msoGradientFromCorner. You can then specify one of four styles, numbered 1 through 4, depending on whether you want the gradient to start at the top left, top right, bottom left, or bottom right. After using a gradient method, you need to specify the ForeColor and the BackColor settings for the object. The following macro sets up a two-color gradient using two theme colors:

```
Sub TwoColorGradient()
    Dim cht As Chart
    Dim ser As Series
    Set cht = ActiveChart
    Set ser = cht.SeriesCollection(1)
    ser.Format.Fill.TwoColorGradient msoGradientFromCorner, 3
    ser.Format.Fill.ForeColor.ObjectThemeColor = msoThemeColorAccent6
    ser.Format.Fill.BackColor.ObjectThemeColor = msoThemeColorAccent2
End Sub
```

When using the OneColorGradient method, you specify a direction, a style (1 through 4), and a darkness value between 0 and 1 (0 for darker gradients or 1 for lighter gradients).

When using the PresetGradient method, you specify a direction, a style (1 through 4), and the type of gradient such as msoGradientBrass, msoGradientLateSunset, or msoGradientRainbow. Again, as you are typing this code in the VB Editor, the AutoComplete tool provides a complete list of the available preset gradient types.

Formatting Line Settings

The LineFormat object formats either a line or the border around an object. You can change numerous properties for a line, such as the color, arrows, and dash style.

The following macro formats the trendline for the first series in a chart:

```
Sub FormatLineOrBorders()
    Dim cht As Chart
    Set cht = ActiveChart
    With cht.SeriesCollection(1).Trendlines(1).Format.Line
        .DashStyle = msoLineLongDashDotDot
        .ForeColor.RGB = RGB(50, 0, 128)
```

```
        .BeginArrowheadLength = msoArrowheadShort
        .BeginArrowheadStyle = msoArrowheadOval
        .BeginArrowheadWidth = msoArrowheadNarrow
        .EndArrowheadLength = msoArrowheadLong
        .EndArrowheadStyle = msoArrowheadTriangle
        .EndArrowheadWidth = msoArrowheadWide
    End With
End Sub
```

When you are formatting a border, the arrow settings are not relevant, so the code is shorter than the code for formatting a line. The following macro formats the border around a chart:

```
Sub FormatBorder()
    Dim cht As Chart
    Set cht = ActiveChart
    With cht.ChartArea.Format.Line
        .DashStyle = msoLineLongDashDotDot
        .ForeColor.RGB = RGB(50, 0, 128)
    End With
End Sub
```

Formatting a Data Series

The Chart Elements icon to the right of a chart is missing the choice to format a data series. Depending on the chart type, the Format Data Series task pane holds special settings that can dramatically affect the look of your chart.

There are a few ways to access the Format Series dialog:

■ Right-click a series in the chart and select Format Series from the context menu.

■ From the first drop-down in the Format tabs, choose the item that you want to format (for example, choose Series 1 from this drop-down to format Series 1). Then click the Format Selection button immediately below the drop-down.

The special settings appear in the Series Options category of the Format dialog box. The following are some of the settings you can control:

■ **Gap Width and Separation**—Control whether the columns in a column chart should be touching each other, as in a histogram, or separated.

■ **Plot on Second Axis**—Specifies that a series should be plotted on a secondary axis. This is useful when the magnitude of one series does not match the magnitude of another series.

■ **Angle of First Slice**—Rotates pie and doughnut charts. Other settings for the round charts control features such as explosion and hole size.

■ **Bar of Pie and Pie of Pie**—Control which categories appear in the secondary chart in these combination charts.

■ **Bubble Size**—Controls how the bubbles are sized in a bubble chart.

■ **Surface and Radar**—Control certain aspects of these chart types.

13

The following sections discuss the various options you can control in the Series Options dialog.

Controlling Gap Width and Series Separation in Column and Bar Charts

Typically, the individual bars in a bar or column chart are separated by gaps. When scientists create histograms, they want to eliminate the gaps between bars.

Excel offers the GapWidth property, whose value can range from 0 to 500 to represent 0% to 500%. Figure 13.15 shows a typical chart and a chart where the gap width has been reduced to 25%.

Figure 13.15
In the bottom chart, the gap width has been reduced from the default to 25%.

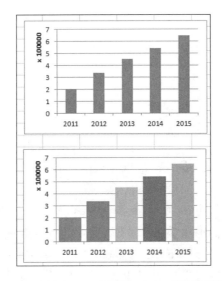

> **TIP**
> Note that reducing the gap size automatically makes the columns thicker. To keep the columns narrow, you should reduce the width of the chart.

The gap width setting applies to chart groups that contain bar or column markers. You can also use it to format the volume markers in volume-high-low-close charts or volume-open-high-low-close charts.

The following macro changes the gap width to 25%:

```
Sub FormatGapWidth()
    Dim cht As Chart
    Set cht = ActiveChart
    cht.ChartGroups(1).GapWidth = 25
End Sub
```

When you create a clustered column chart with two series, the columns for each data point touch, as shown in the top chart in Figure 13.16. You can use the Overlap property to cause the columns to overlap. Values from 1 to 100 cause the columns to overlap anywhere from 1% to 100%. Values from -1 to -100 cause separations between the data points.

The middle chart in Figure 13.16 shows a 50% overlap. The bottom chart shows a –100% overlap.

Figure 13.16
The middle chart has an overlap, and the bottom chart has a negative overlap (that is, a separation).

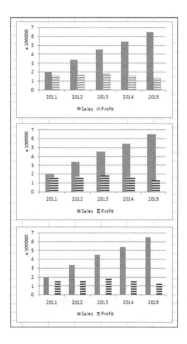

The following macro creates a 25% overlap between the series:

```
Sub FormatOverLap()
    Dim cht As Chart
    Set cht = ActiveChart
    cht.ChartGroups(1).Overlap = 25
End Sub
```

The Overlap property applies to clustered column and clustered bar charts. It should be set to 100% for the volume series in stock charts.

Spinning and Exploding Round Charts

Pie and doughnut charts have rotation and explosion properties. In a typical data series, there might be a few tiny pie slices at the end of the series. These pie slices typically appear in the back of the chart. If you move them around to the front of the chart, they are more visible, and there is more room for the data labels to appear outside the chart.

You control the angle of the first slice of a pie by using the FirstSliceAngle property of the ChartGroup object. Valid values range from 0 to 360, representing rotations of 0 to

13

360 degrees. In the bottom-left chart in Figure 13.17, the original chart was rotated 159 degrees, using the following macro:

```
Sub RotateChart()
    ' Bottom-Left Chart in Figure 13.17
    Dim cht As Chart
    Set cht = ActiveChart
    cht.ChartGroups(1).FirstSliceAngle = 159
End Sub
```

You can also explode pie and doughnut charts. In an exploded view, the individual wedges are separated from each other. You use the Explosion property to change the explosion effect. Valid values range from 0 to 400, representing 0 to 400%. With explosions, tiny values go a long way. The top-right chart in Figure 13.17 represents a 22% explosion and is created with this macro:

```
Sub ExplodeChart()
    ' Top-Right Chart in Figure 13.17
    Dim cht As Chart
    Set cht = ActiveChart
    cht.ChartGroups(1).FirstSliceAngle = 159
    cht.ChartGroups(1).Explosion = 22
End Sub
```

Figure 13.17
You can rotate or explode pie charts to bring the small slices into view.

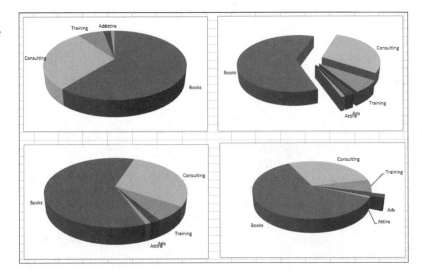

Sometimes, a better effect is to explode a single slice of a pie. You can apply the Explosion property to a single data point. In the bottom-right chart in Figure 13.17, only the Ads slice is exploded. Note that the macro then adjusts the positioning of the adjoining data labels so that they can be seen around the exploded slice:

```
Sub ExplodeOneSlice()
    ' Bottom-Right Chart in Figure 13.17
    Dim cht As Chart
    Dim ser As Series
```

```
    Dim poi As Point
    Dim dl As DataLabel
    Set cht = ActiveChart
    Set ser = cht.SeriesCollection(1)
    cht.ChartGroups(1).FirstSliceAngle = 114
    ' Explode one slice
    Set poi = ser.Points(4)
    poi.Explosion = 22
    ' fix the labels
    Set dl = ser.Points(3).DataLabel
    dl.Left = dl.Left + 30
    dl.Top = dl.Top - 50
    Set dl = ser.Points(5).DataLabel
    dl.Left = dl.Left + 10
    dl.Top = dl.Top + 20
End Sub
```

You can also control the hole size in the center of a doughnut chart. A typical doughnut chart starts out with a hole size that is 50% of the doughnut. You use the `DoughnutHoleSize` property to adjust this from 90% to 10%, using values of 90 to 10. The following macro adjusts the doughnut hole size to 70%:

```
Sub ExplodeChart()
    Dim cht As Chart
    Set cht = ActiveChart
    cht.ChartGroups(1).DoughnutHoleSize = 70
End Sub
```

Controlling the Bar of Pie and Pie of Pie Charts

When your data contains many small pie slices and you care about the differences in those small slices, you can ask for the small slices to be plotted in a secondary pie or a secondary bar chart.

→ For complete details on these unique chart types, read "Using a Pie of Pie Chart" in Chapter 4. These chart types are found in the Pie category.

Because these charts include two charts inside the chart area, Excel offers many additional settings for controlling the size and placement of each chart in relation to the other. There are also myriad ways to determine which pie wedges are represented in the secondary chart. You have complete control of these settings in VBA. You might consider the following:

- How do you decide which wedges are reported in the smaller pie? Excel offers choices to move the last *n* slices, move all slices smaller than *n* percent, or to move all slices smaller than a particular value. Excel also offers the custom method for moving the pie slices.

- Do you want leader lines from the "other" slice to the secondary plot? These are generally a good idea, but you can turn them off or even format them, if desired.

- How large should the secondary plot be compared to the first plot? Suppose you are preparing charts for a meeting to discuss which product lines should be discontinued.

13

In this case, the focus really is on the tiny wedges, and you might want to have the secondary plot be as large as or larger than the original pie.

■ How wide should the gap be between the plots?

The following sections discuss how to adjust each of these settings with VBA.

Using a Rule to Determine Which Wedges Are in the Secondary Plot

Excel offers three built-in rules for determining which pie slices should be in the secondary plot. You can specify that all slices smaller than a certain percentage should be in the secondary plot, that all slices smaller than a certain value should be in the secondary plot, or even that the last *n* slices should be in the secondary plot.

You specify which of these rules to use with the SplitType property, and then you specify a SplitValue setting to indicate where the split should occur.

In Figure 13.18, the top chart used Excel's defaults to show the last four points in the secondary plot. You could use any of these methods to create the bottom chart:

Figure 13.18
In the bottom chart, 80% of the slices appear in the secondary chart.

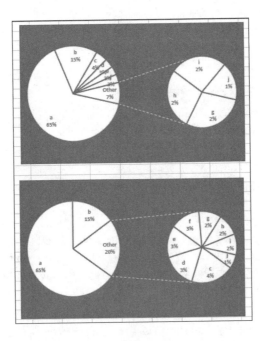

■ You could specify a split type of xlSplitByValue and then indicate that any values less than 10 should be in the secondary plot.

■ You could specify a split type of xlSplitByPercentValue and then indicate that any values less than 5% should be in the secondary plot.

■ You could specify a split type of xlSplitByPosition and then indicate that the last eight values should be in the secondary plot.

Any one of these three macros could be used to create the second chart in Figure 13.18:

```
Sub SmallerThan10ToPlot2()
    Dim cht As Chart
    Dim chtg As ChartGroup
    Set cht = ActiveChart
    Set chtg = cht.ChartGroups(1)
    ' Anything less than 10 to second group
    cht.ChartGroups(1).SplitType = xlSplitByValue
    ActiveChart.ChartGroups(1).SplitValue = 10
End Sub

Sub SmallerThan10PctToPlot2()
    Dim cht As Chart
    Dim chtg As ChartGroup
    Set cht = ActiveChart
    Set chtg = cht.ChartGroups(1)
    ' Anything less than 10% to 2nd plot
    chtg.SplitType = xlSplitByPercentValue
    chtg.SplitValue = 10
End Sub

Sub Last8ToPlot2()
    Dim cht As Chart
    Dim chtg As ChartGroup
    Set cht = ActiveChart
    Set chtg = cht.ChartGroups(1)
    ' Send last 8 slices to secondary plot
    chtg.SplitType = xlSplitByPosition
    chtg.SplitValue = 8
End Sub
```

Defining Specific Categories to Be in the Secondary Plot

You can choose to have complete control over which slices of a pie appear in a secondary chart. If you are trying to decide among three specific products to discontinue, for example, you can move all three of those products to the secondary pie.

To do this with a macro, you first set SplitType to xlSplitByCustomSplit. You can then use the SecondaryPlot property on individual data points. A value of 0 shows the data point in the left pie. A value of 1 sends the data point to the secondary pie.

Because you aren't sure how many items Excel will send to the secondary pie by default, you can write a macro such as the following to first loop through all data points, reset them to the primary pie, and then move three specific slices to the secondary pie:

```
Sub CustomPieofPie()
    Dim cht As Chart
    Dim chtg As ChartGroup
    Dim ser As Series
    Dim poi As Point
    Set cht = ActiveChart
    Set chtg = cht.ChartGroups(1)
```

13

```
    Set ser = cht.SeriesCollection(1)
    chtg.SplitType = xlSplitByCustomSplit
    ' Move all slices to first plot
    For Each poi In ser.Points
        poi.SecondaryPlot = 0
    Next poi
    'Move points 1, 6, 10 to secondary plot
    ser.Points(2).SecondaryPlot = 1
    ser.Points(6).SecondaryPlot = 1
    ser.Points(10).SecondaryPlot = 1
End Sub
```

Controlling the Gap, Size, and Lines of a Secondary Plot

You adjust the gap between an original pie and a secondary plot by using the GapWidth property, whose values range from 0 to 500. In Figure 13.19, the bottom chart has a gap of 500, and the middle chart has a gap of 0.

You can turn on or off the two leader lines extending from the main pie to the secondary plot by setting the HasSeriesLines property to True or False. To format those lines, you use the Format property of the SeriesLines object. The following macro moves the secondary plot to the maximum distance and changes the series lines to a dash/dot style:

```
Sub MindTheGap()
    Dim chtg As ChartGroup
    Set chtg = ActiveChart.ChartGroups(1)
    chtg.GapWidth = 500
    chtg.HasSeriesLines = True
    chtg.SeriesLines.Format.Line.DashStyle = msoLineDashDot
End Sub
```

The size of the secondary plot usually starts off at 75% of the original pie. You can use the SecondPlotSize property to change the plot size from 5 to 200, representing 5% to 200% of the original pie chart. Figure 13.20 shows charts with secondary plot sizes of 75%, 5%, and 200%.

The following macro adjusts the size of the secondary plot to 50% of the size of the main pie:

```
Sub ChangeSize()
    Dim chtg As ChartGroup
    Set chtg = ActiveChart.ChartGroups(1)
    chtg.SecondPlotSize = 50
End Sub
```

13

Figure 13.19
You use the GapWidth property to move the secondary plot closer to or farther from the main pie.

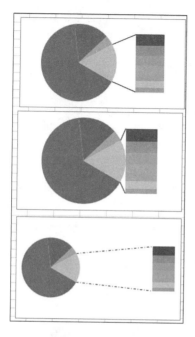

Figure 13.20
You can shift the focus toward or away from the secondary plot by adjusting its size.

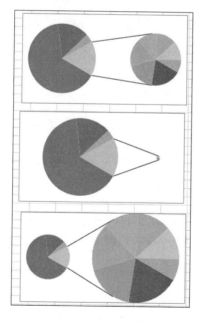

13

Setting the Bubble Size

The bubble chart type includes an incredibly misleading setting that you should always avoid. A bubble chart places circles at particular x and y coordinates. The sizes of the circles are determined by the values specified in the third column of the data series.

By default, Excel scales the size of the circle so that the area of the circle is proportionate to the data. This is an appropriate choice. However, you can override this setting to say that the size represents the width of the circle. This always results in a misleading chart.

For example, in the upper-left chart in Figure 13.21, the smallest circle has a value of 1, and the largest circle has a value of 4. Because this chart uses the xlSizeIsArea setting, the bottom-left circle is four times larger than the top-right circle. The bottom-left chart plots the same data but uses the xlSizeIsWidth setting. With this setting, your circles will be completely out of scale.

Figure 13.21
The bottom-left chart uses xlSizeIsWidth and is misleading. The bottom-right chart shows a negative-sized circle, represented by a circle with no fill.

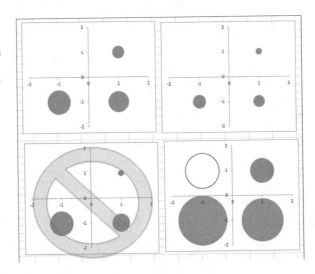

A circle with a width of 1 inch has an area of 0.785 square inches, according to =PI()*(1/2)^2. A circle with a width of 4 inches has an area of 12.56 square inches, according to =PI()*(4/2)^2. This means that with the xlSizeIsWidth setting, the bottom-left circle is 16 times larger than the top-right circle.

> **NOTE**
> It is strange that Excel even offers the xlSizeIsWidth setting. Excel won't let you make columns wider as the column size grows, even in pictograms. Using xlSizeIsWidth is the same type of error.

You can also choose to scale the circles from 0 to 300% by changing the BubbleScale property from 0 to 300. The top-left chart in Figure 13.21 has a 100% scale. The top-right chart uses a 50% scale. The bottom-right chart uses a 300% scale.

Finally, you can specify whether Excel should show negative-sized circles on a chart. In the lower-right chart in Figure 13.21, the –2 in the upper quadrant is represented by a circle with a white fill instead of a circle with a blue fill.

The following macro demonstrates some of the settings available for bubble charts:

```
Sub BubbleSettings()
    Dim chtg As ChartGroup
    Set chtg = ActiveChart.ChartGroups(1)
    ' Never use the following setting
    ' chtg.SizeRepresents = xlSizeIsWidth
    chtg.SizeRepresents = xlSizeIsArea
    chtg.BubbleScale = 50
    chtg.ShowNegativeBubbles = True
End Sub
```

Controlling Radar and Surface Charts

A couple of minor settings affect surface charts and radar charts. A default surface chart uses contour shading within each color band to give a 3D feeling. You can turn this off in a surface chart by using the Has3DShading property. In Figure 13.22, the bottom-left chart has the shading turned off.

Radar charts typically have the name of each category at the end of the axis. You can turn this off by setting the HasRadarAxisLabels property to False. The bottom-right chart in Figure 13.22 shows this setting.

The code for turning off the Has3DShading and HasRadarAxisLabels properties follows:

```
Sub FormatSurface()
    Dim chtg As ChartGroup
    Set chtg = ActiveChart.ChartGroups(1)
    chtg.Has3DShading = False
End Sub
Sub FormatRadar()
    Dim chtg As ChartGroup
    Set chtg = ActiveChart.ChartGroups(1)
    chtg.HasRadarAxisLabels = False
End Sub
```

Figure 13.22

The bottom charts reflect removing the 3D contour (left) and radar axis labels (right).

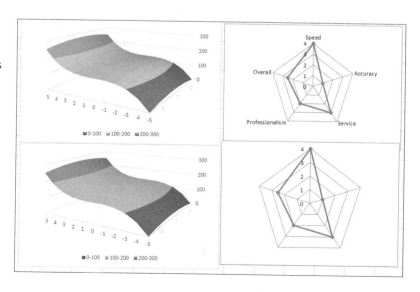

13

Creating a Combo Chart

Sometimes you need to chart series of data that are of differing orders of magnitude. Normal charts do a lousy job of showing the smaller series. Combo charts can save the day.

Consider the data and chart in Figure 13.23. You want to plot the number of sales per month and also show two quality ratings. Perhaps this is a fictitious car dealer where they sell 80 to 100 cars a month, and the customer satisfaction is represented and usually runs in the 80% to 90% range. When you try to plot this data on a chart, the columns for 90 cars sold dwarfs the column for 80% customer satisfaction. (I won't insult you by reminding you that 90 is 112.5 times larger than 80%!)

Figure 13.23
The values for two series are too small to be visible.

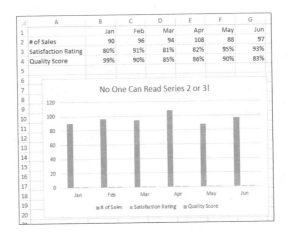

Figure 13.24
A combo chart solves the problem.

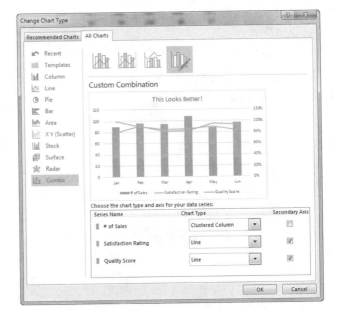

The solution in the Excel interface is to use the new interface for creating a combo chart. You move the two small series to the secondary axis and change their chart type to a line chart. (See Figure 13.24.)

The following case study shows you the VBA needed to create a combo chart.

CASE STUDY: CREATING A COMBO CHART

You want to create a chart showing the number of sales and two percentage measurements. In this process, you have to format each of the three series. At the top of the macro, declare object variables for the worksheet, the chart, and each of the series:

```
Dim WS As Worksheet
Dim CH As Chart
Dim Ser1 As Series
Dim Ser2 As Series
Dim Ser3 As Series
```

Create the chart as a regular clustered column chart. This creates the horrible-looking chart from Figure 13.23. That's okay, because you quickly follow this code with code to fix the chart.

```
Set WS = ActiveSheet
Set CH = WS.Shapes.AddChart2(Style:=201, _
    XlChartType:=xlColumnClustered, _
    Left:=[B6].Left, _
    Top:=[B6].Top, _
    NewLayout:=False).Chart
CH.SetSourceData Source:=Range("Sheet1!$A$1:$G$4")
```

To work with a series, assign the FullSeriesCollection to an object variable, such as Ser2. You could get away with a single object variable called Ser that you use over and over. This code enables you to come back later in the macro to refer to any of the three series.

After you have the Ser2 object variable defined, you will assign the series to the secondary axis group and change the chart type of just that series to a line; then repeat the code for series 3.

```
' Move series 2 to secondary axis as line
Set Ser2 = CH.FullSeriesCollection(2)
With Ser2
    .AxisGroup = xlSecondary
    .ChartType = xlLine
End With

' Move series 3 to secondary axis as line
Set Ser3 = CH.FullSeriesCollection(3)
With Ser3
    .AxisGroup = xlSecondary
    .ChartType = xlLine
End With
```

You now have something close to what you see in the top of Figure 13.24.

Note that at this point, you did not have to touch series 1. Series 1 is fine as a column chart on the primary axis. You come back to series 1 later in the macro.

13

Because too many of the data points in series 3 were close to 100%, the Excel charting engine decided to make the right axis span all the way up to 120%. This is silly, because no one can get a rating higher than 100%. You can override the automatic settings and choose a scale for the right axis. The following code uses 60% as the minimum and 100% as the maximum. Note that 0.6 is the same as 60% and 1 is the same as 100%.

```
' Set the secondary axis to go from 60% to 100%
CH.Axes(xlValue, xlSecondary).MinimumScale = 0.6
CH.Axes(xlValue, xlSecondary).MaximumScale = 1
```

When you override the scale values, Excel automatically guesses at where you want the gridlines and axis labels. Rather than leaving this to chance, you can use the MajorUnit and MinorUnit. Axis labels and major gridlines appear at the increment specified by MajorUnit. The MinorUnit is important only if you plan on showing minor gridlines.

```
' Labels every 10%, secondary gridline at 5%
CH.Axes(xlValue, xlSecondary).MajorUnit = 0.1
CH.Axes(xlValue, xlSecondary).MinorUnit = 0.05
CH.Axes(xlValue, xlSecondary).TickLabels.NumberFormat = "0%"
```

At this point, take a look at the chart in Figure 13.25. It probably makes sense to you because you created the chart. But imagine someone who is not familiar with the chart and not familiar with all the hoops you had to jump through to get there. There are numbers on the left axis and numbers on the right axis. I instantly went to the percentages on the right side and tried to follow the gridlines across. But this doesn't work because the gridlines don't line up with the numbers on the right side. They line up with the numbers on the left side. You can't really tell this for sure, though, because the gridlines coincidentally happen to line up with 100%, 80%, and 60%.

Figure 13.25
Close, but the gridlines are annoying when compared to the right axis.

At this point, you might decide to get creative. Delete the gridlines for the left axis. Add major and minor gridlines for the right axis. Even better, delete the numbers along the left axis. Replace the numbers on the axis with a data label in the center of each column.

```
' Turn off the gridlines for left axis
CH.Axes(xlValue).HasMajorGridlines = False
' Add gridlines for right axis
CH.SetElement (msoElementSecondaryValueGridLinesMajor)
CH.SetElement (msoElementSecondaryValueGridLinesMinorMajor)
```

```
' Hide the labels on the primary axis
CH.Axes(xlValue).TickLabelPosition = xlNone
' Replace axis labels with a data label on the column
Set Ser1 = CH.FullSeriesCollection(1)
Ser1.ApplyDataLabels
Ser1.DataLabels.Position = xlLabelPositionCenter
```

Now you almost have it. Because the book is printed in monochrome, change the color of the series 1 data label to white:

```
' Data Labels in white
With Ser1.DataLabels.Format.TextFrame2.TextRange.Font.Fill
    .Visible = msoTrue
    .ForeColor.ObjectThemeColor = msoThemeColorBackground1
    .Solid
End With
```

And because my charting mentors drilled it into my head, the legend has to be at the top or the left. Move it to the top.

```
' Legend at the top
CH.SetElement msoElementLegendTop
```

The resulting chart is shown in Figure 13.26. Thanks to the minor gridlines, you can easily tell if each rating was in the 80–85%, 85–90%, 90–90% range. The columns show the sales, and the labels stay out of the way, but they are still readable.

Figure 13.26
The final chart conveys information about three series.

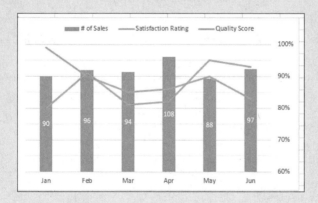

Creating Advanced Charts

In Chapter 7, "Advanced Chart Techniques," I include some amazing charts that do not look like they can possibly be created using Excel. Building these charts usually involves adding a rogue data series that appears in the chart as an X,Y series to complete some effect.

The process of creating these charts manually is very tedious, which ensures that most people never resort to creating such charts. However, if the process is automated, the creation of the charts starts to become feasible.

The next sections explain how to use VBA to automate the process of creating these rather complex charts.

Creating True Open-High-Low-Close Stock Charts

If you are a fan of stock charts in the *Wall Street Journal* or finance.yahoo.com, you will recognize the chart type known as open-high-low-close (OHLC) chart. The "Creating an OHLC Chart" section in Chapter 6, "Creating Stock Analysis Charts," explains how to use a custom left-facing dash image to create an open-high-low-close chart.

> **NOTE** You can download a LeftDash.gif file from `http://www.mrexcel.com/chartbook-data2013.html`.

In VBA, specify the LeftDash.gif as the marker using this code:

```
ActiveChart Cht.SeriesCollection(1).Fill.UserPicture "C:\leftdash.gif"
```

To create a true OHLC chart, follow these steps:

1. Create a line chart from four series: open, high, low, close.
2. Change the line style to none for all four series.
3. Eliminate the marker for the high and low series.
4. Add a high-low line to the chart.
5. Change the marker for Close to a right-facing dash, which is called a dot in VBA, with a size of 9.
6. Change the marker for Open to a custom picture and load `LeftDash.gif` as the fill for the series.

The following code creates a true OHLC chart as shown in Chapter 6:

```
Sub CreateOHCLChart()
    ' Download leftdash.gif from the sample files for this book
    ' and save it in the same folder as this workbook
    Dim Cht As Chart
    Dim Ser As Series

    ActiveSheet.Shapes.AddChart(xlLineMarkers).Select
    Set Cht = ActiveChart
    Cht.SetSourceData Source:=Range("Sheet1!$A$1:$E$33")
    ' Format the Open Series
    With Cht.SeriesCollection(1)
        .MarkerStyle = xlMarkerStylePicture
        .Fill.UserPicture ("C:\leftdash.gif")
        .Border.LineStyle = xlNone
        .MarkerForegroundColorIndex = xlColorIndexNone
    End With
    ' Format High & Low Series
    With Cht.SeriesCollection(2)
        .MarkerStyle = xlMarkerStyleNone
        .Border.LineStyle = xlNone
```

```
      End With
      With Cht.SeriesCollection(3)
          .MarkerStyle = xlMarkerStyleNone
          .Border.LineStyle = xlNone
      End With
      ' Format the Close series
      Set Ser = Cht.SeriesCollection(4)
      With Ser
          .MarkerBackgroundColorIndex = 1
          .MarkerForegroundColorIndex = 1
          .MarkerStyle = xlDot
          .MarkerSize = 9
          .Border.LineStyle = xlNone
      End With
      ' Add High-Low Lines
      Cht.SetElement (msoElementLineHiLoLine)
      Cht.SetElement (msoElementLegendNone)

End Sub
```

Creating Bins for a Frequency Chart

Suppose that you have results from 3,000 scientific trials. There must be a good way to produce a chart of those results. However, if you just select the results and create a chart, you end up with chaos (see Figure 13.27).

Figure 13.27
Try to chart the results from 3,000 trials and you have a jumbled mess.

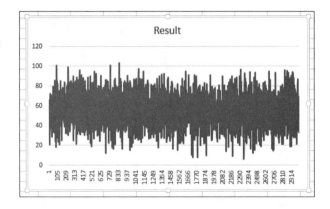

The trick to creating an effective frequency distribution is to define a series of categories, or *bins*. A FREQUENCY array function counts the number of items from the 3,000 results that fall within each bin.

The process of creating bins manually is rather tedious and requires knowledge of array formulas. It is better to use a macro to perform all the tedious calculations.

The macro in this section requires you to specify a bin size and a starting bin. If you expect results in the 0 to 100 range, you might specify bins of 10 each, starting at 1. This would create bins of 1–10, 11–20, 21–30, and so on. If you specify bin sizes of 15 with a starting bin of 5, the macro creates bins of 5–20, 21–35, 36–50, and so on.

13

To use the following macro, your trial results should start in row 2 and should be in the rightmost column of a data set. Three variables near the top of the macro define the starting bin, the ending bin, and the bin size:

```
' Define Bins
BinSize = 10
FirstBin = 1
LastBin = 100
```

After that, the macro skips a column and then builds a range of starting bins (see Figure 13.28). In cell D4 in Figure 13.21, the 10 is used to tell Excel that you are looking for the number of values larger than the 0 in D3, but equal to or less than the 10 in D4.

Figure 13.28

The macro summarizes the results into bins and provides a meaningful chart of the data.

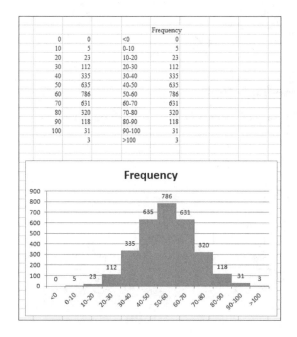

			Frequency
0	0	<0	0
10	5	0-10	5
20	23	10-20	23
30	112	20-30	112
40	335	30-40	335
50	635	40-50	635
60	786	50-60	786
70	631	60-70	631
80	320	70-80	320
90	118	80-90	118
100	31	90-100	31
		>100	3

Although the bins extend from D3:D13, the FREQUENCY function entered in column E needs to include one extra cell, in case any results are larger than the last bin. This single formula returns many results. Formulas that return more than one answer are called *array formulas*. In the Excel user interface, you specify an array formula by holding down Ctrl+Shift while pressing Enter to finish the formula. In Excel VBA, you need to use the FormulaArray property. The following lines of the macro set up the array formula in column E:

```
' Enter the Frequency Formula
Form = "=FREQUENCY(R2C" & FinalCol & ":R" & FinalRow & "C" & FinalCol & _
    ",R3C" & NextCol & ":R" & _
    LastRow & "C" & NextCol & ")"
Range(Cells(FirstRow, NextCol + 1), Cells(LastRow, NextCol + 1)). _
    FormulaArray = Form
```

It is not evident to the reader whether the bin indicated in column D is the upper or lower limit. The macro builds readable labels in column G and then copies the frequency results over to column H.

After the macro builds a simple column chart, the following line eliminates the gap between columns, creating the traditional histogram view of the data:

```
Cht.ChartGroups(1).GapWidth = 0
```

The macro to create the chart in Figure 13.28 follows:

```
Sub CreateFrequencyChart()
    ' Find the last column
    FinalCol = Cells(1, Columns.Count).End(xlToLeft).Column
    ' Find the FinalRow
    FinalRow = Cells(Rows.Count, FinalCol).End(xlUp).Row

    ' Define Bins
    BinSize = 10
    FirstBin = 0
    LastBin = 100

    'The bins will go in row 3, two columns after FinalCol
    NextCol = FinalCol + 2
    FirstRow = 3
    NextRow = FirstRow - 1

    ' Set up the bins for the Frequency function
    For i = FirstBin To LastBin Step BinSize
        NextRow = NextRow + 1
        Cells(NextRow, NextCol).Value = i
    Next i

    ' The Frequency function has to be one row larger than the bins
    LastRow = NextRow + 1

    ' Enter the Frequency Formula
    Form = "=FREQUENCY(R2C" & FinalCol & ":R" & FinalRow & "C" & FinalCol & _
        ",R3C" & NextCol & ":R" & _
        LastRow & "C" & NextCol & ")"
    Range(Cells(FirstRow, NextCol + 1), Cells(LastRow, NextCol + 1)). _
        FormulaArray = Form

    ' Build a range suitable for a chart source data
    LabelCol = NextCol + 3
    Form = "=R[-1]C[-3]&""-""&RC[-3]"
    Range(Cells(4, LabelCol), Cells(LastRow - 1, LabelCol)).FormulaR1C1 = _
        Form
    ' Enter the > Last formula
    Cells(LastRow, LabelCol).FormulaR1C1 = "="">""&R[-1]C[-3]"
    ' Enter the < first formula
    Cells(3, LabelCol).FormulaR1C1 = "=""<""&RC[-3]"

    ' Enter the formula to copy the frequency results
    Range(Cells(3, LabelCol + 1), Cells(LastRow, LabelCol + 1)).FormulaR1C1 = _
        "=RC[-3]"
    ' Add a heading
    Cells(2, LabelCol + 1).Value = "Frequency"
```

13

```
' Create a column chart
Dim Cht As Chart
ActiveSheet.Shapes.AddChart(xlColumnClustered).Select
Set Cht = ActiveChart
Cht.SetSourceData Source:=Range(Cells(2, LabelCol), _
    Cells(LastRow, LabelCol + 1))
Cht.SetElement (msoElementLegendNone)
Cht.ChartGroups(1).GapWidth = 0
Cht.SetElement (msoElementDataLabelOutSideEnd)

End Sub
```

Creating a Stacked Area Chart

In the section "Creating Several Charts on One Chart by Using a Rogue XY Series" in Chapter 7, you learned how to manually create a single chart that contains four area charts (see Figure 13.29). This chart actually contains nine series:

- The first series contains the values for the East region.

- The second series contains 1,000 minus the East values. This series is formatted with a transparent fill.

- Series 3, 5, and 7 contain values for Central, Northwest, and Southwest.

- Series 4, 6, and 8 contain 1,000 minus the preceding series.

- The final series is an X, Y series used to add labels for the left axis. There is one point for each gridline. The markers are positioned at an X position of 0. Custom data labels are added next to invisible markers to force the labels along the axis to start again at 0 for each region.

Figure 13.29
A single chart appears to hold four different charts.

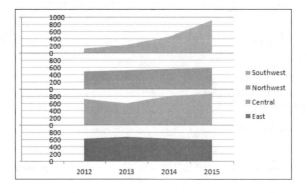

To use the macro provided here, your data should begin in column A and row 1. The macro adds new columns to the right of the data and new rows below the data, so the rest of the worksheet should be blank.

Two variables at the top of the macro define the height of each chart. In the current example, leaving a height of 1000 allows the sales for each region to fit comfortably. The LabSize value should indicate how frequently labels should appear along the left axis. This number must be evenly divisible into the chart height. In this example, values of 500, 250, 200, 125, or 100 would work:

```
' Define the height of each area chart
ChtHeight = 1000
' Define Tick Mark Size
' ChtHeight should be an even multiple of LabSize
LabSize = 200
```

The macro builds a copy of the data to the right of the original data. New "dummy" series are added to the right of each region to calculate 1,000 minus the data point.

The macro then creates a stacked area chart for the first eight series. The legend for this chart indicates values of East, dummy, Central, dummy, and so on. To delete every other legend entry, use this code:

```
' Fill the dummy series with no fill
For i = FinalSeriesCount To 2 Step -2
    Cht.Legend.LegendEntries(i).Delete
Next i
```

Similarly, the fill for each even numbered series in the chart needs to be set to transparent:

```
' Fill the dummy series with no fill
For i = FinalSeriesCount To 2 Step -2
    Cht.SeriesCollection(i).Interior.ColorIndex = xlNone
Next i
```

The trickiest part of the process is adding a new final series to the chart. This series will have far more data points than the other series. Range B8:C28 contains the X and Y values for the new series. If you look in the sample files, you will see that each point has an X value of 0 to ensure that it appears along the left side of the plot area. The Y values increase steadily by the value indicated in the LabSize variable. In column A next to the X and Y points are the actual labels that will be plotted next to each marker. These labels give the illusion that the chart starts over with a value of 0 for each region.

The process of adding the new series is much easier in VBA than in the Excel user interface. The following code identifies each component of the series and specifies that it should be plotted as an X, Y chart:

```
' Add the new series to the chart
Set Ser = Cht.SeriesCollection.NewSeries
With Ser
    .Name = "Y"
    .Values = Range(Cells(AxisRow + 1, 3), Cells(NewFinal, 3))
    .XValues = Range(Cells(AxisRow + 1, 2), Cells(NewFinal, 2))
    .ChartType = xlXYScatter
    .MarkerStyle = xlMarkerStyleNone
End With
```

Finally, code applies a data label from column A to each point in the final series:

```
' Label each point in the series
' This code actually adds fake labels along left axis
For i = 1 To TickMarkCount
```

13

```
        Ser.Points(i).HasDataLabel = True
        Ser.Points(i).DataLabel.Text = Cells(AxisRow + i, 1).Value
Next i
```

The complete code to create the stacked chart in Figure 13.29 is shown here:

```
Sub CreatedStackedChart()
    Dim Cht As Chart
    Dim Ser As Series
    FinalRow = Cells(Rows.Count, 1).End(xlUp).Row
    FinalCol = Cells(1, Columns.Count).End(xlToLeft).Column
    OrigSeriesCount = FinalCol - 1
    FinalSeriesCount = OrigSeriesCount * 2

    ' Define the height of each area chart
    ChtHeight = 1000
    ' Define Tick Mark Size
    ' ChtHeight should be an even multiple of LabSize
    LabSize = 200

    ' Make a copy of the data
    NextCol = FinalCol + 2
    Cells(1, 1).Resize(FinalRow, FinalCol).Copy _
        Destination:=Cells(1, NextCol)
    FinalCol = Cells(1, Columns.Count).End(xlToLeft).Column

    ' Add in new columns to serve as dummy series
    MyFormula = "=" & ChtHeight & "-RC[-1]"
    For i = FinalCol + 1 To NextCol + 2 Step -1
        Cells(1, i).EntireColumn.Insert
        Cells(1, i).Value = "dummy"
        Cells(2, i).Resize(FinalRow - 1, 1).FormulaR1C1 = MyFormula
    Next i

    ' Figure out the new Final Column
    FinalCol = Cells(1, Columns.Count).End(xlToLeft).Column

    ' Build the Chart
    ActiveSheet.Shapes.AddChart(xlAreaStacked).Select
    Set Cht = ActiveChart
    Cht.SetSourceData Source:=Range(Cells(1, NextCol), Cells(FinalRow, _
        FinalCol))
    Cht.PlotBy = xlColumns

    ' Clear out the even number series from the Legend
    For i = FinalSeriesCount - 1 To 1 Step -2
        Cht.Legend.LegendEntries(i).Delete
    Next i

    ' Set the axis Maximum Scale & Gridlines
    TopScale = OrigSeriesCount * ChtHeight
    With Cht.Axes(xlValue)
        .MaximumScale = TopScale
        .MinorUnit = LabSize
        .MajorUnit = ChtHeight
    End With
    Cht.SetElement (msoElementPrimaryValueGridLinesMinorMajor)
```

```
    ' Fill the dummy series with no fill
    For i = FinalSeriesCount To 2 Step -2
        Cht.SeriesCollection(i).Interior.ColorIndex = xlNone
    Next i

    ' Hide the original axis labels
    Cht.Axes(xlValue).TickLabelPosition = xlNone

    ' Build a new range to hold a rogue X, Y series that will
    ' be used to create left axis labels
    AxisRow = FinalRow + 2
    Cells(AxisRow, 1).Resize(1, 3).Value = Array("Label", "X", "Y")
    TickMarkCount = OrigSeriesCount * (ChtHeight / LabSize) + 1
    ' Column B contains the X values. These are all zero
    Cells(AxisRow + 1, 2).Resize(TickMarkCount, 1).Value = 0
    ' Column C contains the Y values.
    Cells(AxisRow + 1, 3).Resize(TickMarkCount, 1).FormulaR1C1 = _
        "=R[-1]C+" & LabSize
    Cells(AxisRow + 1, 3).Value = 0
    ' Column A contains the labels to be used for each point
    Cells(AxisRow + 1, 1).Value = 0
    Cells(AxisRow + 2, 1).Resize(TickMarkCount - 1, 1).FormulaR1C1 = _
        "=IF(R[-1]C+" & LabSize & ">=" & ChtHeight & ",0,R[-1]C+" & LabSize _
        & ")"
    NewFinal = Cells(Rows.Count, 1).End(xlUp).Row
    Cells(NewFinal, 1).Value = ChtHeight

    ' Add the new series to the chart
    Set Ser = Cht.SeriesCollection.NewSeries
    With Ser
        .Name = "Y"
        .Values = Range(Cells(AxisRow + 1, 3), Cells(NewFinal, 3))
        .XValues = Range(Cells(AxisRow + 1, 2), Cells(NewFinal, 2))
        .ChartType = xlXYScatter
        .MarkerStyle = xlMarkerStyleNone
    End With

    ' Label each point in the series
    ' This code actually adds fake labels along left axis
    For i = 1 To TickMarkCount
        Ser.Points(i).HasDataLabel = True
        Ser.Points(i).DataLabel.Text = Cells(AxisRow + i, 1).Value
    Next i

    ' Hide the Y label in the legend
    Cht.Legend.LegendEntries(Cht.Legend.LegendEntries.Count).Delete
End Sub
```

Exporting a Chart as a Graphic

You can export any chart to an image file on your hard drive. The ExportChart method requires you to specify a filename and a graphic type. The available graphic types depend on graphic file filters installed in your Registry. It is a safe bet that JPG, BMP, PNG, and GIF work on most computers.

For example, the following code exports the active chart as a GIF file:

```
Sub ExportChart()
    Dim cht As Chart
    Set cht = ActiveChart
    cht.Export Filename:="C:\Chart.gif", Filtername:="GIF"
End Sub
```

> **NOTE**
> Since Excel 2003, Microsoft has supported an Interactive argument in the Export method. Excel Help
> indicates that if you set Interactive to TRUE, Excel asks for additional settings depending on the file
> type. However, the dialog that asks for additional settings never appears—at least not for the four
> standard types of JPG, GIF, BMP, and PNG. To prevent any questions from popping up in the middle of
> your macro, set Interactive:=False.

Creating Pivot Charts

A *pivot chart* is a chart that uses a pivot table as the underlying data source. Unfortunately, pivot charts do not have the cool "show pages" functionality that regular pivot tables have. You can overcome this problem with a quick VBA macro that creates a pivot table and then a pivot chart based on the pivot table. The macro then adds the customer field to the filters area of the pivot table. It then loops through each customer and exports the chart for each customer.

In Excel 2013, you first create a pivot cache by using the `PivotCache.Create` method. You can then define a pivot table based on the pivot cache. The usual procedure is to turn off pivot table updating while you add fields to the pivot table. Then you update the pivot table to have Excel perform the calculations.

It takes a bit of finesse to figure out the final range of the pivot table. If you have turned off the column and row totals, the chartable area of the pivot table starts one row below the `PivotTableRange1` area. You have to resize the area to include one fewer row to make your chart appear correctly.

After the pivot table is created, you can switch back to the `Charts.Add` code discussed earlier in this chapter. You can use any formatting code to get the chart formatted as you desire.

The following code creates a pivot table and a single pivot chart that summarize revenue by region and product:

```
Sub CreateSummaryReportUsingPivot()
    Dim WSD As Worksheet
    Dim PTCache As PivotCache
    Dim PT As PivotTable
    Dim PRange As Range
    Dim FinalRow As Long
    Dim ChartDataRange As Range
    Dim Cht As Chart
    Set WSD = Worksheets("Data")

    ' Delete any prior pivot tables
    For Each PT In WSD.PivotTables
```

```
            PT.TableRange2.Clear
        Next PT
        WSD.Range("I1:Z1").EntireColumn.Clear

        ' Define input area and set up a Pivot Cache
        FinalRow = WSD.Cells(Application.Rows.Count, 1).End(xlUp).Row
        FinalCol = WSD.Cells(1, Application.Columns.Count). _
            End(xlToLeft).Column
        Set PRange = WSD.Cells(1, 1).Resize(FinalRow, FinalCol)

        Set PTCache = ActiveWorkbook.PivotCaches.Create(SourceType:= _
            xlDatabase, SourceData:=PRange.Address)

        ' Create the Pivot Table from the Pivot Cache
        Set PT = PTCache.CreatePivotTable(TableDestination:=WSD. _
            Cells(2, FinalCol + 2), TableName:="PivotTable1")

        ' Turn off updating while building the table
        PT.ManualUpdate = True

        ' Set up the row fields
        PT.AddFields RowFields:="Region", ColumnFields:="Product", _
            PageFields:="Customer"

        ' Set up the data fields
        With PT.PivotFields("Revenue")
            .Orientation = xlDataField
            .Function = xlSum
            .Position = 1
        End With

        With PT
            .ColumnGrand = False
            .RowGrand = False
            .NullString = "0"
        End With

        ' Calc the pivot table
        PT.ManualUpdate = False
        PT.ManualUpdate = True

        ' Define the Chart Data Range
        Set ChartDataRange = _
            PT.TableRange1.Offset(1, 0).Resize(PT.TableRange1.Rows.Count - 1)

        ' Add the Chart
        WSD.Shapes.AddChart.Select
        Set Cht = ActiveChart
        Cht.SetSourceData Source:=ChartDataRange
        ' Format the Chart
        Cht.ChartType = xlColumnClustered
        Cht.SetElement (msoElementChartTitleAboveChart)
        Cht.ChartTitle.Caption = "All Customers"
        Cht.SetElement msoElementPrimaryValueAxisThousands
        ' Excel 2010 only. Next line will not work in 2007
        Cht.ShowAllFieldButtons = False
    End Sub
```

13

Figure 13.30 shows the resulting chart and pivot table.

Figure 13.30
VBA creates a pivot table
and then a chart from the
pivot table. Excel auto-
matically displays the
PivotChart Filter window
in response.

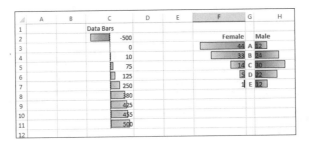

Creating Data Bars with VBA

The data bars in Excel 2013 allow for negative values of a different color, solid or gradient
fills, explicit min and max values, and even data bars that go right to left. The latter setting
makes it easy to create comparative bar charts.

Figure 13.31 shows two sets of data bars created by VBA.

Figure 13.31
Two sets of data bars.

To add default data bars, use this code:

```
Range("C2:C11").FormatConditions.AddDataBar
```

You will want to customize the data bars by changing color, gradient, border color, and
scale. Thus, it is easiest to assign the data bars to an object variable:

```
Dim DB As Databar
With Range("C2:C11")
    .FormatConditions.Delete
    ' Add the data bars
    Set DB = .FormatConditions.AddDatabar()
End With
```

The example in column C of Figure 13.31 includes negative data bars of a contrasting color,
a horizontal axis in the center of the cell, a black border around the data bars, and a custom
scale from –600 to +600. The code to create that data bar is as follows:

```
Sub DataBar()
' Add a Data bar
' Include negative data bars
' Control the min and max point
'

    Dim DB As Databar
    With Range("C2:C11")
        .FormatConditions.Delete
        ' Add the data bars
        Set DB = .FormatConditions.AddDatabar()
    End With

    ' Set the lower limit
    DB.MinPoint.Modify newtype:=xlConditionFormula, NewValue:="-600"
    DB.MaxPoint.Modify newtype:=xlConditionValueFormula, NewValue:="600"

    ' Change the data bar to Green
    With DB.BarColor
        .Color = RGB(0, 255, 0)
        .TintAndShade = -0.15
    End With

    With DB
        ' Use a gradiant
        .BarFillType = xlDataBarFillGradient
        ' Left to Right for direction of bars
        .Direction = xlLTR
        ' Assign a different color to negative bars
        .NegativeBarFormat.ColorType = xlDataBarColor
        ' Use a border around the bars
        .BarBorder.Type = xlDataBarBorderSolid
        ' Assign a different border color to negative
        .NegativeBarFormat.BorderColorType = xlDataBarSameAsPositive
        ' All borders are solid black
        With .BarBorder.Color
            .Color = RGB(0, 0, 0)
        End With
        ' Axis where it naturally would fall, in black
        .AxisPosition = xlDataBarAxisAutomatic
        With .AxisColor
            .Color = 0
            .TintAndShade = 0
        End With
        ' Negative bars in red
        With .NegativeBarFormat.Color
            .Color = 255
            .TintAndShade = 0
        End With
        ' Negative borders in red
    End With

End Sub
```

The next macro creates two sets of simpler data bars. You do not need to format the axis or the negative bar color because these are not ever going to be present in this data set.

The main difference is that the bars on the left have a `.Direction` property of xlRTL, which stands for right to left:

```
Sub DataBarCompare()
' Add two data bars. Right-to-Left for females
'
    Dim DB As Databar
    ' Create left-facing data bars for females
    With Range("F3:F7")
        .FormatConditions.Delete
        ' Add the data bars
        Set DB = .FormatConditions.AddDatabar()
    End With

    ' Set the lower limit
    DB.MinPoint.Modify newtype:=xlConditionFormula, NewValue:="0"
    DB.MaxPoint.Modify newtype:=xlConditionValueFormula, NewValue:="50"

    ' Change the data bar to Red, 15% lighter
    With DB.BarColor
        .Color = RGB(255, 0, 0)
        .TintAndShade = 0.3
    End With

    With DB
        ' Use a gradiant
        .BarFillType = xlDataBarFillGradient
        ' Left to Right for direction of bars
        .Direction = xlRTL
        ' Use a border around the bars
        .BarBorder.Type = xlDataBarBorderSolid
        ' All borders are solid black
        With .BarBorder.Color
            .Color = RGB(0, 0, 0)
        End With
    End With

    ' Create right-facing data bars for males
    With Range("H3:H7")
        .FormatConditions.Delete
        ' Add the data bars
        Set DB = .FormatConditions.AddDatabar()
    End With

    ' Set the lower limit
    DB.MinPoint.Modify newtype:=xlConditionFormula, NewValue:="0"
    DB.MaxPoint.Modify newtype:=xlConditionValueFormula, NewValue:="50"

    ' Change the data bar to Red, 15% lighter
    With DB.BarColor
        .Color = RGB(0, 0, 255)
        .TintAndShade = 0.3
    End With

    With DB
        ' Use a gradiant
        .BarFillType = xlDataBarFillGradient
        ' Left to Right for direction of bars
```

```
        .Direction = xlLTR
        ' Use a border around the bars
        .BarBorder.Type = xlDataBarBorderSolid
        ' All borders are solid black
      With .BarBorder.Color
          .Color = RGB(0, 0, 0)
      End With
    End With
  End With

End Sub
```

Creating Sparklines with VBA

Regular sparklines are relatively easy to create with VBA:

```
Dim SG as SparklineGroup
FinalRow = Cells(Rows.Count, 6).End(xlUp).Row
Set SG = WSL.Range("C3:C5").SparklineGroups.Add( _
    Type:=xlSparkLine, _
    SourceData:="Data!G2:I" & FinalRow
```

Figure 13.32 shows a set of simple sparklines created by VBA.

Figure 13.32
Simple sparklines don't communicate information about the min and max.

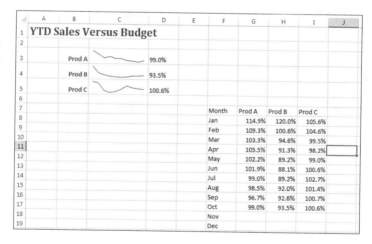

However, if you've read about sparklines in Edward Tufte's book, *Beautiful Evidence*, you will want to go beyond the "regular" sparklines that are the default from Microsoft Excel.

Tufte's sparklines often have a gray band indicating the normal range for a variable. Sparklines don't support the gray band, but you can simulate it by using a transparent shape.

My idea of sparkline perfection involves these elements:

- The entire sparkline presentation requires three adjacent cells.

- The sparkline itself is in the center cell. The min and max of the sparkline are set to be the min and max of the data set. This causes the sparkline to fill 100% of the vertical height of the cell.

- The height of the cell is either 55 or 110. With 110, you can fit 10 lines of 8-point wrapped text.

- In the cell to the left of the sparkline, you would right-justify the maximum value, 8 line feeds, and then the minimum value. This communicates the highest and lowest point experienced in the data set.

- In the cell to the right of the sparkline, you would left-justify the final value. Depending on whether the final value is in the top, middle, or bottom of the range, you would add a sufficient number of line feeds before the value to get the label roughly adjacent to the endpoint.

- In the sparkline cell, center the title for the sparkline.

- In the sparkline cell, add a semitransparent rectangle to show the acceptable values. It is incredibly difficult to position this manually. With VBA, though, you can get the box positioned nearly perfectly.

Figure 13.33 shows a set of four sparklines. Each line is showing readings from manufacturing lines taken every six minutes throughout one day. The min and max value are shown to the left of the cell. The final value is shown to the right of the cell. The colored band represents the acceptable range of 97 to 103.

Figure 13.33
VBA adds labels, titles, and an acceptable range to each sparkline.

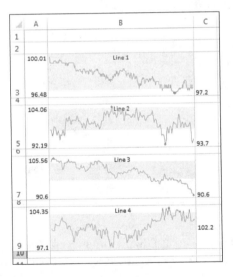

The code to create Figure 13.33 is shown here:

```
Sub ComplexSparklines()
Dim SG As SparklineGroup
Dim SL As Sparkline
Dim WSD As Worksheet ' Data worksheet
Dim WSL As Worksheet ' Dashboard
Dim Rg As Range
Dim Sh As Shape
```

```vba
On Error Resume Next
Application.DisplayAlerts = False
Worksheets("Dashboard").Delete
On Error GoTo 0

Set WSD = Worksheets("Data")
Set WSL = ActiveWorkbook.Worksheets.Add
WSL.Name = "Dashboard"

' Set up the dashboard as alternating cells for sparkline then blank
WSL.Cells(1, 1).ColumnWidth = 5
WSL.Cells(1, 2).ColumnWidth = 35
WSL.Cells(1, 3).ColumnWidth = 5
For r = 3 To 9 Step 2
    WSL.Cells(r, 1).RowHeight = 55
    WSL.Cells(r + 1, 1).RowHeight = 9
Next r

NextRow = 3
NextCol = 2

FinalRow = WSD.Cells(Rows.Count, 1).End(xlUp).Row
Set AF = Application.WorksheetFunction

For i = 2 To 5
    If i > 6 Then Exit For
    ThisLine = WSD.Cells(1, i).Value
    ThisCol = Chr(64 + i)
    ThisSource = "Data!" & ThisCol & "2:" & ThisCol & FinalRow
    Set ThisRg = WSD.Cells(2, i).Resize(FinalRow - 1, 1)
    MyMax = AF.Max(ThisRg)
    MyMin = AF.Min(ThisRg)
    MyRg = MyMax - MyMin
    FinalVal = WSD.Cells(FinalRow, i).Value

    Set SG = WSL.Cells(NextRow, NextCol).SparklineGroups.Add( _
        Type:=xlSparkLine, _
        SourceData:=ThisSource)

    Set SL = SG.Item(1)

    SG.Axes.Horizontal.Axis.Visible = True
    With SG.Axes.Vertical
        .MinScaleType = xlSparkScaleCustom
        .MaxScaleType = xlSparkScaleCustom
        .CustomMinScaleValue = MyMin
        .CustomMaxScaleValue = MyMax
    End With

    ' Line in Green
    SG.SeriesColor.Color = RGB(0, 176, 80)

    ' If the high point is above range, in red
    If MyMax > 103 Then
        SG.Points.Highpoint.Visible = True
        SG.Points.Highpoint.Color.Color = 255
    End If
    If MyMin < 97 Then
```

13

```
            SG.Points.Lowpoint.Visible = True
            SG.Points.Lowpoint.Color.Color = 255
        End If

        ' Add a label to the sparkline cell
        With WSL.Cells(NextRow, NextCol)
            .Value = ThisLine
            .HorizontalAlignment = xlCenter
            .VerticalAlignment = xlTop
            .Font.Size = 8
            .WrapText = True
        End With

        ' Label the cell to the left with min and max
        With WSL.Cells(NextRow, NextCol - 1)
            .Value = _
                Round(MyMax, 2) & vbLf & vbLf & vbLf & vbLf & _ Round(MyMin, 2)
            .HorizontalAlignment = xlRight
            .VerticalAlignment = xlTop
            .Font.Size = 8
            .WrapText = True
        End With

        ' Calculate position for final point
        RtLabel = ""
        For j = MyMax To MyMin Step -(MyRg / 4)
            If j <= MyMin Then
                RtLabel = RtLabel & Round(FinalVal, 1)
                Exit For
            ElseIf j < FinalVal Then
                RtLabel = RtLabel & Round(FinalVal, 1)
                Exit For
            Else
                RtLabel = RtLabel & vbLf
            End If
        Next j

        With WSL.Cells(NextRow, NextCol + 1)
            .Value = RtLabel
            .HorizontalAlignment = xlLeft
            .VerticalAlignment = xlTop
            .Font.Size = 8
            .WrapText = True
        End With

        ' Color the cell
        ' if < 0.95, then red
        With WSL.Cells(NextRow, NextCol).Interior
            If FinalVal <= 95 Then
                .Color = 255
                .TintAndShade = 0.9
            ElseIf FinalVal > 105 Then
                .Color = RGB(0, 0, 255)
                .TintAndShade = 0.7
            End If
        End With
```

```vba
' Add a transparent rectangle to indicate the acceptable range
celltop = WSL.Cells(NextRow, 2).Top
cellht = WSL.Cells(NextRow, 2).Height
CellLt = WSL.Cells(NextRow, 2).Left
CellWid = WSL.Cells(NextRow, 2).Width
' The acceptable range is 97 - 103
If MyMax <= 97 Then
    BandTop = celltop + cellht
ElseIf MyMax <= 103 Then
    BandTop = celltop
ElseIf MyMax > 103 Then
    DeltaTop = MyMax - 103
    BandTop = Round((DeltaTop / MyRg) * cellht, 0) + celltop
End If

If MyMin >= 103 Then
    BandBot = celltop
ElseIf MyMin >= 97 Then
    BandBot = celltop + cellht
Else
    DeltaBot = 97 - MyMin
    x = Round((DeltaBot / MyRg) * cellht, 0)
    BandBot = celltop + cellht - x
End If

BandHt = BandBot - BandTop

If BandHt < 1 Then BandHt = 1

Set Sh = WSL.Shapes.AddShape(Type:=msoShapeRectangle, _
    Left:=CellLt, _
    Top:=BandTop, _
    Width:=CellWid, _
    Height:=BandHt)
'   Sh.ShapeStyle = msoShapeStylePreset23
With Sh.Fill
    .Visible = msoTrue
    .ForeColor.RGB = RGB(102, 255, 255)
    .Transparency = 0.7294117212
    ' .Solid
End With
Sh.Line.Visible = msoFalse

    NextRow = NextRow + 2
Next i

End Sub
```

Next Steps

Although I hope this book has taught you how to create meaningful charts, the next chapter shows many examples of bad charts. People might try to use bad charts to mislead the reader intentionally, or they might create a misleading chart because they think it looks cool. By knowing how to spot bad charts, you can prevent people from misleading you the next time you are sitting through a presentation.

Knowing When Someone Is Lying to You with a Chart

Several settings in Excel enable you to either inadvertently or intentionally create charts that are misleading. Many of the popular charting styles do a poor job of representing the underlying data. Don't get me wrong—the charts often look great, but they do not provide an accurate picture of the data.

This chapter illustrates many of the lies that are easy to incorporate into an Excel chart. My hope is not that you will use these to confuse the chart consumer. Instead, I hope you will avoid these types of charts. I also hope you learn to look with caution on charts created by others that use the techniques included in this chapter.

Lying with Perspective

Excel's 3D charts attempt to show a two-dimensional object on a two-dimensional computer screen and give the perception that the objects are rendered in 3D. Even though Excel provides a lot of support for the 3D charts, they are not covered in great detail in this book because they often misrepresent your data. Instead, I hope you will resist the urge to use 3D charts.

When I took a photography class, during the lesson on wide-angle lenses, the instructor pointed out that a wide-angle lens makes everything in the foreground look proportionally larger than it really is. If you are shooting a portrait of someone who has a big nose, you don't want to use a wide-angle lens for that portrait.

Similarly, with 3D pie charts, any wedges at the front of the pie look much larger than wedges at the back of the pie. For example, in Figure 14.1, both charts show a labor component of 30%. If you want to impress the union during contract negotiations,

14

IN THIS CHAPTER

Lying with Perspective 401

Lying with Shrinking Charts 402

Lying with Scale 403

Lying Because Excel Will Not Cooperate 405

Avoiding Stacked Surface Charts 406

Asserting a Trend from Two Data Points 407

Deliberately Using Charts to Lie 408

Charting Something Else When Numbers Are Too Bad 409

Stretching Pictographs 409

Next Steps 410

you should use a 3D chart where labor is in the front because the labor wedge in that chart is 2.8 times the size of the one in the top chart.

Figure 14.1
Wedges in the front of a 3D pie appear much larger than those in the back.

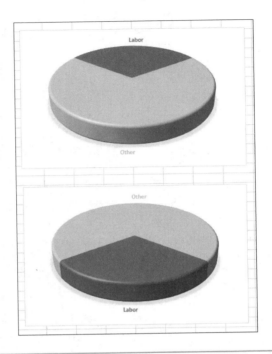

NOTE   If you want to lie with a 3D pie chart, you can accomplish that by changing the rotation of the pie. Right-click the pie, select Format Series, and then change the rotation angle.

In addition, perspective causes problems with 3D column charts. For example, often the reader is not sure whether to look at the front or the back of the column.

Look in the top chart in Figure 14.2. Are any of the quarters more than 3,000? Count the number of gridlines. The sixth line is 3,000. None of the bars ever touches the 3,000 line. However, in the bottom chart, both the Q3 and Q4 columns are over 3,000.

Lying with Shrinking Charts

The pyramid and cone charts should be banned from Excel. You could do without these 14 charts, which inflate the data in the bottom series and deflate the data in the top series.

Consider a standard stacked bar chart like the top one in Figure 14.3. In this chart, a charity's administrative expenses are fairly high at 35%. If the charity wants to minimize its administrative expenses in a chart for its donors, it can change the chart to a cone or pyramid chart because this chart is naturally smaller at the top. In this example, the 35% wedge for administration in black looks like virtually nothing! This occurs because items at the top of the chart get significantly fewer pixels than items at the base of the chart.

Figure 14.2
The 3-D column chart looks great, but it is not accurate.

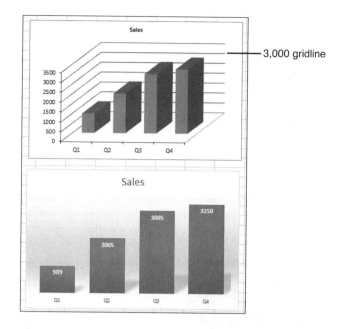

3,000 gridline

Figure 14.3
To misrepresent the 35% category in dark gray at the top, you can put it in a cone chart.

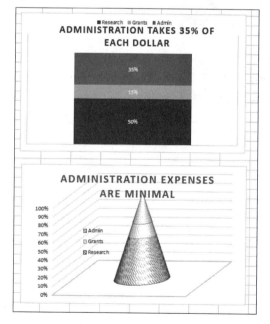

Lying with Scale

In various chapters of this book, you have seen how to change the minimum and maximum values for the scale along the vertical axis. Zooming in enables you to spot variability in tightly clustered values, such as what's shown in Figure 2.23 in Chapter 2, "Customizing Charts." Zooming out enables you to isolate data to a certain zone of the chart.

In Figure 6.10, the volume scale was set two to three times larger than normal to keep the volumes in the lower third of the stock chart.

Although both of those concepts are valid reasons to change the scale, there are also consequences from changing the scale. Changing the scale enables you to paint a very different picture of the data. Figures 14.4 through Figure 14.6 show the same demand curve.

In Figure 14.4, the manufacturing plant zoomed the scale in to have a minimum of 4000 and a maximum of 7500. With a title proclaiming that sales are erratic, they can argue that the cost of staffing-up and staffing-down to meet the ripsaw demand for product is causing problems.

If the sales team presented their chart first, a different picture would have emerged. Figure 14.5 shows a chart where the scale has been zoomed out to have a minimum of 0 and a maximum of 20,000. With this chart, the demand looks almost constant.

Figure 14.4
The chart produced by the manufacturing plant focus on the variability.

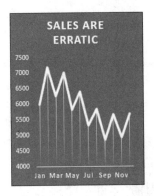

Figure 14.5
By zooming out, the demand looks smooth.

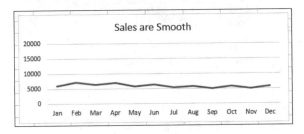

In addition, note that it is much less apparent in Figure 14.5 that the demand is trending down. Figure 14.6 attempts to hide this trend even more. By switching to a 3D chart and adjusting the 3D rotation settings, you can create a line that appears to be trending up at the end.

Figure 14.6
The downward trend appears to reverse.

Lying Because Excel Will Not Cooperate

The chart in Figure 14.7 was presented at a board meeting. The treasurer intended to present the good news that a particular department produced a consistent profit for several years. Instead of showing one line with 42 months, he built a cross-tab table to show 12 months and a different line for each year.

Because the current year was not yet complete, data for July through December is blank in the original table. For this reason, it showed up as zeros in the chart data.

The problem occurs from a clever formula in the charting data. This formula allowed the 48 rows of vertical monthly data to be presented in a 4-row by 12-column arrangement. The result is that the formula converts blank cells to zeroes for future months.

The solution shown in Figure 14.8 is to convert the zero results to NA(). Zeros are plotted on a chart, whereas #N/A errors are not plotted. By checking for a zero and then converting those results to #N/A errors, the future months are not plotted on the chart.

Zeros can be converted automatically to #N/A. Suppose you are building a table with any formula such as =Formula. Edit that formula to be =IF(Formula=0,NA(),Formula).

Figure 14.7
Zeros in the future months make it look like all the money disappears.

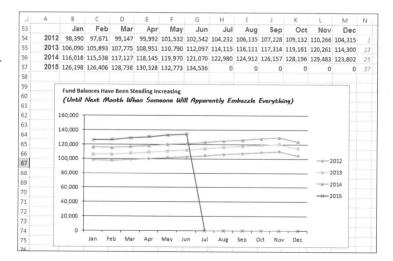

> **NOTE**
> Note that the subtitle in Figure 14.7 was not in the original chart. I penciled this editorial comment in as I was listening to the presentation.

Figure 14.8
Convert the formula to show futures months as #N/A.

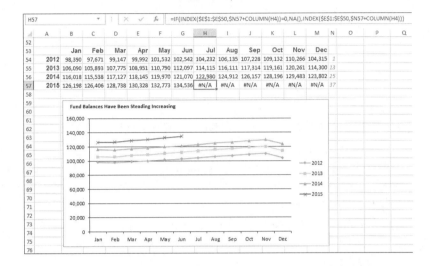

Avoiding Stacked Surface Charts

The message of the chart at the top of Figure 14.9 is that marketing costs more than tripled in three years. If the vice president of marketing wants to defend the marketing expenses, he might mix the marketing department in with other departments to show the marketing budget as a middle series in a stacked area chart.

In a stacked area chart, you can usually figure out what is happening with the numbers in the series at the base of the chart. However, after that first series, everything becomes difficult to judge.

In the chart at the bottom of Figure 14.9, the dramatic increase in marketing spending is not immediately apparent. Some people might see the downward slope at the top of the marketing region and incorrectly infer that marketing costs are decreasing.

The bottom line is that you should not use stacked area charts. Show the data as individual line charts instead.

14

Figure 14.9
Adding data obscures the marketing excesses.

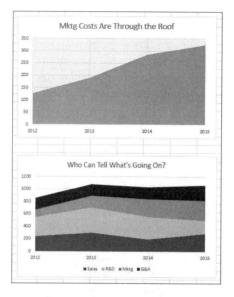

Asserting a Trend from Two Data Points

In the top chart in Figure 14.10, sales appear to be trending up. Even the automatic Excel trendline indicates this is occurring.

If you are presented with this chart, ask the presenter for more data. For example, it would be good to put those two data points in the context of a larger historical trend.

If you see more data, you might realize that the increase in the past year is actually the bottoming out of a six-year skid, as shown in the bottom chart in Figure 14.10.

Figure 14.10
Inferring a trend based on a two-point line is dangerous. You need to add more data points to tell the real story.

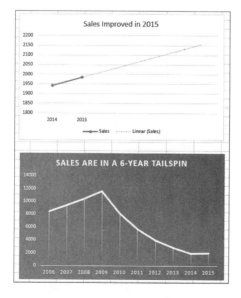

14

Deliberately Using Charts to Lie

Some people are just good at lying. For example, sales are increasing in Figure 14.11. Or are they? Notice that the chart author reversed the categories along the x-axis, with the most recent year appearing at the left. Most people are conditioned that charts proceed from earliest to latest. If the presenter is flipping through slides in a PowerPoint presentation, the chances are no one will notice that sales are not trending up.

Excel makes it easy to create the chart in Figure 14.11. The Format Axis dialog for the chart offers a simple check box for Categories in Reverse Order, as shown in Figure 14.12.

Figure 14.11
It appears that all is going well.

Figure 14.12
The reversed years in Figure 14.11 come from this setting.

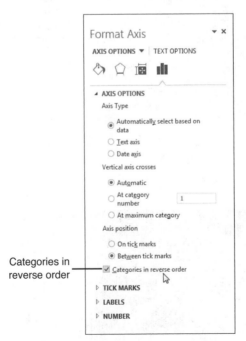

Charting Something Else When Numbers Are Too Bad

As another example, in Figure 14.13, a city is drastically losing population. Jobs are scarce, education is bad, and people are moving out. The top chart paints a pretty bleak picture. The mayor, who has been around for 24 years, wants to put a happy spin on the message. His staff prepares the bottom chart, which shows how population growth has slowed.

Figure 14.13
When the absolute numbers are bleak, you plot the percentage rate of change.

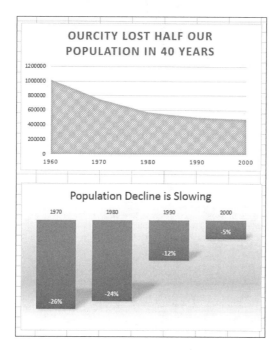

Stretching Pictographs

The next example is definitely a non-Excel lie. Even Excel is smart enough not to allow picture markers to change in both height and width. Someone had to make the markers invisible and use clip art to pull off the lie shown in Figure 14.14.

The image on the left is 100 pixels tall and 100 pixels wide. This seems like a reasonable way to represent $100 million in exports. When the chart designer scaled the picture up to 300 pixels for the March data, the designer allowed both the height and width to change. The size of the final image contains nine times the area of the first image, even though the exports increased by a factor of three.

The rule for pictographs is that you should increase the height of the picture, but never the width. Even though Excel does this properly, charts in newspapers and magazines are frequently created in Photoshop. The designers try to create a pretty chart that does not distort the image by increasing the height and width of the marker. In the process, they create a misleading chart.

14

Figure 14.14
The size of the images increased in both height and width. This causes a 200% increase to look like an 800% increase.

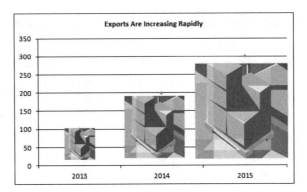

Next Steps

Appendix A, "Charting References," lists several additional resources where you can find more information on charting.

Charting References

Other Charting Resources

If you enjoyed this book, there are many more resources for you to investigate. This appendix includes people, books, and websites that have had an influence on my charting life.

> **NOTE**
>
> Websites come and go. I will maintain a list of links to these references and any others that I find at http://www.mrexcel.com/chartbook2013data.html.

Gene Zelazny: The Guru of Business Charting

During a 50-year career at McKinsey & Company, Gene Zelazny has taught two generations of people how to effectively communicate with charts. I learned a lot about charting during a six-month stint on a McKinsey project team. The McKinsey consultants—such as Gino Picasso and Firoz Dosani, who taught me about charting—learned the craft from Gene Zelazny.

I enjoy Gene's work because he focuses on positive ways to effectively communicate by using charts and visuals. Whereas Tufte spends a lot of ink showing why popular charts are bad, Gene cuts right to the chase and shows examples of effective charts.

Pick up anything that you find written by Gene. He first wrote *Say It with Presentations*. His best kit is The Say It with Charts Complete Toolkit. If you wonder where Microsoft got the idea for SmartArt graphics, you will see that Gene began advocating what Microsoft calls SmartArt long before Microsoft coined the name. The kit includes a book, images on CD-ROM, and more (see http://www.zelazny.com/charts.html).

A

IN THIS APPENDIX

Other Charting Resources 411

Gene Zelazny: The Guru of Business Charting 411

PowerFrameworks.com 412

Books by Edward Tufte 412

Websites with Charting Tutorials 413

Interactive Training 413

Live Training 413

Blogs About Charting 413

Visual Design Stores 414

Professional Chart Designers 414

Charting Utilities and Products 415

PowerFrameworks.com

If you are the go-to person for charts in your company, you need to subscribe to PowerFrameworks.com. The $169.99 annual subscription gives you access to hundreds of charting and presentation templates. Kathy Villella and Lisa Baker are constantly adding new, leading-edge elements to the site. For example, Kathy recently posted an umbrella chart element that you can import into PowerPoint. In addition to the element, Kathy provides several professionally designed ideas about how you could use the chart.

PowerFrameworks hires professional artists to bring its ideas to life. It makes sure that in a lock-and-key chart, the key actually fits in the lock. You can build brilliant-looking animated or still charts using these elements.

The company's ideas alone are worth the price of a PowerFrameworks subscription. Download the templates, label the charts, color with the Formatting tab, and you are ready to go.

A subscription to PowerFrameworks can help supercharge your career.

Books by Edward Tufte

I own everything that Professor Edward Tufte writes. He self-publishes his books and spares no expense in creating fantastic, full-color, beautiful books.

If Gene Zelazny was the source of Microsoft's ideas for SmartArt, then Edward Tufte is the source for Microsoft's ideas about sparklines. In his book *Beautiful Evidence*, Tufte demonstrated sparklines as "intense, word-sized graphics."

Tufte's books are informative and filled with eye candy. I can spend an hour studying the beautiful Napoleon's March chart that manages to communicate seven different series with a single line. Tufte has found examples of good and bad charts throughout history. He coined the term *chartjunk*.

My only complaint is that Tufte comes off as a bit of a curmudgeon. He shows bad charts and explains why they are bad. I am sure that Tufte would skewer some of my charts in this book. After reading Tufte, I am filled with doubt and knowledge about what not to do. Zelazny counters this by telling you only what is effective.

Tufte has written the following books:

- *The Visual Display of Quantitative Information*, now in its second edition, contains 250 illustrations of the best and sometimes the worst ways of displaying information.
- *Envisioning Information* covers maps, charts, tables, timetables, and more. This book is aimed at those in the design profession.
- *Visual Explanations: Images and Quantities, Evidence and Narrative* is about the representation of verbs. This book talks about how to pack the most information into a small space and how to use visual information for making decisions.
- *Beautiful Evidence* is a book in which Tufte introduces the concept of sparklines.

Tufte also maintains a website and forum at `http://www.EdwardTufte.com`.

Websites with Charting Tutorials

Excel gurus maintain numerous websites. A very few offer a better-than-usual concentration on charting and the process of creating unique charts:

- **Jon Peltier**—Jon, a Microsoft MVP, has several excellent charting examples on his website. If I am Googling a particularly difficult chart problem, I end up at Jon's site more often than not. Visit his site at `http://www.PeltierTech.com`.

- **Mike Alexander**—Mike runs a site with a funny name (DataPig Technologies) but great content. Many of his charting ideas made it into Chapter 7, "Using Advanced Chart Techniques." The benefit of Mike's site is that all the tutorials are five-minute videos that allow you to actually watch the charts being built. Visit `http://www.DataPigTechnologies.com`.

- **Andy Pope**—Andy maintains a website with amazing chart examples. These examples run circles around even the advanced charts shown in Chapter 7 of this book. Andy is a Microsoft MVP. Visit his website, `http://www.andypope.info/charts.htm`.

- **Tushar Mehta**—Tushar, a Microsoft MVP, has some nontraditional charting examples on his website, at `http://www.tushar-mehta.com/excel/charts/`.

- **Tom Bunzel**—If you need to present your data with PowerPoint, check out Tom Bunzel's site, `http://www.professorppt.com`. Tom writes books about PowerPoint and numerous articles for InformIT.

Interactive Training

As I was working on the manuscript for this book, I also recorded an interactive DVD + Book that Que markets as *LiveLessons Power Excel 2013*. That product has more than an hour of content on charting in Excel.

Live Training

If you are an MBA student at a business school, you might be lucky enough to catch Gene Zelazny as a guest speaker at your college. I highly recommend attending his seminar if he visits your town.

Edward Tufte provides a one-day course on charting at various sites around the country. Check out `http://www.edwardtufte.com/tufte/courses` for a schedule.

Blogs About Charting

A few people are gracing the blogosphere with posts that often touch on charting:

- **Juice Analytics**—Zach and Chris Gemignani seem to be proponents of Edward Tufte. They often critique charts at their Juice Analytics blog, `http://www.juiceanalytics.com/weblog/`.

- **Daily Dose of Excel**—Many Excel MVPs contribute topics on various Excel topics to Dick Kusleika's Daily Dose of Excel blog. You can find an archive of the charting posts at `http://www.dailydoseofexcel.com/archives/category/charting/`.

- **Visual Business Intelligence**—Steven Few shows off new and innovative visual designs at his blog, `http://www.perceptualedge.com/blog/`.

- **Instant Cognition**—This wide-ranging blog has several excellent posts on visual report design. See `http://blog.instantcognition.com/category/visualization/charts/`.

- **An-Sofie Guilbert**—A curated collection of interesting data visualizations. See `http://ansofieguilbert.wordpress.com/category/data-visualization-infographics-diagrams/`.

- **Dustin Smith**—Dustin Smith regularly collects beautiful charts, graphs, and maps and posts them at his site. See `http://chartporn.org`.

- **Politikal Arithmetik**—Professor Charles Franklin's blog always has the latest political charts and analysis. Visit for inspiration on cool charting ideas: `http://pollsandvotes.com/PaV/` and `http://politicalarithmetik.blogspot.com/`.

In addition, I produce a daily two-minute video podcast about Excel that occasionally dips into the charting realm. You can find a link to charting episodes at `http://www.mrexcel.com/chartbook2013data.html`. Also, when I find interesting charts, I pin them to this board at `http://pinterest.com/mrexcel/unusual-charts-graphs/`.

Visual Design Stores

If you are a fan of visual information and graphic design, a must-see store on your next trip through Toronto is SWIPE. This store is dedicated to books on advertising and design.

David Michaelides has been running SWIPE for almost 20 years. If there is a book on advertising or design, he either has it or knows where to get it. The store is located at 401 Richmond Street West, Toronto. You can find more information at `http://www.swipe.com`. Plan to spend at least an hour browsing the store.

Professional Chart Designers

If you are creating charts and getting paid for it, then you, the reader, are a professional chart designer. However, if you are in a pinch and need to find some outside help, check out the services of these designers:

- **Bob D'Amico**—Bob D'Amico is an illustrator and a designer. Although he drew the humorous charts in Chapters 4 and 6, he has a complete portfolio of serious charting designs he has completed for clients. Whether you need something serious or irreverent, contact Bob via email at CartoonBob@mac.com.

■ **Andy Attiliis**—Andy Attiliis operates a professional charting design service at `http://www.ideasiteforbusiness.com/andy/dc.htm`.

Charting Utilities and Products

Some charts just aren't easy to create in Excel. The following are some of my favorite utilities for creating different charts:

■ **Speedometer Chart Creator**—Mala Singh provides an add-in that can generate speedometer charts in seconds instead of the hour it can take to draw a speedometer with AutoShapes. His charts show a current value plus yesterday's value, so you can get an idea of whether the value is trending up or down. Mala also offers the MacroEconomic Supply Curve Chart add-in, in which the width of the column indicates units sold and the height of the column indicates price. You can see these charts and more at `http://www.mrexcel.com/graphics.shtml`.

■ **Dashboard Reporting with Excel**—This is Charley Kyd's excellent kit about how to create dashboards in Excel. It features an e-book plus a dozen sample Excel files to get you started. Charley is the king of getting small charts readable in Excel; my favorite example puts 112 readable postage stamp–size charts on a single letter-size sheet of paper. Visit `http://www.ExcelUser.com`.

■ **Xcelsius**—This product can use your Excel data to make interactive charts and output them to the Web or PowerPoint. Check it out at `http://www.businessobjects.com/xcelcius`.

> **NOTE**
> If you have resources that should be listed here, send them to the email address listed at `http://www.mrexcel.com/chartbook2013data.html`.

A

Index

Symbols

#N/A errors, zero values and, 405-406

Numbers

2D pie charts, 120

3D charts, 40-41

    3D column charts, 13

    3D pie charts, 120

    back walls, 41

    column depth, 41

    depth, 65

    floors, 41

    height, 65

    perspective, 65, 401-403

    rotation, controlling, 65-66

    side walls, 41

    X rotation, 65

    Y rotation, 65

3D rotation, surface charts, 168-169

10-icon sets, 269-271

100% stacked charts, 80

    component comparisons, showing, 119, 126-127

    thumbnails, 13

1900, dates prior to (date fields), 83, 89-91

A

Accent Process style (SmartArt layouts), 288

Add Chart Element drop-down (Design tab), 29, 36

AddChart2 chart creation method, 346-348

Alexander, Mike, 413

all caps, titling charts in, 59-60

Alt+F1 key combination, creating charts, 15

analysis elements, 39-40

    drop lines, 40

    error bars, 40

    trendlines, 40

    up/down bars, 40

animating scatter charts via Power View, 245-246

Annual Reports, showing years in reverse, 53

An-Sofie Guilbert blog, 414

area charts, 69, 79

arrows

    columns, replacing with arrows, 101-102

    upward arrows, illustrating growth by, 304

art

    charts, exporting as, 331-332, 389-390

    PowerPoint, copying charts as pictures, 325-326

    Shapes, 287

        converting SmartArt to, 314-315

        creating, 311-312

        displaying cell contents, 309-311

        formatting, 311

        Freeform Shapes, 311-312

    SmartArt, 287, 288, 308-309

        adding art to, 298-299

        applying styles, 293

        balance charts, 304

        Basic Cycle layouts, 305

        changing color in, 292-293

        changing Shapes, 295-296

        changing styles, 293-294

        choosing layouts, 302-303

        controlling Shapes from Text pane, 296-298

        converting to Shapes, 314-315

        Cycle category, 289-290

        Design tab, 294

        Divergent Radial layouts, 305

        elements in, 289

        Equation style, 302

        formatting in, 288, 294-296

        funnel charts, 302

        gear charts, 302

        Hierarchy category, 290

        inserting, 291-292

        labeled Hierarchy charts, 307-308

        Leveraging SmartArt Graphics in the 2007 Microsoft Office System, 303, 308

        limitations of, 301-302

        List category, 289

        Matrix category, 290, 302

        Office.com category, 290

        organizational charts and, 299-301

        Picture category, 290

        Process category, 289

        Pyramid category, 290, 302

        Relationship category, 290, 302

        styles of layouts, 288-289

        Table List layouts, 306

        upward arrows, 304

        Venn diagrams, 306-307

    WordArt, 287-288, 312-313

art lying by stretching pictographs, 409-410

Attiliis, Andy, 415

automatic trendlines, adding to charts, 105-106

axes, 37-39

Category axis, 52

category-based axes, 80-95

date-based axes, 54, 80-95

depth axis, 168

formatting, 47-55

Horizontal (category) axis, 39

Horizontal Axis title, 38

Logarithmic axis, 50-52

monthly charts, 54-55

sparklines, 254-256

text-based axes, 54

time-based axes, 81

time-scale axes, 93-95

Values axis, 48-50

Vertical (value) axis, 39

Vertical Axis title, 38

Y-axis scale, 143-144

years, showing in reverse (Annual Reports), 53

B

back walls (3D charts), 41

backwards compatibility, coding and, 341

bad chart types, 10-9

balance charts, 304

bar charts, 79, 80

in-cell bar charts, 259-263

comparisons, illustrating, 113-117, 115-116

data series, 368-369

gap width, formatting, 368-369

paired bar charts, 161-163

subdividing bars for emphasis, 116-117

bar of pie charts, 120, 371-374

customizing splits in, 134

using, 134-135

Basic Cycle layouts (SmartArt), 305

Basic Process style (SmartArt layouts), 288

Beautiful Evidence, 249, 257, 395, 412

benchmark charts, 219-220

Bing maps, 275

bins, creating for frequency charts, 383-386

blank series, moving series with (stacked and clustered charts), 139-143

blogs (web resources), 413-414

bubble charts, 15, 147, 159-160, 375-377

bullet charts, 212-217

Bunzel, Tom, 413

C

callouts (data labels), 8-9

candlestick charts, 173

color, changing in, 191-192

columns, rearranging downloaded data in, 175

creating, 191-196

caps (capital letters), titling charts in, 59-60

categories, reversing, 24-25

Category axis, controlling labels, 52

category-based axes, trend charts, 80-95

cells

in-cell bar charts, creating via data bars, 259-263

cell formulas as data label captions, 356-358

charts

creating from conditional formatting in cells, 271-273

fitting into cells via sparklines, 250-259

contents, displaying via Shapes, 309-311

data bars

creating in-cell bar charts, 259-263

showing for subsets of cells, 262-263

icon sets, showing icons only for best cells, 268-269

Change Chart Type (Design tab), 31

Change Color drop-down (Design tab), 31

Chart area, 37-38, 61-64

Chart Elements, 26

Add Chart Element drop-down (Design tab), 29

Format Task Pane, icons available per Chart Element table, 30

Chart Filters, 26

chart objects, referencing charts in (VBA coding), 342

Chart Styles, 26, 31

Chart title, 38

charting tutorial websites, 413

Charts menu, Quick Analysis icon

creating charts, 10-11

previewing charts, 11

closing prices (stocks), showing with line charts, 177-181

clustered charts

creating, 138-145

thumbnails, 13

clustered columns, combining with stacked columns, 138-139

Code window (VBA Editor), 335

coding

backwards compatibility, 341

chart objects, referencing, 342

charts

referencing, 342

specifying built-in charts, 342-344

specifying chart location, 343

specifying chart size, 343

comments, adding to code, 341

data ranges, 337-338

End With statements, 340

End+Down Arrow versus End+Up Arrow, 338

lines of code, continuing, 340

objects

object-oriented coding, 336-337

referring to, 340

With statements, 340

super-variables, 339-340

VBA coding

AddChart2 chart creation method, 346-348

applying chart color, 352-355

bar of pie charts, 371-374

changing chart fills, 363-366

combo charts, 378-381

creating bins for frequency charts, 383-386

customizing charts, 350

data bars, 392-395

Excel 2003-2013 chart creation method, 349-350

Excel 2007-2013 chart creation method, 348-349

exploding round charts, 369-371

exporting charts as graphics, 389-390

filtering charts, 355-356

Format method, 363-367

formatting charts, 351-358

formatting data series, 367-368

formatting data series separations, 368-369

formatting gap width, 368-369

formatting line settings, 366-367

OHLC charts, 382-383

pie of pie charts, 371-374

pivot charts, 390-392

radar charts, 377

referring to specific charts, 343-346

SetElement method, 358-363

setting bubble size in bubble charts, 375-377

sparklines, 395-399

specifying chart styles, 351-352

specifying chart titles, 350-351

spinning round charts, 369-371

stacked area charts, 386-389

surface charts, 377

color, 125-126

candlestick charts, changing in, 191-192

Change Color drop-down (Design tab), 31

color scales, 249

customizing, 264-265

showing extremes via, 263-265

gradients, Plot area, 61-63

highlighting slices in pie charts, 125-126

Power View maps, 285-284

SmartArt, changing color in, 292-293

themes, changing in, 74

VBA coding, applying via, 352-355

column charts, data sets up to 12 time periods, 77

columns

arrows, replacing with, 101-102

clustered charts

combining with stacked column charts, 138-139

narrowing, 143

data series, formatting separations, 368-369

depth (3D charts), 41

floating columns, 200-202

gap width, formatting, 368-369

highlighting, 100-101

sparkcolumns, 250

stacked column charts, 108-110

combining with clustered columns, 138-139

narrowing, 143

stock charts

adjusted close columns, 175-177

rearranging downloaded data in columns, 174-175

combining chart types in a single chart, 197-199

combo charts, 8-9

creating, 378-381

magnitude (order of), charting, 23

monthly sales trend charts, creating, 106-108

year-to-date sales charts, creating, 106-108

comments, adding to code, 341

communicating effectively with charts, 96-105

company relationships, illustrating via SmartArt, 305

comparisons

bar charts, illustrating with, 113-117, 115-116

component comparisons, showing, 117-135

compatibility (backwards), coding and, 341

component decomposition, displaying with waterfall charts, 136-145

con/pro decisions, illustrating via balance charts, 304

contrasting components with surface charts, 167-169

converting

charts to

PDF, 332

XPS, 332

Power View tables to charts, 238-239

SmartArt to Shapes, 314-315

copying/pasting

charts

creating from pasted Excel data in PowerPoint, 327-328

as pictures in PowerPoint, 325-326

sparklines, 259

copying/pasting Excel documents to PowerPoint, 319-328

correlations, testing in scatter charts, 157-158

current sales to prior-year sales comparison charts, 110

Current Selection drop-down (Format tab), formatting chart elements, 36

customizing

charts, VBA coding, 350

color scales, 264-265

data bars, 261-262

high-low-close charts, 183-184

sparklines, 253-254

cutting/pasting rows, 33

Cycle category (SmartArt), 289-290

D

daily dates, rolling to months, 91-93

Daily Dose of Excel blog, 414

Daily Giz Wiz podcast, 118

D'Amico, Bob, 414-415

dashboard elements, Power View, 238

Dashboard Reporting with Excel, 415

data bars, 249

in-cell bar charts, creating, 259-263

creating, 260-261, 392-395

customizing, 261-262

gradients, 259

negative values, 260

numeric values

formatting, 260

hiding, 260

scale, specifying, 260

showing for subsets of cells, 262-263

text in, 260

zero values, 260

Data group icons (Design tab), 31

data labels, 38

callouts (data labels), 8-9

cell formulas as data label captions, 356-358

charts

adding data labels to, 43-46

fitting in, 45-46

content of, changing, 45

gridlines, correcting data labels crossed out by, 44

data markers (series), replacing with

pictures, 73-74

Shapes, 73

data points (series)

formatting, 73

trends, asserting from two data points, 407

data sequence, changing with Select Data icon, 25

data series separations (columns/bar charts), formatting, 368-369

data sets

charts, locating in, 34

unsummarized data sets, 7

data tables, 38-39, 46-47

data visualizations, 249

    color scales, 249

        customizing, 264-265

        showing extremes via, 263-265

    data bars, 249

        in-cell bar charts, 259-263

        creating, 260-261

        customizing, 261-262

        formatting numeric values, 260

        gradients, 259

        hiding numeric values, 260

        negative values, 260

        showing for subsets of cells, 262-263

        specifying scale, 260

        text in, 260

        zero values, 260

    icon sets, 249

        10-icon sets, 269-271

        five-icon sets, 265

        four-icon sets, 265

        moving numbers closer to icons, 266-268

        reversing sequence of icons, 268

        setting up, 265-266

        showing icons only for best cells, 268-269

        three-icon sets, 265

date fields

    dates prior to 1900, 83, 89-91

    dates represented by numeric years, 81-83

    dates that are really time, 83

    text dates, 81, 83-84

date lookup tables, PowerPivot, 234-235

date systems, comparing, 85

date-based axes, 54, 80-95

Debartolo, Dick, 118

decomposition (components), displaying with waterfall charts, 136-137

Decrease Font Size icon (Home tab), 31

deleting titles, 99-100

delta charts, 220-221

departments within companies, illustrating via SmartArt, 306

depth (3D charts), 65

depth axis, surface charts, 168

Design tab (Excel 2013)

    Add Chart Element drop-down, 29, 36

    Change Chart Type, 31

    Change Color drop-down, 31

    Chart Styles Gallery, 31

    Data group icons, 31

    Move Chart, 31

    Quick Layout drop-down, 29-30

Design tab (SmartArt), 294

designer websites, 414-415

detail, showing via sparklines, 256-257

Developer tab, enabling, 334

displaying

    cell contents via Shapes, 309-311

    gridlines, 55

    time-scale axes, 93-95

Divergent Radial layouts (SmartArt), 305

doughnut charts, 120, 127-128

    component comparisons, 119

    exploding, 369-371

    spinning, 369-371

down/up bars, adding to line charts, 70

dragging

    charts

        outside visible window, 33

        in visible window, 33

Power View elements, creating by, 240

drawing with scatter charts, 155-156

drop lines, 40, 69

E

editing, chart titles, 16

elements

analysis elements, 39-40

axes, 37-39

changing scale of Values axis, 48-50

controlling labels on Category axis, 52

date-based axes, 54

formatting, 47-55

labeling monthly charts with JFMAMJJASOND, 54-55

Logarithmic axis, 50-52

showing years in reverse (Annual Reports), 53

text-based axes, 54

back walls (3D charts), 41

Chart area, 37-38, 61-64

Chart title, 38

column depth (3D charts), 41

data labels, 38

adding to charts, 43-46

changing content of, 45

correcting data labels crossed out by gridlines, 44

fitting in charts, 45-46

data tables, 38-39, 46-47

drop lines, 40, 69

error bars, 40, 71-72

floors (3D charts), 41

formatting, 41-72

accessing formatting tools, 35-36

Add Chart Element drop-down (Design tab), 36

Current Selection drop-down (Format tab), 36

Format Task Pane, 36

Plus icon, 35

gridlines, 39

creating unobtrusive gridlines, 56-57

displaying, 55

major gridlines, 55-56, 57-58

minor gridlines, 55-56

Horizontal (category) axis, 39

Horizontal Axis title, 38

labels, 37-39

legends, 38

formatting, 43

moving, 41-42

rearranging, 42

Plot area, 38

adding pictures to, 64

formatting, 61-64

gradients, 61-63

textures, 64

series

formatting, 72-74

replacing data markers with pictures, 73-74

replacing data markers with Shapes, 73

time comparisons, 115-116

side walls (3D charts), 41

SmartArt common elements, 289

trendlines, 40

adding equations to charts, 68

automatic trendlines, 105-106

exponential trendlines, 68

forecasting with, 66-69

formatting, 67-68

logarithm trendlines, 68-69

moving average trendlines, 69

multiple trendlines on single chart, 110

polynomial trendlines, 69

power trendlines, 69

types of elements table, 37-36

up/down bars, 40, 70

Vertical (value) axis, 39

Vertical Axis title, 38

embedding charts/workbooks in PowerPoint, 325

emphasis, subdividing bars in bar charts for, 116-117

End With statements, 340

End+Down Arrow versus End+Up Arrow, 338

enlarging sparklines, 256-257

Envisioning Information, 412

Equation style (SmartArt), 302

error bars, 40, 71-72

Excel 2003-2013 chart creation method, 349-350

Excel 2007-2013 chart creation method, 348-349

Excel 2013

cell formulas as data label captions, 356-358

charts

AddChart2 chart creation method, 346-348

filtering, 355-356

improvements to charts, 2-3

data labels, cell formulas as data label captions, 356-358

Developer tab, enabling, 334

new features of, 7-9

exploding

doughnut charts, 369-371

pie charts, 369-371

slices in pie charts, 124

exponential trendlines, 68

exporting, charts as graphics via VBA, 331-332, 389-390

extremes, showing via color scales, 263-265

F

Facebook, chart presentations and, 329

Few, Stephen, 414

fills, changing (VBA coding), 363-366

Filter pane (Power View), 242

filtering

Chart Filters, 26

charts in Excel 2013, 355-356

data

pivot charts, 230-231

tile boxes (Power View), 243-244

unwanted rows, 8

finance.yahoo.com website, 171, 173, 180

floating columns/bars, 200-202

floors (3D charts), 41

fonts

Decrease Font Size icon (Home tab), 31

Font group (Home tab), 31

forecasting, trendlines and, 66-69

formatting, 36

Chart area, 61-64

charts

changing fills, 363-366

data series, 367-368

Format method (VBA), 363-367

line settings, 366-367

VBA coding, 351-358

conditional formatting, creating charts, 271-273

data in PowerPivot, 235-236

data series, 367-368

elements, 41-72

   accessing formatting tools, 35-36

   Add Chart Element drop-down (Design tab), 36

   Current Selection drop-down (Format tab), 36

   Format Task Pane, 36

   Plus icon, 35

Format method (VBA), 363-367

Format tab, 31, 36

Format Task Pane, 27-30

   formatting chart elements, 36

   icons available per Chart Element table, 30

   icons table, 29

legends, 43

line charts

   drop lines, 69

   up/down bars, 70

numeric values

   data bars, 260

   formatting in labels, 7-8

Paintbrush icon, 8

Plot area, 61-64

series, 72-74

Shapes, 311

SmartArt Format tab, 288, 294-296

task pane commands, 9-8

templates, saving changes in, 75

themes, changing color, 74

trendlines, 67-68

Formula bar, editing titles, 16

Freeform Shapes, 311-312

frequency charts, 163-166, 383-386

funnel charts, SmartArt and, 302

Funnel icon, 8, 26

further reading

   Beautiful Evidence, 412

   Envisioning Information, 412

   Visual Explanations: Images and Quantities, Evidence and Narrative, 412

G

gap width (columns/bar charts), formatting, 368-369

gear charts, SmartArt and, 302

Gemignani, Chris, 413-414

Gemignani, Zach, 413-414

GeoFlow mapping software, 275

   creating maps, 284-286

   zoom feature, 285

gradients, Plot area, 61-63

graphics, 288, 289, 302

   exporting charts as, 331-332, 389-390

   PowerPoint, copying charts as graphics, 325-326

   Shapes, 287

      converting SmartArt to, 314-315

      creating, 311-312

      displaying cell contents, 309-311

      formatting, 311

      Freeform Shapes, 311-312

   SmartArt, 287, 288, 308-309

      adding graphics to, 298-299

      applying styles, 293

      balance charts, 304

      Basic Cycle layouts, 305

      changing color in, 292-293

      changing Shapes, 295-296

changing styles, 293-294

choosing layouts, 302-303

controlling Shapes from Text pane, 296-298

converting to Shapes, 314-315

Cycle category, 289-290

Design tab, 294

Divergent Radial layouts, 305

elements in, 289

Equation style, 302

formatting in, 288, 294-296

funnel charts, 302

gear charts, 302

Hierarchy category, 290

inserting, 291-292

labeled Hierarchy charts, 307-308

Leveraging SmartArt Graphics in the 2007 Microsoft Office System, 303, 308

limitations of, 301-302

List category, 289

Matrix category, 290, 302

Office.com category, 290

organizational charts and, 299-301

Picture category, 290

Process category, 289

Pyramid category, 290, 302

Relationship category, 290, 302

styles of layouts, 288-289

Table List layouts, 306

upward arrows, 304

Venn diagrams, 306-307

WordArt, 287-288, 312-313

graphics lying by stretching pictographs, 409-410

gridlines, 39

data labels, correcting, 44

displaying, 55

major gridlines, 55-58

minor gridlines, 55-58

unobtrusive gridlines, creating, 56-57

grouping daily dates in pivot charts, 228-230

growth, illustrating by upward arrows, 304

guidelines (arbitrary), XY series and, 202-206

H

height (3D charts), 65

help

charting tutorial websites, 413

Dashboard Reporting with Excel, 415

interactive training, 413

live training, 413

Speedometer Chart Creator, 415

web resources, 411

Xcelsius, 415

Helper icons

Funnel icon, 26

Paintbrush icon, 26

Plus icon, 26

Hierarchy category (SmartArt), 290

Hierarchy charts, labels and, 307-308

highlighting

columns, 100-101

sections of charts by adding second series, 102-103

slices in pie charts

color, 125-126

exploding, 124

high-low lines, 192-196

high-low-close charts, 79

columns, rearranging downloaded data in, 175

creating, 182-183

customizing, 183-184

volume, adding, 186-190

Home tab

commands, 31

Decrease Font Size icon, 31

Font group, 31

Horizontal (category) axis, 39

Horizontal Axis title, 38

Horizontal Multiples (Power View), 244-245

I

---

icon sets, 249

10-icon sets, 269-271

five-icon sets, 265

four-icon sets, 265

moving numbers closer to icons, 266-268

reversing sequence of icons, 268

setting up, 265-266

showing icons only for best cells, 268-269

three-icon sets, 265

images

exporting charts as, 331-332, 389-390

PowerPoint, copying charts as pictures, 325-326

Shapes, 287

converting SmartArt to, 314-315

creating, 311-312

displaying cell contents, 309-311

formatting, 311

Freeform Shapes, 311-312

SmartArt, 287-288, 308-309

adding images to, 298-299

applying styles, 293

balance charts, 304

Basic Cycle layouts, 305

changing color in, 292-293

changing Shapes, 295-296

changing styles, 293-294

choosing layouts, 302-303

controlling Shapes from Text pane, 296-298

converting to Shapes, 314-315

Cycle category, 289-290

Design tab, 294

Divergent Radial layouts, 305

elements in, 289

Equation style, 302

formatting in, 288, 294-296

funnel charts, 302

gear charts, 302

Hierarchy category, 290

inserting, 291-292

labeled Hierarchy charts, 307-308

Leveraging SmartArt Graphics in the 2007 Microsoft Office System, 303, 308

limitations of, 301-302

List category, 289

Matrix category, 290, 302

Office.com category, 290

organizational charts and, 299-301

Picture category, 290

Process category, 289

Pyramid category, 290, 302

Relationship category, 290, 302

styles of layouts, 288-289

Table List layouts, 306

upward arrows, 304

Venn diagrams, 306-307

WordArt, 287-288, 312-313

images lying by stretching pictographs, 409-410

importing data to MapPoint, 275-279

Insert tab, creating charts via, 14-15

Instant Cognition blog, 414

interactive training (web resources), 413

Internet presentations, charts and, 328-331

iterative processes, showing by Basic Cycle layouts (SmartArt), 305

J

JFMAMJJASOND, labeling monthly charts with, 54-55

Juice Analytics blog, 413-414

K

Kusleika, Dick, 414

Kyd, Charley, 415

L

labels, 37-39

   arbitrary labels and XY series, 202-206

   callouts from cell values, 8-9

   Category axis, controlling on, 52

   cell formulas as data label captions, 356-358

   Data labels, 38

   Hierarchy charts, 307-308

   monthly charts, labeling with JFMAMJJASOND, 54-55

   number formatting, 7-8

   pie charts, 121-124

   sparklines, 257-259

layouts

   Page Layout tab, changing themes via, 32, 74

   Quick Layout drop-down (Design tab), 29-30

Legend boxes, removing items from (stacked and clustered charts), 143

legends, 38

   formatting, 43

   moving, 41-42

   rearranging, 42

   single-series charts, 7

Leveraging SmartArt Graphics in the 2007 Microsoft Office System, 303, 308

line charts, 77-78, 171-172

   closing prices (stocks), showing with, 177-181

   columns, rearranging downloaded data in, 175

   formatting

      drop lines, 69

      up/down bars, 70

   scatter charts, replacing with, 154-155

   volume as a column, 180-182

line charts with volume, rearranging downloaded data in columns, 175

LinkedIn, chart presentations and, 329

List category (SmartArt), 289

live training (web resources), 413

logarithm trendlines, 68-69

Logarithmic axis, showing magnitude of order, 50-52

lying, charts and

   charting something else when numbers are bad, 409

   deliberate lying, 408

   perspective, 401-403

   scale, 403-405

   shrinking charts, 402-403

   stacked surface charts, 406-407

   stretching pictographs, 409-410

   trends, asserting from two data points, 407

   zero values and #N/A errors, 405-406

M

macro recorder, 336-338

magnitude (order of)

    charting, 23

    Logarithmic axis, showing order of magnitude, 50-52

major gridlines, 55-58

maps

    Bing maps, 275

    GeoFlow, 275

        creating maps, 284-286

        zoom feature, 285

    MapPoint, 275

        importing data to, 275-279

        zoom feature, 278-279

    Power View, 275

        color, 285-284

        creating maps, 279-284

        enabling add-ins, 280

        loading data into, 280-281

        zoom feature, 283-284

    showing data on, 285-284

markers (data), replacing with

    pictures, 73-74

    Shapes, 73

Matrix category (SmartArt), 290, 302

Mehta, Tushar, 413

Michaelides, David, 414

minor gridlines, 55-58

misleading charts

    charting something else when numbers are bad, 409

    deliberate lying, 408

    perspective, 401-403

    scale, 403-405

    shrinking charts, 402-403

    stacked surface charts, 406-407

    stretching pictographs, 409-410

    trends, asserting from two data points, 407

    zero values and #N/A errors, 405-406

mixing chart types in a single chart, 197-199

monthly charts, labeling with JFMAMJJASOND, 54-55

monthly sales trend charts, creating, 106-108

months, rolling daily dates to, 91-93

Move Chart (Design tab), 31

moving

    charts

        within current worksheets, 33

        dragging in visible window, 33

        dragging outside visible window, 33

        between worksheets, 34

    charts between worksheets, 200

    legends, 41-42

    rows, cutting and pasting, 33

    series with blank series (stacked and clustered charts), 139-143

    slice labels in pie charts, 123-124

moving average trendlines, 69

Multiples (Power View), replicating charts, 244-245

N

narrowing columns (stacked and clustered charts), 143

negative values in data bars, 260

noncontiguous data, charting, 19-21

nonsummarized data, charting, 22-23

numeric values, 260

    data bars

        formatting in, 260

        hiding in, 260

    labels, formatting in, 7-8

numeric years

    data, plotting by, 88-89

    dates represented by (date fields), 81-83

O

object-oriented coding, 336-337, 339-340

    object variables, 339-340

    referrals to objects, 340

Office.com category (SmartArt), 290

OHLC (Open-High-Low-Close) charts, 172-173

    columns, rearranging downloaded data in, 175

    creating, 184-186, 382-383

order of magnitude

    charting, 23

    Logarithmic axis, showing order of magnitude, 50-52

organizational charts, SmartArt and, 299-301

Other Customer Summaries, 130

P

Page Layout tab, themes

    changing, 32

    changing color in, 74

Paintbrush icon, 8, 26

paired bar charts, 161-163

Paste Options menu

    PowerPoint, 317

    Word, 317

pasted Excel data, creating charts from (PowerPoint), 327-328

PDF, converting charts to, 332

Peltier, Jon, 145, 413

performance reviews, radar charts and, 166-167

perspective (3D charts), 65, 401-403

Picture Accent List style (SmartArt layouts), 288

Picture Accent Process style (SmartArt layouts), 288

pictures

    charts, exporting as, 331-332, 389-390

    data markers, replacing with (series), 73-74

    Plot area, adding to, 64

    PowerPoint, copying charts as pictures, 325-326

    Shapes, 287

        converting SmartArt to, 314-315

        creating, 311-312

        displaying cell contents, 309-311

        formatting, 311

        Freeform Shapes, 311-312

    SmartArt, 287, 288, 308-309

        adding pictures to, 298-299

        applying styles, 293

        balance charts, 304

        Basic Cycle layouts, 305

        changing color in, 292-293

        changing Shapes, 295-296

        changing styles, 293-294

        choosing layouts, 302-303

        controlling Shapes from Text pane, 296-298

        converting to Shapes, 314-315

        Cycle category, 289-290

        Design tab, 294

        Divergent Radial layouts, 305

        elements in, 289

        Equation style, 302

        formatting in, 288, 294-296

        funnel charts, 302

        gear charts, 302

        Hierarchy category, 290

        inserting, 291-292

labeled Hierarchy charts, 307-308

Leveraging SmartArt Graphics in the 2007 Microsoft Office System, 303, 308

limitations of, 301-302

List category, 289

Matrix category, 290, 302

Office.com category, 290

organizational charts and, 299-301

Picture category, 290

Process category, 289

Pyramid category, 290, 302

Relationship category, 290, 302

styles of layouts, 288-289

Table List layouts, 306

upward arrows, 304

Venn diagrams, 306-307

WordArt, 287-288, 312-313

pictures lying by stretching pictographs, 409-410

pie charts, 113

2D pie charts, 120

3D pie charts, 120

bar of pie charts, 120, 371-374

customizing splits in, 134

using, 134-135

component comparisons, showing, 117-126

data representation in, 129-135

exploding, 369-371

highlighting slices

color, 125-126

exploding, 124

labeling, 121-124

Other Customer Summaries, 130

pie of pie charts, 130-133, 135, 371-374

rotating, 123

slices, moving labels, 123-124

spinning, 369-371

time comparisons, 80

pivot charts, 22-23, 223

creating, 223-225, 390-392

daily dates

grouping, 228-230

rolling to months, 91-93

data, filtering

Filter fly-out menu, 230

Slicers, 230-231

fields, changing in, 225-226

multiple pivot charts, connecting via Slicers, 231-232

sorting, 226-227

Plot area, 38

formatting, 61-64

gradients, 61-63

pictures in, 64

textures, 64

Plus icon, 26

data labels, adding to charts, 43

elements, adding with, 8

formatting chart elements, 35

SetElement method (VBA), emulating changes from via, 358-363

podcasts, 118

Politikal Arithmetik blog, 414

polynomial trendlines, 69

Pope, Andy, 413

power trendlines, 69

Power View, 232-233, 246-247

chart points as Slicers, 240-241

dashboard elements, 238

elements, creating by dragging, 240

enabling, 233

Filter pane, 242

maps, 275

color, 285-284

creating, 279-284

enabling add-ins, 280

loading data into, 280-281

zoom feature, 283-284

Multiples, replicating charts via, 244-245

scatter charts, animating, 245-246

Slicers, adding, 241-242

tables, converting to charts, 238-239

tile boxes, filtering charts via, 243-244

worksheets, creating, 237

PowerFrameworks.com website, 412

PowerPivot, 232-233

data

formatting, 235-236

loading into, 233-234

date lookup tables, 234-235

enabling, 233

VLOOKUPs, replacing with relationships, 236-237

PowerPoint

charts

creating with pasted Excel data, 327-328

embedding, 325

copying/pasting Excel documents to, 319-325

Excel presentations, 317-328

Paste Options menu, 317

pictures, copying charts as, 325-326

workbooks, embedding, 325

presentations

charts

Facebook presentations, 329

LinkedIn presentations, 329

Twitter presentations, 329

PowerPoint, 317-328, 319-325

Web presentations, charts and, 328-331

Word, 317-328

previewing charts, Quick Analysis icon, 11

prior-year sales to current sales comparison charts, 110

Process category (SmartArt), 289

pro/con decisions, illustrating via balance charts, 304

Project Explorer (VBA Editor), 334-335

Properties window (VBA Editor), 335

Pyramid category (SmartArt), 290, 302

Q

Quick Analysis icon, charts

creating, 10-11

previewing, 11

Quick Layout drop-down (Design tab), 29-30

R

radar charts, 147, 161, 166-167, 377

reading (further)

Beautiful Evidence, 412

Envisioning Information, 412

Visual Explanations: Images and Quantities, Evidence and Narrative, 412

rearranging legends, 42

Recommended Charts, 7

creating, 11-13

pivot charts, creating via, 223-225

recording macros, 336

Relationship category (SmartArt), 290, 302

relationship charts, 168-169

bubble charts, 147, 159-160

frequency distribution charts, 163-166

paired bar charts, 161-163

radar charts, 147, 161, 166-167

scatter charts, 147

adding labels to, 149-150

connecting data points with lines, 153-154

creating, 149

drawing with, 155-156

replacing line charts, 154-155

showing labels, 150-152

testing correlations, 157-158

surface charts, 147

3D rotation, 168-169

depth axis, 168

showing contrast with, 167-169

relationships (company), illustrating via SmartArt, 305

removing items from Legend boxes, 143

replicating via Multiples (Power View), 244-245

reports (Annual), showing years in reverse, 53

REPT function, creating charts, 273-274

resizing titles, 98-99

reversing

data sorting order in bar charts, illustrating comparisons, 115

order of years in Annual Reports, 53

sequence of icons in icon sets, 268

series and categories, 24-25

rogue XY series

arbitrary guidelines, 202-206

charts, showing several on one chart, 207-212

rotating

3D rotation

3D charts, 65-66

surface charts, 168-169

pie charts, 123

rows

moving rows via cutting/pasting, 33

unwanted rows, filtering, 8

S

sales trend charts (monthly), creating, 106-108

saving formatting changes in templates, 75

scale

data bars, 260

misleading charts and, 403-405

Scatter chart icon, 15-14

scatter charts, 147

animating via Power View, 245-246

correlations, testing, 157-158

creating, 149

drawing with, 155-156

labels

adding, 149-150

showing, 150-152

line charts, replacing, 154-155

lines, connecting data points, 153-154

Select Data icon, 25

sequence (data), changing, 25

series

blank series, moving with (stacked and clustered charts), 139-143

charts

adding to bar charts, 115-116

highlighting charts by adding second series, 102-103

data markers, replacing with

pictures, 73-74

Shapes, 73

formatting, 72-74

reversing, 24-25

single data points, formatting, 73

XY series
  arbitrary guidelines, 202-206
  showing several charts on one chart, 207-212

SetElement method (VBA), emulating changes from Plus icon, 358-363

Shapes, 287
  cell contents, displaying, 309-311
  creating, 311-312
  formatting, 311
  Freeform Shapes, 311-312
  replacing data markers with (series), 73
  SmartArt Shapes
    changing, 295-296
    controlling Shapes from Text pane, 296-298
    converting to, 314-315

shrinking charts, 402-403

side walls (3D charts), 41

Singh, Mala, 415

single data points (series), formatting, 73

single-series charts, legends, 7

Slicers
  chart points as Slicers in Power View, 240-241
  pivot charts
    connecting multiple pivot charts, 231-232
    filtering data, 230-231
  Power View, adding Slicers in, 241-242

SmartArt, 287-288, 308-309
  balance charts, 304
  Basic Cycle layouts, 305
  color, changing in, 292-293
  Cycle category, 289-290
  Design tab, 294
  Divergent Radial layouts, 305

  elements in, 289
  Equation style, 302
  formatting in, 288, 294-296
  funnel charts, 302
  gear charts, 302
  Hierarchy category, 290
  images, adding, 298-299
  inserting, 291-292
  labeled Hierarchy charts, 307-308
  layouts
    choosing, 302-303
    styles of, 288-289
  Leveraging SmartArt Graphics in the 2007 Microsoft Office System, 303, 308
  limitations of, 301-302
  List category, 289
  Matrix category, 290, 302
  Office.com category, 290
  organizational charts and, 299-301
  Picture category, 290
  Process category, 289
  Pyramid category, 290, 302
  Relationship category, 290, 302
  Shapes
    changing, 295-296
    controlling from Text pane, 296-298
    converting to, 314-315
  styles
    applying, 293
    changing, 293-294
  Table List layouts, 306
  Text pane (SmartArt), 296-298
  upward arrows, illustrating growth by, 304
  Venn diagrams, 306-307

Smith, Dustin, 414

sorting

    data order in bar charts, illustrating comparisons, 115

    pivot charts, 226-227

sparkcolumns, 250

sparklines, 3, 249-251

    axis values, controlling, 254-256

    charts, fitting into cells, 250-259

    copying, 259

    creating, 395-399

    customizing, 253-254

    detail, showing, 256-257

    enlarging, 256-257

    groups, creating, 251-252

    labeling, 257-259

    Tufte, Edward, 249

    win/loss charts, 250, 256

Speedometer Chart Creator, 415

spinning

    doughnut charts, 369-371

    pie charts, 369-371

splits (stocks), handling in stock charts, 175-177

stacked area charts, creating, 386-389

stacked charts, 126-127

    100% stacked charts

        component comparisons, 119, 126-127

        thumbnails, 13

    creating, 138-145

    stacked surface charts, 406-407

    thumbnails, 13

stacked column charts, 108-110, 138-139

Stock and Surface charts, 15

stock charts

    adjusted close columns, 175-177

    candlestick charts, 173

        changing color in, 191-192

        creating, 191-196

        rearranging downloaded data in columns, 175

    columns, rearranging downloaded data in, 174-175

    finance.yahoo.com website, 171, 173, 180

    high-low lines, 192-196

    high-low-close charts

        adding volume, 186-190

        creating, 182-183

        customizing, 183-184

        rearranging downloaded data in columns, 175

    line charts, 171-172

        rearranging downloaded data in columns, 175

        showing closing prices (stocks), 177-181

        volume as a column, 180-182

    line charts with volume, rearranging downloaded data in columns, 175

    OHLC charts, 172-173

        creating, 184-186

        rearranging downloaded data in columns, 175

    overview of, 171-173

    stock data, obtaining, 173-177

    up/down bars, 192-196

    volume-high-low-close charts, rearranging downloaded data in columns, 175

Stock Market data, high-low-close charts, 79

stretching pictographs, lying by, 409-410

subdividing bars in bar charts for emphasis, 116-117

super-variables (coding), 339-340

surface charts, 147, 377

    3D rotation, 168-169

    depth axis, 168

showing contrast with, 167-169

stacked surface charts, 406-407

SWIPE visual design store, 414

T

Table List layouts (SmartArt), 306

tables

date lookup tables, PowerPivot, 234-235

Power View tables, converting to charts, 238-239

task pane, formatting commands, 8-9

templates, saving formatting changes in, 75

text

data bars, 260

dates stored as text (date fields), 81

converting to dates, 83-84

fonts

Decrease Font Size icon (Home tab), 31

Font group (Home tab), 31

line type, changing midstream, 103-105

text boxes versus titles, 99-100

Text pane (SmartArt), controlling Shapes from, 296-298

text-based axes, 54

textures, Plot area, 64

themes

color, changing, 74

Page Layout tab, changing themes in, 32

thermometer charts, 217-219

thumbnails

3D column charts, 13

100% stacked charts, 13

clustered charts, 13

stacked charts, 13

tile boxes (Power View), filtering charts via, 243-244

time, dates that are really (date fields), 83

time comparisons, pie charts, 80

time comparisons bar charts, illustrating with, 115-116

time-based axes, 81

time-scale axes, 93-95

titling

Chart title, 38

charts, 16-18

all caps, 59-60

assigning titles from Worksheet cells, 18

editing titles, 16

effective communication, 96-100

Formula bar, 16

picking up titles from Worksheets, 17

VBA coding, 350-351

deleting titles, 99-100

resizing titles, 98-99

text boxes versus, 99-100

WordArt, creating titles and headlines via, 312-313

training

interactive training, 413

live training, 413

trend charts

category-based axes, 80-95

date-based axes, 80-95

trendlines, 40

automatic trendlines, adding to charts, 105-106

charts, adding equations to, 68

exponential trendlines, 68

forecasting with, 66-69

formatting, 67-68

logarithm trendlines, 68-69

moving average trendlines, 69

multiple trendlines on single chart, 110

polynomial trendlines, 69

power trendlines, 69

trends, asserting from two data points, 407

Tufte, Edward, 249, 412-413

tutorials, charting tutorial websites, 413

Twitter, chart presentations and, 329

U

unsummarized data sets, 7

up/down bars, 40

line charts, adding to, 70

stock charts, 192-196

upward arrows, illustrating growth by, 304

V

Values axis, changing scale of, 48-50

VBA, 333, 395

charts

bar of pie charts, 371-374

exporting as graphics, 331-332

coding

AddChart2 chart creation method, 346-348

adding comments to code, 341

applying chart color, 352-355

backwards compatibility, 341

changing chart fills, 363-366

combo charts, 378-381

continuing lines of code, 340

creating bins for frequency charts, 383-386

customizing charts, 350

data bars, 392-395

data ranges, 337-338

End With statements, 340

End+Down Arrow versus End+Up Arrow, 338

Excel 2003-2013 chart creation method, 349-350

Excel 2007-2013 chart creation method, 348-349

exploding round charts, 369-371

exporting charts as graphics, 389-390

filtering charts, 355-356

Format method, 363-367

formatting charts, 351-358

formatting data series, 367-368

formatting data series separations, 368-369

formatting gap width, 368-369

formatting line settings, 366-367

object variables, 339-340

OHLC charts, 382-383

pie of pie charts, 371-374

pivot charts, 390-392

radar charts, 377

referencing chart objects, 342

referencing charts, 342

referring to objects, 340

referring to specific charts, 343-346

SetElement method, 358-363

setting bubble size in bubble charts, 375-377

sparklines, 395-399

specifying built-in charts, 342-344

specifying chart location, 343

specifying chart size, 343

specifying chart styles, 351-352

specifying chart titles, 350-351

spinning round charts, 369-371

stacked area charts, 386-389

With statements, 340

super-variables, 339-340

Developer tab (Excel 2013), 334

enabling, 333-334

tools, 335-336

VBA Editor, 334-335

Code window, 335

Project Explorer, 334-335

Properties window, 335

Venn diagrams, SmartArt and, 306-307

Vertical (value) axis, 39

Vertical Axis title, 38

Verticle Multiples (Power View), 244-245

visible window

dragging charts

inside, 33

outside, 33

zoom, adjusting, 33

Visual Business Intelligence blog, 414

visual design stores, 414

Visual Display of Quantitative Information, **412**

Visual Explanations: Images and Quantities, Evidence and Narrative, **412**

visualizations (data), 249

color scales, 249

customizing, 264-265

showing extremes via, 263-265

data bars, 249

in-cell bar charts, 259-263

creating, 260-261

customizing, 261-262

formatting, 260

gradients, 259

hiding numeric values, 260

negative values, 260

showing for subsets of cells, 262-263

specifying scale, 260

text in, 260

data labels, zero values, 260

icon sets, 249

10-icon sets, 269-271

five-icon sets, 265

four-icon sets, 265

moving numbers closer to icons, 266-268

reversing sequence of icons, 268

setting up, 265-266

showing icons only for best cells, 268-269

three-icon sets, 265

VLOOKUPs, replacing with relationships in PowerPivot, 236-237

volume, high-low-close charts

adding to, 186-190

columns, rearranging downloaded data in, 175

W

waterfall charts, 136-145

Web (World Wide) presentations, charts and, 328-331

web resources, 411

blogs, 413-414

charting tutorial websites, 413

Daily Giz Wiz podcast, 118

Dashboard Reporting with Excel, 415

finance.yahoo.com website, 171, 173

interactive training, 413

LinkedIn, chart presentations and, 329

live training, 413

PowerFrameworks.com website, 412

professional chart designers, 414-415

Speedometer Chart Creator, 415

stock charts, 171, 180

Twitter, chart presentations and, 329

Xcelsius, 415

web resources Facebook, chart presentations and, 329

win/loss charts, sparklines and, 250, 256

With statements, 340

Word

Excel presentations, 317-328

Paste Options menu, 317

WordArt, 287-288, 312-313

workbooks, embedding in PowerPoint, 325

worksheets

charts

creating from conditional formatting in cells, 271-273

moving between worksheets, 34, 200

moving within current worksheets, 33

Power View, creating in, 237

X

X rotation (3D charts), 65

Xcelsius, 415

XPS, converting charts to, 332

XY series

arbitrary guidelines, 202-206

charts, showing several on one chart, 207-212

Y

Y rotation (3D charts), 65

Y-axis scale, adjusting (stacked and clustered charts), 143-144

years, 88-89

current sales to prior-year sales comparison charts, 110

data, plotting by numeric year, 88-89

dates represented by numeric years (date fields), 81-83

reverse, showing in (Annual Reports), 53

year-to-date sales charts, creating, 106-108

Z

Zelazny, Gene, 411

zero values, #N/A errors and, 405-406

zoom

GeoFlow mapping software, 285

MapPoint, 278-279

Power View, maps, 283-284

visible window, adjusting in, 33

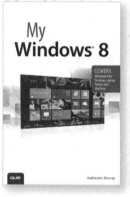

MrExcel
Library Series

**Learn from
Bill Jelen,
Excel MVP,
founder of MrExcel**

FORMULAS
AND FUNCTIONS
Microsoft Excel 2013

PIVOT TABLE
DATA CRUNCHING
Microsoft Excel 2013

VBA AND MACROS
Microsoft Excel 2013

CHARTS AND GRAPHS
Microsoft Excel 2013

**Get to the Next Level in Excel
Proficiency with Bill Jelen, Excel MVP
and Best-Selling Author**

Titles in the **MrExcel Library** are designed
to launch readers to the next level in Excel
proficiency by pinpointing a certain task and
expanding on it—providing the reference
material readers need to become more productive
with advanced features of Excel.

Every book in the **MrExcel Library** pinpoints a specific
set of crucial Excel skills, and presents focused tasks and
examples for performing them rapidly and effectively.
Selected by Bill Jelen, Microsoft Excel MVP and mastermind behind
the leading Excel solutions website MrExcel.com, these books will:

- Dramatically increase your productivity—saving you 50 hours a year,
  or more
- Present proven, creative strategies for solving real-world problems
- Show you how to get great results, no matter how much data you have
- Help you avoid critical mistakes that even experienced users make

Visit quepublishing.com/mrexcel

FREE
Online Edition

Your purchase of *Excel 2013 Charts and Graphs* includes access to a free online edition for 45 days through the **Safari Books Online** subscription service. Nearly every Que book is available online through **Safari Books Online**, along with thousands of books and videos from publishers such as Addison-Wesley Professional, Cisco Press, Exam Cram, IBM Press, O'Reilly Media, Prentice Hall, Sams, and VMware Press.

Safari Books Online is a digital library providing searchable, on-demand access to thousands of technology, digital media, and professional development books and videos from leading publishers. With one monthly or yearly subscription price, you get unlimited access to learning tools and information on topics including mobile app and software development, tips and tricks on using your favorite gadgets, networking, project management, graphic design, and much more.

Activate your FREE Online Edition at
informit.com/safarifree

STEP 1: Enter the coupon code: EIGJGWH.

STEP 2: New Safari users, complete the brief registration form. Safari subscribers, just log in.

If you have difficulty registering on Safari or accessing the online edition, please e-mail customer-service@safaribooksonline.com